Political Governance in Post-Genocide Rwanda

Filip Reyntjens's new book analyzes political governance in post-genocide Rwanda and focuses on the rise of the authoritarian Rwanda Patriotic Front (RPF). In the aftermath of the 1994 Rwandan genocide, the RPF has employed various means – rigged elections, elimination of opposition parties and civil society, legislation outlawing dissenting opinions, and terror – to consolidate power and perpetuate its position as the nation's ruling party. Although many international observers have hailed Rwanda as a "success story" for its technocratic governance, societal reforms, and economic development, Reyntjens complicates this picture by casting light on the regime's human rights abuses, social engineering projects, information management schemes, victimization of the Hutu majority, and retributive justice system. He argues that the regime's deeply flawed political governance is likely to destroy the achievements of decent bureaucratic governance and may lead to new large-scale violence.

Filip Reyntjens is Professor of African Law and Politics at the Institute of Development Policy and Management, University of Antwerp.

Political Governance in Post-Genocide Rwanda

FILIP REYNTJENS

University of Antwerp

CAMBRIDGE
UNIVERSITY PRESS

CAMBRIDGE
UNIVERSITY PRESS

32 Avenue of the Americas, New York NY 10013-2473, USA

Cambridge University Press is part of the University of Cambridge.

It furthers the University's mission by disseminating knowledge in the pursuit of
education, learning and research at the highest international levels of excellence.

www.cambridge.org
Information on this title: www.cambridge.org/9781107678798

© Filip Reyntjens 2013

This publication is in copyright. Subject to statutory exception
and to the provisions of relevant collective licensing agreements,
no reproduction of any part may take place without the written
permission of Cambridge University Press.

First published 2013
First paperback edition 2015

A catalogue record for this publication is available from the British Library

Library of Congress Cataloguing in Publication data
Reyntjens, Filip, author.
Political governance in post-genocide Rwanda / Filip Reyntjens.
pages   cm
Includes bibliographical references.
ISBN 978-1-107-04355-8
1. Rwanda – Politics and government – 1994–   2. Front patriotique
rwandais.   3. Rwanda – Ethnic relations.   4. Ethnicity – Political aspects –
Rwanda.   5. Human rights – Rwanda.   I. Title
JQ3567.A91R49   2014
320.967571–dc23   2013029438

ISBN 978-1-107-04355-8 Hardback
ISBN 978-1-107-67879-8 Paperback

Cambridge University Press has no responsibility for the persistence or accuracy of
URLs for external or third-party internet websites referred to in this publication,
and does not guarantee that any content on such websites is, or will remain, accurate
or appropriate.

Contents

Acknowledgments

It is not easy to identify those who have contributed to the research that has led to this book. Indeed, having worked for thirty-five years on Rwanda and the Great Lakes region, I have developed extensive networks of friends, colleagues, and political and social actors, both there and in the wider world. They are a rich source of information, a sounding board for ideas, and a platform for sharing analysis. It is therefore impossible to say who contributed what to this book, and I cannot thank these persons individually. However, it is my pleasure to express the debt I owe to those who have generously given their precious time to comment on parts or whole of the draft: An Ansoms, Bert Ingelaere, René Lemarchand, Luc Reydams, Stef Vandeginste, a Rwandan reader who must remain anonymous, and two anonymous reviewers for Cambridge University Press. Of course, errors of fact and analysis are my responsibility.

To the best of my knowledge, this book takes into account developments up to the end of 2012.

Filip Reyntjens

List of Abbreviations

ADEP-Mizero	Alliance pour la démocratie, l'équité et le progress
AFDL	Alliance des forces pour la libération du Congo-Zaïre
AFP	Agence France Presse
AFRICOM	Africa Command
AGI	Africa Governance Initiative
AI	Amnesty International
ALIR	Armée pour la libération du Rwanda
AP	Associated Press
APRM	African Peer Review Mechanism
ARG	Association des rescapés du genocide à Butare
ARI	Agence rwandaise d'informations
AU	African Union
BBC	British Broadcasting Corporation
BBTG	Broad Based Transitional Government
CAURWA	Community of Indigenous Peoples of Rwanda
CCAC	Concertation chrétienne pour l'Afrique centrale
CCOAIB	Conseil de concertation des organisations d'appui aux initiatives de base
CHRI	Commonwealth Human Rights Initiative
CIA	Central Intelligence Agency
CID	Criminal Investigation Department
CIP	Crop Intensification Programme
Cladho	Collectif des ligues et associations de défense des droits de l'homme
CNDP	Conseil national pour la défense du people

COOPIBO	Association for Development Cooperation
CRDDR	Comité pour le respect des droits de l'homme et la démocratie au Rwanda
CSO	Civil Society Organisation
DFID	Department for International Development
DGP	Democratic Green Party
DMI	Directorate of Military Intelligence
DRC	Democratic Republic of Congo
EICV	Enquête intégrale sur les conditions de vie des ménages
ESO	External Security Organisation
EU	European Union
FAO	Food and Agriculture Organisation
FAR	Forces armées rwandaises
FARG	Fonds d'assistance aux rescapés du genocide
FDLR	Forces démocratiques pour la libération du Rwanda
FDU-Inkingi	Forces démocratiques unifiées-Inkingi
FIDH	Fédération internationale des ligues des droits de l'homme
FOR	Forum des organisations rurales
FOS	Socialistische Solidariteit
FPR	Front patriotique rwandais
FRD	Forces de Résistance pour la Démocratie
FRF	Forces républicaines et fédéralistes
Frodebu	Front pour la démocratie au Burundi
GDP	Gross domestic product
GOR	Government of Rwanda
HRW	Human Rights Watch
ICC	International Criminal Court
ICG	International Crisis Group
ICRC	International Committee of the Red Cross
ICTR	International Criminal Tribunal for Rwanda
ICTY	International Criminal Tribunal for the Former Yugoslavia
IDP	Internally displaced person
IFEX	International Freedom of Expression Exchange network
IMF	International Monetary Fund
INGO	International Nongovernmental Organization
IOB	Institute of Development Policy and Management

IPEP	International Panel of Eminent Persons
IRC	International Rescue Committee
IRDP	Institute of Research and Dialogue for Peace
IRIN	Integrated Regional Information Network
LDF	Local Defence Forces
LDGL	Ligue des droits de la personne dans la région des grands lacs
Liprodhor	Ligue rwandaise pour la promotion et la défense des droits de l'homme
MDR	Mouvement démocratique républicain
MEP	Member of the European Parliament
MONUSCO	Mission de l'Organisation des Nations Unies pour la stabilisation en RD Congo
MP	Member of Parliament
MRNDD	Mouvement républicain national pour la démocratie et le développement
MSF	Médecins sans frontières
NCOS	Nationaal Centrum voor Ontwikkelingssamenwerking
NDI	National Democratic Institute
NEC	National Electoral Commission
NEPAD	New Partnership for Africa's Development
NGO	Nongovernmental Organization
NORDEM	Norwegian Resource Bank for Democracy and Human Rights
NRM	National Resistance Movement
NSS	National Security Service
NURC	National Unity and Reconciliation Commission
OAU	Organisation of African Unity
OIF	Organisation international de la francophonie
ORINFOR	Office rwandais d'information
OTP	Office of the Prosecutor
PAC	Presidential Advisory Council
PAM	Programme alimentaire mondial
PDC	Parti démocrate chrétien
PDP-Imanzi	Parti de défense du peuple-Imanzi
PDR-Ubuyanja	Parti démocratique pour le renouveau-Ubuyanja
PL	Parti liberal
PRGF	Poverty Reduction and Growth Facility
PRI	Penal Reform International

PRSP	Poverty Reduction Strategy Paper
PSD	Parti social démocrate
PS-Imberakuri	Parti social-Imberakuri
PSP	Parti pour la solidarité et le progress
RDF	Rwanda Defence Forces
RDR	Rassemblement pour la démocratie et le retour des réfugiés
RFI	Radio France Internationale
RIG	Rwanda Investment Group
RNA	Rwanda News Agency
RNC	Rwanda National Congress
RNLM	Rwanda National Liberation Movement
RPA	Rwanda Patriotic Army
RPF	Rwanda Patriotic Front
RPG	Rocket-propelled grenade
RPR	Rassemblement du Peuple Rwandais
RPT	Rwanda pour tous
RSF	Reporters sans frontiers
RUD	Ralliement pour l'Unité et la Démocratie
RWF	Rwanda Franc
SADC	Southern African Development Community
SNJG	National Service of the *Gacaca* Jurisdictions
TNA	Transitional National Assembly
TPIR	Tribunal pénal international pour le Rwanda
UDR	Union démocratique rwandaise
UN	United Nations
UNAMIR	United Nations Assistance Mission to Rwanda
UNAR	Union nationale rwandaise
UNDP	United Nations Development Programme
UNHCHR	United Nations High Commission for Human Rights
UNHCR	United Nations High Commission for Refugees
UNHRFOR	United Nations Human Rights Field Operation in Rwanda
UNICEF	United Nations Children's Fund
Uprona	Union pour le progrès national
USAID	United States Agency for International Development
VOA	Voice of America
VRT	Vlaamse Radio en Televisie
WFP	World Food Programme

Introduction

There are two radically opposed perceptions of Rwanda. One is that of Bono, Pastor Rick Warren, Bill Clinton, and Tony Blair, who are just a few of the "Friends of the New Rwanda," as well as most aid agencies. This perception focuses on technocratic/bureaucratic governance and hails economic progress; visionary leadership; reforms in education, health, and agriculture; women empowerment; and market policies, to name but a few.[1] This view is also informed by the genocide credit the regime enjoys and by feelings of guilt over international inaction in 1994. The other perception, shared by most academic observers, projects a highly critical view of the polity that emerged after the genocide. It focuses on political governance and denounces autocratic rule, gross human rights abuse, growing inequality and rural poverty, victimization of the Hutu majority, and injustice. This has created structural violence and will eventually lead to political instability and new conflict.[2] This book makes clear that I belong to the second school of thought.[3]

---

[1] When President Kagame received a Global Citizen Award in 2009, the statement of the Clinton Foundation read as follows: "From crisis, President Kagame has forged a strong, unified and growing nation with the potential to become a model for the rest of Africa and the World" (Clinton Foundation, "Former President Clinton Announces the Winners of the Third Annual Clinton Global Citizen Awards", 23 September 2009).

[2] This view is well presented in S. Straus, L. Waldorf (Eds.), *Remaking Rwanda: State Building and Human Rights after Mass Violence*, Madison, University of Wisconsin Press, 2011.

[3] As this book is critical of the current regime, I have tried to discuss my findings with Rwandan officials. However, these attempts were in vain, as I never received replies to my repeated requests for a discussion of my manuscript.

Part hagiography, part journalism, Stephen Kinzer's widely read book on Kagame tries hard to reconcile the two Rwandas, and the two Kagames: "The greatest enigma to those who wonder about Rwanda's prospects is President Kagame himself. He is a visionary endowed with enormous energy and ambition. Yet he can also be an angry, vengeful authoritarian. Because he so totally dominates Rwandan life, his choices will decisively shape the country's future."[4] The opposing views on Rwanda can be understood in light of the way in which Rwanda was "discovered" by the world in 1994. Although it was a widely researched country, particularly after 1945,[5] knowledge was generated by a limited number of scholars working in Belgium and, to a lesser extent, France and the United States. The genocide led to an explosion of interest and a dramatic increase in writing of different kinds, ranging from political pamphlets and current-affairs articles to intense high-quality doctoral research, with many articles in scholarly journals in between. Many of the authors, be they journalists, aid workers, diplomats, or academic researchers, were newcomers to Rwanda and the wider region. While many initial publications suffered from lack of historical background, fell into a trap of simple answers, or even showed outright bias, the quality of research dramatically improved over the years. In addition, Rwanda is no longer the reserve of a handful of scholars (myself included) exercising some kind of oligopoly, and the geographic extension of interest has been considerable, with most researchers now coming from the English-speaking world.[6]

The discovery took place in very peculiar circumstances, through the lens of genocide. To some extent, this context still determines the way in which Rwanda is seen. As will be discussed in this book, nearly twenty years after the genocide, international feelings of guilt still come into play, obscuring both the historical background and the perception of current

---

[4] S. Kinzer, *A Thousand Hills: Rwanda's Rebirth and the Man Who Dreamed It*, Hoboken NJ, John Wiley & Sons, 2008, pp. 4–5. Kinzer later feared that the second Kagame displaced the first one, and that he risked becoming "a tragic figure who built the foundations of a spectacular future for his country, but saw his achievements collapse because he could not take his country from one-man rule toward democracy" (S. Kinzer, "Kagame's Authoritarian Turn Risks Rwanda's Future", *The Guardian*, 27 January 2011).

[5] M. d'Hertefelt, D. de Lame (Eds.), *Société, culture et histoire du Rwanda: Encyclopédie bibliographique 1863–1980/87*, 2 vols., Tervuren, Royal Museum for Central Africa, 1987.

[6] Twenty-two of the twenty-seven authors of *Remaking Rwanda* are native speakers of English. While I myself mainly published in French until the mid-1990s, most of my writings are now in English, as a response to the shift in readership.

political and social dynamics. It comes as no surprise that those, such as the "Friends" mentioned earlier, who have a very limited and simplified knowledge of Rwanda should embrace the current regime. The academic researchers, who have engaged much more profoundly with present-day Rwanda and who have worked for long periods in and on the country, have developed a more sophisticated and critical view. In many cases, this evolution took time, and many of those who now write critically about the Rwanda Patriotic Front (RPF) initially were supporters.[7]

The quality of modern-day scholarship on Rwanda is high, and it is mainly the product of younger researchers who have accumulated extensive field experience, far from towns and main roads, in extraordinarily difficult circumstances. The background and ever-present sequels of the genocide were traumatizing, and working under an oppressive and autocratic regime exercising a high degree of control was demanding and destabilizing for both the scholars and their Rwandan interpreters, "fixers," and participants in the field. Being unable to work in Rwanda myself,[8] the research of these scholars has allowed me to stay in tune with the micro level[9] and, eventually, to write this book.

This book makes no apology for the two features that some will hold against me. The first is that it is unabashedly empirical. I believe that only by accumulating a great deal of factual data can I show the characteristics of governance in post-genocide Rwanda and the response (or lack of it) by the international community. It is precisely this accumulation that allows one to go beyond anecdotal evidence and to demonstrate the existence of systemic features. This also means that this book is a case study of limited comparative and theoretical interest. Large numbers of intense case studies

---

[7] For instance Susan Thomson, who is now attacked by the regime for her writings, wrote that "when I left Rwanda for Canada in January 2001, I was a strong supporter" (S. Thomson, *Resisting Reconciliation: State Power and Everyday Life in Post-Genocide Rwanda*, PhD thesis, Dalhousie University, 2009, p. xxiv).

[8] I have been persona non grata in Rwanda since early 1995 for having written, after a visit in October 1994, a moderately phrased memo expressing concern about the RPF's way of running the country (F. Reyntjens, "Sujets d'inquiétude au Rwanda, octobre 1994", *Dialogue*, 179 [November–December 1994], pp. 3–14, translated and summarized in English as F. Reyntjens, "Subjects of Concern: Rwanda, October 1994", *Issue*, 23:2 [1995], pp. 39–43).

[9] As far as the macro political level is concerned, I have come to realize with surprise and relief that the information flows are such that it is possible to follow developments closely even while remaining abroad. This is not to say that I would not rather prefer to go to Rwanda regularly, but the handicap of not being allowed in has proven much less constraining than I anticipated.

are needed to complement the broad statistical Collier-like[10] approaches
that offer very valuable overall insight but cannot address, much less
explain, country or regime specificities and deviances. When reading
Collier, I often realized that the "laws" he deducts from statistical corre-
lations do not always fit situations I observe in the part of Africa that
I study.[11] This is inevitable as a correlation that is "statistically significant"
does not apply to all cases. In-depth case studies are as important as large-
N studies, and they may contribute to answering the question of why
deviances occur.[12]

A second feature is that this book focuses on political governance.
Rwanda is hailed for its good technocratic/bureaucratic governance, and
donors consider their money there "well spent." The regime's achievements in this field are undisputable, and they have been highlighted in
many publications. There is no doubt that the RPF has a vision that it has
successfully implemented, particularly in economic development, and an
ambitious modernization drive more generally. The praise it has received
internationally is understandable, as progress can be physically witnessed.
Kigali has seen a building spree, and the city is clean and safe. Elites are
competent and cosmopolitan, civil servants are at their desks, and there is
little petty corruption. In particular since 2000, economic and social
statistics have shown significant improvement. The regime knows how to
deal with donors and speaks their language. For visitors and expats who
do not leave towns or main roads, Rwanda is indeed a miracle after the
utter human, social, and material devastation it suffered in 1994.

I argue, however, that Rwanda's dangerously flawed political governance not only risks destroying the achievements of technocratic/bureau-
cratic governance, but that it has also engendered large-scale structural
violence. Straddling the African Rift Valley, the metaphor that naturally

---

[10] For instance P. Collier, *Wars, Guns, and Votes: Democracy in Dangerous Places*, New
      York, Harper, 2009.
[11] While it offers numerous useful insights (and is great fun to read), Collier's book has the
      weakness typical of large-N studies: it is often uninformed and on occasion flawed on
      particular cases, about which it contains many errors of facts and analysis.
[12] Flyvbjerg has published a strong defense of case study research, arguing that a scientific
      discipline without a large number of thoroughly executed case studies is a discipline
      without systematic production of exemplars, and a discipline without exemplars is an
      ineffective one (B. Flyvbjerg, "Five Misunderstandings about Case-Study Research",
      Qualitative Inquiry, 12:2 [2006], pp. 219–245). This does not mean that he rejects
      research that focuses on large random samples or entire populations: "The advantage of
      large samples is breadth, whereas their problem is one of depth. For the case study, the
      situation is the reverse. Both approaches are necessary for a sound development of social
      science" (*idem*, p. 241).

comes to mind about Rwanda is that of a volcano waiting to erupt, thus opening the way for renewed violence, the scale and consequences of which are as yet impossible to predict. I do realize that the focus on political governance, at the expense of achievements in other fields, may cause some to consider this book as partial.

The book is organized as follows: Chapters 1, 2, and 3 address the way in which the RPF took power after the genocide, and then how it set out to consolidate it. While there is, of course, no clear-cut line, I distinguish between two periods, with the first studied in Chapter 1 and the second in Chapters 2 and 3. The first period ends around 2000, when reconstruction was by and large completed, the threats emanating from insurgent forces in the DRC and at home had disappeared, and the RPF exercised full control allowing it to embark on an ambitious engineering project. This was laid out in *Rwanda Vision 2020*, a document that came out in 2000, which was also the year marked by the unfolding of a profound political crisis, when the president, the prime minister, and the speaker of parliament were forced to resign. The first ended up in jail; the two others fled abroad. This episode allowed Kagame to become president and cleared the remaining hurdles on the road to full control. One of the means to achieve this was the creation, also in 2000, of the Forum for political parties that was to become a powerful tool in the RPF's hegemonic project. Strict laws on "divisionism" and on NGOs came out in 2001, and during the same year the adoption of a new national flag, seal, and anthem symbolized the full takeover. Chapters 2 and 3 analyze the post-2000 period. Chapter 2 studies the way in which elections were used, as instruments not of democratization but of regime consolidation. All the elections held at the local and national levels since 1999 were fundamentally flawed, but a pliant international community let the RPF get away with it. Chapter 3 addresses other means used to manage political space, mainly through the elimination of the remaining dissident voices. The following chapters study defining traits in a number of important areas: human rights (Chapter 4), the way in which the regime dealt with the world and the region (Chapter 5), the regime's ambitious engineering project (Chapter 6), its successful bid to manage information and to impose its vision of truth (Chapter 7), and the politics of justice in Rwanda, the International Criminal Tribunal for Rwanda (ICTR), and third countries (Chapter 8). A conclusion follows.

Besides analyzing regime behavior at home and abroad, the book pays considerable attention to the failure of the international community to rein in the RPF's violent and authoritarian project, thus contributing to the risk of another tragedy in the Great Lakes region. It attempts to shed light on the strategies deployed to capture and consolidate power by one of Africa's most enigmatic and misunderstood dictators, and it invites one to revise drastically the assumptions about the impact of Kagame's rule in the new Rwanda and throughout the entire region. This book starts where other books ended. Indeed, much has been written on the genocide, its antecedents, and its effects, but just one edited volume (*Remaking Rwanda*, mentioned earlier) addresses post-genocide Rwanda generally.[13]

However, a brief reminder of events up to the genocide may assist the reader. The Rwandan civil war started on October 1, 1990, when the RPF, mainly made up of Tutsi refugees who had fled the country between 1959 and 1973, attacked from Uganda with Ugandan support. This happened at a moment when the Habyarimana regime was attempting to settle the refugee problem while at the same time moving from single-party rule to multiparty politics, in line with an evolution seen elsewhere in Africa after the end of the Cold War. Indeed the RPF had to attack when it did, as progress in both those fields would have gravely diminished the legitimacy of a violent attempt at overthrowing the regime. Nevertheless, the political transition continued: in June 1991, a new constitution introduced multipartyism, and in April 1992, a coalition government came into place with a prime minister from the opposition. The transition took place against the background of an atypical civil war. Indeed the rebel force, while being Rwandan, (1) invaded the country from a neighboring country, by which it was supported and of whose army it was part; (2) was seen largely by the majority ethnic group of Hutu[14] and even by many in the Tutsi ethnic minority as a threat; and (3) represented a small constituency (in particular the Tutsi refugee community). Trust in the RPF and its legitimacy was limited, although the internal opposition initially saw it as an objective ally in its struggle against the former single party.

Negotiations with the RPF started after the coalition government was formed. Through several protocols (on the rule of law, power sharing, refugee repatriation, and integration of government and rebel forces into

---

[13] A number of aspects, particularly in the areas of justice, local-level politics, and rural policies, have been addressed in a sizable number of journal articles. Johan Pottier has written an important book on the current regime's information management to which I refer on several occasions. This book was under review when another edited volume was published: M. Campioni, P. Noack (Eds.), *Rwanda Fast Forward: Social, Economic, Military and Reconciliation Prospects*, Houndmills, Palgrave Macmillan, 2012. The disconnect between the editors' introduction and most chapters in the book is striking.

[14] Hutu constitute about 90 percent of the population, Tutsi about 10 percent; the pygmoid Twa are well below 1 percent.

one national army), an overall accord was signed in Arusha on August 4, 1993. In addition to being a peace accord, this was a fundamental reshuffling of political cards. From executive, the presidency became ceremonial. The transitional government and assembly were to be put in place by the main political parties including the RPF, along consociatonal lines (for instance, decisions in the "broad-based transitional government" were to be taken by two-thirds of its members, and the support of at least four parties was needed to attain a majority in the "Transitional National Assembly"). The new national army was to be made up of 60 percent government army and 40 percent RPF, except in command functions from battalion level upward, where both components were to share half the positions. Many Hutu felt that the RPF secured a deal that was better than it deserved.

Even among the domestic opposition, the belief in the good faith of the RPF rapidly dwindled, particularly after the rebels launched a new offensive in early 1993. By mid-1993, from tripolar (the former single party[15] – the unarmed opposition – the RPF), the political landscape became bipolar (MRNDD and allies versus RPF and allies), thus destroying the balance that lay behind the Arusha peace accord. This bipolarity increasingly developed along ethnic lines, and was further compounded by the October 1993 coup d'état in neighboring Burundi where a Hutu president was assassinated by the predominantly Tutsi army. This led many Rwandan Hutu to believe that the RPF would never accept genuine democracy. By the end of 1993, the Arusha accord was dead, the process of putting into place the transitional institutions was stalled by both parties, and the downing of President Habyarimana's plane on April 6, 1994, heralded the resumption of the civil war, the genocide against the Tutsi by the Hutu extremist interim government, and war crimes and crimes against humanity committed by both parties to the conflict. The RPF declared victory on July 18, 1994.[16]

---

[15] The Mouvement républicain national pour la démocratie et le développement (MRNDD).

[16] On the run-up to the genocide, see F. Reyntjens, *L'Afrique des grands lacs en crise: Rwanda, Burundi 1988–1994*, Paris, Karthala, 1994; G. Prunier, *The Rwanda Crisis, 1959–1994: History of a Genocide*, London, Hurst, 1995 (new edition 1997 with an additional chapter very critical of the RPF); A. Guichaoua, *Rwanda: de la guerre au génocide. Les politiques criminelles au Rwanda (1990–1994)*, Paris, La Découverte, 2010. On the genocide, see A. Des Forges, *Leave None to Tell the Story: Genocide in Rwanda*, New York and Paris, Human Rights Watch–International Federation of Human Rights, 1999.

I

The Capture of Power and the Path to Hegemony

When taking power, the RPF inherited a country it hardly knew. Being an "outsider" coming from abroad, it had a poor understanding of the social and political relations, and it was probably genuinely disappointed by the lukewarm way in which it was welcomed by most Rwandans. The years in exile and the guerrilla experience pushed it toward self-reliance and distrust toward anything outside its known environment, and therefore toward a strong degree of isolationism. Establishing control and only counting on those who can be trusted (i.e., the core of the movement) was a logical, even essential course of action, and this is what the RPF set out to do from day one. The war between the Forces armées rwandaises (FAR) and the Rwanda Patriotic Army (RPA), the military wing of the RPF, which had resumed on April 7, 1994, ended with the fall of Gisenyi (northwest) on July 18. The RPA controlled the country's territory, with the temporary exception of the "safe humanitarian zone" created in the southwest by the French operation Turquoise. On the next day, a new government was inaugurated in Kigali. Although its composition appeared at first sight to obey the spirit if not the letter of the Arusha peace accord signed in August 1993, the departures were considerable, and they all aimed at establishing hegemony.

According to Article 2 of the Declaration of the RPF Concerning the Putting into Place of the Institutions made on July 17, from being purely ceremonial, the presidency became executive and even dominant. It provided that the president was to be consulted on and to approve the composition of the government. More important, if the government was unable to reach a decision, "the President of the Republic decides in a sovereign way." The RPF took three of the five cabinet seats previously allotted to the former ruling party MRNDD, thus ensuring a blocking minority of one-third plus one. Indeed, the fundamental law provided that cabinet decisions needed a two-thirds majority. So the RPF, with eight portfolios out of a total of twenty-one, was in a position to prevent decisions from being taken, which allowed the president to "decide in a sovereign way." Both the president, Pasteur Bizimungu,[1] and the incumbent of the newly created post of vice-president, General Paul Kagame, were from the RPF. Introduced by the RPF declaration, the function of vice-president was not defined, and one would be tempted to consider it as honorific, were it not for its incumbent, who was the real power holder.[2] Other important modifications concerned the legislative branch. Although the parliamentary seats originally reserved for the MRNDD and other parties excluded from participation in power were redistributed among all the parties represented in the Transitional National Assembly (TNA), the RPF Declaration introduced an important correction by reserving six seats for the RPA, which had become the national army. Thanks to the military MPs, the RPF and allied parties secured a majority in Parliament.

The constitutional setup was consolidated in a bizarre "Fundamental Law" adopted by the TNA in May 1995, which entered into force retroactively on July 17, 1994. This brief text of only three articles contained no provision of substantive law and limited itself to the enumeration of the documents enjoying constitutional status and the determination of their hierarchy. The four texts were the constitution of 1991 and the Arusha Accord, which together formed the fundamental law under the terms of the accord, as well as the RPF declaration of July 17 and a protocol of agreement signed on November 24, 1994, by the RPF and seven political parties in view of the installation of the TNA. The hierarchy between these was as follows, from bottom to top: the 1991 constitution, the Arusha Accord, the RPF declaration, and the protocol of agreement. However, this was just the hierarchy at first sight. Indeed, article 1 of the protocol stated that "[t]he signatories adhere to the 'Declaration of the RPF concerning the putting into place of the institutions' of 17 July 1994." As it was

---

[1] Appointed "by consensus in the Political Bureau of the RPF" (article 9, RPF Declaration).

[2] Thanks to his being vice-president, Kagame was able to formally succeed President Bizimungu after he was forced to resign in 2000 (see the following discussion). For Kagame, who in 1994 "claim[ed] no interest in a postwar political career" (D. Lorch, "Rwanda Rebels: Army of Exiles Fights for a Home," *The New York Times*, 9 June 1994), this later simply confirmed a political reality.

incorporated in the protocol, it was therefore the RPF Declaration that was at the apex of the constitutional hierarchy. In other words, the RPF unilaterally imposed its constitutional order.

The Fundamental Law was a piece of subtle and smart constitutional engineering that attempted to hide the monolithic nature of the exercise of power. Under the labels of "power-sharing" and "national unity," needed for international consumption, it allowed the RPF to pull the strings while avoiding creating an image of unfettered control.[3] The restructuring of the (vice-)presidential institution through the extension of its powers and its predominance within the executive branch, as well as through its control of Parliament, allowed the RPF to exercise a political monopoly while avoiding to create an image of unfettered power. This was just the constitutional side of a hegemonic project. Political and physical ways of establishing and maintaining control will be discussed later.

The prime minister of the government put in place on July 19, 1994 (and completed the next day), was Faustin Twagiramungu of the Mouvement Démocratique Républicain (MDR), in line with the Arusha Accord. Four other ministers were from the MDR, three from the Parti libéral (PL), three from the Parti social démocrate (PSD), and one from the Parti démocrate chrétien (PDC), in addition to the eight RPF members and one independent. Twelve ministers were Hutu; nine were Tutsi. In the TNA put in place on November 25, 1994, thirty-five MPs were Tutsi and twenty-nine were Hutu, whereas the ethnic identity of six MPs was unknown.[4] In a context where security concerns were genuine and trade-offs needed to be made between freedom and control, the RPF seemed to waver between, on one hand, political openness and inclusiveness (witness the setting up of a government of national union and the return to Rwanda of a number of non-RPF civilian and military officials) and, on the other hand, a violent and exclusionary mode of management, as is detailed later. After all, the RPF was the military victor, and it could have kept power for itself. A strong feeling prevailed in the international community that some latitude needed to be given to a regime facing the colossal task of reconstructing the country. When the first indications of a worrying drift appeared soon after the RPF seized power, most thought it premature to question the good faith and political will of the new regime.

---

[3] For more details, see F. Reyntjens, "Constitution-Making in Situations of Extreme Crisis: The Case of Rwanda and Burundi," *Journal of African Law* 40:2 (1996), pp. 236–239.

[4] These statistics are based on A. Guichaoua (Ed.), *Les crisis politiques au Burundi et au Rwanda (1993–1994)*, Paris, Karthala, 1995, pp. 762–764.

Already during the second half of 1994, however, early warnings came from several quarters. In August and early September, a team led by UNHCR consultant Robert Gersony observed "systematic and sustained killing and persecution of civilian Hutu populations by the RPA."[5] Human rights organizations voiced similar concerns.[6] The RPF's human rights record is discussed in Chapter 4. In September, Laurien Ntezimana, a well-known lay pastoral worker recognized for his opposition to the genocide, had the courage to issue a document under the title "From Charybdis to Scylla." He denounced the climate of terror caused by the RPA killings, the massive arrests on mere denunciation (*gutunga agatoki*, meaning "pointing fingers"), the pillaging and raping, and the triumphalism displayed by the military victors and Tutsi returnees. He found striking similarities between the old and the new regimes.[7] In November, despite it being present in the government and even holding the portfolio of prime minister, the main opposition party MDR published a document critical of the new regime. Some problems it outlined included the lack of respect for the Fundamental Law and the Arusha peace accord, the blocking of party political activities, the increasing insecurity, the delayed formation of a new national army, the obstacles to national reconciliation and unity, and the chaotic return of old caseload refugees.[8] In fact, the MDR denounced practices that were at the core of the RPF's hegemonic project: the control of the army dominated by Tutsi, the concentration of power in the (vice-)president's office, the elimination of the opposition, the reign of terror exercised by killings and by massive arrests often based on mere denunciation. The issue of insecurity and killings by the RPA became an increasing bone of contention between Prime Minister Twagiramungu and

[5] Summary of UNHCR presentation before Commission of Experts 10 October 1994: "Prospects for early repatriation of Rwandan refugees currently in Burundi, Tanzania and Zaire".

[6] Amnesty International, *Reports of Killings and Abductions by the Rwandese Patriotic Front, April-August 1994*, London, October 1994; Human Rights Watch, *The Aftermath of Genocide in Rwanda*, New York, September 1994; Human Rights Watch, *Rwanda: A New Catastrophe?*, New York, December 1994. In the same period after a field trip in October, I expressed concern in a November 1994 memo ("Sujets d'inquiétude au Rwanda, October 1994", *Dialogue*, 179 [November–December 1994], pp. 3–14, translated and summarized in English in "Subjects of Concern: Rwanda, October 1994", *Issue*, 23:2 [1995], pp. 39–43).

[7] L. Ntezimana, "De Charybde en Scylla? Point de vue d'un 'Rwandais positif' sur les événements en cours au Rwanda," Butare, 15 September 1994.

[8] "Position du M.D.R. sur les grands problèmes actuels du Rwanda," Kigali, 6 November 1994; also see "Le MDR face à la déception," *Le Messager-Intumwa*, 24 November 1994, pp. 7–9.

Vice-President Kagame, so much so that in early January 1995, they had a public debate, during which the former denounced the insecurity and the latter defended the honour of the army.[9]

Despite these worrying signs, US$634 million were pledged in bilateral and multilateral aid at a donors' roundtable in Geneva in January 1995. The failure to tie these pledges to improvements in a rapidly deteriorating human rights and political situation may well have persuaded the regime that it could act without restraint and that impunity was assured. We shall see later that this line was to be continued up to the present day. The RPF was squarely supported by the "Friends of the New Rwanda," in particular the United States, the United Kingdom, and the Netherlands. These countries were not burdened by much knowledge of Rwanda and the region,[10] and driven by an acute guilt syndrome after the genocide, they reasoned in terms of "good guys" and "bad guys," the RPF naturally being the "good guys."

While they faked inclusion, behind the curtains, the "good guys" were busy taking full control and cordoning off political space.[11] Internal reports of the Intelligence and Security Department of the National Gendarmerie between January and March 1995 are very revealing.[12] Thus, a monthly report on "Enemy internal activity" produced in early January labeled non-RPF and particularly MDR politicians, civil servants, and diplomats as "subversive" and "enemy agents." Whenever they met, the meetings were considered "clandestine." In addition, "[m]any of NGOs operating in Rwanda are subversive." A January 19 Intrep addressed to Kagame by Colonel Kayumba Nyamwasa noted "lack of contentment among opposition politicians especially those from MDR and naturally from other extremists who have taken hiding in other political parties (...) [T]hese MDR politicians are, like always, making it a tribal issue and are holding secret consultations." Like the previous report, it singled out wings in the MDR as being pro- and anti-RPF. It also expressed concern that the MDR's increasing strength at grassroots level "will affect

---

[9] G. Prunier, *Africa's World War. Congo, the Rwandan Genocide, and the Making of a Continental Catastrophe*, Oxford, Oxford University Press, 2009, p. 9.

[10] Up to then, the United Kingdom and the Netherlands had been minor donors and did not have an embassy or even a professional consulate in Kigali.

[11] The RPF was present on the ground well before its victory, and it possessed a great deal of intelligence and infiltration capacity. According to Reed, by the time of the signing of the Arusha peace accord in August 1993, the RPF had 146 cells operating in Kigali alone (W.C. Reed, "Exile, Reform, and the Rise of the Rwandan Patriotic Front", *Journal of Modern African Studies*, 34:3 [1996], p. 496).

[12] All the documents quoted in this paragraph are on file with the author.

RPF's hold on the local population." Ministers, including Hutu from the RPF (Seth Sendashonga and Alexis Kanyarengwe), were said to organize meetings with the aim of "finding a way of fighting for the rights of the (Hutu) majority." On February 21, another Intrep noted that six parliamentarians were holding "secret meetings (...) at Hotel Kiyovu in room 21" and accused foreigners of showing "negative tendencies" and "working with the enemy." One member of the Belgian Red Cross was said to have been dismissed "because he was pro our government." A "joint security meeting to review lawyers for the appointments in the judiciary" held on March 11 vetted potential candidates for the higher courts and the general prosecutor's office. Although the government of national union was in place for international consumption, the security apparatus was monitoring "opponents," including in the government, and interfering in the functioning of the apparatus of the state. Invisible at the time, a "securocracy"[13] was rapidly being put in place.

Although claiming inclusiveness in a "government of national union," the RPF had no other choice but to establish full control and eliminate all possible political competition. This was clear well before it seized power. Although it claimed to wage a war of liberation, it considered those it "liberated" hostile and unreliable, in addition to being immature, and even plain stupid (see also the following discussion). During the war in the early 1990s, it considered having to manage populations as a hindrance, which is why it pushed people into the government-controlled area or to Uganda. The few who remained in RPF-held territory were regrouped and tightly controlled. This strategy was made clear by Kagame as early as in April or May 1992 at an RPF Central Committee meeting: "since there was no possibility of winning local support, the population was to be viewed as a security risk and so areas needed to be cleared."[14] Guichaoua lists a number of violent incidents engineered by the RPF between 1991 and early 1993 aimed at creating tensions and provoking stalemate, including by political killings.[15] Two experiences confirmed the RPF leadership's conviction that it could not allow an open electoral process to take place.

---

[13] Term coined by E. Sidiropoulos, "Democratisation and Militarisation in Rwanda: Eight Years after the Genocide", *African Security Review*, 11:3 (2002), pp. 77–87.

[14] B.M. Collins, *The Rwandan War 1990–1994: Interrogating the Dominant Narrative*, PhD thesis, London, University of London, SOAS, 2009, p. 115.

[15] A. Guichaoua, *Rwanda: De la guerre au génocide. Les politiques criminelles au Rwanda (1990–1994)*, Paris, La Découverte, 2010, pp. 134–137. These attempts at violent destabilisation were described by a former member of the RPA: A.J. Ruzibiza, *Rwanda. L'histoire secrète*, Paris, Editions du Panama, 2005, pp. 143–145, 151, 184, 202, 224.

In September 1993, indirect mayoral elections were organized in the eight communes of the demilitarized zone in the north. Although this was a region that neither the FAR nor the MRNDD physically controlled, and although the RPF conducted an electoral campaign and fielded candidates, the MRNDD captured all the posts. The RPF realized then that it stood no chance in an open political contest.[16] Similar inspiration was found in the elections that took place in Burundi in mid-1993. Despite the control exercised by the former single party Uprona, which was Tutsi dominated, its Hutu-dominated challenger Frodebu handsomely won the elections. For the RPF, the lesson was clear: not only was it unpopular, but the risk of ethnic voting at its expense was also real. As will be seen later, this remained an obsession, and an understandable one at that. RPF rule soon was based on a combination of "democratic centralism" dear to many pre-1990 guerrilla movements or vanguard parties, fear for democracy, and a pervasive focus on security and control.[17] Even before taking power, the RPF reasoned in military terms and did not believe in the implementation of the Arusha Accord. An internal document stated that "our military strategists must tell us how the military striking force of the Front can survive the merger of the two armies. At any rate, it is extremely important to maintain this striking force."[18] It outlined four main scenarios in the short term, none of which included respecting the accord.[19]

[16] Guichaoua notes that this experience was a turning point, "marking the profound disdain of the RPF's military leadership for the 'democrats', as well as its rejection of the electoral process foreseen by the Arusha peace accords for the post-transition period" (A. Guichaoua, *Rwanda*, p. 135).

[17] Prunier explained the RPF's attitude on account of its "oddity": "It was created outside the country where it intended to operate, its members were initially recruited among the armed forces of a foreign power, most of its combatants had never set foot in the land where they were going to fight, and they never managed to get any support from the masses of the population in whose name they were struggling. It nonetheless achieved power, but only after most of its civilian supporters had been annihilated in a perversely popular genocide by another segment of the population it later had to rule over" (G. Prunier, "The Rwandan Patriotic Front," in C. Clapham [Ed.], *African Guerillas*, Oxford, James Currey, 1998, p. 119).

[18] FPR, "L'environnement actuel et à venir pour l'organisation," p. 17, translated from French. This text is not dated, but it was probably made in February 1994. Although it is not signed, the style suggests that the author may well be Tito Rutaremara, a leading RPF ideologue belonging to the (small) progressive wing of the party. Rutaremara is currently Rwanda's ombudsman.

[19] Rupture of the accord and its renegotiation in Habyarimana's advantage; weakening of the broad-based transitional government (BBTG) in Habyarimana's advantage; marginalization of Habyarimana's Group; rupture of the accord through the fall of the BBTG and resumption of hostilities at the expense of Habyarimana (FPR, "L'environnement actuel", pp. 6–8).

CLEANSING THE REGIME

During the first half of 1995, and particularly after the RPA killed thousands of civilian internally displaced persons (IDPs) in Kibeho at the end of April (see Chapter 4), there were major disagreements within the government, for instance about abuse committed by the army and over appointments in the judiciary and the local administration, but they were initially kept behind closed doors. Interior Minister Sendashonga wrote more than 400 memos to Kagame about the killings and insecurity, but Kagame was careful never to answer in writing; later he simply stopped reacting.[20] As killings and "disappearances" went on, Sendashonga decided to disband the Local Defence Forces that committed many of the abuses. However, they were controlled by the RPF's local *abakada* ("cadres"), and they constituted a powerful means for RPF control at the local level. Kagame was furious, and a campaign of calumny started against Sendashonga.[21] After resigning from his position of chief of staff (*directeur de cabinet*) of the prime minister's office, Jean Damascène Ntakirutimana, a member of the political bureau of the MDR, explained his concerns in a letter with a memo sent to Twagiramungu from Nairobi on June 12, 1995. He denounced the "totalitarian drift" and "the summary executions, torture, arbitrary arrests, stalemate in the justice system, prohibition of political parties, double talk on the tricky problem of refugees, repression of the free press, hidden activities of extremist groups, etc." The conclusion of his memo was ominous: "absent genuine national reconciliation, the emergence of extremists that can be observed risks leading the country to a new cycle of violence that always causes vengeance."[22]

The crisis came to a head at the end of August 1995. A cabinet meeting on August 25 was the scene of angry exchanges: personally challenged by Prime Minister Twagiramungu and Interior Minister Sendashonga, Vice-President and Defense Minister Kagame walked out of the session. The rupture between the RPF and the MDR was now complete. Wanting to outpace his adversaries, Prime Minister Twagiramungu offered his resignation on August 28, after which President Bizimungu summoned Parliament later that day. He asked the chamber to vote a motion of no confidence toward the prime

---

[20] G. Prunier, *Africa's World War*, p. 18.

[21] *Idem*, p. 45.

[22] J.D. Ntakirutimana, Letter and memo "Le régime du FPR mène le Rwanda vers l'impasse", Nairobi, 12 June 1995.

minister, which it did without debate. The MPs, told that "now we will see who are the enemies of the people," did what was expected: only six among them did not vote the motion. The next day, Bizimungu revoked the ministers of Information, Justice, Home Affairs, and Transport and Communications. The latter, Immaculée Kayumba, a Tutsi from the RPF, was probably sacrificed in order to avoid the impression that these measures affected just Hutu Ministers. On August 31, the president appointed a new prime minister, Pierre-Célestin Rwigema, like his predecessor a Hutu from the MDR, and twenty ministers (five of whom were new, while three others changed portfolios). This episode, which was replete with unconstitutionalities,[23] confirmed the RPF's stranglehold on the system and eliminated the critical voices in the government. Prime Minister Twagiramungu, Interior Minister Seth Sendashonga (RPF) and Information Minister Jean-Baptiste Nkuliyingoma (MDR) left the country, whereas Justice Minister Alphonse-Marie Nkubito (an independent) stayed inside the country, where he died in early 1997. Sendashonga was later assassinated in Nairobi by Rwandan security operatives (see the following discussion).

This was just the tip of the iceberg. Many politicians, civil servants, judges and military officers who had stayed on or who returned after the RPF's victory were threatened or disillusioned, and they left the country in increasing numbers from early 1995 on. Over the years, at least a dozen government ministers fled the country, an impressive number in the absence of regime change. One way the RPF tightened its hold on power was through "accusatory practices" in which Hutu were branded "*génocidaires*."[24] This made them extremely vulnerable, as they risked arrest or worse. Among those who went into exile during 1995 alone were the Kigali prosecutor (Nsanzuwera), leaders of human rights organizations (such as Matata, Nyirimbibi, and Katabarwa), the governor (Niyitegeka) and treasurer (Ruberangeyo) of the Central Bank, two superior officers (Rusatira and Lizinde), and several permanent secretaries and other high-ranking civil servants. As soon as they were out of the country, they made allegations of concentration and abuse of power, outrages by the army and intelligence services, massive violations of human rights, insecurity and

---

[23] See F. Reyntjens, "Un ordre constitutionnel dissimulé: la 'loi fondamentale' du 26 mai 1995", *Dialogue*, 186, (October-November 1995), pp. 13–22 at pp. 21–22.

[24] L. Waldorf, "Revisiting Hotel Rwanda: Genocide Ideology, Reconciliation, and Rescuers", *Journal of Genocide Research*, 11:1 (2009), p. 107.

intimidation, and discrimination against Hutu and even against Tutsi genocide survivors.[25] Many did not have the luck to escape. From early 1995 on, Hutu elites became the victims of harassment, imprisonment, and even physical elimination. Provincial governors (*préfets*), local mayors, head teachers, clerics, and judges were killed in increasing numbers. In most cases, the responsibility of the RPA was well documented.[26] Former RPA lieutenant Abdul Ruzibiza later offered examples of people killed during 1994 through 1996 in what he called "the period of massive imprisonment, arrests and killings, both public and discreet, of an unprecedented magnitude."[27] In May 1996, former justice minister Nkubito cited thirty cases of judges and prosecutors that were arrested under all sorts of pretexts, in addition to those who were killed or who "disappeared."[28]

Suspected opponents were not just eliminated inside Rwanda, but even abroad. On October 6, 1996, Colonel Theoneste Lizinde was shot and killed in Nairobi. A former MP for the RPF, he defected and fled to Kinshasa first, and to Kenya later after falling out with Kagame, apparently over the killing of Hutu civilians. Although this was never proved, sources from within the RPF indicated that the assassination was committed by Rwandan external intelligence. The responsibility of Kigali was clearer when Seth Sendashonga was killed on May 16, 1998, in Nairobi too. Already in February 1996, he was the victim of an attempt against his life by François Mugabo, a diplomat at the Rwandan embassy. As Rwanda refused to lift his diplomatic immunity, Mugabo returned to Kigali unhindered. Alphonse Mbayire, an RPA officer who was working at the Rwandan embassy in Nairobi at the time of Sendashonga's assassination,

---

[25] For a few early examples, see V. Ndikumana and J. Afrika, *Lettre ouverte au Conseil de sécurité de l'ONU sur la situation qui prévaut au Rwanda*, Nairobi, 14 November 1994; E. Ruberangeyo, *Mes inquiétudes sur la gestion actuelle rwandaise des fonds publics*, Brussels, 31 May 1995; S. Musangamfura, *J'accuse le FPR de crimes de génocide des populations d'ethnie hutu, de purification ethnique et appelle à une enquête internationale urgente*, Nairobi, 8 December 1995; F. Twagiramungu and S. Sendashonga, *F.R.D. Plate-forme politique*, Brussels, March 1996; T. Lizinde, *Rwanda: la tragédie*, Brussels (in fact: Kinshasa), 1 May 1996. In early 1995, Planning Minister Jean Birara wrote a text very critical of the RPF that he did not sign for obvious reasons (J. Birara, *Note sur la situation au Rwanda*, 2 January 1995).

[26] Early examples can be found in reports by Human Rights Watch, *Rwanda: The Crisis Continues*, New York, April 1995; *Local Rwandan Leaders Assassinated*, New York, August 1995; Human Rights Watch, Fédération internationale des ligues des droits de l'homme, *HRW and FIDH condemn new killings in Rwanda*, New York, July 1996.

[27] A.J. Ruzibiza, *Rwanda. L'histoire secrète*, pp. 415–420.

[28] A. Nkubito, *Le harcèlement, les tracasseries, les menaces, bref la persécution du personnel judiciaire*, Kigali, 10 May 1996. Fearing for his life, Nkubito did not sign this text with his name.

was killed by "unknown persons" in Kigali a few days after his name was mentioned during the Nairobi murder trial. Two or three weeks before the assassination, ESO (External Security Organisation) chief Lieutenant Colonel Patrick Karegeya was in Nairobi, where he returned a couple of days before the crime.[29] As will be seen later, political assassinations and attempts abroad continued in the following years, up to the present day.

SPLITS WITHIN THE RPF

From early on, some Tutsi began to worry about where the regime was heading. Already in April 1995, Jean-Pierre Mugabe, a Tutsi survivor and an RPF veteran, wrote in *Le Tribun du Peuple*: "There are many Tutsi extremists. They are everywhere in the civil service and we have decided to denounce them. They have arbitrarily arrested many Hutu, as if all Hutu were *Interahamwe*. For these extremists even the Tutsi survivors of the genocide are *Interahamwe*. Today many of the Tutsi are just as vulnerable as the Hutu."[30] By mid-1998, Tutsi widely expressed unease about the evolution. A document circulated in Kigali in June or July 1998 and largely commented after it was posted on the internet claimed that a new *akazu*[31] was in power, united by among others family bonds, and accumulating material wealth, functions and privileges.[32] Other Tutsi voiced concern through their newspapers: journals such as *Le Tribun du Peuple* and *Ukuri* denounced widely spread instances of corruption, abuse of office, favoritism, illegal grabbing of houses and land, and fake privatizations.[33] The

---

[29] More details on the killing and Kigali's involvement can be found in G. Prunier, *Africa's World War*, pp. 365–368. Although the murder trial held in Nairobi did not lead to definitive conclusions, the likelihood of a Rwandan operation emerged, see "Analysis: The Trial of Sendashonga's Assassins – a Trail of Missing Links", Nairobi, Internews, 18 September 2000; "Investigating Officer Calls Former Rwandan Minister Assassination Political", Nairobi, Internews, 25 January 2001. A thoroughly researched piece of investigative journalism made a strong case against Kigali: *Celui qui savait*, film by Julien Elie, Montreal, Alter-Ciné, 2001. On the killing abroad of eight persons because of their knowledge of the RPF's role in downing former president Habyarimana's plane, see J. Swain, "The Riddle of the Rwandan Assassin's Trail", *The Sunday Times*, 4 April 2004.

[30] Jean-Pierre Mugabe in *Le Tribun du Peuple*, April 1995, no. 48, quoted by G. Prunier, *Africa's World War*, pp. 43–44.

[31] This term was used before 1994 to refer to President Habyarimana's inner circle; litterally speaking, *akazu* means "little hut"; see F. Reyntjens, *L'Afrique des grands lacs en crise. Rwanda, Burundi, 1988–1994*, Paris, Karthala, 1994, pp. 189–190.

[32] "Analyse politique du phénomène Akazu," document signed by "a deceived patriot (i.e., member of the RPF").

[33] A survey of the Rwandan press at the end of 1998 can be found in *Dialogue*, 207 (November-December 1998), pp. 83–87.

nickname given to the grand houses and office buildings newly built in Kigali was "Long live the genocide." An editorial published in the November 1998 issue of *Le Tribun du Peuple* asked the question, "More and more, you love the faults that you used to denounce on the waves of Radio Muhabura[34] (. . .); why did you combat Habyarimana?." The article went on to say that a new mafia was becoming "like the untouchable princes of President Habyarimana's days." When, disgusted and threatened, the paper's director Jean-Pierre Mugabe went into exile in the United States, he published a press release in which he summarized his observations and stated that "the law of the jungle now prevails." According to Mugabe, "the genocide perpetrated against our loved ones has been transformed into a 'commercial asset' by these corrupt and money-hungry authorities that practice the politics of the belly."[35] In May, Mugabe detailed his accusations in a text sent this time to the real holder of power: he dealt with issues such as the pillage of national assets and the misuse of foreign aid, the insecurity of people and goods, assassinations and arbitrary arrests, nepotism in the army, the job market and the schools, the elimination of military originating from Rwanda and Burundi, and the fate of the genocide survivors.[36] The reaction of the regime was furious: the director of the official information office ORINFOR accused Mugabe of being inspired by "personal opportunistic motives" and to have published reports "full of lies, defamation and politically motivated vendettas."[37] Dissident Tutsi increasingly became the victims of the accusatory practices mentioned earlier. As they could not be treated as *génocidaires*, they were either denounced as supporters of the exiled king[38] or accused of corruption, financial abuse, or other common law offenses.

A second wave of departures came in early 2000, in part against the background of increasing tensions between Tutsi returnees, those from

---

[34] The RPF's radio station during the rebellion.

[35] J.-P. Mugabe, "Cri d'alarme au président de la République rwandaise, à tous les Rwandais tant ceux qui résident au Rwanda ou [*sic*] ceux qui sont à l'étranger", Press release, 19 March 1999.

[36] J.-P. Mugabe, "Itangazo. Mbwirire Gen. Major Kagame Paul ku karubanda amarorerwa Urwanda ruzize" ("Solemn Message to Major General Kagame Paul on the Ills that Undermine Rwanda"), May 1999. Also see J.-P. Mugabe, "The Killings Resume: Preparing for the Next Rwandan War", *Defense & Foreign Affairs Strategic Policy*, 4 (1999), pp. 4–7.

[37] W. Rutayisire, "Mugabe Has Stretched his Opportunism too Far", Kigali, n.d. (1999).

[38] The last king of Rwanda, Kigeri V Ndahindurwa, who was deposed in 1960, lives in exile in the United States. Some opponents of the current regime advocate the return of the monarchy, a plea considered subversive in Kigali. The pro-monarchy movement is briefly discussed later in this chapter.

Uganda in particular, and genocide survivors. The latter felt for some time that they were becoming second-rate citizens who had been sacrificed by the RPF, which was suspected of having been interested in military victory rather than in saving them.[39] These apprehensions of Tutsi survivors were visible from early on. Already in mid-1996, McGreal quoted a survivor who had this to say about the returnees: "Those outsiders did not suffer like we did. They used our suffering and they promised us lots of things. But I think they want to forget us. Perhaps it would have been easier for them if everyone had died."[40] Indeed, according to Collins, based on several sources including RPF dissidents, portraying the image of the good guys and, already before the genocide, of victims, the RPF went as far as inciting ethnic violence: "The strategy was to provoke attacks upon Tutsis in order that it [the RPF] could present itself as the champion of the

---

[39] Kuperman claims that "the rebels expected their challenge to provoke genocidal retaliation but viewed this as an acceptable cost of achieving their goal of attaining power" (A. Kuperman, "Provoking Genocide: A Revised History of the Rwandan Patriotic Front", *Journal of Genocide Research*, 6:1 [2004], p. 63). When General Dallaire, the commander of the UN peacekeeping force UNAMIR, expressed concern about the fate of Tutsi and mentioned the ability of the RPF to save them, Kagame told him, "There will be many sacrifices in this war. If (they) have to be killed for the cause, they will be considered as having been part of the sacrifice" (R. Dallaire, *Shake Hands with the Devil. The Failure of Humanity in Rwanda*, Toronto, Random House Canada, 2003, p. 358). If the RPF downed the plane of President Habyarimana on April 6, 1994, which is very likely, it would have known what everyone knew, namely that the toll for Tutsi living inside Rwanda would be very high. On March 15, 1994, the CIA predicted a death toll of possibly 500,000 in case the conflict escalated (J. Cohen, *One Hundred Days of Silence. America and the Rwanda Genocide*, Lanham MD, Rowman & Littlefield Publishers, 2007, p. 29). Even as the genocide unfolded, "the RPF clung to its strategy: refusing to compromise its demands for political power, while accepting retaliation against Tutsi civilians as the price of achieving that goal, even as the price climbed much higher than expected" (A. Kuperman, "Provoking Genocide", p. 78). Scheffer describes the way in which the RPF "slowed down the peace-keeping train in New York" and says that "by early May [1994] (it) officially rejected intervention by U.N. or African peacekeeping forces in Rwanda. RPF officers asserted that their victory was the only way to stop the ongoing genocide" (D. Scheffer, *All the Missing Souls. A Personal History of the War Crimes Tribunals*, Princeton and Oxford, Princeton University Press, 2012, p. 62). Reydams offers a well-documented demonstration, based in part on U.S. intelligence documents, of the RPF's cynical choice of power at the expense of Tutsi lives. He suggests "a calculation that it was more useful to let the *génocidaires* do their work – preferably in front of western TV cameras – and prosecute them later" (L. Reydams, *Let's Be Friends. The United States, Post-Genocide Rwanda, and Victor's Justice in Arusha*, IOB Discussion Paper 2013.01, Antwerp, p. 17).

[40] "The Nightmares of a Tutsi Survivor," *Guardian Weekly*, 28 July 1996, quoted by J.K. Gasana, N. Nsengimana, *Breaking Hutu-Tutsi Enmity in Rwanda through Reconciliation*, Projet NOUER, Lausanne, October 1997, p. 14.

oppressed and to justify its war."[41] Collins lists several examples of provocative killings committed by the RPF.[42]

Intra-Tutsi tensions heralded a profound political crisis that started on 6 January 2000, when the Speaker of the National Assembly, Tutsi genocide survivor[43] Joseph Sebarenzi, suddenly resigned under pressure from groups within the RPF who were under parliamentary scrutiny. Some members of his own party, the PL, participated in the plot to remove him. In the autumn of 1999, the assembly not only forced three ministers from other parties to resign, but also started inquiries about two RPF ministers, Patrick Mazimhaka (minister in the president's office) and Emmanuel Mudidi (Education). Sebarenzi was suddenly accused of seeking "cheap popularity," of displaying "dictatorial tendencies," of poor management, and of aiming at confrontation with the government and the Supreme Court. A politically more dangerous allegation spread by sources in the RPF and the PL said that he conspired with exiles for the return of the monarchy. Fearing for his life, Sebarenzi fled to Uganda and later settled in North America.[44] At the inauguration of Sebarenzi's successor Vincent Biruta (PSD), President Bizimungu stated that "the role of parliament is not to conduct inquiries and dismiss ministers."[45]

The Sebarenzi affair was hardly over when Prime Minister Pierre-Célestin Rwigema announced his resignation on February 28, 2000. Already accused of complicity in the genocide, he was under parliamentary scrutiny for corruption and abuse of power since October 1999. Rwigema narrowly escaped a vote of no confidence on December 22, 1999, but his position became untenable when on February 17, 2000, Parliament put in place a commission to investigate him. In his letter of resignation to President Bizimungu, Rwigema wrote that "the controversial interpretations of the subject of the parliamentary probe and the media campaigns that followed it have created a climate that handicaps the exercise of my function, and are at the basis of my decision to put an end to it."[46] Bernard

---

[41] B.M. Collins, *The Rwandan War*, p. 116.

[42] *Idem*, pp. 116–117, 147–148, 157–160.

[43] As he left Rwanda in 1992 to join the RPF, strictly speaking Sebarenzi was not a "survivor". However, being a Tutsi from the interior, he was perceived as such and was considered close to the survivors' needs and concerns.

[44] For a description of his saga, see J. Sebarenzi, *God Sleeps in Rwanda. A Journey of Transformation*, New York, Atria Books, 2009.

[45] Kigali, DPA, 19 January 2000.

[46] Kigali, AFP, 28 February 2000.

Makuza,[47] also of the MDR, replaced Rwigema who sought asylum in the United States at the end of May.[48] The new government put in place on March 20 reflected the creeping RPF-ization and tutsization: eleven of eighteen ministers were from the RPF, twelve were Tutsi; a good five years on, Kagame was the only survivor of the cabinet put in place in July 1994. During the government's inauguration ceremony, Bizimungu again expressed his frustration with regard to the parliament's functioning, accusing it of settling scores with certain (implicitly Hutu) ministers, whereas others (Tutsi) were left alone.

What was in the offing for some time arrived less than a month later. On March 23, in a brief letter to the Speaker of the Assembly, Bizimungu resigned "for personal reasons." On the same day, he wrote to Kagame, in his capacity of chair of the RPF, that he resigned from his functions of responsibility in the party, but that he would "continue to serve the country and the movement as an ordinary member of the RPF."[49] Accusations were immediately leveled against him: Bizimungu was said to have committed tax fraud, to have illegally dispossessed farmers, and to have opposed parliamentary inquiries into corruption for fear of being investigated himself.[50] In addition, during a special parliamentary session on March 24, he was accused of "political crimes" and of "serious violations of the constitution."[51] Although Uganda offered him political asylum,[52] Bizimungu remained in the country; he was arrested a year later, convicted, and sentenced to a fifteen-year jail sentence in 2005.[53] In contradiction to the Arusha Accord, which provided that the interim of the presidency was to be filled by the Speaker of the National Assembly[54], Vice-President Kagame assumed the office, a move endorsed on March 25 by the Supreme Court in a decision without clear legal basis. However, unanimity was quickly created, and on March 29, seven parties asked the

---

[47] Son of Anastase Makuza, one of the historic leaders of the MDR-Parmehutu and an important player in the 1959–1961 revolution.

[48] As happened to other opponents, Rwigema was accused of having participated in the genocide, an international arrest warrant was launched against him in April 2001, and his name suddenly appeared on a new list of "category 1" genocide suspects published during that period. He, however, returned to Rwanda in 2011, and he was forgiven for his sins.

[49] Kigali, ARI-RNA, 23 March 2000.

[50] Kigali, AP, 23 March 2000.

[51] Kigali, PANA, 24 March 2000.

[52] This hostile act must be seen in the context of the conflict that opposed Uganda and Rwanda at the time against the background of the war in the DRC.

[53] He was, however, pardoned by President Kagame in 2007. He has led a secluded life ever since and has not made any public appearance or statement.

[54] Art. 48, 2 of the protocol on power sharing.

RPF to designate Kagame as candidate for the presidency. The political bureau of the party followed suit on April 1, and on April 17, Kagame was elected president by eighty-one votes against five in a joint session of the government and the National Assembly.

The departures of the Speaker, the prime minister and the head of state within three months were a strong indication that the regime was facing a profound political crisis. Although Waugh felt that Bizimungu's resignation "was the confirmation that the multi-ethnic façade of reconstruction in Rwanda was now at an end,"[55] the crisis did not so much express the ethnic conflict but rather two other developments, namely, the next step in the taking of full control by Kagame and increasingly visible signs of intra-Tutsi strife opposing, on one hand, the genocide survivors and (more particularly "Ugandan") fractions of the old diaspora and, on the other, groups within the RPF, including within the army.[56]

After what happened to Sebarenzi, the fears of the survivors increased when an advisor in the president's office, Assiel Kabera, himself a survivor close to Sebarenzi, was assassinated on March 6, 2000, by men in uniform. Although the murder remained officially unsolved, a private enquiry carried out by his friends and family concluded that Kabera was killed by the DMI (Directorate of Military Intelligence) on the orders of President Kagame.[57] Although the situation was, of course, very different, the tension recalled that which prevailed in early 1994 during the months preceding the genocide. Sebarenzi summed up this feeling in an interview: "The situation is becoming uncontrollable, there are deep divisions today particularly among Tutsi and these tendencies could lead to a catastrophe (...) There are many similarities with the period which preceded the 1994 genocide."[58] Indeed, the regime was increasingly challenged from within. At the beginning of 2001, the directors of the newspaper *Rwanda Newsline*, who used to be close to the RPF, were threatened after the publication of articles criticizing the government, in particular concerning the RPA's involvement in the Congo. They wrote that they were accused of

[55] C.M. Waugh, *Paul Kagame and Rwanda. Power, Genocide and the Rwandan Patriotic Front*, Jefferson, NC, McFarland & Company, 2004, p. 152.

[56] As seen later, RPA officers left the country, whereas others were arrested in an atmosphere of coup rumours and accusations of connivance with the monarchic movement. Some were forcibly returned from abroad (for an example, see an Urgent Action by Amnesty International, 24 February 2000, AFR 47/07/00).

[57] "Raporo ya commission yigenga ku rupfu rwa bwana Assiel Kabera," Kigali, 16 August 2000.

[58] Kigali, AFP, 4 April 2000.

being in the pay of "negative forces" ("a term loosely coined by the RPF by which it terrorizes all its critics or opponents into silence").[59] The editorial staff of *Imboni*, another newspaper considered close to the RPF, left Rwanda for Brussels, where they published *Imboni in Exile*. In its first editorial, the staff sarcastically "apologized" for "having publicly expressed our indignation at the spirit of sycophancy, the deliberate process of impoverishment of society and public opinion to vassaldom."[60] Even a journalist of the governmental press was forced to go into exile: on September 2, 2000, Valens Kwitegetse of the newspaper *Imvaho Nshya* sought asylum in Uganda.

High-ranking RPF officials and RPA officers followed suit: MPs Evariste Sissi and Deus Kagiraneza (who was also an officer in the RPA and a DMI cadre) left for Uganda and Belgium, respectively; Bosco Rutagengwa, the founder of the genocide survivors' organization Ibuka, found asylum in the United States; RPA Majors Furuma,[61] Mupende, Ntashamaje and Kwikiriza left for Uganda, Belgium or Canada; banker and former MP Valens Kajeguhakwa, an ertswhile funder of the RPF, fled as well.[62] In August 2001, RPA chief of staff General Kayumba Nyamwasa went on "study leave" in the United Kingdom, after a violent verbal dispute with Kagame against the background of a malaise in the army around the operations in the DRC.[63] On April 12, 2001 the editorial of *Rwanda Newsline* interpreted the "disappearance" on April 4 of retired major Alex Ruzindana, who was later found dead, as "a possible attempt to discourage new defections." In June, retired FAR Colonel Stanislas Biseruka was condemned to three years in prison for breach of trust. Even RPF members abroad were disillusioned enough to quit. At the beginning of September 2000, the leadership of the RPF United States (including its chairperson, Alexandre Kimenyi, and vice chairman, Augustin Kamongi) resigned from the party in disgust.

---

[59] The expression "negative forces" is contained in the July 1999 Lusaka Accord on the DRC, which mentioned the Interahamwe militia, among others.

[60] *Imboni en exil*, 2001, no. 1.

[61] In a letter to Kagame dated 9 January 2001, Furuma wrote that he resigned from the RPF/RPA and fled the country because the government "appears to be certainly leading the country to deepening national poverty, continued denial of fundamental rights, further ethnic violence (...)". In an open letter dated January 23, 2001, Furuma leveled more specific accusations: large-scale killings of Hutu, looting in Rwanda and the DRC, and the evolution toward dictatorship.

[62] As soon as he left the country and joined the opposition, he was accused of abuse at the BACAR bank.

[63] Although Kayumba returned in mid-2002, the rift with Kagame was not closed. Kayumba eventually entered in open opposition against Kagame in early 2010 (see Chapter 3).

Despite the endeavours of the regime to convince opponents abroad, Hutu in particular, to return home, few did. The opposition in exile was unanimous in staying away from the "National Summit on Unity and Reconciliation" held in Kigali in October 2000. One of the invitees, Joseph Sebarenzi, explained his absence: "This conference is a media event aimed at convincing international opinion that the RPF wants to promote national reconciliation, but we cannot come to any positive results in the present situation."[64]

RPF-IZATION AND TUTSIZATION

Internally, the RPF tightened its grip. At the occasion of a reshuffle on March 28, 1997, the RPF chairman Alexis Kanyarengwe left the government, in which he was minister of the Interior. Officially he was not sacked, but resigned "because he wanted to devote himself to other functions." However, he had no other function than being the chairman of the RPF, and that was essentially an honorific function in the shadow of strongman Kagame. In reality, Kanyarengwe was removed following his protest, and that of Ignace Karuhije, the *préfet* of Ruhengeri, against massacres committed by the RPA in his home region (see Chapter 4). Karuhije was sacked on the same day because of "incompetence and inability to curb insecurity." The cabinet reshuffle of March 1997 was also a new departure from the Arusha Accord and went toward even more executive dominance. Indeed, the dismissals of ministers were decided by the president and not by the assembly, and the new appointments were made without consulting the political parties. Less than a year later, on February 15, 1998, Kanyarengwe was replaced at the helm of the RPF by Kagame, while President Bizimungu became deputy chairman of the party. Kanyarengwe, who since 1990 had been the "Hutu face" of the RPF, completely disappeared from public life.[65] The "election" of the new RPF leadership happened in a very opaque way. It was unclear which

---

[64] Kigali, AFP, 20 October 2000. Some Tutsi were worried about attempts to "recuperate" Hutu personalities. Thus, in *Imboni* (in exile), no. 3, Déo Mushayidi complained about the rapid "Hutuization" of the RPF, of which he saw signs in "the large-scale enrolment of ex-FAR in the RPA" and "the creation of new militia that are referred to as the Local Defence Forces recruited mainly among young Hutu." In a document widely circulated and discussed on the Internet, Frank Ikondere claimed that "the RPF leadership today is composed of a few people who feel that Tutsi are more of a danger than Hutu" (Posting on Rwanda-l, 3 September 2000).

[65] The use of "token Hutu" became so widespread that Tutsi survivors protested on several occasions against the co-optation into politics and the army of suspected *génocidaires*.

body took the decision,[66] and the new composition confirmed the Tutsi nature of the party: among the three members of the executive committee and the eight commissioners, Bizimungu was the only Hutu.

Indeed, the dominance of the RPF did not just express itself in political terms, but in ethnic terms too. The "tutsization" drive was visible from early on. Although it officially rejected ethnic discrimination and even the notion of ethnicity, the RPF rapidly reserved access to power, wealth, and knowledge to Tutsi elites. The only exception was the cabinet, in which a number of Hutu served as ministers in order to give a symbolic expression of national unity, but we shall see later that their real power was very limited. The RPF vigorously and categorically denied any ethnic factor, a denial that was an essential element of the hegemonic strategies of small Tutsi elites, such as that powerful in Rwanda during the 1950s and in Burundi between 1965 and 1988. Political analysts J.-H. Bradol and A. Guibert insisted that "to stress the absence of ethnic identities has become a means of masking the monopoly by Tutsi military of political power. In this case, political discourse opposed to ethnism attempts to hide the domination of society by the self-proclaimed representatives of the Tutsi community."[67] This state of affairs was explained away in a paradoxical fashion: when, in the past, Hutu were a majority in public institutions, this was called "ethnic discrimination"; however, now that Tutsi were a majority, this became "meritocracy." Of course, the elimination of ethnicity was a worthwhile goal, shared by many Rwandans, but this objective was manipulated as a tool for the monopolization of power in the hands of a small group.

The former priest Privat Rutazibwa, one of the ideologues of the RPF, put forward a revealing justification for this ethnic bias. "The Hutu elites as a whole entirely subscribe to the fundamental thesis of the ethnist ideology, namely that power belongs to the Hutu because they are a majority." Such an observation obviously allows the exclusion of "the Hutu elites" in their entirety, in order to base the exercise of power on "the qualification of competence and personal merit."[68] The government-owned weekly *La Nouvelle Relève* meant exactly the same when it

---

[66] According to a February 16, 1998 communiqué of the RPF, the decision was taken by "the national consultative council of the representatives of the members of all the regions, with reference to the month of December 1993".

[67] J.-H. Bradol and A. Guibert, "Le temps des assassins et l'espace humanitaire, Rwanda, Kivu, 1994–1997", *Hérodote* 86:7 (1997), p. 119.

[68] P. Rutazibwa, "Cet ethnisme sans fin," *Informations Rwandaises et Internationales*, 5 (November-December 1996), pp. 19–20.

expressed the hope that the road followed would be "the result of a popular consensus between the leaders and the *enlightened part* of the people."[69] This "enlightened part" clearly did not include the Hutu, or at least their elites. Therefore, the combination of "meritocracy" and the exclusion of the elite of one ethnic group delivered the right to govern to the elite of the other ethnic group.

This Tutsization, which was also a means of consolidating the hold of the RPF on the system, was quite spectacular at most levels of the state: by 1996, the majority of MPs, four of the six Supreme Court presiding judges, more than 80 percent of mayors, most permanent secretaries, and university teachers and students, almost the entire army command structure and the intelligence services were Tutsi. This phenomenon was further amplified and supported by a sociopolitical reality, namely, the Tutsization of urban Rwanda, which had become the sociological and economic foundation of the RPF. Many of the returned diaspora ("old caseload refugees") indeed settled in towns and cities where they became the majority, "squatting" homes, shops, and businesses.[70] A survey showed that, by mid-2000, of 169 of the most important officeholders, 135 (or about 80 percent) were RPF/RPA and 119 (roughly 70 percent) were Tutsi.[71] Another survey conducted independently from the previous one arrived at similar findings for 2002: of 401 major functions in the state machinery, 252 (about 63 percent) were occupied by Tutsi.[72] These data were confirmed again in 2008, when the U.S. embassy analyzed 118 senior positions in ministries, parastatals, and regulatory bodies. The review showed that two-thirds of the positions were occupied by Tutsi. The document concluded that "[f]or all the government's exhortations to Rwandans to abandon ethnic identities (. . .), the political reality is self-evidently otherwise" and that "if this government is ever to surmount the challenges and divides of Rwandan society, it must begin to share real authority with Hutus to a much greater degree than it does now."[73] Although the official position is that such

---

[69] *La Nouvelle Relève*, 31 May 1996 (emphasis added).

[70] This phenomenon is discussed in W. Harambe, *Les propriétés illégalement occupées au Rwanda: une manne pour le Front Patriotique Rwandais*, s.l., s.d. (1996).

[71] For details see F. Reyntjens, "Rwanda, ten years on: From genocide to dictatorship," *African Affairs*, 103:2 (2004), p. 189.

[72] A.E. Gakusi, F. Mouzer, "Rwanda: Contraintes structurelles et gouvernance," Paris, May 2003, mimeo, p. 8. Also see A.E. Gakusi, F. Mouzer, *De la revolution rwandaise à la contre-révolution. Contraintes structurelles et gouvernance 1950–2003*, Paris, L'Harmattan, 2003, pp. 27–29, 128–133.

[73] "Ethnicity in Rwanda – Who Governs the Country?", US Embassy Kigali, Ref. Kigali 480, August 5, 2008, available through WikiLeaks (http://wikileaks.org/cable/2008/08/08/

statistics cannot be made "as there are no longer Tutsi, Hutu and Twa, but only Rwandans," RPF members acknowledge in private that Tutsi dominate the system. They explain this by saying that most positions are filled by members of the RPF and that it is natural that they tend to be Tutsi as the RPF is a predominantly Tutsi organization. They also explain that it is understandable that even RPF Hutu are not entirely trusted and that their genuine loyalty is in doubt. So "delicate" positions are reserved to Tutsi faithful and "delicate" decisions are taken in an inner circle of Tutsi.[74]

MILITARIZATION OF THE POLITICAL LANDSCAPE

The way in which the RPF imposed its dominance led to the militarization of the political landscape. While during 1991 through 1993, political parties and a vigorous civil society had emerged in the public arena, the resumption of the war, the genocide and the taking of power by the RPF eliminated these actors. Dorsey has shown how the army and the intelligence services soon became the pillars of the regime and how the strict control of people was an obsession from the beginning of the war in 1990. The instruments of power and accumulation were concentrated in small networks based on a common past in certain refugee camps, schools, and family ties.[75] The RPF decreed a new transition period that was to last five years (1994–1999, but this period was extended for another four years in 1999) and suspended the activities of political parties, without however banning them, at least initially. Parties did not function, and the most important one, the MDR, was reduced to silence after its November 1994 position mentioned earlier. It was altogether banned in 2003 (see Chapter 2). Civil society progressively disappeared as a result of militarization, ethnic polarization, and sheer repression. Just like the population, it was physically separated in 1994. Most of its leaders fled abroad and were scattered across many countries in Africa, Europe, and North America. Inside Rwanda, some of the older organizations resumed their

KIGALI525.html). After the cable became known, Kagame reacted furiously, stating that the West had no credibility to judge the Rwandan government because it stood by a "genocidal government" and that he wanted "a break with these fellows" ("Kagame Accuses US for Backing 'Genocidal Government'", *The Chronicles*, 7 November 2011).

[74] Some lucidly argue that, despite different institutional engineering, the situation in Rwanda and Burundi is not that different: Hutu are dominant in Burundi, Tutsi are in Rwanda, and there are "token Tutsi" in Burundi and "token Hutu" in Rwanda.

[75] M. Dorsey, "Violence and Power-Building in Post-Genocide Rwanda," in R. Doom, J. Gorus (Eds.), *Politics of Identity and Economics of Conflict in the Great Lakes Region*, Brussels, VUB Press, 2000, pp. 311–348.

activities, but they were closely monitored by the intelligence system, whereas newly created organizations attempted to cater for the needs of genocide victims. The way in which the little that was left of an autonomous civil society was destroyed is addressed in Chapter 3.

Although the internal opposition was eliminated, political movements were created early on in the new diaspora. In November 1994, the Union démocratique rwandaise (UDR) was created in Paris under the initiative of former prime minister Dismas Nsengiyaremye. Former minister François Nzabahimana chaired the Rassemblement pour la démocratie et le retour des réfugiés (RDR), founded in April 1995 in Mugunga (North Kivu). Rwanda pour tous (RPT), created in Brussels in June 1995, was chaired by former minister James Gasana. The Forces de Résistance pour la Démocratie (FRD) were set up in Brussels by Twagiramungu and Sendashonga in March 1996. The discourse of these movements was similar: they were "neither *génocidaire* nor RPF," and they condemned the dictatorial management and the crimes committed by both the former and the current regime, although the RDR, or at least some of its leaders, used an ambiguous discourse and were uncomfortably close to genocide suspects.[76] Besides these movements, mainly rallying Hutu for obvious reasons, a "Tutsi" opposition emerged too. On one hand, the old monarchist party Union nationale rwandaise (UNAR), which was refused registration in Rwanda, distanced itself from the RPF. In a communiqué dated May 26, 1996, its chairperson Claude Rukeba accused the RPF of having put in place a dictatorial and violent dictatorship, and of discriminating against Hutu and (Tutsi) genocide survivors. The message concluded by asking "the united (i.e. members of UNAR) to cease solidarity with the RPF. It is high time."[77] On the other hand, the Rwanda National Liberation Movement (RNLM), presided by a former refugee in Uganda, John Karuranga, accused the RPF of having committed atrocities and being a veiled Ugandan occupation force. On July 27, 1996, the former *mwami* (king) Kigeli V appealed for a political dialogue. In early January 1997, this initiative was relayed by a group of Hutu and Tutsi petitioners who launched an "Appeal to King Kigeli V for him to act as reconciler of the Rwandan people." This was the first bi-ethnic platform bringing together very diverse political tendencies, which made it difficult for the

---

[76] Until their arrest in Yaoundé and referral to the International Criminal Tribunal for Rwanda (ICTR), some of these suspects presented themselves as the "Cameroon section of the RDR."

[77] "Itangazo. Umutwe w'Abashyirahamwe b'Urwanda," 26 May 1996; also see an op-ed published by Rukeba in *Le Devoir* (Montreal), 12 June 1996.

RPF to qualify initiatives such as these as "genocidal." During a debate broadcast by the national radio, the general secretary of the RPF called the advocates of the return of the monarchy "pawns of the Christian-Democrat International, the missionaries and other friends of the old regime intent on dividing the Tutsi, the RPF and the Rwandan people generally."[78] For many years to come, these diaspora groups and many that were to follow only had a limited impact on Rwandan politics. Those that did eventually matter are discussed later.

The militarization of the political landscape increased proportionally with the decline of the role played by political parties and civil society. The country was increasingly dominated by the army, the powerful DMI, and the Local Defence Forces (LDF). The budget showed this prominence: in 1996, more than half the current expenditure was military. A small circle of RPF leaders took the important decisions in an opaque way, while the government dealt with the day-to-day management of administrative affairs and Parliament was sidelined. This was illustrated by the fact that important issues, such as deploying the army on several occasions (up to 2012) in Zaire/DRC, was never discussed in the cabinet or in Parliament. The emergence of an executive presidency at the expense of the legislature was illustrated in February 1997 by an incident that led to the eviction of Juvénal Nkusi (PSD) as speaker of the TNA. In November 1996, Parliament adopted a bill organizing the control of the government, in application of article 81 of the constitution. Although the constitutional court upheld the validity of the bill, President Bizimungu refused to promulgate it, despite the provision of article 6, d) of the Arusha protocol on power sharing, which also stipulated that in such a case "the laws shall be sanctioned and promulgated by the Speaker of the TNA." Under heavy pressure from the government, the Speaker refused to fulfil his constitutional duty, as a result of which he was sacked by the assembly. We have seen that a similar fate befell his successor Joseph Sebarenzi.

CONCLUSION

Although the RPF initially gave the impression that it at least contemplated a regime of power sharing, the reality is that it wanted full and total power from day one, just as it had done before its victory in the areas it controlled during the civil war. It achieved this through a combination of

[78] "Débat radiodiffusé autour du Roi Kigeri V et de la monarchie," *ARI/RNA*, 146, 23 June 1999.

mechanisms. The most important was physical. The RPF literally "occupied" the country, taking swift control of the national territory and the Rwandan population by putting its cadres in all strategic locations, both national and local. Using widespread terror, it imposed compliance with that control. The massacre of (potential) opponents was systematic. Between 1994 and 1998, hundreds of thousands of Hutu civilians were killed in both Rwanda and Zaire/Congo (see Chapter 4), but Tutsi were also selectively targeted. These killings instilled fear, forced real or imaginary trouble-making counter-elites at the local and national levels into compliance or at least made them keep silent. After they were sufficiently subdued, it was no longer necessary to resort to massacres: just keeping the lid on and reminding who had the power to kill were sufficient. With the help of examples, Prunier shows that "[t]he evidence points to an original tactical pattern."[79]

Another mechanism was political. Those "not with the RPF were against it,"[80] and those whose loyalty was in doubt – in politics, civil society, the judiciary, the civil service, the security sector – were ruthlessly excluded through dismissal, assassination, imprisonment, or exile. Not just the elites but rural people too were forced to join the RPF. Not being a member is dangerous, as an example given by a refugee in Nakivale settlement shows: "The RPA killed my wife (in 2000). She was a primary school teacher, so she was one of the (rural) intellectuals. She didn't join the RPF. More than 100 people were killed at that time. (. . .) To be Rwandan is to be part of the RPF."[81] A third mechanism was a shrewd communication strategy aimed at keeping the international community at bay. This is discussed in Chapter 5.

In order to understand the violent modes of the RPF, Prunier suggests to look at its Ugandan origins. "The whole life history of these men even before they set foot on Rwandese soil had been full of the sound and the fury of civil war, with its attendant atrocities and civilian massacres, committed against them, around them, or by them. For them violence

---

[79] G. Prunier, *Africa's World War*, p. 21. This is by no means a thing of the past but a current phenomenon. In 2010, recent refugees in Uganda recounted stories of ongoing oppression, extrajudicial killings and disappearances all of which were traced to officials and presented an image of "a sophisticated but profoundly repressive political system that is systematically silencing any opposition" (*A Dangerous Impasse: Rwandan Refugees in Uganda*, Citizenship and Displacement in the Great Lakes Region, Working Paper No. 4, June 2010, p. 35).

[80] P. Gready, "'You're Either with Us or against Us': Civil society and policy making in post-genocide Rwanda", *African Affairs*, 109:437 (2010), pp. 637–657.

[81] *A Dangerous Impasse*, p. 32.

was not exceptional; it was a normal state of affairs."[82] In addition, "[a]s soldiers they only knew the gun, and the gun had worked well for them in the past."[83] In a similar vein, Verhoeven argues that the RPF elites' "formative years were spent in violent environments, under constant threat of infiltration and extermination by their enemies."[84]

However, apart from the Ugandan background, there was also a great deal of continuity with the previous regime. Indeed, the manner in which power was exercised by the RPF echoed that of the days of single-party rule before 1990 in several respects. Under both Habyarimana and Kagame, a clientelistic network referred to as the *akazu* accumulated wealth and privileges. Both manipulated ethnicity, the former by scapegoating and eventually exterminating the Tutsi, the latter by discriminating against the Hutu under the guise of ethnic amnesia.[85] Both used large-scale violence to eliminate their opponents, and they did so with total impunity, which is another element of continuity. Whereas, under the former regime, attacks, murders and massacres of civilians during the early 1990s were never judicially investigated, let alone prosecuted, so too did the new regime permit RPA soldiers and powerful civilians who ordered or committed assassinations and massacres to go unpunished. Human rights abuse is discussed in Chapter 4.

Continuity was visible not just in the exercise of power, but also in the nature of the state. An ancient state tradition played an undeniable role here: a mere two years after the extreme human and material destruction of 1994, the state was rebuilt. Rwanda was again administered from top to bottom; territorial, military, and security structures were in place; the judicial system was reestablished; tax revenues were collected and spent. The regime was able in a short time to establish total control over state and society. The next two chapters examine the ways and means of regime consolidation.

---

[82] G. Prunier, *Africa's World War*, p. 13.

[83] *Idem*, p. 22.

[84] H. Verhoeven, "Nurturing Democracy or into the Danger Zone? The Rwandan Patriotic Front, Elite Fragmentation and Post-liberation Politics", in M. Campioni, P. Noack (Eds.), *Rwanda Fast Forward. Social, Economic, Military and Reconciliation Prospects*, Houndmills, Palgrave Macmillan, 2012, p. 265.

[85] This brings to mind the situation in Burundi in the Bagaza years, when ethnicity was denied, just like in Rwanda today. Nevertheless, clandestine censuses were organized, for instance, in the schools, where the names of Hutu students were marked with "U" and those of Tutsi students with "I." Although denied at the time, these practices were later admitted by the minister of education under Bagaza ("Education. Système 'U' et 'I'," *Iwacu. Le Magazine*, April 2012, p. 25).

2

Elections as a Means of Regime Consolidation

PREPARING THE GROUND

From early on, the regime tackled political parties, civil society and the press. By the end of 1997, the number of "disappearances" was growing so rapidly that Amnesty International voiced serious concern.[1] All types of troublemakers were targeted: in 1997, one journalist was killed and two were arrested, as were two leaders of human rights associations and judges. The regime disliked civil society, and it adopted a strategy of intimidation and destruction, in part through infiltration. Indeed, RPF general secretary Denis Polisi lambasted "those business enterprises called NGOs" and lashed out at "the latest invention of NGOs, namely civil society."[2] In order to prepare the ground for risk-free elections, the RPF first set out to eliminate what was left of the political opposition.

The destruction of the MDR, the last party that attempted to maintain some autonomy towards the RPF, started in earnest in 1998. During a meeting in May of a "Forum for National Orientations," the MDR

---

[1] Amnesty International, *Rwanda: "Disappearances" Reach Alarming Proportions, Say Amnesty International Delegates*, London, 12 March 1998.

[2] Remarks made to members of the Rwandan community in Brussels, June 15, 1997. Six years later, the message may have been softer, but the core remained. Minister of State for Good Governance Protais Musoni stated, "On one side civil society is seen as a counter power to government, and on the other civil society is seen as an effective partner in service delivery and the development process. Rwanda favours the latter approach" (P. Musoni, *Building a Democratic Culture: Rwanda's Experience and Perspectives*, Conference on "Elections and Accountability in Africa", Wilton Park, 21–25 July 2003, pp. 14–15).

proposed a document[3] in which it defended a number of positions on the past and the present[4] that were quite opposed to those of the RPF. The MDR was summoned to rewrite its homework in no uncertain terms,[5] which it did in less than a week: the new document toed the RPF line and every word critical of the regime had disappeared. This was not enough, though. In July, Prime Minister Rwigema, an MDR member himself, caused the party to split.[6] Members opposed to the "reformation" of the party were accused of being against national unity and were expelled from the MDR. In February and March 1999, four of them were first excluded from Parliament and then arrested. Rwigema had outlived his usefulness by then. Suddenly accused of having distributed weapons to militiamen during the genocide and of being in league with the armed rebellion, the Kigali prosecutor opened a file against him.[7] Kagame stated that these accusations "must be taken seriously,"[8] and embattled Rwigema asked for "the forgiveness of all Rwandans for the ideology of divisions" spread by former leaders of his party, that now condemned "all leaders who preach destructive ideologies."[9] As seen earlier, Rwigema was sacked and left the country a year later. A next step in the destruction of the MDR followed in 2001. In June, Minister Désiré Nyandwi (MDR but who later joined the RPF) caused a new split in the party, whose general secretary Pierre Gakwandi was arrested in December after having published an article critical of the government. We shall see that the party was finally banned altogether in 2003.

---

[3] MDR, *Contribution du Mouvement Démocratique Républicain dans la recherche de solutions aux problèmes que rencontre le Rwanda*, 23 May 1998.

[4] For instance, the document stated that even before colonial days, Rwanda was not unified, that the 1959 revolution introduced the idea of democracy, that royalty rather than external factors undermined the country, and that the amalgamation making all Hutu *génocidaires* contributed to insecurity.

[5] "The MDR must recognise its historical responsibility in what happened in the country. The MDR must admit that the Parmehutu vision is sectarian and reactionary. This vision must be officially rejected by that party" ("Note explicative concernant le procès-verbal sanctionnant la réunion dirigée en date du 23/05/1998 par Son Excellence le Président de la République", Kigali, 23 May 1998).

[6] He later explained that one of the reasons why he left the country in 2000 was that "he had been forced to destroy his party" ("Un ancien premier ministre va demander asile aux Etats-Unis", Kigali, AFP, 24 July 2000).

[7] "Judicial sources" indicated that Rwigema was a suspect "for some time," but that investigations had been hampered by Justice Minister Faustin Nteziryayo, who resigned and left the country in January (Kigali, AFP, 12 March 1999).

[8] Kigali, ARI/RNA, 5 April 1999.

[9] Kigali, Reuters, 11 April 1999.

While dealing with the MDR, the regime made sure that no other opposition forces emerged. In an open letter sent on May 5, 2000, to the leaders of the political parties, MP Jean Mbanda (PSD), a Tutsi genocide survivor, denounced "the progressive decrease of political space," and claimed that the political parties had practically ceased to exist: the forum of political parties was a club that did not represent anything, which Mbanda likened to the ancient *abiru*.[10] The parties' leaders have thus "contributed to the re-instauration of dictatorship," and Mbanda claimed that the country was "in a crisis without precedent." On May 29, he was arrested, officially because of financial abuse committed in 1994.[11] On May 30, 2001, former president and RPF leader Pasteur Bizimungu announced the creation of a new party, the PDR (Parti démocratique pour le renouveau)-Ubuyanja. Bizimungu and former minister Charles Ntakirutinka were immediately placed under house arrest, whereas other founders were threatened to the extent that three of them left the party two weeks after its aborted creation. Interestingly, this campaign mainly targeted Tutsi members, which then allowed to present the PDR as an "ethnist" Hutu party. Another PDR leader, Gratien Munyarubuga, was assassinated, yet another, Major Frank Bizimungu (a Tutsi officer without blood ties to Pasteur Bizimungu), "disappeared." On April 7, 2002, Kagame gave clear notice to his predecessor in a speech during the annual genocide commemoration: "The day will come when I will have to take decisive action against these people. When this day has come, even their (western) sponsors with whom they spend time drinking tea will be powerless."[12] Two weeks later Bizimungu and Ntakirutinka were finally arrested and jailed, and during the following weeks, dozens of others suspected of supporting the PDR ended up in prison. The justifications of these arrests were always the same: "association of criminals," "attempt against the security of the state," and "sowing division among the population."[13]

The way in which the opposition was treated can be understood in the context of the process that was to lead to the "transition towards democracy." Started at the end of 2001, the proceedings of a constitutional commission included a "popular consultation" that, according to the

[10] The holders of the royal ritual under the monarchy.
[11] Mbanda was released without trial in January 2003, and he subsequently left the country.
[12] "Rwanda Leader Kagame Warns Opponents on Genocide Anniversary", Kigali, AFP, 7 April 2002.
[13] On this, see Liprodhor, "Déclaration sur les récentes arrestations", Kigali, 3 June 2002; Amnesty International, *Rwanda: Number of Prisoners of Conscience on the Rise*, London, 7 June 2002.

International Crisis Group (ICG), was "highly supervised" and "has not really opened up the debate on the future of Rwanda."[14] A first draft constitution was published in November 2002, followed by new versions in December 2002 and February 2003. Parliament adopted the final text on April 23, 2003, and it was approved by referendum on May 26. According to the chairperson of the electoral commission, 87 percent of voters participated, of which 93 percent voted yes, after a campaign that was exclusively in favor of the text, without a single dissident opinion being voiced. This result was not only predictable, but also inevitable. François Grignon of the ICG observed that "[t]here was no real possibility to reject [the draft] because there was no campaigning to explain why it is bad (...). It was a state-managed referendum, and we have a state-managed result."[15] The International Federation of Human Rights found that "the constitution offers the image of a virtuous facade, opposed to the reality of strong restrictions on freedoms and democratic principles."[16]

These points of view were shared in more diplomatic language by an EU observer mission. Although lauding the technical and organizational aspects of the referendum, it expressed "concern" over a number of political issues, noting, for instance, that "control mechanisms in the constitutional text (...) result in restrictions on the freedom of expression, on the freedom of association and on the activities of political parties"; it also "feared that these restrictions on party activities on the ground have blocked the political game and reinforced the position of the RPF." The mission "expressed concern over a number of recent events" and quoted the banning of the MDR (see below), the "disappearance" of opponents, and the difficulties met by civil society organizations. During the run-up to the referendum, the media were "all engaged in a real campaign for the promotion of the electoral process and the constitution (...). Media communication in Rwanda is essentially at the service of the institutions." Regarding the high turnout, the report subtly indicated that "at the eve of the referendum a large part of the population in all provinces seemed convinced that the vote was compulsory." On the freedom of the vote, it noted that "inside a number of polling stations, observers have signalled

---

[14] International Crisis Group, *Rwanda at the end of the transition: a necessary political liberalisation*, Nairobi and Brussels, 13 November 2002, p. 6.

[15] "Rwandans Endorse New Constitution", Kigali, AP, 27 May 2003.

[16] Fédération internationale des droits de l'homme, "Rwanda. Quelle réconciliation nationale sans pluralisme démocratique?", Paris, 4 June 2003.

the presence of unauthorized persons.[17] This could be an element of intimidation of the voters."[18] The criticism by the EU observer mission was adequate. It saw the signs of what was to come during the "transition" and future electoral exercises. However, the warnings were not heeded, and there was no follow-up. As will be seen later, the lack of meaningful response to its authoritarian drift convinced the regime that it could act with impunity when closing the political landscape.

This is all the more surprising because observers were unanimous in their interpretation of the constitutional and electoral process. A critical report of the ICG quoted earlier observed that "[t]he press, associations and opposition parties have been silenced, destroyed or co-opted."[19] "[T]he political parties that exist in Rwanda today are only tolerated if they agree not to question the definition of political life drawn up by the RPF."[20] It concluded that "the election campaign of June-July 2003 will be hardly much more than a farce."[21] In a slightly more veiled way, a report made for USAID arrived at similar conclusions: "The regime has demonstrated a high degree of sensitivity to criticism. Those critical of the regime are often silenced, marginalized, intimidated, or forced into exile"[22]; "The regime in power (...) continues to view open debate as a threat."[23] The forum of political parties, enshrined in the constitution, was one of the instruments of control: "it has served as a means of limiting the range of allowable ideas among politicians" and was compared by one of the sources of the report to the central committee of a single party.[24]

With elections in view later that year, the MDR was dealt the final blow in the spring of 2003. Despite its full control of all instruments of local, provincial, and national management and its constitutional engineering (cf. infra), the RPF was not confident about the outcome of the polls.[25] It

---

[17] These persons were not identified, but they were probably *abakada* (local cadres of the RPF) and elements of the Local Defence Forces.

[18] Mission d'observation électorale de l'Union Européenne, *Référendum constitutionnel, Rwanda 2003*, Kigali, n.d.

[19] International Crisis Group, *Rwanda at the End of the Transition: A Necessary Political Liberalisation*, Nariobi and Brussels, 13 November 2002, p. 1.

[20] *Idem*, p. 2.

[21] *Idem*, p. 9.

[22] USAID, *Rwanda Democracy and Governance Assessment*, November 2002, p. 46.

[23] *Idem*, p. 50.

[24] *Ibid.*

[25] The RPF's limited belief in elections was made clear in an internal document quoted earlier: "The strong foundations put in place during the transitional period must allow the Front to organise the timely departure of Habyarimana Juvénal with or without elections (these need to be organised at the moment of the RPF's choosing, in light of the situation in the

therefore needed to close off the last potential spaces of political contestation, and it did so radically and quite openly. President Kagame gave notice in a speech on March 31, 2003, when he addressed his opponents in a veiled way that was, however, very understandable for Rwandans: "If they come with the objective of hindering our programmes, they will be injured. (...) Our clemency decreases (...) To whoever prides himself of having harvested sorghum or maize, we will say that we have mills to crush them." The outcome of the political process was without doubt: "I can tell you that the result of the elections is known (...). I can tell you for 100% that the elected will be those who follow the policy of reconstructing the country. (...) Those who want to bring divisionism (...) have no place in this country."[26] Just like that of "consensus," the notion of "divisionism" became central in the regime's project to eliminate all forms of dissent.

Kagame's threats were immediately followed by deeds. On April 15, Parliament recommended the banning of the MDR. The report of a parliamentary commission "entrusted with the study of the problems of the MDR" and the debate in the assembly were very revealing. On one hand, they showed what can be called a "Frodebu obsession."[27] The report stated that "the adherents of the ethnist ideology [within the MDR] (...) have started to teach that the population should vote like in Burundi, when they elected Ndadaye in 1993."[28] Presenting the report, the chair of the commission confirmed this feeling: "Some have told us without fear or anxiety that they intend to play the political card of Frodebu during the elections." Clearly, the MDR was perceived as a major threat to the dominance of the RPF if the playing field were level. On the other hand, the meaning of "divisionism" became quite clear: indeed, the report of the parliamentary commission stated that the MDR had said in November 1994 "that it is an opposition party [which means] that it has the intention to divide the Rwandans again."[29] Besides political parties, all contexts in

country)" (FPR, "L'environnement actuel et á venir de l'organisation", n.d. [early 1994], p. 11).

[26] Speech by President Kagame on International Water Day, Rebero, Bwisige District, Byumba, 31 March 2003. On the use of the notion of "divisionism" as a tool for political repression, see infra.

[27] As said earlier, in Burundi, Hutu candidate Melchior Ndadaye won the presidential election in June 1993, and his party Frodebu won the parliamentary elections, much to the surprise of the incumbent, Tutsi Pierre Buyoya and his party Uprona. They felt they had been fooled by many Hutu voters, seen as "Uprona during the day, and Frodebu during the night." They interpreted the poll as an "ethnic census."

[28] *Rapport de la Commission parlementaire sur les problèmes du MDR*, Kigali, 17 March 2003.

[29] *Idem.*

which dissident opinions could be voiced were targeted. In the commission's report and during the parliamentary debate, the human rights organization Liprodhor and the independent weekly *Umuseso* were quoted, along with international NGOs that funded "divisionist" organizations. The government did not play hard to get: on May 16, "the Council of Ministers, having studied the conclusions of Parliament on the case of the MDR, approves these conclusions and confirms the banning of the MDR because of its divisionism, and requests the competent authorities to give effect to this decision in accordance with the law."[30]

This decision was accompanied by a crackdown on those considered close to the MDR. Former defence minister General Emmanuel Habyarimana and Colonel Balthazar Ndengeyinka, both quoted in the parliamentary report, were lucky to escape to Uganda and from there to Europe. Others were less fortunate: on April 1, Major Félicien Ngirabatware was arrested and detained incommunicado; on April 3, the former secretary of General Habyarimana, Damien Musayidi, "disappeared," followed on April 7 by MDR MP Léonard Hitimana. On April 23, former Supreme Court judge Colonel Augustin Cyiza, considered close to the MDR, also "disappeared," while a mise en scène tried to make believe that he had fled to Uganda.[31] In addition, two parties that attempted to fill the void left by the MDR were refused recognition: on August 11, just before the elections, the government rejected the applications of ADEP-Mizero (Alliance pour la démocratie, l'équité et le progrès) and of the PSP (Parti pour la solidarité et le progrès).

Clearly the regime had decided to cross the Rubicon. On April 22, 2003, Amnesty International denounced a "government-orchestrated crackdown on the political opposition" with the help of the concept of "divisionism (. . .), vague terminology used by the government to disenfranchise the political opposition in an election year."[32] In May, Human Rights Watch arrived at the same conclusion, which it substantiated in detail.[33]

---

[30] Communiqué: "Le gouvernement approuve la dissolution du parti MDR", Kigali, ARI, 19 May 2003. At the time of this decision, the Prime Minister and the Minister of the Interior were members of the MDR.

[31] On this episode, see T. Cruvellier et al., *Augustin Cyiza: Un homme libre au Rwanda*, Paris, Karthala, 2004.

[32] Amnesty International, *Rwanda: Escalating Repression against Political Opposition*, London, 22 April 2003.

[33] Human Rights Watch, *Preparing for Elections: Tightening Control in the Name of Unity*, New York, May 2003.

The regional human rights league Ligue des droits de la personne dans la région des grands lacs (LDGL) observed "some sort of a vicious circle: the regime proceeds to the closure of democratic space; in order to counter that, initiatives are taken to combat the regime which in turn closes even further, in order to smother every attempt at contestation and every possibility of free expression."[34] The closing of the political landscape was finally achieved in 2004, when former president Bizimungu was condemned to fifteen years in jail; seven other co-accused were sentenced to between five and ten years. According to Amnesty International, this was "further proof of the government's willingness to subvert the Rwandese criminal justice system in an attempt to eliminate all potential political opposition."[35] Even the usually cautious European Union expressed "concern" about the trial that "appears to have fallen short of international standards of fairness and impartiality," as well as about "the nature of the charges" against Bizimungu and his codefendants.[36] The Supreme Court confirmed the sentences of Bizimungu and Ntakirutinka. Although the judgment in first instance was deeply flawed (a single prosecution witness who was himself implicated, manipulation and intimidation of other witnesses), the Supreme Court failed to show "the judicial competence and independence of the country's highest court."[37] Bizimungu (but not Ntakirutinka) was pardoned in 2007 and has led a secluded and very silent life since.[38]

In the eyes of the regime, the elimination of the political opposition was legitimate. As a matter of fact, it claimed there was no genuine opposition. During an interview with a Belgian journalist, President Kagame claimed that his opponents were "ignorant," "misguided," or "disgruntled." Anyway, they were just a minority: "[t]he majority of people in Rwanda

---

[34] LDGL, *Dynamiques de paix et logiques de guerre. Rapport annuel sur la situation des droits de l'homme dans la région des grands lacs. Année 2002*, May 2003.

[35] Amnesty International, *Rwanda: Government Slams Door on Political Life and Civil Society*, London, 9 June 2004.

[36] Council of the European Union, *Declaration by the Presidency on behalf of the European Union on the case of Pasteur Bizimungu*, Brussels, 9 July 2004.

[37] Human Rights Watch, *Rwanda: Historic Ruling Expected for Former President and Seven Others*, New York, 16 January 2006.

[38] Refusing an interview, Bizimungu later told *The Chronicles* that "he was barred from talking to the media". Justice Minister Karugarama however stated that Bizimungu was allowed to talk to the press, "but it all depends on what he talks about": "if his talk is not criminal then he can talk." He added that "he is free to move, but not everywhere" ("I'm not Allowed to Talk to the Media – Bizimungu", *The Chronicles*, 28 March 2012).

are engaged in these processes (of building the country) and are happy."[39] As noted by the ICG, those who do not adhere to the RPF view have no place in the political dispensation: "[w]hen the regime's viewpoint is not respected, accepted or understood, it is simply imposed."[40]

LOCAL "ELECTIONS" TO PAVE THE WAY

During "reflection meetings" held in the office of the president between May 1998 and March 1999 (the so-called Urugwiro meetings), worries were expressed about the dangers involved in organizing elections. These dangers included "politicians saying one thing during the day and the opposite during the night," the risk of ethnic voting whereby "those who are called 'the minority' could be kept away," and inadequate "educating the people."[41] In order to allay these fears, it was agreed that elections would start at the lowest level, that they would be preceded by "sensitiza-tion" and that they would be "nonpartisan."[42]

Despite the disappearance of opposition parties, come election time the RPF did not feel secure. As the transitional period of five years decreed by the RPF when it took power was supposed to come to an end in July 1999, the regime needed to be seen to embark on a "democratization" process, if only for external consumption. In March 1999, elections were organized at the most basic local levels, the cell and the sector. Inspired by the Ugandan model of "no-party democracy," votes were cast on individual candidates without declared political affiliation. More importantly, the polls were not secret, as voters queued up behind the candidates "of their choice," thus leaving serious doubts as to the electorate's free choice, particularly in a context of authoritarian political management and social conformism. A brief report by Liprodhor (Ligue rwandaise pour la pro-motion et la défense des droits de l'homme), which observed the polls in thirty-one cells in the northwest, mentioned "pressure by the military" and the "fear (of the population) for imprisonment." "Many people are said to have been detained in municipal lockups because they considered being

---

[39] "'Seek Broad, Long-term Solutions', Kagame urges Congolese", Kigali, 13 April 2002, interview with Marc Hoogsteyns published on the Rwanda government website, www. gov.rw/government/president/interviews/2001/drcserious.html.

[40] International Crisis Group, *Rwanda at the End of the Transition*, p. 2.

[41] Republic of Rwanda, Office of the President of the Republic, *Report of the Reflection Meetings Held in the Office of the President of the Republic from May 1998 to March 1999*, Kigali, August 1999, § 59.

[42] *Idem*, § 63–65.

candidates (...) The population says that the elections was merely a means to legitimise an existing situation."[43]

The RPF prolonged the transitional period by another four years, and in 2001, the regime embarked on a new "democratisation process." It held municipal elections on March 6–7, 2001, claiming this to be an important step on the road to democratization –an assertion accepted by some of its international partners. In reality, the elections offered ominous signs for the future of democracy. The voting system itself was very indirect and of Byzantine complexity, allowing RPF placemen to exercise full control over the process. According to an observer accredited by the electoral commission, the "elected" councillors represented only 20 percent of the electoral college in charge of choosing the mayors.[44] Various observers' reports mentioned the pressure on candidates, on aspiring candidates, and on voters. Candidates did not run under a party label, and political parties were barred from campaigning, but the RPF recruited candidates anyway and campaigned in numerous districts.

The local authorities appointed by the RPF and elements of the Local Defence Forces and the army gave the voters to understand which candidate they were expected to elect. An NGO observer considered that "the people in the party machinery" were known to all, a fact "which distorts the play of democracy and tends to transform Rwanda into an RPF state."[45] By far the most important flaw in the ballot was its lack of secrecy. Even though voting booths, ballot papers, and ballot boxes were used, electors expressed their preference by putting their thumbprint opposite the name and the picture of the candidate of their choice. In Rwanda, just as elsewhere in Africa, the imposition of a thumbprint is the equivalent of a signature[46]; it was therefore as if a voter, in Europe or North America, signed the ballot paper with his or her own name.

Human Rights Watch found that "this election has been flawed from the beginning, and these flaws far outweigh the few election-day irregularities that have been reported."[47] The International Crisis Group shared this concern. Its report on the elections observed that an important goal was "to begin to develop a new RPF 'cadre' in the countryside and to build

---

[43] Liprodhor, "Observations des élections locales (Région du nord-ouest du Rwanda)", Gisenyi, 4 April 1999.

[44] Kigali, AFP, 7 March 2001.

[45] CCAC, *Rapport sur l'observation des élections communales au Rwanda*, no date.

[46] Illiterate people sign documents by apposing their thumbprint.

[47] Human Rights Watch, *No Contest in Rwandan Elections. Many local officials run unopposed*, New York, 9 March 2001.

the party's political base ahead of presidential and parliamentary elections in 2003." The RPF-controlled National Electoral Commission "abused its powers to veto unwanted candidates and guarantee that only supporters of government policies were selected." "In this context, 'Consensual democracy' has become the imposition of one party's ideology."[48] The LGDL concurred: the elections "should not deceive (...) They took place under the total and tight control of the RPF."[49] These assessments "from above" were confirmed by local-level observations. Longman's informers said that RPF officials actively manipulated the candidate lists, pushing some people to run for office and telling others to withdraw their candidacy. "Even more troubling was the degree to which the RPF failed to respect the choices of the public, as they freely removed elected office-holders from their positions if they found them to be insufficiently compliant. (...) Four of the five elected mayors in the districts I studied were arrested during the two-year period of my research."[50]

The local polls were a rehearsal for the national elections. They allowed consolidation of control at the municipal level, where the polls are effectively conducted. The electoral commission was the weapon of control at the national level, indeed "political control at its best" in the terms of the ICG.[51] It was "both too powerful and too partisan (...) a tool of political control, not an independent and transparent institution."[52] Observers warned that the 2003 elections were about to create an irreversible situation and urged the international community not to support them. The ICG recommended to "refuse to finance the 2003 elections and the establishment of post-transitional institutions unless they are preceded by the liberalisation of political activities and a marked improvement in respect for basic freedoms of association and expression."[53] In a similar vein, Human Rights Watch stated that "International donors should not fund the Rwandan elections if the MDR is dissolved or if 'disappearances', arbitrary arrests and prosecutions are carried out against individuals solely because of their political ideas."[54] These warnings were not heeded: the

---

[48] International Crisis Group, *"Consensual Democracy" in Post-Genocide Rwanda. Evaluating the March 2001 District Elections*, 9 October 2001, p. 35.

[49] LGDL, *La problématique de la liberté d'expression au Rwanda*, Kigali, December 2001.

[50] T. Longman, "Limitations to Political Reform. The Undemocratic Nature of Transition in Rwanda", in S. Straus, L. Waldorf (Eds.), *Remaking Rwanda. State Building and Human Rights after Mass Violence*, Madison, the University of Wisconsin Press, 2011, p. 39.

[51] International Crisis Group, *"Consensual Democracy"*, p. 12.

[52] *Idem*, p. 23.

[53] International Crisis Group, *Rwanda at the End of the Transition*, p. iii.

[54] Human Rights Watch, *Preparing for Elections*, p. 16.

elections went ahead, they were grossly flawed, and Kigali got away with it, thus giving the RPF the (justified) feeling that no one was going to stop it.

THE WATERSHED: THE 2003 ELECTIONS

At the presidential election of August 25, 2003, President Kagame was elected with 95.05 percent of the vote, against 3.62 percent for Faustin Twagiramungu[55] and 1.33 percent for Jean Népomuscène Nayinzira after a campaign marred by arrests, "disappearances," and intimidation. The monolithic nature of the political landscape showed clearly in the fact that all parties represented in Parliament supported Kagame's bid. Just prior to the election, two parties that aimed at replacing the banned MDR were refused registration (cf. supra). Several persons who collected signatures needed for the registration of Twagiramangu's candidature were arrested, and on the day before the poll, his twelve provincial representatives were arrested "for illegal gatherings" and were accused by the police of "coordinating violent acts in all provinces for tomorrow."[56] Amnesty International summarized the preelection period as follows: "The Rwandese government has stage-managed the first post-genocide elections in a climate of fear and intimidation. How can the Rwandese people freely exercise their fundamental political freedoms when individuals are being arrested simply because they would not attend campaign rallies of the ruling RPF party?"[57] The U.S. National Democratic Institute (NDI) too called the elections "significantly flawed"[58] and noted "a climate of permanent fear and apprehension."[59] It observed ruling party dominance, political harassment, blurred lines between the ruling party and the state, and inhibited political discourse at the grassroots level, as well as a "pervasive" government influence on civil society.[60]

During an observation of 340 polling stations (out of 10,000), a European mission witnessed irregularities and fraud, among others, through ballot box stuffing and nontransparent counting procedures. It

---

55 We have seen that Twagiramungu left the country after resigning as prime minister in August 1995. He briefly returned to Rwanda to contest in the presidential poll.

56 Kigali, AFP, 24 August 2003.

57 Amnesty International, *Rwanda: Run-up to Presidential Elections Marred by Threats and Harassment*, London, 22 August 2003.

58 National Democratic Institute (NDI), *Assessment of Rwanda's Pre-electoral Political Environment and the Role of Political Parties, August 3–11, 2003*, n.d., p. 2.

59 *Idem*, p. 5.

60 *Idem*, pp. 6–9.

found that "generally speaking, the polling day was marked by the deterioration of the electoral process between the opening of the polling stations and the consolidation of results."[61] Two of the anecdotal examples seen by the mission spoke for themselves. When an observer arrived at a station before opening hour, the voting had started, but voters did not use the polling booths; instead, they arrived with their ballot paper already filled in which they then put in the box. In another case, a paper filled out in favor of Twagiramungu was opened by an official who told the voter "not to waste his time," on which he handed him a paper marked in favor of Kagame. These practices were confirmed by other field observations. In Ntabona, soldiers forced the local election committee to destroy votes for Twagiramungu and add votes for Kagame.[62] A mayor told the population that "we must not change the way things are or there will be problems", which was interpreted by Begley's participants as "a threat. It means that we will face problems if we try and vote for the other parties."[63] An election official told that, before the presidential poll, "[m]embers of the army came and gave a briefing on what to do about those who would complain about being forced to support Kagame. (...) [Officials] took the ballots that were for Twagiramungu and brought new ones and (...) marked them for Kagame."[64] Two former bodyguards of Kagame said that the Republican Guard had stuffed hundreds of ballot boxes at their barracks two days before the elections.[65] These anecdotal facts hide a general and systematic practice, unobservable for outsiders, as noted by a Rwandan: "They can put as many monitors they want next to the ballot boxes, but the decisions will already have been made long before that."[66]

---

[61] Mission d'observation électorale de l'Union Européenne, *Rwanda. Election présidentielle 25 août 2003. Elections législatives 29 et 30 septembre, 2 octobre 2003. Rapport final*, n.d., p. 34.

[62] B. Ingelaere, "The Ruler's Drum and the People's Shout. Accountability and Representation on Rwanda's Hills", in S. Straus, L. Waldorf (Eds.), *Remaking Rwanda*, p. 72.

[63] L. Begley, *"Resolved to Fight the Ideology of Genocide and all of its Manifestations": The Rwandan Patriotic Front, Violence and Ethnic Marginalisation in Post-Genocide Rwanda and Eastern Congo*, DPhil Thesis, University of Sussex, 2011, p. 121.

[64] *Idem*, p. 125. Someone who voted for Twagiramungu was taken to the local police commissioner who asked him, "Why did you vote for him?" The voter answered "Because it's democracy", to which the commissioner replied "Yes, but we tell you who to vote for. If you do this again you will be killed" (*idem*, p. 134).

[65] "'Kagame Is a Killer.' Defectors Tell of Life on Run from Rwandan Assassins", *The Times* (London), 8 October 2012.

[66] B. Oomen, "Donor-Driven Justice and its Discontents: The Case of Rwanda", *Development and Change*, 36:5 (2005), p. 901.

EU observers arrived at similar conclusions during the parliamentary elections of September. They took place without genuine opposition to the RPF, as all competing parties supported Kagame for the presidency, and opposition parties were not allowed to participate. The main independent candidates were disqualified on the eve of the polls. Although the observers' work was made difficult, and even impossible in certain places, the mission witnessed numerous cases of fraud, intimidation, manipulation of electoral lists, ballot-box stuffing, and flawed counting and consolidation.[67] The report of a mission by NORDEM, the Norwegian Resource Bank for Democracy and Human Rights, arrived at similar conclusions.[68] Just like during the presidential elections, anecdotal observations were revealing. In Gisenyi, an observer saw 584 ballot papers folded in the same fashion and bearing the same thumbprint next to the RPF symbol. Elsewhere, others saw unsealed boxes full of papers, papers favorable to other parties stashed in a corner, and completed lists of voters, as if everyone had voted, while people were still queuing up outside. Members of the PSD, who came to observe operations in the station where they voted themselves, were surprised to learn that the RPF obtained 100 percent of the votes.

At the direct polls for fifty-three MPs, the cartel of the RPF and four small parties obtained 73.78 percent of the vote, followed by the PSD with 12.31 percent and the PL with 10.56 percent. As all parties represented in parliament either joined the RPF list or supported the RPF candidate during the presidential election, all the directly elected MPs were part of one political platform. This monolithic nature was reinforced by the fact that most if not all MPs indirectly elected or designated by organizations representing women, youth and handicapped were members or sympathisers of the RPF, thus reinforcing its dominance in an obscure fashion.[69] Even at this indirect level, the pressure exercised by the regime was considerable, forcing many candidates to desist. For instance, for the 24 women seats only 58 candidates out of an initial 154 remained on polling day. The manipulation clearly showed in that, in every province, the two women who were elected obtained high and similar results, whereas the

---

[67] Mission d'observation électorale, *Rwanda Election*, pp. 36–39.

[68] I. Samset, O. Dalby, *Rwanda: Presidential and Parliamentary Elections 2003*, Oslo, NORDEM Report 12/2003.

[69] Stroh notes that ten out of twenty-four so-called nonpartisan women "elected" in 2003 appeared on the RPF list in 2008 (A. Stroh, "Electoral Rules of the Authoritarian Game: Undemocratic Effects of Proportional Representation in Rwanda", *Journal of Eastern African Studies*, 4:1 [2010], p. 5).

other candidates got negligible scores; in other words, it was very clear which candidates had to be elected. The same phenomenon was visible with the representatives of the youth: the two elected candidates obtained 154 and 139 votes, respectively, whereas the five other candidates shared the remaining 27 votes.

The members of the Senate were not elected directly but were designated by institutions largely dominated by the RPF, such as district and city councils, the president, the consultative forum of political organizations, the universities, and institutions of higher learning. The mechanism observed earlier with regard to women and youth representatives was also at play here. In five provinces, there was only one candidate, whereas there were just two in four others. Everywhere, the elected senator obtained a majority that was so overwhelming (between 81 percent and 98 percent) that competition must have been very limited. The "elections" of representatives of women and youth, and of senators were the first instance of a phenomenon that became widespread, namely, the use of "bridesmaids," that is, the putting up of candidates that are not supposed to be elected in order to give an impression of competition (see also infra).

A development widely lauded as a result of the elections was the massive entry of women in parliament. As they occupied half the seats in the Chamber of Deputies, this assembly became the most feminine worldwide. However, the presence of women, as well as of representatives of the youth and the handicapped, also served to hide control by the RPF. Indeed, the election of candidates representing a group in the population allowed to dissimulate their political allegiance.[70] Although, historically speaking, several women played an important role in the RPF's hierarchy and later in government, and the RPF genuinely supported women's rights[71], they increasingly "serve[d] more as an instrument of legitimizing and preserving RPF power."[72] At any rate, noting that "the lack of political freedom limits the ability of women to influence policy," Longman observed that the large presence of women "provided no check on the use of parliament for

---

[70] Mission d'observation électorale, *Rwanda Election*, p. 8. Likewise, Burnet noted that "most of these women owe allegiance to the RPF, rather than to the constituencies who elected them" (J.E. Burnet, "Women Have Found Respect. Gender Quotas, Symbolic Representation, and Female Empowerment in Rwanda", *Politics & Gender*, 7:3 [2011], p. 310).

[71] For instance, by giving women the right to inherit property and to own land.

[72] T. Longman, "Rwanda: Achieving Equality or Serving an Authoritarian State?", in H.C. Britton, G. Bauer (Eds.), *Women in African Parliaments*, Boulder CO, Lynne Rienner, 2006, p. 147.

political intimidation and repression."[73] As a result, "women politicians in Rwanda are in fact participating in the adoption and implementation of policies that are compromising individual liberties and increasing national and international insecurity."[74] In a similar vein, Burnet found that, as a result of increasing authoritarianism, women's ability to influence policy making decreased despite their increased participation.[75] A study by Coffé found little emphasis among Rwandan female representatives on substantive policy issues. During interviews, it was often repeated that all MPs have generally the same ideas, an attitude that "reflects very much the political environment and culture in Rwanda where political diversity is limited."[76] Rwandan women themselves came to realize that criticism of any aspect of governing in Rwanda, including the promotion of women, was risky. In 2005, when the head of a women's organization questioned the effectiveness of the female legislators in solving women's problems and likened them to flowers, which look good but do little else, she was condemned and threatened. Shortly afterward, she fled the country.[77]

Although Parliament was designed as a heterogeneous body in which political parties were officially present only for two-thirds of the seats, making it difficult to determine the formal political affiliation of each MP and senator, the RPF's domination was crushing. As all parties represented in parliament belonged to the RPF's cartel, the EU observer mission arrived at the paradoxical conclusion that, after the elections, "political pluralism is more limited than during the transition period."[78] In reality, the elections returned Rwanda to de facto single-party rule.[79] Rather than leading to more democracy and openness, 2003 was the year when an authoritarian regime was consolidated and remaining spaces of political contestation were cordoned off. In other words, the "transition" signaled continuity and even entrenchment rather than a break with the past.

---

[73] *Idem*, p. 149.

[74] *Idem*, p. 133.

[75] J.E. Burnet, "Gender Balance and the Meanings of Women in Governance in Post-genocide Rwanda", *African Affairs*, 107:428 (2008), pp. 361–386.

[76] H. Coffé, "Conceptions of Female Political Representation. Perspectives of Rwandan Female Representatives", *Women's Studies International Forum*, 35 (2012), p. 294.

[77] "Women's Voices Rise as Rwanda Reinvents Itself", *The New York Times*, 26 February 2005.

[78] Mission d'observation électorale, *Rwanda Elections*, p. 12.

[79] An interesting illustration could be found on the Parliament's Web site (www.rwandapar liament.gov.rw): initially (visit of October 17, 2003), Speaker Alfred Mukezamfura was classified as RPF, although he was a member of the PDC, a party that belonged to the RPF cartel; this error was later corrected (visit of October 31, 2003), but it showed the degree to which the RPF's dominance was considered "natural."

International reactions to the fraudulent polls were nevertheless muted. In an article published before the elections, Claudine Vidal wondered "whether the donors have the feeling that they help the Rwandan voters to exercise their civil and political rights." Her answer was that "to believe it, they will need a strong will to be blinded."[80] In its issue of November 7, 2003, *Le Monde* referred to "the electoral consecration of fear" and "the faking of a reconciliation democracy." Likewise, some bilateral donors expressed concern. Before the polls, the Netherlands suspended part of its funding of the elections, as long as the issue of the "disappearances" of opponents was not clarified.[81] On August 20, 2003, a spokesperson of the U.S. Department of State expressed concern over reports of intimidation and harassment and insisted that the elections be conducted in a free and fair fashion. On August 29, another spokesperson noted "with concern the reports (...) on irregularities in the vote." On October 13, the EU presidency regretted "the restrictions on the activities of the opposition, the intimidations, threats, and arrests that have characterised the electoral campaign, as well as the irregularities observed in a number of polling stations." However, just as had happened with the warnings issued before the elections, no action was taken.[82]

This reinforced the RPF in its conviction that things would blow over, which they did. This message, sent by the international community since the January 1995 roundtable in Geneva (cf. supra) was to embolden the regime in the years to come. Front Line noted that

[t]he donor community gave Rwanda about $7 million to hold superficially democratic elections, but then largely turned a blind eye to the widespread fraud, and human rights violations committed by the RPF to ensure its election victory – even though those problems were thoroughly documented and reported by the European Union's own election observer mission. If donors were unwilling to cry

---

[80] C. Vidal, "Rwanda. L'espoir en trompe-l'oeil", *Le Nouvel Observateur*, 19–25 June 2003.

[81] However, the amount withheld was a mere €250,000, and Dutch aid was actually increased after the elections. Although the Netherlands could "feel good" to have acted morally, this gesture, of course, had no impact on the regime's behavior.

[82] In a brief communiqué of September 26, the Amani Forum, a group of MPs from the region, avoided pronouncing itself. Earlier, the group's chairperson eluded the question: "The fact is that there have been difficulties before and during the elections. It is difficult to say that the elections have been free and fair" ("A look at Kagame's landslide win", *The New Vision* [Kampala], 3 September 2003). One academic commentator gave the elections a cautious nod of approval. While acknowledging that the polls "were found wanting on many counts", Kiwuwa opined that "the elections were a fundamental step towards democratic rule" (D.E. Kiwuwa, "Democratization and Ethnic Politics: Rwanda's Electoral Legacy", *Ethnopolitics*, 4:4 [2005], p. 448). However, this poorly informed and rather naive article was premised on the assumption that the polls were free and fair.

foul over flawed elections that they had helped finance, the Rwandan government clearly calculated that it did not have much to fear from donors when it came time to suppress human rights defenders.[83]

After failing Rwanda in 1994, the international community did so again in 2003 by allowing a dictatorship to take hold.[84]

President Kagame appointed the first post-transition government on October 19. Bernard Makuza (ex-MDR) was maintained as prime minister. Contrary to a tendency that was visible in recent years, the number of Hutu ministers increased significantly: thirteen of eighteen ministers were now Hutu, including five from the RPF; however, only two of eleven state secretaries (vice-ministers) were Hutu. Sixteen of twenty-nine members of government were from the RPF, which was a violation of article 116 of the constitution providing that "a political organization holding the majority of seats in the Chamber of Deputies may not exceed fifty (50) per cent of all the members of the Cabinet." The increase of the number of Hutu ministers was diversely interpreted in Kigali. Some saw it as an attempt by the RPF to broaden its ethnic base; others felt that Kagame gave a signal to dissident Tutsi that he could do without them by building an alternative power base. The Hutu recently incorporated in the RPF were from a new generation, whereas the old one, that was politically active in 1994, was evicted, in prison, killed or in exile (cf. supra). Irrespective of ethnicity, there was also a broader rejuvenation within the RPF. As veterans were sidelined, young and well-trained technocrats often coming from abroad were given considerable responsibility in higher echelons of the public service. Benefiting from rapid upward social and economic mobility, they were eager to demonstrate their loyalty and not inclined to challenge the party's leadership. The regime thus reinforced itself by incorporating obedient, fervent, and competent cadres and at the same time reinforced its polished exterior toward donors.[85] McDoom similarly observed that the uncertainty over the security of anyone's position has contributed to the emergence of new cadres who are highly motivated to demonstrate loyalty to Kagame: "This desire to show loyalty has in turn inspired them

[83] Front Line Rwanda, *Disappearances, Arrests, Threats, Intimidation of Human Rights Defenders 2001–2004*, Dublin, 2005, pp. 98–99.

[84] Jens Meierhenrich noted that "[i]nstead of inaugurating constitutional democracy, the 2003 presidential and parliamentary elections paved the way for constitutional dictatorship" (J. Meierhenrich, "Presidential and Parliamentary Elections in Rwanda, 2003", *Electoral Studies*, 25:3 [2006], p. 633).

[85] I thank Therese Kayikwamba Wagner for having drawn my attention to these aspects of changing the guard.

to pursue his opponents with formidable zeal, tolerating little criticism of either him or his party."[86]

THE ROUTINE OF COSMETIC ELECTIONS, 2006 AND 2008

The local elections of February and March 2006 confirmed the essentially cosmetic nature of the polls. After having noted a great deal of irregularities and pressure exercised both on candidates and voters, the only organization that felt it worthwhile to observe the elections, LDGL, found that "the results (...) were known in advance in all the sites visited", and that "there was no free choice for candidates by the voters."[87] Research conducted in ten rural sectors showed that this was also the perception of people, who realized that Tutsi cadres of the RPF consolidated their hold on the local level and that the polls were orchestrated by the "RPF family." In Ntabona where he witnessed the behind-the-scenes manipulations, Ingelaere found that all the candidates were RPF members and that they were subtly screened by military who had been sent to the region some weeks before the election. A member of the electoral committee told him, "We presented more than one candidate to give the impression of free elections."[88] Certain Hutu interviewees reacted with fatalism to what they saw as the disappearance of the "achievements of the [1959] revolution": "*Bashaka kutugira ibikoresho*" ("They can use us as their servile instruments"), a reference to the so-called feudal period before 1959.[89] Likewise, in interviews conducted by Burnet in 2007, numerous citizens confirmed that the outcome of the elections was always predetermined.[90] Although the resignation noted by Ingelaere obviously hid a considerable potential

---

[86] O.S. McDoom, *Rwanda's Exit Pathway from Violence: A Strategic Assessment*, World Development Report 2011, Background Case Study, April 2011, p. 37.

[87] LDGL, *Deuxième rapport partiel de la LDGL sur le monitoring des élections des autorités des échelons administratifs de secteurs, districts et la ville de Kigali organisées du 20 février au 04 mars 2006*, Kigali, 15 March 2006.

[88] B. Ingelaere, "The Ruler's Drum", p. 72.

[89] B. Ingelaere, "Living the Transition: Inside Rwanda's Conflict Cycle at the Grassroots", *Journal of Eastern African Studies*, 3:3 (2009), p. 457.

[90] Noting that "[t]he orchestrated nature of elections is an open secret in Rwanda today," Burnet gives the example of an election in one *umudugudu*, where the citizens failed to elect the preferred candidate. The election official declared: "No, no, no! You haven't done it right. Let's try again to see if you can do what we've asked" (J.E. Burnet, "Gender balance", p. 366, fn. 15).

of violence, the way in which the RPF consolidated its hold on the local level allowed it to move with serenity to the next parliamentary elections.

These took place in September 2008. Despite its full control, the RPF still felt the need to resort to widespread fraud during these elections, and this fraud was covered by the international community. The official result of the direct election[91] of the Chamber of Deputies was as follows: RPF: 78.76 percent of the votes (forty-two seats), PSD: 13.12 percent (seven seats), and PL: 7.50 percent (four seats). However, in reality, the RPF's machine worked too well, as a sample of almost 25 percent of the votes, collected by an EU observer mission, showed that the RPF obtained 98.39 percent of the votes.[92] This was not a surprising result as an election official told Begley that "[t]he officials said that we had to keep the election results between ninety and a hundred percent for the RPF."[93] Realizing that its score was too "Stalinist," the RPF lowered it and "offered" some seats to the PSD and the PL that were not in the opposition anyway. The EU mission formulated some fundamental criticism that in itself would suffice to discredit the entire operation. For instance, the ballot boxes were not sealed in 76 percent of the observed polling stations, one hour passed between the end of the vote and the start of the counting, the results forms were not secured inside sealed envelopes in 68 percent of the cases observed, consolidation procedures were not properly followed in 64 percent of the cases, and so on.[94] The lack of transparency in the aggregation of results denounced by the observer mission "is known to be a crucial gateway to manipulation."[95] Of course, threats, intimidations, and "orientations" that preceded the election could not be observed.

Despite these crucial shortcomings, the EU mission saw the polls as "an important step in the ongoing process to further institutionalise the democratic process in Rwanda."[96] When presenting the report in Kigali, the

---

[91] As in 2003, representatives of women, the youth, and the handicapped were elected in indirect and opaque polls.

[92] The PL, the PSD, and an independent candidate obtained 0.61 percent, 0.53 percent and 0.48 percent respectively. These data come from two sources inside the mission.

[93] L. Begley, *Resolved to Fight*, p. 126. Begley's participants mentioned a whole array of rigging techniques, such as ballot changes, removal of non-RPF ballots, unsealed boxes, and fraudulent counting (*idem*, pp. 126–127).

[94] It should be noted that these percentages of irregularities were found in the stations observed by the mission, that is, 576 out of 15,000. One can only guess what happened in other stations.

[95] A. Stroh, "Electoral Rules", p. 9.

[96] European Union, Election Observation Mission, *Republic of Rwanda. Final Report. Legislative Elections to the Chamber of Deputies*, 15–18 September 2008, 26 January 2009, p. 7.

president of the mission, British MEP Michael Cashman, stated that "the process of democratisation in Rwanda since the end of the genocide is remarkable."[97] One understands the long delay between the mission and the publication of the final report, which was discreetly presented in Kigali without the international press even mentioning it. Indeed, we have seen that a large sample with a margin of error of less than one percent collected by the mission showed the profoundly flawed nature of the election. There were heated debates within the mission on whether this should be in the report,[98] but Cashman prevailed and kept this damning information out of the report. So this was a fake report on fake elections. The signal given by the EU was, of course, disastrous, as the Rwandan regime knew that the mission was aware of the fraud but that it did not denounce it. It realized again that it could afford this kind of behavior, and it was going to remember this two years later.[99]

Others were not duped, however. The Bertelsmann Transformation Index (BTI), which monitors the state of democracy, the economic system, and governance in 128 countries in transition and development, summarized its assessment as follows:

Rwanda strengthened its authoritarian development strategy. The 2008 parliamentary elections failed to meet international standards and confirmed the façade character of its democratic institutions. (...) At the same time, the government sidelines parts of the domestic society that it does not trust and rejects dialogue with a significant number of groups in exile that are regarded as either perpetrators of the genocide or promoters of "divisionism." (...) President Kagame and the RPF gained an absolute majority through questionable means and systematically misled donors with a sophisticated democratic façade. (...) All in all, the most recent elections contributed to the consolidation of authoritarian rule instead of democratization.[100]

[97] European Union, Delegation of the European Commission, "Press Release", Kigali, 26 January 2009.

[98] So much so that Cashman had to refute allegations about divisions in the mission: EU Election Observation Mission, Republic of Rwanda, "EU Chief Observer Refutes Allegations about Divisions in EU Election Observation Mission", Kigali, 14 September 2008.

[99] The way it felt covered by its most important donor encouraged the regime to treat critical voices with disdain. For instance, a declaration by the regional human rights organization LDGL (*Déclaration de la LDGL sur les élections législatives 2008 au Rwanda*, Kigali, 19 September 2008) was called "a bunch of inadmissible lies" by the chairman of the National Electoral Commission, although its observations were not different from those in the EU observer mission report. Karangwa concluded that "these statements by the LDGL must be seen in the perspective of regional geopolitical destabilisation" ("La Commission électorale scandalisée par le rapport de la LDGL", Kigali, ARI, 25 September 2008).

[100] Bertelsmann Stiftung, *BTI 2010 – Rwanda Country Report*, Gütersloh, 2009.

MEETING THE CHALLENGE OF 2010

Although the opposition seemed to have disappeared in 2003, it resurfaced in 2009–2010 in the perspective of the presidential elections of 2010. Up to then, none of the registered parties considered themselves to be in the opposition. During a meeting of the PL in 2008, one of the speakers affirmed that "we are not here to oppose President Kagame but to build the nation. Rwanda does not need a European-type opposition."[101] After overcoming many obstacles put on its path, one single opposition party, the Parti Social (PS)-Imberakuri succeeded in registering in mid-2009, whereas two other pretenders, the Democratic Green Party (DGP) and the Forces démocratiques unifiées (FDU)-Inkingi did not obtain registration as a result of systematic sabotage. However, these initiatives challenged the monopoly of the RPF and introduced, inside the country,[102] a debate that contested the ruling party's discourse. Although the RPF controlled the political space from the local to the national levels, this was seen as a real menace, particularly at a moment when the regime was also facing internal tensions (see the following discussion). The leaders of the (would-be) opposition parties were threatened, the regime engineered splits within them, administrative obstacles prevented them from functioning, and meetings were disturbed with the complicity of the security services. Reminiscent of the way in which the regime weakened the MDR before banning it (cf. supra), in March 2010 the RPF attempted to destroy the only registered opposition party PS-Imberakuri by having some members of the party create a dissident wing that replaced Ntaganda by a new leadership that abstained from criticizing the government. The minister of Local Government recognized the breakaway wing and the government press described the dissident wing as the "real" party, whereas the real party was presented as a "breakaway faction." Those who remained loyal to the party leader Bernard Ntaganda were banned from a congress organized in August 2010 under the auspices of the National Unity and Reconciliation Commission (NURC).[103]

On 4 March 2010, Déo Mushayidi, a Tutsi former journalist and chair of the Parti de défense du peuple (PDP)-Imanzi that operated in exile, who was in the region to prepare the registration of his party in Rwanda, was

---

[101] F. Janne d'Othée, "Rwanda. Elections en trompe-l'oeil", *Le Vif-L'Express* (Brussels), 12 September 2008.

[102] Numerous opposition movements were active abroad, but they were no threat to the RPF.

[103] "PS Imberakuri moves to end infighting", *The New Times*, 29 août 2011.

arrested in Tanzania and extradited the next day to Rwanda via Burundi.[104] Mushayidi was accused of "terrorism," "attempt against the security of the state," and "revisionism, genocide ideology and divisionism." He was claimed to have collaborated with the FDLR[105] and to be part of a terrorist network with, among others, Kayumba Nyamwasa and Karegeya, two former RPF officers in exile in South Africa (see the following discussion).[106] Mushayidi was sentenced to life in prison on September 17, 2010, a verdict confirmed by the Supreme Court on February 24, 2012.

Repression intensified in April 2010,[107] after the chair of FDU-Inkingi, Victoire Ingabire, returned to Rwanda after sixteen years in exile, with the stated aim to run for the presidency. Right after her arrival, she made the following statement at a genocide memorial site:

[W]e are here honouring at this memorial the Tutsi victims of the Genocide. There are also Hutu who were victims of crimes against humanity and war crimes, not remembered or honoured here. Hutu are also suffering. They are wondering when their time will come to remember their people. In order for us to get to that desirable reconciliation, we must be fair and compassionate towards every Rwandan's suffering. It is imperative that for Tutsi survivors, Hutu who killed their relatives understand the crimes they committed and accept the legal consequences. It is also crucial that those who may have killed Hutu understand that they must be equally punished by the laws.[108]

Although the statement squarely recognized the genocide, the reference to Hutu victims was seen as a provocation. Ingabire was arrested and accused of "genocide ideology." Her U.S. lawyer was in turn arrested in June (but released after a few weeks on "humanitarian grounds").

Ingabire's trial started in September 2011, and it was replete with incidents. The judge was hostile to the defence throughout. Although the

---

[104] This very expeditious "extradition" (that was in reality a kidnap) did not respect any of Burundi's legal requirements.

[105] Forces démocratiques pour la libération du Rwanda, a Hutu rebel movement operating in eastern DRC.

[106] "Mushayidi Arrested for Terrorism, Extradited", *The New Times*, 6 March 2010; "Deo Mushayidi's Arrest Major Blow to Terrorists' Alliances", *Sunday Times* (Kigali), 7 March 2010.

[107] On April 24, the Human Rights Watch resident researcher was expelled, a move that further handicapped inside observation.

[108] Quoted in L. Waldorf, "Instrumentalizing Genocide. The RPF's Campaign against 'Genocide Ideology'", in S. Straus, L. Waldorf (Eds.), *Remaking Rwanda*, p. 58. I quote this statement in full, because Ingabire was later prosecuted for "genocide ideology" based on these words.

statements of prosecution witnesses,[109] who were also Ingabire's co-accused who pleaded guilty, were prepared like a script, the defense was forced to communicate its questions for cross-examination in advance. During the trial, just as he had done on several occasions in the past, President Kagame stated that Ingabire was guilty and that she had admitted as much, which of course was a violation of the presumption of innocence and severely weighed on the independence of the court. When a witness challenged the claims of the prosecution on Ingabire's collaboration with the FDLR, he was threatened, his cell (he was serving a prison sentence) was searched, and his documents were seized. The court then refused to continue hearing him. When the defense raised the issue of the constitutionality of the 2008 genocide ideology law, the Supreme Court refused to rule on the substance of the claim, which it declared inadmissible because a copy of the law was not attached to the petition, although, of course, the law must not be proved. Faced with this unlevel playing field, Igabire threw in the towel on April 16, 2012, stating that she had given up hopes of a fair trial. She decided she would no longer present herself and asked her lawyers to do likewise. On October 30, 2012, the High Court found her guilty of conspiracy to undermine the government and denying the genocide and sentenced her to eight years in prison after a trial seen as flawed by international human rights organizations.[110]

The media, too, were targeted during the run-up to the polls. Of the three remaining independent newspapers, two, *Umuseso* and *Umuvugizi*, were suspended for six months by the High Media Council, thus preventing them from covering the run-up to the presidential election. On the same day, the director of *Umuvugizi*, Jean-Bosco Gasasira, fled the country for Uganda after having received repeated death threats; he was followed on May 24 by his colleague at *Umuseso*, Didas Gasana. At the end of June, the codirector of *Umuvugizi*, Jean-Léonard Rugambage, was murdered in Kigali on the very day his newspaper's Web site (whose access was blocked

[109] They had been unlawfully detained in a military camp without access to a lawyer for seven months before incriminating Ingabire (Amnesty International, *Rwanda: Shrouded in Secrecy. Illegal Detention and Torture by Military Intelligence*, London, October 2012, p. 27).

[110] Human Rights Watch, *Rwanda: Eight Year Sentence for Opposition Leader. Victoire Ingabire Found Guilty of Two Charges in Flawed Trial*, Nairobi, 30 October 2012; Amnesty International, *Rwanda: Ensure Appeal after Unfair Ingabire Trial*, London, 30 October 2012; "Rwanda: la FIDH dénonce des 'irrégularités' dans le procès Ingabire", Nairobi, AFP, 3 November 2012; also see "Rwandan Justice. Fairness on Trial. Opposition Leaders in Rwanda Are Hounded in the Courts", *The Economist*, 3 November 2012.

inside Rwanda) published a story about the regime's "hit squads" operating in South Africa (see the following). The government pretended that Rugambage was the victim of an act of vengeance, but his colleague Gasasira stated that "the Rwandan intelligence services were on a killing spree (…) with the knowledge of President Paul Kagame himself."[111] In July, two journalists of *Umurabyo* were arrested, accused of "insurrection, publishing material insulting for the President, incitement to public disorder, ethnic divisionism, and the promotion of genocide ideology".[112] They were sentenced to seventeen and seven years' imprisonment, respectively, in February 2011.[113]

In the meantime, dozens of members of opposition parties were arrested on June 24, 2010 when demonstrating against the impossibility for their leaders to register as presidential elections candidates. The PS-Imberakuri chair Bernard Ntaganda was arrested on the same day, and indicted for "ethnic divisionism, organising a demonstration without authorisation, setting up a criminal group, and attempted murder."[114] He was sentenced to four years in prison in February 2011.[115] In April 2012, the Supreme Court upheld his sentence.[116] The vice-president of the DGP André Rwisereka was assassinated on July 13, 2010; his nearly beheaded body was found near Butare.[117] Although the police suggested that he was the victim of armed robbery, the president of his party stated that he, along with Rwisereka, had received death

---

[111] "Editor's Murder 'Approved by Rwandan President'", *The Independent* (London), 2 July 2010.

[112] "Police Speaks out on Umurabyo Arrests", *The New Times*, 14 July 2010.

[113] The Supreme Court reduced their sentences to four and three years in April 2012. Reporters sans frontières called this "false good news," as "these two women must be set free and the charges against them withdrawn" (Reporters sans frontières, "Sentiment mitigé après la réduction des peines contre deux journalistes femmes d'Umurabyo", Paris, 6 April 2012).

[114] "Rwanda: les arrestations d'opposants se multiplient", Kigali, AFP, 25 June 2010.

[115] Amnesty International immediately called for his unconditional release and called the charges "politically motivated" (*Rwandan Opposition Politician Jailed for Exercising Rights*, London, 14 February 2011).

[116] Human Rights Watch, "Rwanda: Opposition Leader's Sentence Upheld. Bernard Ntaganda, Journalists in Prison for Expressing Critical Views", Nairobi, 27 April 2012.

[117] Rwisereka was a former RPF member, who had become a "traitor." The way in which he was killed could have been a macabre reminder of the RPF's oath of allegiance: "I solemnly swear before the men that I will work for the RPF family ["*umuryango wa FPR*"], that I will always defend its interests, and that, if I divulge its secrets, I will be decapitated like any other traitor" (A.J. Ruzibiza, *Rwanda. L'histoire secrète*, Paris, Editions du Panama, 2005, p. 65). This formula was confirmed to this author by several other (former) members of the RPF.

threats.[118] On July 28, the entire print of the first issue of *The Newsline*, a new journal set up in Kampala by reporters of *Umuseso*, was confiscated at the border with Uganda. On the same day, the High Media Council published a list of media allowed to operate in the country. None of the independent papers was on the list, meaning that they were no longer suspended but were banned altogether.[119]

Now that the opposition candidates were prevented from participating in the presidential polls, the National Electoral Commission announced on June 7, 2010, that four contenders were registered. Next to Kagame they were from three parties that belonged to the RPF-led cartel. These "stooge" candidates were no opponents, and they knew (and accepted) that their chances against Kagame were nil. The lining up of such candidates that are there for show and that are not supposed to win is an ancient ploy of the regime; these candidates are known in Rwanda as "bridesmaids."[120] This trick was also used within the RPF. Thus, in December 2009, Kagame was reelected president of the party after a vote where the single other "candidate" obtained less than 2 percent of the vote. During the "primaries" organized in the provinces for the designation of the party's presidential candidate, at each occasion Kagame secured between 98 percent and 100 percent of the votes against candidates that were very close associates. For instance, in Kigali city, Senator José Kagabo managed to gain a mere 6 votes out of 380, but he graciously "welcomed" the result and stated that he lost "in a transparent way."[121]

Even in this extremely constraining environment, the RPF took no risks, and Kagame attracted monumental crowds to his campaign rallies. Quite paradoxically, it was in Gicumbi, where the RPF massacred thousands of Hutu civilians in 1994, that an electoral meeting drew 150,000 persons,[122] but people "were forced to assist, and they were taken there in trucks of the

---

[118] "Rwanda: Mort suspecte d'un opposant", Kigali, Reuters, 14 July 2010. The party's chairperson Frank Habineza went into exile in Sweden in August, but returned in September 2012 in the hope of having the DGP registered and to participate in the 2013 parliamentary elections.

[119] For surveys on the actions undertaken by the regime to muzzle dissident voices during the run-up to the presidential election, see Human Rights Watch, *Rwanda: Silencing Dissent Ahead of Elections*, 2 August 2010; F. Reyntjens, "Chronique politique du Rwanda, 2009–2010", in S. Marysse, F. Reyntjens, S. Vandeginste (Eds.), *L'Afrique des grands lacs. Annuaire 2009–2010*, Paris, L'Harmattan, 2010, pp. 280–288.

[120] Human Rights Watch, *Law and Reality. Progress in Judicial Reform in Rwanda*, New York, 24 July 2008, p. 46.

[121] "Kagame Wins Kigali City Primaries", *The New Times*, 10 May 2010.

[122] "Kagame's Gicumbi rally attracts monumental crowd of over 150,000", *The New Times*, 3 August 2010.

state."[123] In Kigali, people ("invited" by text messages to attend the party's meetings) were transported by public buses.[124] Also in Kigali, "neighbourhoods were literally cordoned off during hours by the army (...): whoever was inside the perimeter was prohibited from leaving, and strongly incited to go to the presidential meeting."[125] The capacity of the system to mobilize and use modern technology for this aim already showed in November 2008, when state officials and text messaging were massively used to organize regime-led protests after the arrest of Rose Kabuye in France (cf. infra).[126]

Despite the protests of international human rights organizations[127] and even some signs of concern in Washington,[128] the polls went ahead on August 9, 2010. The result was predictable: Kagame obtained 93.08 percent against 5.15 percent, 1.37 percent, and 0.40 percent, respectively, for his "opponents." Although technically not compulsory, participation in the vote reached a whopping 98 percent: Rwandans know very well what is expected of them, they know the risks involved in "uncivil" behavior, and others voted in their place if necessary (see the following discussion). The results were strikingly similar in the five provinces (results per districts were not made public by the electoral commission): Kagame's score was everywhere between 92.53 percent and 93.99 percent of the vote, a spread of less than 1.5 percent. The same applied to the results of his "competitors": Ntawukuriryayo got between 4.31 percent and 6.07

---

[123] "Kagame au double visage", *Le Vif/L'Express*, 6 August 2010.

[124] "Elections présidentielles au Rwanda: mobilisation générale à Kigali", *Syfia Grands Lacs*, 22 July 2010.

[125] "Le problème au Rwanda, c'est la peur", *La Croix*, 8 August 2010.

[126] A. Purdekova, "'Even if I Am not Here, there Are so Many Eyes': Surveillance and State Reach in Rwanda", *Journal of Modern African Studies*, 49:3 (2011), p. 490.

[127] Human Rights Watch, *Rwanda: Stop Attacks on Journalists, Opponents. Government Actions Undermine Democracy as Presidential Election Draws Near*, New York, 26 June 2010; Fédération Internationale des ligues des droits de l'homme, *Rwanda: La FIDH appelle à mettre un terme à l'actuelle vague de violence et demande une enquête indépendante et impartiale sur les assassinats d'opposants politiques et de journalistes*, Paris, 16 July 2010; Commonwealth Human Rights Initiative, *The CHRI Condemns Human Rights Abuses in the Run Up to Elections in Rwanda*, London, 22 July 2010; Amnesty International, *Rwanda: Pre-election attacks on politicians and journalists condemned*, London, 5 August 2010.

[128] On 25 May the U.S. assistant secretary of state for African Affairs stated that "the political environment ahead of the elections has been riddled by a series of worrying actions taken by the Government of Rwanda, which appears to be attempts to restrict the freedom of expression" (Johnnie Carson, assistant secretary, Bureau of African Affairs, Testimony before the House Foreign Affairs Committee Subcommittee on Africa and Global Health, 25 May 2010).

percent, Higiro between 1.12 percent and 1.73 percent, and Mukabaramba between 0.25 percent and 0.74 percent. The consensus across the country was moving, including with regard to the bridesmaids.

Although the opposition was excluded and the RPF controlled the entire electoral machinery (the electoral commission at the national level, the districts at the local level), just like in 2003 and 2008, it was not completely confident and applied widespread fraud at both levels. On one hand, the slogans of unanimity during the Habyarimana years (*Tuli kumwe 100%* – "all together for 100%") were back (*Tora Kagame 100%* – "Vote for Kagame 100%"), which incited local leaders to force the population not just to vote, but to vote for Kagame. Awards were even given to the "best sectors."[129] The logic of the "performance contracts" (*imihigo*) imposed on local authorities in many fields was often translated in terms of electoral performances. In a number of known cases, during the hours preceding the vote, local leaders went from door to door to collect voters' cards. They filled the ballot paper, stamped the cards, and informed the electors that they had voted and did not need to go to the polling station.[130] The coordinator of a station in Musanze confirmed these practices and added that "[t]he authorities had urged us to control each ballot cast. After the voter would drop his ballot in the box, we would open it in order to verify which candidate had been voted. If it was not candidate Paul Kagame, we would take the ballot out and replace it with a 'new ballot.'" The fifteen to twenty votes cast in favour of Higiro were replaced by ballots in favor of Kagame.[131] In addition, similar to earlier occasions, voters "expressed their choice" by putting their thumbprint (cf. supra). Although it would be practically impossible to check each print, the perception of many voters is that the polls are not secret.

On the other hand, fraudulent practices were not limited to the local level. In the absence of observation by the European Union,[132] the only serious international report was produced by a Commonwealth observer

---

[129] "Rwanda: le zèle des dirigeants de base nuit au vote libre", *Syfia Grands Lacs*, 9 September 2010.

[130] These practices are detailed in "Kagame Wins a Contest that Never Was", *The Newsline* (Kampala), 13–20 August 2010.

[131] "Rwanda RPF's Election Rigging Tactics Exposed", Newsline, 25 August 2010, (http://www.newslineea.com/index.php?option=com_contents&view=article&id=175: rpfs-election-rigging-tactics-exposed-&catid=65:headline).

[132] The official reasons given for this absence were the lack of funding and the fact that many elections needed to be observed in 2010, but the futile nature of the observation missions in 2003 and 2008 was also mentioned. The Organisation internationale de la francophonie (OIF) did send a mission, but its report was less than incisive, probably in order to

mission.[133] Although the mission accepted the official discourse on a number of issues (such as the "impartial" composition of the electoral commission and the reasons for the lack of registration of opposition parties) too willingly, it noted essential flaws: lack of verification whether ballot boxes were empty at the start of polling (which allowed the stuffing of boxes described earlier); the use of the thumbprint "could lead to a perception that a ballot could be traced to an individual"[134]; and, most importantly, the lack of transparency in the tabulation procedure. The report also expressed concern over the fact that "[t]he election campaign notably lacked critical opposition voices."[135] On the issue of tabulation, the report noted that "it was not possible to ascertain quite where, how and when the tabulation was to be completed,"[136] both between the voting stations and the districts and between the latter and the national level. In the Western Province, the observers found that "[a]fter the boxes left the Polling Center, what happened to the boxes and reports is a mistery. The District Office where the final consolidation was to take place was obviously not used for consolidation, and it was done elsewhere (we presume at Sector Office), contrary to what was declared by the District NEC Coordinator."[137] Indeed, no one knew what happened with the papers and counts during the two days between the election and the official proclamation of the results on August 11. According to a well-placed source of a Dutch journalist, the result was so monolithic that, just like in 2008, the electoral commission "adapted" the result downward,[138] which probably explains the uniform nature of results countrywide.

In September 2011, the election of fourteen senators (the twelve other are appointed) again showed the cosmetic nature of polls. Senators are elected by small colleges at provincial level, and the results showed that it was

---

avoid relations between France and Rwanda from getting worse (see below). However it noted "the absence of real competition between the contenders" (Organisation internationale de la francophonie, *Election présidentielle du 9 août 2010 au Rwanda. Rapport d'une Mission francophone d'information et de contacts*, n.d., p. 4), "numerous cases of serious violations of rights and freedoms" (*idem*, p. 5), and "an electoral process that appears fragile from a democratic point of view" (*idem*, p. 13).

[133] Commonwealth Secretariat, Rwanda Presidential Elections 9 August 2010, *Report of the Commonwealth Observer Group*, n.d.

[134] *Idem*, p. 24.

[135] *Idem*, p. 17.

[136] *Idem*, p. 25.

[137] *Idem*, p. 28.

[138] A. Verbraeken, "Handen in en uit de stembus" ("Hands in and out of the Ballot Boxes"), *Vrij Nederland*, 21 August 2010.

decided in advance who would be elected and who were the "*/*
maids." In every province, the "elected" candidates obtained a*/*
whelming majority, while the other candidates got negligible scores. ᴦʋᴧ
instance, in Kigali, the elected candidate got 80.78 percent of the vote; the
six other candidates managed scores between zero and 5.41 percent. The
image was the same in all provinces: East (three elected candidates with
scores between 62.96 percent and 77.55 percent; nine others with scores
between 3.05 percent and 6.97 percent), West (three elected candidates
with scores between 81.44 percent and 89.95 percent; six others with
scores between 1.96 percent and 8.73 percent), North (two elected candidates with scores between 90.90 percent and 92.30 percent; three others
with scores between 6.52 percent and 1.63 percent), South (three candidates with scores between 69.83 percent and 84.21 percent; thirteen others
with scores between 0.80 percent and 14.57 percent). Even a paper
appearing in Kigali observed that "the vote tally difference between the
winners and the losers was overwhelming," without however offering an
explanation. An unsuccessful candidate indicated that it was not his intention to win: "I already knew who the winner would be," whereas another
thought that "probably the Electoral Colleges had agreed on the candidate
to be voted".[139]

CONCLUSION

Rwanda is a strong case of hegemonic authoritarianism, where under the
guise of seemingly regular elections in a multiparty context the polls do not
perform any meaningful function other than consolidating a dictatorship.
It does not even meet Schedler's requirements of electoral authoritarian
regimes, where elections are "minimally pluralistic (opposition parties are
allowed to run), minimally competitive (opposition parties, while denied
victory, are allowed to win votes and seats), and minimally open (opposition parties are not subject to massive repression, although they may
experience repressive treatment in selective and intermittent ways)."[140]
The international community, and Rwanda's main sponsors in particular,
knew full well that every election since the first local polls in 1999 was
deeply flawed. Indeed, everyone knew: the RPF, of course, because it

---

[139] "A New House of Senate 2011. How Open Were the Recent Senatorial Elections?", *The Chronicles*, 13–20 October 2011.

[140] A. Schedler (Ed.), *Electoral Authoritarianism. The Dynamics of Unfree Competition*, Boulder, CO, Lynne Rienner, 2006, p. 3.

organized the fraud, but most ordinary Rwandans knew as well. Despite timid expressions of concern by some donors, this issue was never seriously addressed, thus giving the Rwandan regime the justified impression that it could proceed unhindered. This is exactly what it did, becoming bolder at each new electoral moment, even resorting to political murder in 2010. So, the regime's belief that it was legitimate to eliminate dissenting voices found support in the silence of the international community. The systematic rigging of the polls by a party that was exercising full control, from the center to the most remote hill, showed its own uncertainty about the outcome of even moderately free and fair elections. Contrary to other authoritarian regimes, where protests are occasionally heard, the RPF's physical and, on occasion, violent control succeeded in avoiding any publicly aired contestation, at least domestically.

The consequence of electoral manipulation has been the restoration of de facto single-party rule, with the added and dangerous effect that, in a country deeply divided along ethnic lines, those who rule are seen as representing minority interests by a frustrated majority reduced to silence. Elections were by no means the only way in which the RPF entrenched its dominance. Other mechanisms are analyzed in the next chapter.

3

Managing Political Space

Civil society was soon eliminated as an autonomous force. Since the second half of the 1990s, human rights defenders, advocates of rural development, and NGOs generally were threatened by arrests, "disappearances," and intimidation.[1] The regime tackled religious groups early on. Some churches were close to the previous regime and a number of clerics aided and abetted genocide. More importantly, churches were considered a potential challenge to the RPF's hegemonic project. Already in January 1995, the papal nuncio complained that "the national radio and the press close to the regime often and publicly accuse the Catholic Church of having participated in the genocide, in order to denigrate and discredit it in the eyes of the people and to prevent it from playing its role in society." Citing a number of examples, he mentioned "brutal aggressions against ecclesiastic staff."[2] Both Rwandan and foreign clergy were killed, the most notorious incident being the massacre of the archbishop of Kigali, three bishops, and other clergy in Gakurazo on June 5, 1994. Churches were also forced to select leaders that were acceptable to the regime.[3] Other civil

---

[1] A survey of these practices can be found in Front Line Rwanda, *Disappearances, Arrests, Threats, Intimidation of Human Rights Defenders, 2001–2004*, Dublin, 2005. In addition to human rights defenders, the report highlights the persecution of rural defenders, independent journalists, and NGOs.

[2] Letter of the acting papal nuncio to the minister of justice, Kigali, 9 January 1995.

[3] On the way in which the regime established its dominance over religious groups, see T. Longman, "Limitations to Political Reform. The Undemocratic Nature of Transition in Rwanda", in S. Straus, L. Waldorf (Eds.), *Remaking Rwanda. State Building and Human Rights after Mass Violence*, Madison, The University of Wisconsin Press, 2011, p. 28.

57

society groups followed. In 1998, two leaders of the human rights associations Collectif des ligues et associations de défense des droits de l'homme (Cladho, a human rights umbrella organization created in 1993) and of Liprodhor went into exile. The chair of another human rights group (ADL), André Sibomana, died of an illness that might have been cured, had he been allowed to seek treatment abroad, but who was prevented from leaving the country.

In addition to direct persecution, the secret services infiltrated civil society groups; "such tactics have largely succeeded in breaking up the Rwandan local NGO network."[4] Cladho is one example. After the organization was taken over by the RPF, its new executive secretary Silas Sinyigaya stated that "[t]he government is now a partner state. Before it was a dictatorship of the majority, but now the government is inclusive." Cladho became a "briefcase NGO," and by late 2003, the Belgian NGO umbrella 11.11.11 stopped financing it because of its lack of seriousness and its reluctance to defend the human rights league Liprodhor in the wake of mounting government criticism (see the following discussion).[5] Even the Tutsi survivors' organization Ibuka, which had become increasingly critical of the government, was neutralized in 2000. Its vice-president Josué Kayijaho went into exile and Kayijaho's brother Assiel Kabera was assassinated. The Ibuka founder Bosco Rutagengwa and general secretary Anastase Muramba too fled the country. The organization's leadership was replaced by RPF faithfuls such as Antoine Mugesera,[6] a member of the party's central committee, and Ibuka ceased criticizing the regime.

A law promulgated in April 2001 gave the authorities wide-ranging powers to control the management, finances, and projects of national and international NGOs. LDGL observed that "Rwanda surprises particularly by the weird collusion between the government and important sections of civil society. Spaces of free expression are almost all invaded or reduced to

---

[4] International Crisis Group, "'Consensual Democracy' in Post-genocide Rwanda. Evaluating the March 2001 District Elections", 9 October 2001, p. 20. This tactic of infiltration was widely used from the very beginning of RPF rule. The ICG noted that from July 1994, RPF cadres "applied to work in UN agencies, local and foreign NGOs and key businesses to monitor attitudes towards the government and general activities" (*Idem*, p. 7).

[5] Front Line Rwanda, *Disappearances, Arrests*, p. 35. Already in May 1995, 11.11.11 had expressed surprise and concern after Cladho issued a communiqué supporting the government's version of the Kibeho massacre (Cladho, "Déclaration sur les incidents du camp des déplacés de Kibeho", Kigali, 28 April 1995).

[6] Mugesera had previously helped to neutralize the cooperatives' training and research center Iwacu (T. Longman, "Limitations to Political Reform", p. 31).

a minimum in order to prevent contestation." In clear terms, "civil society" was infiltrated and manipulated by the regime. LDGL noted that "the [2001] law on associations and the measures accompanying it have considerably diminished the margins within which they can function."[7] Likewise, Gready noted the use of various strategies of management and control, most prominently infiltration: "RPF cadres, or those with close ties to the government, have infiltrated the top jobs in local NGOs, 'umbrella' groups, and collectives."[8] The practice of controlling and co-opting also affected international NGOs: "LandNet Rwanda, for example, an umbrella network of local and international NGOs, now has a Ministry of Lands official as an *ex officio* member."[9] After the publication of the 2005 land law, LandNet planned a conference to discuss implementation, at which point the government essentially closed LandNet down, using strong language, such as "betrayal."[10] Government assertiveness forced NGOs to constantly shift registers, from controversial to less controversial interventions or from advocacy to policy implementation, as shown by the examples of LandNet and Penal Reform International.[11]

The loss of autonomy of civil society appeared very clearly in 2003, the election year. On May 9, the organization Pro-Femmes organized a meeting of "civil society" to discuss the "problem of the MDR" with representatives of, among others, Cladho, Duterimbere, Ibuka, the "Maison de la presse" and Liprodhor. Only the last one did not subscribe to measures and "recommendations" that read like a communiqué of the RPF.[12] Independent components of national (Liprodhor) and international (Human Rights Watch) civil society were severely criticized. Thus, a report

---

[7] LDGL, *La problématique de la liberté d'expression au Rwanda*, Kigali, December 2001.

[8] P. Gready, "'You're Either with Us or against Us': Civil Society and Policymaking in Post-genocide Rwanda", *African Affairs*, 109:437 (2010), pp. 641–642.

[9] J. Pottier, "Land Reform for Peace? Rwanda's 2005 Land Law in Context", *Journal of Agrarian Change*, 6:4 (2006), p. 510.

[10] P. Gready, "Beyond 'You're with Us or against Us': Civil Society and Policymaking in Post-genocide Rwanda", in S. Straus, L. Waldorf (Eds.), *Remaking Rwanda*, p. 96.

[11] P. Gready, "You're Either with Us".

[12] A few extracts make the point very clear: "1. Civil society reiterates its support to the policy of unity and reconciliation of Rwandans;

2. Civil society energetically condemns all forms of division among Rwandans and those that cause it;

3. Civil society totally supports the recommendation of the National Assembly on the banning of the MDR;

(...) 5. Civil society recommends the sacking of the artisans of division employed in the civil service (...);

6. Civil society forcefully condemns the report recently released by Human Rights Watch".

of Human Rights Watch[13] was labeled "partisan, flawed, and manipulated by a wing of the MDR," and it was said to be "no different from the reports that used to be written in Mugunga [refugee camp of Hutu in Zaire in 1994–6]". Liprodhor was accused of all ills: collaboration with the MDR, Human Rights Watch, and the international Christian Democracy, discrimination, divisionism. "Civil society" linked to the RPF or infiltrated by it thus became instrumental in destroying autonomous civil society. A report produced by the civil society umbrella organization CCOAIB (Conseil de concertation des organisations d'appui aux initiatives de base) in 2011 only confirmed the closeness of civil society with the regime: "Generally, civil society's external working environment in Rwanda is conducive. (. . .) [I]ndicators such as civil society registration, restrictions on civil society, dialogue between state and civil society, public trust and public spiritenness were reported to be positive."[14] The survey does not contain one word critical of the government and offers high scores on themes such as "basic freedoms and rights" and "political context."[15]

Holvoet and Rombouts observed that, in addition to the threat of persecution, the law on NGOs helps to explain "the self-censoring attitudes of civil society organisations," including international NGOs. "Reacting critically can jeopardise next year's registration and puts thus in danger the presence and survival of an entire organisation (. . .). In short, there is little room for advocacy NGOs and the few that are still active are heavily criticised as if they want to divide the country."[16] In their analysis of civil society participation in the drafting of the Rwandan Poverty Reduction Strategy Paper (PRSP), Renard and Molenaers noted that "[t]hreats to civil society, and outright repression by part of the state apparatus, were occurring at the same time that civil society was 'participating' in the preparation of the PRSP. Donors apparently were of the opinion that more than this semblance of participation was at this stage either not possible or desirable". They concluded that "[b]y pretending, for the sake of convenience, to see levels of civil society participation that just are not there, donors became blind to the violations of minimum benchmarks in the treatment of civil society by the regime, in particular in the

---

[13] Human Rights Watch, *Preparing for Elections: Tightening Control in the Name of Unity*, New York, May 2003.

[14] CCOAIB, *The State of Civil Society in Rwanda in National Development. Civil Society Undex Rwanda Report*, Kigali, March 2011, p. 9.

[15] *Idem*, p. 28.

[16] N. Holvoet, H. Rombouts, *The Denial of Politics in PRSP Monitoring and Evaluation. Experiences from Rwanda*, IOB Discussion Paper 2008–2, Antwerp, p. 25.

realm of civil liberties."[17] Vandeginste observed similar blindness in the International Financial Institutions, quoting the IMF's Europe assistant director who stated that Rwanda's November 2000 interim PRSP was an example of how human rights concerns could be integrated in the country's development strategies.[18] Vandeginste also quoted the Joint Staff Assessment by the World Bank and the IMF of the full PRSP, which noted that "the participation in the PRSP process and sense of ownership are impressive," that "the country ownership of the PRSP process has been consistently strong," and that "the PRSP has been written with the Rwandese populations as the primary audience."[19]

These optimistic assessments were very distant from the reality on the ground. Under the heading "You're with us or against us," a senior government official echoed earlier statements by RPF leaders: "When civil society sees itself as something different to government, as almost opposed, then it is a problem."[20] What the government sees in store for civil society is service delivery and gap filling. Even "consultation" often takes the form of information sharing and instruction ("This is what we are going to do; any questions?").[21] Although, overall, quite positive about the development of civil society, a report noted that "[t]he state clearly warned CSOs [civil society organizations] to refrain from any political activity and to avoid creating dissensions in the population. It gave these CSOs a definite role, that is to contribute to the social and economic development of the country as part of the national decentralization policy."[22]

The final assault on civil society came in 2004, a year after the elimination of the political opposition, and it was conducted in exactly the same vein. We have seen earlier that the last remaining independent human rights organization, Liprodhor, was already targeted during the

---

[17] R. Renard, N. Molenaers, *Civil Society Participation in Rwanda's Poverty Reduction Strategy*, IOB Discussion Paper 2003–5, Antwerp, pp. 23–24.

[18] S. Vandeginste, "Rwanda, The World Bank, PRSP and Human Rights", in S. Marysse, F. Reyntjens (Eds.), *L'Afrique des grands lacs. Annuaire 2004–2005*, Paris, L'Harmattan, 2005, pp. 124–125. This statement was made after several international human rights organizations had been expressing concern over major human rights abuse during the preceding years.

[19] *Idem*, p. 135.

[20] P. Gready, "Beyond 'You're Either with Us", p. 89. It is interesting to note that the "You're with us or against us" line was exactly the one used by interim president Sindikubwabo when he launched the genocide in Butare on April 19, 1994.

[21] P. Gready, "Beyond 'You're Either with Us", p. 89.

[22] International Rescue Committee, *Report on the Sustainability of the Rwandan Civil Society*, July 2007, p. 32.

parliamentary debate that led to the banning of the MDR in 2003. The threats were hardly veiled, and Liprodhor "alert[ed] general opinion on the possible risks of intimidation, harassment and other forms of destabilisation against its members, its leaders and its staff."[23] This fear proved justified. Reminiscent of the 2003 report on the MDR, at the end of June 2004, a "Parliamentary Commission of Inquiry on Genocidal Ideology" recommended the banning of a number of associations "preaching the ideology of genocide and ethnic hatred." Among them was Liprodhor, as well as half-dozen other groups, including some involved in the promotion of peasant interests. In addition, several international NGOs, as well as France and the Netherlands, stood accused. The INGOs that were targeted – CARE, Trócaire, 11.11.11, and Norwegian People's Aid – seemed to have in common that they adopted a rights-based approach to development and that they supported Liprodhor.[24] International human rights groups protested, to no avail. Human Rights Watch felt that "the commission interpreted 'genocidal ideas', prohibited by law in Rwanda, so broadly as to include even dissent from government plans for consolidating land holdings. (...) Under such a broad interpretation, any opposition to the government can be labelled 'a genocide ideology' and its proponents can be severely punished."[25] According to Amnesty International, "the Rwandese National Assembly is inappropriately manipulating the concept of genocide to silence not only organizations and individuals critical of the government but organizations who have a close relationship with the Rwandese people and whose loyalty the government questions."[26] Even African Rights, an organization usually sympathetic to the RPF, this time objected and found this to be "a flagrant misunderstanding of the exact meaning of the expression 'genocide ideology' (...). The accusation seems to reside in the fact that these organisations are allegedly involved in anti-government political activities (...). But this should not be the equivalent of muzzling every criticism of the government."[27]

Contrary to the MDR a year earlier, it proved unnecessary to formally ban Liprodhor. After Parliament sent a list of a dozen Liprodhor cadres to

---

[23] Liprodhor, "La Liprodhor proteste", Kigali, 16 April 2003.

[24] Front Line Rwanda, *Disappearances, Arrests*, p. 84.

[25] Human Rights Watch, *Rwanda: Parliament Seeks to Abolish Rights Group*, New York, 2 July 2004.

[26] Amnesty International, *Rwanda: Deeper into the Abyss – Waging War on Civil Society*, London, 5 July 2004.

[27] African Rights, *Faux pas pour le Rwanda. Remarque sur la recommandation parlementaire prônant l'interdiction de six ONG*, Kigali, 9 July 2004.

the government with the request that they be arrested and prosecuted, in early July most of its leadership fled to Uganda and Burundi. This was the end of Liprodhor as an autonomous organization, something the government openly welcomed: in a declaration of September 18, it noted "that Liprodhor has separated itself from those among its members corroded by the ideology of genocide (and that) the General Assembly of Liprodhor, during its meeting of 11 September 2004, has asked forgiveness to the people and government of Rwanda for the bad behavior of some of its representatives and members."[28] This contentment was understandable, as most new members of the board of Liprodhor were now RPF faithful. Rather than banning it, the RPF took over and thus neutralized Liprodhor.[29]

Akin to the Forum for political parties that offered the RPF an institutional instrument of control, the government created a "Rwandan Civil Society Platform" in 2007. Although this alledgedly brought together Rwandan CSOs, it was launched by the Ministry of Local Administration in the absence of many stakeholders. The platform's leadership was appointed by the ministry. Christiane Adamczyk finds it "questionable whether the platform really represents the variety of Rwandan civil society" and observes a "widening gap between the grassroots level and a distant leadership with political aspirations."[30]

ELIMINATING THE INDEPENDENT PRESS

The media underwent the same fate as civil society.[31] Hardly a year after the RPF seized power, Reporters sans frontières (RSF) sounded the alarm bell and denounced arrests, physical and psychological harassment, and torture of journalists, in addition to the restrictions on the circulation of

[28] *Déclaration du conseil des ministres à l'issue de sa réunion au Village Uruguiro, le 17 septembre 2004, relative au rapport de la Chambres des Députés sur les tueries de Gikongoro et de l'idéologie génocidaire au Rwanda*, Kigali, 18 September 2004.

[29] The destruction of Liprodhor is extensively discussed in Front Line Rwanda, *Disappearances, Arrests*, pp. 45–56.

[30] C. Adamczyk, "Independent Actors or Silent Agents: Where To Go for Rwandan Civil Society?", in M. Campioni, P. Noack (Eds.), *Rwanda Fast Forward. Social, Economic, Military and Reconciliation Prospects*, Houndmills, Palgrave Macmillan, 2012, p. 71.

[31] An excellent survey of the fate of the media under RPF rule can be found in L. Waldorf, "Censorship and Propaganda in Post-genocide Rwanda", in A. Thompson (Ed.), *The Media and the Rwanda Genocide*, London, Pluto Press, Kampala, Fountain Publishers, 2007, pp. 404–416. Also see a chapter on "Silencing Independent Journalists" in Front Line Rwanda, *Disappearances, Arrests*, pp. 67–81.

information.[32] Indeed, the "turning point" (in the words of André Sibomana, the editor of the Catholic weekly *Kinyamateka*) already came in January 1995, with an attack, presumably under the direct orders of Kagame, on Edouard Mutsinzi, the editor of *Le Messager-Intumwa*[33]: "the message got through: from now on, anyone criticising the government knew what to expect."[34] In 2006, Amnesty International cited a list of about forty journalists who were "arbitrarily detained, unjustly judged, forced to flee the country, 'disappeared' or assassinated" since the RPF came to power.[35] Under the title "An atrophied and muzzled press," the ICG noted that "[s]ince 1998, each stage in the concentration of power seems to have been accompanied by additional restrictions on the subjects the press could cover."[36] The regime even attempted to control the press operating abroad. In March 2000, the bimonthly journal *Dialogue*, whose editors left Kigali for Brussels in 1994, received notification of the "decisions" taken by a new Kigali-based "executive committee" recognized by the Rwandan minister of justice, telling it "to immediately cease publication (…) and stop withdrawals from the bank accounts of the journal." The letter was signed by the new "legal representative" Antoine Mugesera, who also happened to be a member of the central committee of the RPF.[37] In 2004, when members of the RPF launched a Kigali-based version of *Dialogue*, its board was chaired by Mugesera, who in the meantime had become chair of Ibuka and a senator, and it included RPF spokesman Servilien Sebasoni. The layout of issue 178 of April-June 2004 looked like a twin of the Brussels version, about which its editorial claimed against all

---

[32] Reporters sans frontières, *Rwanda: l'impasse? La liberté de la presse après le génocide, 4 juillet 1994–28 août 1995*, n.d. (1995).

[33] Mutsinzi was stabbed several times by a group of extremist Tutsi who were left undisturbed. While Mutsinzi had been highly critical of the former regime, he also criticised the new one. In an article published shortly before he was assaulted, he called certain elements of the RPA "the new *interahamwe*." A witness of the Office of the Prosecutor (OTP) of the ICTR described the attack on Mutsinzi in detail. It was organised by Major Steven Balinda and Captain Dan Munyuza, under the direct orders of Kagame, "to teach a lesson to [Mutsinzi] who had criticised Kagame in this journal". Kagame gave orders "not to kill him, but to cut his tongue, eyes and right hand" (witness statement 9 February 2002, ICTR ref R0000232).

[34] Front Line Rwanda, *Disappearances, Arrests*, p. 68.

[35] Amnesty International, *Rwanda: La liberté de la presse réprimée depuis 12 ans*, London, 3 May 2006.

[36] International Crisis Group, *Rwanda at the End of the Transition: A Necessary Political Liberalisation*, Nairobi and Brussels, 13 November 2002, p. 14.

[37] Earlier we have seen the role played by Mugesera in the neutralisation of Ibuka and Iwacu.

evidence that it had become "the road of shame" publishing articles "that include a dose of revisionism and denial."

When traveling from the DRC through Rwanda, Guy Theunis, who was a missionary priest in Rwanda until 1994 and active in the press and the promotion of human rights, was arrested in September 2005. Although he was officially accused of "incitement to genocide," there was nothing in his file, and the affair was a settling of scores with *Dialogue*, of which Theunis had been the editor from 1989 to 1992, and possibly also with the White Fathers (Theunis's congregation) and the Catholic Church more generally. Grotesque accusations were launched during a hastily convened *gacaca* session, and Theunis was classified in category 1 of the *génocidaires*. The regime even found a foreign scholar, in the person of Christian Scherrer, to play in this comedy. At the other extreme, Human Rights Watch researcher Alison Des Forges, who happened to be in Rwanda at the time, saved the honor of scholars by taking the defense of Theunis in a very hostile context. After a great deal of pressure, Rwanda accepted to transfer Theunis to Belgium to stand judgment. He was interrogated and a file was opened, but in the absence of substance, the case was abandoned. Both Belgium and Rwanda were happy to forget about it.[38]

In November 2001, the RSF called President Kagame a "predator of press freedom" and noted that only one weekly, *Umuseso*, was "relatively independent." The report concluded that "[j]ournalists continue to suffer threats and pressures."[39] Around the same period, a report by the LDGL found that "the press is again targeted by the regime" and that

while fewer journalists are arrested or killed lately, this is not due to a larger openness of the authorities, but rather to the fatigue and/or the resignation of a profession that prefers to adopt a low profile instead of seeking confrontation with an authoritarian regime (. . .) The degree of press freedom is inversely proportional to the omnipotence of the internal (DMI) and external (ESO) intelligence services.[40]

The "relatively independent" *Umuseso* was under continuous threat. Its editor in chief Ismail Mbonigaba was twice arrested, in 2002 and 2003, and three of its journalists were detained in mid-2002. A U.S. embassy cable described how a special intelligence unit within the police's criminal

---

[38] On the Theunis affair, see Reporters Without Borders, *Rwanda. The Arrest of Father Guy Theunis. An Investigation of the Charges, the Legal Action and Possible Reasons*, Paris, November 2005. A personal account can be found in G. Theunis, *Mes soixante-quinze jours de prison à Kigali*, Paris, Karthala, 2012.

[39] Reporters sans frontières, *Rwanda. Discreet and Targeted Pressure: President Kagame Is a Predator of Press Freedom*, Paris, 7 November 2001.

[40] LDGL, *La problématique*.

investigation department (CID) was tasked with "shutting down" the paper. The CID recruited and armed an *Umuseso* employee to spy for the government, and offered money to a journalist to help destroy the paper. The cable concluded that "the GOR wants to eliminate the paper entirely, not just weaken it."[41] In April 2003 the entire print of the first issue of a new journal, *Indorerwamo*, published by a former director of *Umuseso*, was seized, and the paper was unable to produce further issues. RSF protested against this measure that "amounts to censorship and proves that press freedom is not respected in Rwanda."[42] In January 2004, police again seized entire prints of *Umuseso* after it published several articles alleging corruption by Gerald Gahima, vice-president of the Supreme Court and former general prosecutor, and his brother Théogène Rudasingwa, director of the president's cabinet.[43] The 2002 Press Law provided for criminal sanctions for a wide array of vaguely worded offenses. Although it also forbade "propaganda," this prohibition was applied only to the independent media: *The New Times*, Rwanda's only daily and Kagame's mouthpiece, uses sources very selectively and always in support of the regime. This is, of course, propaganda, but the paper never got into trouble with the law.

In its 2004 annual report, RSF summarized the situation as follows: "A monopoly of radio and television, a monochrome written press, and the systematic harassment of the only independent publication in the country mean that, ten years after the end of the genocide against the Tutsi, the country of Paul Kagame remains a country where press freedom does not exist".[44] Harassment came in many ways: pressures on announcers, intimidation, demonization, and seizure of entire prints, but the strongest threat came in the wake of the campaign against the MDR (cf. supra). Among the "promoters of division," the 2003 parliamentary committee included "the journalists of *Umuseso*." In September 2005, *Umuseso* journalist Jean-Léonard Rugambage was arrested after having written about the corruption of certain *gacaca* judges and after his paper criticized the arrest of

---

[41] "Special Intelligence Unit Infiltrates Rwanda's Independent Newspaper", Ref. US Embassy Kigali 00105, 13 August 2004, available through WikiLeaks (http://wikileaks.org/cable/2004/08/04KIGALI1162.html).

[42] Reporters sans frontières, *Rwanda: un nouveau journal indépendant saisi dès son premier numéro*, 23 April 2003.

[43] L. Waldorf, "Censorship and Propaganda", p. 410. Interestingly, Gahima and Rudasingwa were later accused of the very same misdeeds after they fell out with Kagame (see the following discussion).

[44] Reporters sans frontières, *Rapport annuel 2005*, Paris, n.d.

Theunis. As seen earlier, he was killed in 2010. Also in September 2005, the director of *Umuco*, Bonaventure Bizumuremyi, was arrested, and he continued to receive death threats after his liberation. He was again harassed, intimidated, and physically aggressed after *Umuco* wrote that the RPF controlled the judiciary, forced local cooperatives to fund the party, and was unable to manage the country. He escaped alive by fleeing to Uganda in 2010 (cf. supra). In October 2005, Gilbert Rwamatwara, a freelance journalist with VOA who also published in *Umuco*, warned that he risked "disappearing," fled the country. Again in August 2006, RSF expressed concern about the "increasingly hostile climate" for independent papers, after several journalists were threatened, arrested, or physically aggressed. In January 2007, the director of *Umurabyo* was arrested after the publication of an article on the violations of press freedom (she was eventually convicted to a lengthy jail sentence in 2011, cf. supra). The following month, a professor of the University of Bukavu and director of Bukavu-based *Mashariki News* was arrested while in Kigali on a teaching assignment. He was accused of "segregation, sectarianism and threatening internal state security" because of an article titled "Alerte Rwanda" published on the Internet in 2005, in which he severely criticized the regime. After having been threatened in August and October 2006, in February 2007 Jean-Bosco Gasasira, director of the weekly *Umuvugizi*, was aggressed with iron bars and severely injured by unidentified assailants just days after his paper published an article denouncing nepotism inside the RPF.[45] He later fled to Sweden, where he was again harassed (see the following discussion). Paradoxically, at the occasion of a ceremony organized at the occasion of World Press Freedom Day on 2 May 2008, the directors of *Umuseso*, *Rushyashya*, and *Umuvugizi* were thrown out. Information minister Louise Mushikiwabo indicated that she was to exclude all "negativist" papers from governmental activities.[46]

As spaces of expression were effectively closed and a great deal of courage was needed to contest the existing situation, the regime needed less and less to use large scale repression. The reports on 2007 of both Human Rights Watch and the U.S. State Department observed that the press and civil society exercised self-censorship that was reinforced by threatening statements made by members of the government, including

---

[45] A striking detail is that Gasasira is the brother of Chris Bunyenyezi, a superior RPA officer killed by his own during the first days of the war in October 1990 under circumstances that were never elucidated.

[46] Reporters sans frontières, *RSF s'inquiète du mépris grandissant du gouvernement envers certains journalistes*, 6 May 2008.

Kagame. For the same year, Rwanda stood at 147 out of 169 countries in RSF's world ranking of press freedom.[47] One reads with surprise in a cable of U.S. ambassador Arietti that "[p]ress freedom in Rwanda (...) has in recent years taken root" and that "[t]he GoR states – probably accurately – that Rwanda's media has never enjoyed more freedom than it does today."[48]

Foreign media, too, were targeted. In January 2006, two Rwandan journalists working for the VOA and the BBC were accused of "treason": according to the police spokesperson, they were no "patriots," and "the ideology of these journalists needs revision."[49] In May 2006, a dozen journalists, including a number of foreign correspondents, were thrown out from the NEPAD (New Partnership for Africa's Development) forum in Kigali. In June, the RFI correspondent was expelled without any explanation. In April 2008, the chairperson of Ibuka publicly denounced "genocide denying, and even genocidal" journalists working in Rwanda for the BBC and VOA. In June 2008, the information minister accused the BBC and VOA of "destroying the unity of Rwandans" and announced that the government had "the ability and the right" to suspend their broadcasts "if the situation does not change."[50] The BBC was banned from FM relay in Rwanda during two months in 2009 because of a programme that, in the words of the information minister, contained "most outrageous statements." This reference was to an interviewee who claimed that some of the bodies that ended up in Lake Victoria in 1994 were those of victims of the RPF; this accusation was true[51] but, of course, was unacceptable to the RPF. In early May, East African newspaper publishers, who happened to be in Kigali for a regional conference, called the measure "dictatorial."[52] Having read a transcript of the broadcast, U.K. ambassador Nicholas Cannon said that his government was

---

[47] Reporters sans frontières, *Rapport annuel 2008*.

[48] US Embassy Cable 06Kigali480, "The State of Press Freedom in Rwanda", 18 May 2006, available through Wikileaks (http://wikileaks.org/cable/2006/05/06KIGALI480.html).

[49] Reporters sans frontières, *Rwanda; Le chef de l'Etat inaugure une salve d'attaques verbales des autorités contre les journalistes*, 31 January 2006.

[50] "La BBC et la VOA accusées par Kigali de 'détruire l'unité des Rwandais'", Kigali, AFP, 19 August 2008.

[51] Sources are given in Chapter 4.

[52] "Eastern Africa Editors Slam Kigali's Move against BBC", Journalism.co.za, 3 May 2009. It is interesting to note that *The New Times* of Kigali, in its report of the meeting, did not mention this condemnation ("Regional Scribes Appeal for More Media Freedom", *The New Times*, 4 May 2009).

"disappointed" by the measure and that there was "completely no sign that it was fomenting hate or denying the genocide."[53] The VOA was threatened with being banned from Rwandan airwaves in mid-2009, as was the BBC once again.[54] The crackdown on the press in 2010 was discussed earlier.

"DECENTRALIZATION" AS A MEANS TO FURTHER CENTRAL CONTROL

Decentralization is commonly seen and promoted as a means of furthering local democracy, accountability, and ownership. Several authors have shown that it has served the opposite in Rwanda, namely, to expand and entrench the control by the central state at the deepest local level. It should be noted that the previous regime too, through its so-called democratic centralism, maintained a strong pyramidal system in which orders traveled fast from top to bottom (and, at the end, made an efficient "decentralized" genocide possible). In a sector where he conducted field research, Sommers noted that officials kept files on every household. These forms were very detailed and contained what an official called "everything that people are supposed to be doing." "Obligations" are enforced by local-level fines. According to a local observer, the annual cost of these "obligations" amounted to more than US$200, more than the annual revenue of an average Rwandan. The centralized nature of "decentralization" was made clear by the fact that the performance contracts (*imihigo*) to be implemented at *umudugudu* (village; see Chapter 6) level came from the Ministry of Local Government supposedly in charge of decentralization. It was very detailed and covered five areas of "good governance," thirty objectives, and sixty-eight strategies for officials to implement the objectives. The centralized nature of decentralization also showed in that even a sector official would refer to those higher up in the hierarchy (at district and national levels) as "the authorities," although that sector official is a central part of what the government presents as a dramatic decentralization policy.[55]

Purdekova has documented the pervasive presence of the state at the local level, with the local RPF hierarchies mimicking those of the state. All

---

[53] "British Envoy Defends BBC Programming", Kigali, RNA, 18 May 2009.

[54] "Pressure on VOA Radio Mounts from Government", Kigali, RNA, 19 June 2009; "BBC Risks Indefinite Ban from Rwanda", Kigali, RNA, 26 June 2009.

[55] M. Sommers, *Stuck. Rwandan Youth and the Struggle for Adulthood*, Athens, GA, and London, University of Georgia Press, 2012, pp. 82–86.

citizens are drafted into the system in three ways. First, nearly everyone is forced to become a member of the RPF family (*umuryango*), a membership that comes with the price of countless exactions, for instance, under the form of "contributions" to the party, "the most widespread and effective fundraising mechanism in Rwanda."[56] Second, large numbers of people are co-opted into the administrative and security systems, all becoming "responsible for something" (*mutuelle de santé*, community policing, education or hygiene committees, *imihigo* and *ubudehe* committees, youth and women representatives, and much more).[57] Forced into being the "eyes and ears" of the regime, everyone spies on everyone: people suggested that there is an official, trained spy per organization and perhaps per office and that all newcomers are assigned someone to watch them.[58] Third, people's time is saturated with multiple state-ordained activities, and peasants' time and energy are appropriated in the production of public goods that are largely symbolic and unproductive. These include unpaid administrative and police duties (such as night patrols); compulsory presence at a myriad of meetings related to security, special occasions, commemorations, and political happenings; and labor-exacting duties such as *umuganda*, which is an indirect but effective taxing system. As a result of all these demands, "the poor do not have time."[59] Purdekova concluded that "grass-roots" does not always mean "free of central power": "Despotism can also be decentralised, and so can disempowerment."[60] Sommers concurs: "the decentralization process appears to provide the national government with opportunities to expand, rather than transfer or devolve, its power and influence."[61]

The central figure at the district and the sector level is the executive secretary, appointed and paid by the central government. Ingelaere noted that there is a clear hierarchy between appointed and elected local office-holders, with only those in appointed positions receiving a salary. Most if not all are Tutsi of the RPF,[62] and they are not of local origin, whereas in the past, these positions were almost exclusively occupied by local

---

[56] A. Purdekova, "'Even if I Am not Here, there Are so Many Eyes': Survellience and State Reach in Rwanda", *Journal of Modern African Studies*, **49**:3 (2011), p. 482.

[57] *Idem*, pp. 482–483.

[58] *Idem*, p. 488.

[59] *Idem*, p. 491.

[60] *Idem*, p. 494.

[61] M. Sommers, *Stuck*, p. 89.

[62] The executive secretaries were Tutsi in five of the six field sites of Ingelaere (the sixth was not categorized) (B. Ingelaere, "Peasants, Power and Ethnicity: A Bottom-up Perspective on Rwanda's Political Transition", *African Affairs*, 109:435 [2010], p. 289).

Hutu. The executive secretaries are responsible for imposing the RPF line on the rural populations.[63] The fact that those holding real power tend to be Tutsi outsiders, whereas local Hutu occupy lesser positions inevitably exacerbates the ethnic dimension of local politics.

AN ARMY WITH A STATE

The way in which the political opposition, civil society, and the press were treated epitomized a more general attempt at controlling people and space. This showed in the maintenance of a large and efficient army, able to operate inside and far beyond national borders; in the establishment of "re-education," "solidarity," and "regroupment" camps (see the following discussion); in the villagization policy (*imidugudu*; also see the following discussion); in the tense relations of distrust with nonstate and foreign actors; and in the emergence of a powerful intelligence capacity, with the DMI operating inside the country and the ESO abroad. Despite its civilian appearance, Rwanda is an army with a state rather than a state with an army, and it is effectively run by a military regime. This vision is well rendered by the back cover of a book[64] by Brig. Gen. Frank Rusagara, the military historian of the RDF (Rwanda Defence Forces, the new name of the RPA since 2002) who coined the term "Rwandanicity." He writes that

[i]t is the military that played the most central socio-political role in what became of Rwanda during its heydays when no slave trader could tread its soil, to its lowest moment during the 1994 genocide. It is also the military that led the way in re-uniting a shattered people and the country to become a democratic state of reputable international standing. (...) Borrowing from the *ingabo z'u Rwanda* (Rwandan army) of old, the RDF today not only ensures security for all, but provides a model of national unity and integration that continues to inform Rwanda's socio-political and economic development.

This feeling is again understandable against the background of the RPF's experience, which had shown that bold military action can deliver more than can negotiations and peace accords.[65]

---

[63] B. Ingelaere, "The Ruler's Drum and the People's Shout. Accountability and Representation on Rwanda's Hills", in S. Strauss, L. Waldorf (Eds.), *Remaking Rwanda*, pp. 69–74.

[64] F.K. Rusagara, *Resilience of a Nation. A History of the Military in Rwanda*, Kigali, Fountain Publishers Rwanda, 2009.

[65] H. Verhoeven, "Nurturing Democracy or into the Danger Zone? The Rwandan Patriotic Front, Elite Fragmentation and Post-liberation Politics", in M. Campioni, P. Noack (Eds.), *Rwanda Fast Forward*, p. 267.

The central place taken by the military and intelligence services allowed one analyst to call Rwanda a "securocracy."[66] Indeed, military skills permeate the way in which Rwandans must be "educated." A "manual for the solidarity camps and other training" issued by the Civic Education Service of the NURC contains a section on "self-defence." Among other things, students at *ingando*[67] are taught how to "perform military drills," the "stripping and assembling of AK-47 rifle," and the "use [of] combat tactics in a section and a platoon."[68] Rusagara was very explicit when he called *ingando* "a military approach to reintegration and promotion of the Rwandan identity based on the institutions and the alleged values of the pre-colonial period."[69]

Still at the end of the 1990s, official military expenditure stood at around 30 percent of the budget, a huge figure in itself, but formal accounts only showed part of this reality. The RPA found other sources of funding outside of the official budget in its presence in the DRC (see the following discussion), the embargo against Burundi, the imposition of unofficial "taxes" and even a "voluntary" contribution to the war effort,[70] theft and extortion, and payments by parastatal companies such as Rwandex, Sonarwa and Rwandatel.[71] That Rwanda is an army with a state rather than a state with an army also showed elsewhere. In July 2005, a new building for the Ministry of Defence, of which the construction cost was about US$24 million, was inaugurated. In March 2007, the chief of army staff announced that a "formidable" air force was to be created, "one of the best on the continent."[72] Many enterprises are owned by army officers who pocketed a good part of the projects funded by donors.[73] Two generals even succeeded each other at the head of the Rwandan soccer association.

---

[66] E. Sidiropoulos, "Democratisation and Militarisation in Rwanda: Eight Years after the Genocide", *African Security Review*, 11:3 (2002), pp. 77–87.

[67] *Ingando* is discussed in Chapter 7.

[68] République du Rwanda, Commission nationale pour l'unité et la réconciliation, *Manuel pour les camps de solidarité et autres formations*, Kigali, October 2006, p. 120.

[69] Colonel Frank Rusagara presentation about solidarity camps at the international conference on genocide, Kigali, April 2004, summarized in Penal Reform International, *From Camp to Hill, the Reintegration of Released Prisoners*, May 2004, p. 111.

[70] On this, see Human Rights Watch, *Rwanda. The Search for Security and Human Rights Abuses*, New York, April 2000.

[71] Examples can be found in M. Dorsey, "Violence and Power-building in Post-genocide Rwanda", in R. Doom, J. Gorus (Eds.), *Politics of Identity and Economics of Conflict in the Great Lakes Region*, Brussels, VUB Press, 2000, pp. 311–348.

[72] "Airforce Set for Strong Boost", *The New Times*, 5 March 2007.

[73] Confidential sources in Kigali.

The army is even directly and heavily involved in the economy. According to a UN panel of experts, Rwandan companies such as Rwanda Metals, Grands Lacs Metals, and Tri-Star illegally exploited Congolese resources,[74] and the partners with whom the panel met "were in Rwandan army uniforms and were top officers."[75] It found that these companies and others such as the bank BCDI seemed "to report separately to the same people at the top of the pyramid."[76] Tri-Star, which was created out of the RPF's "production department" was later rebranded as Crystal Ventures, with subsidiary companies in areas such as civil works, telecommunications, security services, property development and management, and media systems, to name but a few. In 2008, the RDF set up another business venture, Horizon Group. The group established several subsidiary companies and entered into a number of joint venture partnerships with public enterprises. The army also owns the Credit and Savings Society, which operates as a commercial bank.[77]

LAW AS A TOOL OF CONTROL

Of course, control was not maintained just through military means. Law, too, became a powerful tool. I have referred earlier to the "Fundamental Law" pushed through by the RPF less than a year after it took power. The 2003 constitution proceeded from the same obsession with control. Among other mechanisms, this was achieved by the role assigned to the Senate and to the Consultative Forum for Political Organizations, both dominated by the RPF, to "discipline" political parties.[78] As mentioned

[74] The External Security Organisation (ESO) had a unit with the telling name, "Production," in its Congo Desk. On the exploitation of resources by the RPA in the DRC, see F. Reyntjens, *The Great African War. Congo and Regional Geopolitics, 1996–2006,* New York, Cambridge University Press, 2009, pp. 224–231.

[75] United Nations, Security Council, *Report of the Panel of Experts on the Illegal Exploitation of Natural Resources and Other Forms of Wealth of the Democratic Republic of the Congo,* S/2001/357, 12 April 2001, para. 82.

[76] *Idem,* para. 86.

[77] On these weblike structures, see D. Booth, F. Golooba-Mutebi, *Developmental patrimonialism? The case of Rwanda,* London, ODI, APPP Working Paper No. 16, March 2011; D. Booth, F. Golooba-Mutebi, "Developmental Patrimonialism? The Case of Rwanda", *African Affairs,* 111:444 (2012), pp. 379–403; N. Gökgür, *Formulating a Broad-based Private Sector Development Strategy. Inception Report,* 20 June 2011; N. Gökgür, *Rwanda's Ruling Party-owned Business Enterprises: Do They Enhance or Impede Development?,* IOB Discussion Paper 2012.03, Antwerp, 2012.

[78] According to a USAID document, the forum "has served as a means of limiting the range of allowable ideas among politicians", and a source of the report compared it to the central committee of a single party (USAID, *Rwanda Democracy and Governance Assessment,* November 2002, p. 50). According to the experience of the former Speaker of Parliament

earlier, the inclusion of twenty-seven indirectly elected MPs (of eighty) allowed to hide the RPF's dominance of the House, whereas the Senate is entirely appointed by institutions dominated by the RPF.[79] As the RPF was consolidating its hold on the political landscape, it devised other legal instruments to outlaw contestation.

Law became a major instrument for redefining collective identities in a way rarely seen elsewhere. It reconfigured the ethnic map and entrenched the regime's policing of relations between individuals and groups. Law no. 47/2001 of December 18, 2001, made "sectarianism," later called "divisionism" a criminal offense. Article 3 states that "sectarianism is a crime committed through the use of any speech, written statement or action that causes an uprising that may degenerate into strife among people." The notion is so broad and vague that a judge interviewed by Human Rights Watch was unable to define it, despite having adjudicated and convicted defendants on divisionism charges.[80] The political use was made clear during the parliamentary debate that led to the banning of the MDR and the destruction of Liprodhor (cf. supra). A parliamentary commission showed how far-reaching the interpretation of "divisionism" could be: "[The granaries built by the peasants organisation FOR] were put in place to show to the population that the state doesn't do anything for them and that FOR shows people how to get together to tackle their problems."[81] After the Community of Indigenous Peoples of Rwanda (CAURWA), founded in 1995 to promote the rights of the Twa,[82] published two reports critical of government policies in 2004, the justice ministry refused to grant legal recognition to the organization, claiming that its name and objectives were contrary to the prohibition of divisionism. Later during that year, the

Joseph Sebarenzi, "[c]reating the Forum of Political Parties was a way for Kagame to remove members of parliament who stood in his way", and he offers many examples of how this worked (J. Sebarenzi, *God Sleeps in Rwanda. A Journey of Transformation*, New York, Atria Books, 2009, pp. 146–151).

[79] A more detailed analysis of the constitution can be found in F. Reyntjens, "Les nouveaux habits de l'empereur: analyse juridico-politique de la constitution rwandaise de 2003", in: S. Marysse, F. Reyntjens (Eds.), *L'Afrique des grands lacs. Annuaire 2002–2003*, Paris, L'Harmattan, 2003, pp. 71–87.

[80] Human Rights Watch, *Law and Reality. Progress in Judicial Reform in Rwanda*, New York, 24 July 2004, p. 34.

[81] République du Rwanda, Chambre des députés, *Rapport de la Commission parlementaire ad hoc créée en date du 20 janvier 2004 chargée d'examiner les tueries perpétrées dans la province de Gikongoro, l'idéologie génocidaire et ceux qui la propagent partout au Rwanda*, adopted by the Chamber on 30 June 2004 (unofficial translation from Kinyarwanda).

[82] A small pygmoid ethnic group that makes up less than 1 percent of the population. The Twa have historically been marginalized, and they still are.

government ordered CAURWA to suspend its activities because its director raised the situation of the Twa at a session of the African Commission on Human and People's Rights.[83]

In the wake of the destruction of civil society, the accusation of adhering to "genocide ideology" was also used to "weed out" the schools. On October 2, 2004, the Ministry of Education published a "list of school directors, teachers and pupils considered to be propagators of the ideology of genocide within the educational institutions." During a broadcast on Radio Rwanda on October 10, in which the ministers of Education and of Justice, as well as a spokesperson for the national police participated, it was announced that staff and pupils had been arrested, and that the "tracing" was to continue. After a number of people were convicted without a legal basis during the preceding years, "genocide ideology" was finally made a criminal offense by Law No. 18/2008 of July 23, 2008. Article 2 defined genocide ideology as "an aggregate of thoughts characterised by conduct, speeches, documents and other acts aiming at exterminating or inciting others to exterminate people basing on ethnic group, origin, nationality, region, colour, physical appearance, sex, language, religion or political opinion." Not only do these categories far exceed those provided for in the genocide convention, but this poorly drafted text is also extremely vague. What is punishable: the "aggregate of thoughts," the conduct, speeches and the like, the aims, or incitements? And yet, the penalties are very harsh: from ten to twenty-five years in prison and double that in the case of recidivism (article 4); even children are punishable (article 9), as are parents, guardians, tutors, teachers, or headmasters who have "inoculated" them with the genocide ideology. Political and nongovernmental organizations found guilty are to be dissolved and given a fine of up to 5 million RWF.

Examples of genocide ideology given by a Senate report illustrate the scope for political exploitation (e.g. "partisan and unfair political criticism"; claims that the RPF is "a totalitarian regime stifling the opposition, the press, freedoms of association and expression"; references to "the guilt feelings of the international community that is too lenient on the post-genocide regime" are all punishable).[84] Waldorf concluded that the report "conflates genocide ideology with any ethnic discourse, political criticism, revisionism, and negationism. According

---

[83] Front Line Rwanda, *Disappearences, Arrests*, pp. 41–43.

[84] République du Rwanda, Sénat, *Idéologie du génocide au Rwanda et stratégies de son éradication*, Kigali, 2006, p. 21. The author of this book is guilty of all these crimes.

to its definition, any mention of alleged RPF war crimes or human rights abuses would constitute 'genocide ideology.'"[85] The risk of manipulation was indeed obvious, as a few examples show. After a Spanish judge produced arrest warrants against Rwandan army officers (cf. infra), the justice minister stated that "indicting the ruling party is a way of denying Genocide."[86] When a parliamentary commission found out in December 2007 that the "genocide ideology" was widespread in schools, MPs called for disciplinary and legal sanctions against headmasters and teachers, as well as the "re-education" of all pupils involved.[87] Education minister Jeanne d'Arc Mujawamariya, a Hutu, was severely taken to task, and certain MPs even suggested that she shared the genocide ideology herself. A follow-up commission was to continue the inquiry.[88] Mujawamariya suspended dozens of teachers and pupils and threatened that "a teacher transmitting the genocide ideology must not be transferred to another school, but immediately sacked and sent to prison for appropriate prosecution."[89] In mid-January 2008, Parliament expressed dissatisfaction with the actions of the minister, who then announced the creation of a "situation file" for each teacher and pupil. She also accepted to withdraw the textbooks for the teaching of Kinyarwanda.[90] On March 7, 2008, Mujawamariya was demoted to the portfolio of Gender, and the state secretary for primary and secondary education Joseph Murekeraho, a Hutu too, left the government. They were both replaced by Tutsi from the RPF, which thus took full control of the education sector. In the meantime, fearing to be accused of genocide ideology, deprived of history and language manuals, and threatened by their inclusion on the ministry's "black list," teachers were paralyzed, and some quit their jobs.[91] The climate of suspicion had a profound impact on the functioning of schools:

---

[85] L. Waldorf, "Revisiting Hotel Rwanda, Genocide Ideology, Reconciliation, and Rescuers", *Journal of Genocide Research*, 11:1 (2009), p. 111.

[86] "Journalists Urged to Fight against Genocide Deniers", *The New Times*, 5 April 2008.

[87] "Shocked MPs Condemn Genocide Ideology in Secondary Schools", *The New Times*, 13 December 2007.

[88] "Genocide Ideology: Lawmakers Form Another Ad Hoc Commission", *The New Times*, 21 December 2007.

[89] "Rwanda: suspension d'enseignants accusés de prôner le génocide", Kigali, Panapress, 27 December 2007.

[90] The history manuals had been withdrawn earlier because of their "divisionist" and "genocidal" contents.

[91] "La lutte contre l'idéologie génocidaire paralyse les enseignants", *Syfia Grands Lacs/ Rwanda*, 27 March 2008.

"All along this term, pupils and teachers watched their behavior and their words, for fear of being misinterpreted."[92] During seminars organized by a Berkeley history curriculum project, the team noted increasing resistance to discussing ethnicity or identity, considered "taboo subjects." A senior Rwandan historian warned that "the conversation was approaching genocide ideology."[93] The malaise also reached the National University, where the academic authorities annulled the elections of student representatives and dissolved their committees, referring to the prevalence of "ethnic divisionism" and "genocide ideology."[94]

Amnesty International found that the broad and ill-defined laws of 2001 and 2008 created a vague legal framework deliberately aiming at criminalizing criticism of the government and legitimate dissent and that individuals also used the laws for personal gain, for instance, to discredit teachers, gain local political capital, and manipulate land disputes or personal conflicts.[95] Human Rights Watch pointed out that, given that discussing RPA war crimes was equated with genocide ideology, victims could not take these cases to court.[96] A report commissioned by AFRICOM opined that "because the RPF controls all mechanisms of the state, including the judiciary, there is no broadly credible independent adjudicator to determine what constitutes genuine divisionist speech or 'genocide denial' versus legitimate debate. The accusation is used liberally by the RPF to suppress a wide range of speech that is deemed critical of the government."[97] Likewise, the UN independent expert on minority issues found these laws "problematic and ill-defined. (…) [They] must be revised as a matter of urgency and safeguards should be implemented to guarantee that they are not used to silence dissent or restrict the legitimate activities of political opposition."[98]

---

[92] *Idem.*

[93] S. Warshauer Freedman et al., "Teaching History in Post-Genocide Rwanda" in S. Straus, L. Waldorf (Eds.), *Remaking Rwanda*, p. 308.

[94] "NUR Dissolves Entire Students' Leadership", *The New Times*, 24 April 2008.

[95] Amnesty International, *Safer to Stay Silent. The Chilling Effect of Rwanda's Laws on "Genocide Ideology" and "Sectarianism"*, London, 2010.

[96] Human Rights Watch, *Law and Reality*, pp. 90–91. It is interesting to note that the initial 2001 law on the *gacaca* jurisdictions included war crimes in their mandate, but this competence was dropped in the 2004 amendment, thus making the prosecution of RPA crimes impossible. A public information campaign then insisted that these crimes were not to be talked about during *gacaca* proceedings (also see Chapter 8).

[97] Center for Strategic & International Studies, *Rwanda. Assessing Risks to Stability*, Washington, DC, June 2011, p. 13.

[98] United Nations, General Assembly, Human Rights Council, *Report of the Independent Expert on Minority Issues, Gay McDougall*, A/HRC/19/56/Add.1, 28 November 2011, p. 21.

The use of divisionism or genocide ideology related charges is not just a marginal phenomenon affecting a few troublemakers. According to a report on judicial activity in 2007–2008 cited by Human Rights Watch, Rwandan courts initiated 1,304 cases involving genocide ideology during that period. In addition, 243 persons were charged with genocide denial and revisionism. As of August 2009, there reportedly were 912 people in prison (356 awaiting trial, 556 convicted) on genocide ideology charges.[99] Official government statistics quoted by Amnesty International confirmed the widespread impact of charges related to "divisionism" and "genocide ideology": during 2007 through 2009, 1,845 cases were brought before the courts.[100] Rwandan jurists told Human Rights Watch researchers that the broad and ill-defined charges of divisionism or genocide ideology were frequently used to serve political or personal interests; five concrete examples of such politically inspired prosecutions are given in the Human Rights Watch report.[101] Admitting the link made between genocide ideology and accusations of RPF abuse, Rwandan authorities said they were exploring the possibility of prosecuting Spanish judge Andreu Merelles for genocide ideology[102] (see infra). Waldorf offered a similar explanation after the filing of amicus briefs by Human Rights Watch opposing transfers of genocide suspects by the ICTR to Rwanda was met with accusations by Ibuka and the justice minister that Alison Des Forges trivialized the genocide and had become "a spokesperson for genocide ideology." These outbursts "seemed to substantiate Human Rights Watch's argument that the government uses sweeping accusations of genocide ideology to intimidate or silence its critics."[103] When, during a 2007 National Summit for Children and Young People, a child complained about the detention of parents, it was severely rebuked by a representative of the National Human Rights Commission for "propagating genocidal ideology."[104] In September 2008, two pupils at the primary school of Busanza were arrested for having called, in private, a classmate (who was a genocide

---

[99] Amnesty International, *Report 2010*, London, n.d., p. 273.
[100] Amnesty International, *Safer to Stay Silent*, p. 19.
[101] Human Rights Watch, *Law and Reality*, p. 40.
[102] Republic of Rwanda, Rwandan Embassy, The Hague, to the embassies and international organizations accredited to the Kingdom of the Netherlands, No. 256, February 11, 2008 enclosing a communiqué from the Ministry of Foreign Affairs and Cooperation.
[103] L. Waldorf, "Revisiting Hotel Rwanda", p. 112.
[104] K. Pells, "Building a Rwanda 'Fit for Children'", in S. Straus, L. Waldorf (Eds.), *Remaking Rwanda*, p. 81.

survivor) a "cockroach."[105] At a *gacaca* trial in October 2006, a witness said that the defendant had fled to Burundi because he had seen RPF soldiers killing local people. The defendant was acquitted, but the witness was arrested several days later. Brought to trial in March 2007, he was sentenced to twenty years in prison for "gross minimization of the genocide."[106] The dangers of vague norms were again highlighted when, in April 2009, the chairperson of Ibuka accused singer Jean-Paul Samputu, a genocide survivor himself, of "revisionism" because he publicly stated that he forgave those who killed members of his family.[107]

In early 2005, the start of the *gacaca* proceedings (cf. infra) gave rise to a new round of accusatory practices and became a source of concern for Hutu elites, or what was left of them. Defense minister Marcel Gatsinzi, General Laurent Munyakazi, Ruhengeri governor Boniface Rucagu, the Speaker of the Chamber of Deputies Alfred Mukezamfura, and four other MPs were accused of having participated in the genocide. In March, the former dean of the National University's law school Alberto Basimongera was arrested, apparently on account of a text critical of the regime he published in 1995 while in exile in Bukavu. In May, former minister Jean-Népomuscène Nayinzira who was a candidate at the 2003 presidential election was questioned by the police and was subjected to endless threats after he criticised the government in an interview with the Voice of America and an electronic journal.[108] General Munyakazi, a former FAR officer integrated in the RPA, was sentenced to life in prison by a military court in November 2006. Despite being recognized for his courageous opposition to the genocide, Major Cyriaque Habyarabatuma was arrested in 2004 and was given a life sentence in June 2010. In July 2005, the archbishop of Kigali Thaddée Ntihinyurwa was taken to a *gacaca* court in Cyangugu, where he was bishop in 1994. Many more examples could be given of Hutu political and military leaders, including from the RPF, who stood thus accused. These constant threats made them very vulnerable and imposed total loyalty to the RPF. The signal was very clear: as soon as they outlived their usefulness, prison, exile, or death awaited them.

---

[105] "Two Primary School Girls Jailed over Genocide Ideology", *Sunday Times*, 13 September 2008.

[106] Human Rights Watch, *Law and Reality*, pp. 40–41.

[107] "Samputu Dismisses IBUKA 'Negationist' Accusations", *The New Times*, 15 April 2009.

[108] "L'ex-ministre du gouvernement FPR Jean-Népomuscère Nayinzira fustige la politique actuelle du régime de Kigali", *Libre antenne*, 23 May 2005.

HIDING THE MONOPOLY OF POWER

Despite the appearance of political pluralism, for example, through a "coalition government," the RPF managed to monopolize real, although sometimes less visible, decision making. The ploy of the "second man," put forward to hide who wielded real power, was used by the RPF from the beginning, as two examples at the very top of the system show. Although Alexis Kanyarengwe was officially the RPF's chairperson, its "vice chairman" Paul Kagame was the real boss, as he himself told journalist Stephen Smith in 1992: "Don't worry. (...) You're seeing the boss. Kanyarengwe is only our front man. You'd be wasting your time [talking to him]."[109] Likewise, when Pasteur Bizimungu served as president between 1994 and 2000, he was the "front man" with "Vice-President" Kagame calling the shots. In the 1990s, it was useful to have "token Hutu" seen as being in charge until they could be dispensed with (cf. supra on the subsequent demise of Sendashonga, Kanyarengwe, and Bizimungu).

This also showed at other levels. When the Gendarmerie (National Police) became operational again in August 1994, its formal chief of staff ex-FAR Colonel Ndibwami "was practically marginalised. The real Chief of Staff was (RPA) Colonel Kayumba Nyamwasa."[110] The ICG found that, from July 1994, RPF cadres were posted at all levels of the administration, both in Kigali and in the provinces, to control the actions of civil servants, ministers, and politicians.[111] Still according to the ICG, "[t]he administrative chain of authority – from the office of the President, to the hills – is under control of an omnipresent security apparatus, which shadows the official system."[112] In 2002, although ministers were drawn from several parties, the vast majority of secretary-generals (permanent secretaries) at the ministries were RPF members. Twelve of sixteen ministries had an RPF permanent secretary, and at the remaining four ministries, the ministers were from the RPF. Exiled opponents who were once ministers said that this practice amounted to giving them a post but no power,

---

[109] S.W. Smith, "Rwanda in Six Scenes", *London Review of Books*, 33:6 (17 March 2011), p. 3. I had the same impression when meeting with Kanyarengwe on a couple of occasions in 1990, just after the beginning of the war (F. Reyntjens, *Les risques du métier. Trois décennies comme 'chercheur-acteur' au Rwanda et au Burundi*, Paris, L'Harmattan, 2009, pp. 24–25).

[110] Statement made by former RPA officer to the OTP of the ICTR (witness statement, 9 February 2002, ICTR ref R0000232).

[111] International Crisis Group, "'Consensual Democracy'", p. 7.

[112] *Idem*, p. 22.

whereas the RPF secretary-generals wielded the real power.[113] This was confirmed by a U.S. embassy cable mentioned earlier: "Hutus in very senior positions often hold relatively little real authority, and are commonly 'twinned' with senior Tutsis who exercise real power." The cable included a number of examples of "twins" of a powerless Hutu and a powerful Tutsi.[114] Just as Dorsey noted with regard to the way the RPF treated its Congolese proxies, domestic non-RPF "partners" were "not allies, but mere auxiliaries."[115] This hidden exercise of power was nearly complete in 2010, when seventeen of eighteen permanent secretaries were from the RPF (in addition, fifteen were Tutsi). The same ploy is practiced at embassies, particularly those run by a Hutu or a non-RPF ambassador, where the first secretary – usually an RPF Tutsi working for the DMI – holds real power and even spies on his "boss."[116] We have seen that the same phenomenon can be observed in local government, where the executive secretaries, the most powerful persons at the local level, are generally RPF Tutsi unfamiliar with the area and are appointed and paid by the central government, whereas elected positions are often occupied by Hutu originating from the area, but they are not paid and have no real power.[117]

Another way of hiding control by the RPF is the use of youth and women organizations to conceal the party's dominance under the guise of the representation of these interest groups. In 1998, an RPF congress put Aloysia Inyumba, the minister for women and social services, in charge of building up a national network of women's groups, using aid funds for women's empowerment allocated to her ministry. By the first quarter of 1999, Catholic youth leaders were recruited to mobilize the young. Women and youth leaders were promised positions within the future

---

[113] International Crisis Group, *Rwanda at the End of the Transition*, p. 11.

[114] "Ethnicity in Rwanda – Who Governs the Country?", US Embassy Kigali, Ref. Kigali 480, 5 August 2008, available through WikiLeaks (http://wikileaks.org/cable/2008/08/08KIGALI525.html).

[115] M. Dorsey, "Violence and Power-Building", p. 344.

[116] An example among many is what happened to Rwanda's ambassador in Burundi Willy Eraste Kabera. After less than a year in function, he was recalled in May 2011, apparently because he had "wrong contacts" who were denounced by his own first secretary who worked for the DMI. In addition, a colonel of the Congolese Tutsi rebel movement FRF (Forces républicaines et fédéralistes; see the following discussion), suspected of being in league with Rwandan dissidents Kayumba Nyamwasa and Karegeya, who was imprisoned in Burundi, escaped to Uvira (DRC) at the end of March. On his arrival in Kigali, Kabera was interrogated by a panel that included his former first secretary, and his passport was withdrawn. Only in November that same year was he replaced by Augustin Habimana, who was considered more trustworthy.

[117] B. Ingelaere, "Peasants, Power and Ethnicity", pp. 287–291.

district councils or even seats in parliament if they supported the RPF. In parallel, the "solidarity camps" organized by the NURC became the training grounds for RPF political sensitization and education and for the selection of electoral candidates.[118] As seen earlier, the twenty-four MPs representing women, elected in an indirect and opaque way, are "RPF approved," and they serve to hide the RPF's dominance of Parliament.

Likewise, despite official adherence to the principle of separation of powers, the RPF has taken control of the judiciary. Although the law prohibits judges from belonging to political parties, most of them are RPF members. A Human Rights Watch report noted in 2008 that

[a] judge said that loyalty to the RPF was important in getting appointed and that he had been recruited after several meetings with a representative of the RPF who had no link to the judicial system. According to another lawyer, of the two candidates presented to the Senate for appointment to the Supreme Court, one clearly was meant to be chosen while the second was there only for show. The second candidate is known in the profession as "the bridesmaid."[119]

The desire to control people and space is inspired not just by the need to fend off challenges to its power or to avert the return of Hutu extremism but also by the way in which the RPF views the Rwandan population, which it treats with distrust and paternalism. Aloysia Inyumba, an influential RPF leader, expressed this very well when she stated that "the ordinary citizens are like babies. They will need to be completely educated if we want to move towards democracy."[120] In other words, democracy will come after reeducation (cf. also the following on the *ingando* camps), but for the time being, "a strong, 'enlightened' leadership is required"[121] This is a long-standing belief. An internal RPF text quoted earlier read in part as follows:

The majority of the Rwandans have neither democratic culture nor the will to change. Let us not be fooled, many of them have not detached themselves from Habyarimana because they see him as "their chief". Many have adhered to the

---

[118]　International Crisis Group, "'Consensual Democracy'", p. 7. This information was based on interviews with a former RPF official, a youth district candidate, and a NURC official.

[119]　Human Rights Watch, *Law and Reality*, p. 46. The report also contains many examples of executive interference in the judicial process (pp. 46–69).

[120]　J. Corduwener, "Wederopbouw in Rwanda, met ijzeren hand" ("Reconstruction in Rwanda, with an Iron Fist"), *NRC-Handelsblad*, 27 March 2002.

[121]　International Crisis Group, *Rwanda at the End of the Transition*, p. 5. The same report quotes constitutional commission member Jacques Kabale as pointing out that "the commission has the merit of asking the opinions of an uneducated population" (*Idem*, p. 7).

MDR because they thought, rightly so, that it is the Parmehutu. Therefore, very few of them are really progressive, whence the need for the Front to approach this conservative population and to bring to it a message of change.[122]

RARE LOOKS INTO THE INSIDE

The core of the Rwandan political-military system is well cordoned off, but a few insiders have offered views behind the curtains of governance. The former Speaker of Parliament Joseph Sebarenzi and former minister Patrick Habamenshi, respectively a Tutsi of the PL and a Hutu of the RPF, who were both forced into exile, offer a unique and damning insight into practices that remind of Nero's Rome: occult and parallel hierarchies and networks of decision making; surveillance and interception of electronic, telephone, and mail communications; lies, threats, and intimidation; settling of scores, corruption, and nepotism; denunciations and slander; diffusion of rumours and false accusations; manipulation and duplicity; and murders and "disappearances."[123] After his departure into exile, General Kayumba Nyamwasa used similar terms: "Intrigue, treachery, manipulation and betrayal."[124]

As said earlier, decision making at the top of the system was opaque, and both government and parliament were sidelined on major issues. In a remarkably frank article in *Rwanda Focus*, an Internet journal close to the RPF, editor Shyaka Kanuma forcefully challenged those practices.[125] He wrote that there

is an over-reliance on a few, powerful "godfathers" to make major decisions. (...) [A] few of these godfathers have been advancing their own interests above those of the collective Rwandan populace. (...) The main godfather, the chief manipulator, the master of intrigue, the boss of machinations, is one whom I will not name. (...) He-who-must-not-be-named has for years built a formidable network of political minions in important institutions.

He went on to wonder "[h]ow (...) He-who-must-not-be-named manages to do all this? Does it mean his boss has no idea what is going on?" The "boss" clearly was Kagame, and He-who-must-not-be-named was James Musoni, the powerful minister of Local Administration, considered very

---

[122] FPR, "L'environnement actuel", p. 10.

[123] J. Sebarenzi, *God Sleeps in Rwanda*; P. Habamenshi, *Rwanda. Where Souls Turn to Dust. My Journey from Exile to Legacy*, New York, iUniverse, 2009.

[124] "Gen. Nyamwasa Responds to Kagame", *Sunday Monitor* (Kampala), 30 May 2010.

[125] "When the Politics of Personal Destruction Get out of Hand", *Rwanda Focus*, 27 April 2012.

close to Kagame.[126] The article ended with a warning that "this man's personal politics may very well end up doing real damage to the government itself."[127]

Although strong control does not allow much insight into how political governance is perceived inside the country, a few rare and revealing looks are available. These insights do not refer to a distant past, but relate to current day situations. With a view to disarming and repatriating fighters of the Ralliement pour l'Unité et la Démocratie (RUD) and of the Rassemblement du Peuple Rwandais (RPR), a "roadmap" agreed in Kisangani in May 2008 with the Rwandan government provided for an "exploratory mission" to Rwanda, which took place in January 2009. Although the report of the visit noted that the government put obstacles to the implementation of the initially agreed programme, for example, by refusing access to certain sites, the observations are interesting as they were widely known by many Rwandans, but could not be aired inside the country. Among other things, the report noted the return to the DRC of repatriated former combatants to fight in the ranks of the CNDP (see the following discussion) or to chase after Rwandan refugees, the seizure of real estate without compensation in Kigali, the terror against the population by intelligence services and the Local Defence Forces, the enrolment into the RPF by force and intimidation, the obligation to vote for the RPF during the parliamentary elections of September 2008, and the fact that "only Tutsi and RPF members (...) are allowed to work in administrative functions, the police and the army." With regard to reconciliation, "trials in the *gacaca* courts do not dispense fair justice" and "the 1994 Gisozi memorial site incites toward ethnic hatred." Among the causes of resistance to voluntary repatriation, the report noted "the absence of freedom to participate in political life."[128]

Another interesting view from within is offered by a study on why Rwandan refugees in Uganda refuse to return home or why they leave again after having done so.[129] Based on fieldwork in the Nakivale refugee settlement at the end of 2009, where many had only recently fled into exile – often for the second or third time – the research found that the refugees overwhelmingly view the regime as oppressive, and that ethnicity specifically is

---

[126] Indeed, a number of reactions to the article explicitly identified Musoni.

[127] "When the Politics of Personal Destruction Get out of Hand", *Rwanda Focus*, 23 April 2012.

[128] "Rapport de la visite exploratoire effectuée au Rwanda par la délégation et leurs dépendants de RUD/RPR du 23 au 28 janvier 2009", Kasiki, 1 February 2009.

[129] *A Dangerous Impasse.*

used as a basis for repression. Most refugees who had previously returned to Rwanda recounted stories of torture, imprisonment, and the killing of family members. They mentioned mechanisms, including through *gacaca* proceedings (cf. Chapter 8), used as means of repression, such as the operation of Ibuka, genocide remembrance events and the promotion of anti-Hutu stereotypes. Ascription of collective guilt was seen as a cover for expropriating property, and victimization based on ethnicity continued to feed localized divisions and create further polarization. In addition, respondents mentioned the lack of political space regardless of ethnicity. The picture created through the interviews is one of a government that controls almost every aspect of its citizens' lives. There is widespread pressure to join the RPF: "to be Rwandan is to be part of the RPF."[130]

THE RPF CHALLENGED FROM WITHIN

Increased control by the RPF should however not suggest that it is monolithic. There is anecdotal evidence that quite some debate is occurring inside the party that is, however, largely invisible to outsiders, as major political decisions are not taken in the cabinet or in parliament, but within a small inner circle. One of the areas where this was visible was the decision to embark on the experiment of *gacaca* justice (see Chapter 8). Initially, many in the RPF were opposed (and some still are). The *gacaca* law was amended on several occasions, because the RPF did not figure out how to tackle the problem of the prosecution of genocide suspects. It therefore behaved in a reactive fashion. Likewise, there was a great deal of debate on how the criminal code of 2012 should deal with the issue of abortion. In other fields, too, the RPF is a "learning organisation."[131]

On a number of occasions, splits were very visible. We have seen earlier that, already in the late 1990s, a number of RPF members turned into opponents. This evolution became more pronounced from 2000 on. The cases of Seth Sendashonga, Alexis Kanyarengwe and Pasteur Bizimungu could be seen as that of Hutu getting frustrated over Tutsi domination and the unacknowledged crimes committed against their ethnic kin, but prominent Tutsi also abandoned ship. Internal tensions reached the highest echelons of the regime. In August 2001, chief of army staff Kayumba Nyamwasa went on "study leave" in the United Kingdom after a violent

---

[130] *Idem*, p. 32.
[131] I thank Frederick Golooba-Mutebi for having drawn my attention to this.

verbal exchange with Kagame over the RPA's operations in the DRC (see infra).[132] Although Kayumba Nyamwasa returned in mid-2002, rumors of him plotting a coup d'état continued. In July 2003, tracts emanating from an unknown "Armée du Peuple Rwandais pour la Libération" circulated in Kigali, calling on Kayumba Nyamwasa and the defense minister, former FAR general Marcel Gatsinzi, to help it overthrow Kagame. In November 2003, the entire print of *Umuseso*, which discussed the conflict between Kagame and Kayumba Nyamwasa, was seized at the Uganda-Rwanda border.[133] According to the article, Kagame accused Kayumba Nyamwasa to plot against him and warned he would "crush" him. Another sign of trouble was the replacement of general prosecutor Gerald Gahima at the end of November 2003.[134] Based on documents of the Central Bank obtained through a leak probably organized by people close to Kagame, the January 2–8, 2004, issue of *Umuseso* published an article on the non-reimbursement of debts by some high officials, Gahima among them. Two weeks later, Kagame forced Gahima to resign; Gahima's brother, Théogène Rudasingwa, chief of staff in the president's office, was sacked at the same occasion. Officers considered close to Kayumba Nyamwasa, such as Colonel Dan Munyuza,[135] were arrested; others were retired. In early March 2004, the powerful heads of the two main intelligence services were replaced: Colonel Patrick Karegeya by Lieutenant-Colonel Emmanuel Ndahiro at the ESO and Colonel Jack Nziza by Colonel Jacques Musemakweli at the DMI. Despite the fact that Kayumba Nyamwasa was maintained at the head of another intelligence outfit, the National Security Service (NSS), coup rumors continued to circulate.

In January 2005, Kayumba Nyamwasa was replaced at the head of the NSS and was appointed ambassador in faraway New Delhi, but he waited for months before taking up his post. It is through the Ugandan press that the news came out that Patrick Karegeya, who was the army spokesperson

---

[132] In March 2002, Kagame's personal helicopter pilot Djuma Kamanzi and the private secretary of first lady Janet Kagame too left the country. According to members of his family, Kamanzi declared that he would only obey orders from Kayumba Nyamwasa.

[133] *Umuseso* was printed in Kampala. Three journalists, including the papers' director, were arrested on November 21 for "defamation and inciting divisionism" but released a few days later.

[134] He became vice-president of the Supreme Court, a less powerful position. In order to have him appointed, article 149 of the constitution was amended on November 28, 2003, reducing the professional experience required from twelve to eight years.

[135] Munyuza was however later involved in a plot to assassinate Colonel Patrick Karegeya, who then was a close associate to Kayumba Nyamwasa (see the following discussion).

since his ouster from the ESO, was arrested in early May 2005.[136] In June 2006, he was condemned to eighteen months in prison for "insubordination" and "desertion." However, the real reason of his disgrace was that Kagame suspected him of being an opponent with excellent ties in Uganda and of aiming to overthrow him in cahoots with Kayumba Nyamwasa, among others. After having served his sentence, Karegeya was released in November 2007. Beating the vigilance of the security services, he fled to Uganda, and from there to South Africa, where he kept quiet until 2010. Karegeya's departure was a serious setback for Kagame, for two reasons. On one hand, his flight was possible only because of the incompetence or, worse, the complicity of some in the security apparatus.[137] On the other, his previous function of head of the ESO had given Karegeya access to very delicate information. In a context where Kagame was threatened by the justice of France and Spain (see the following discussion), the fallout of Karegeya making statements was feared to be disastrous.

The Ugandan daily *The New Vision* wrote that the "Ugandans" in Kagame's entourage were targeted, information immediately denied and considered an interference in the internal affairs of Rwanda by *The New Times*.[138] Denials could not hide the fact that the list of those sacked, sent away, or harassed in different ways grew longer. Former police chief General Frank Rugambage went on study leave abroad; Gahima and Rudasingwa went into exile; the house of Colonel Richard Masozera, husband of historical RPF leader Aloysia Inyumba, was raided in a search for weapons. Some RPA officers left the country made damning revelations about the regime. Lieutenant Abdul Ruzibiza fled in February 2001, and eventually found refuge in Norway, where he published a text highly critical of the RPF's human rights record in March 2004.[139] In a similar vein, Lieutenant Aloys Ruyenzi, who fled at the end of 2001, published a document containing very serious allegations against Kagame.[140] Majors Alphonse Furuma, Fred Kwikiriza, and Michael Mupende also defected in

---

[136] *The New Vision* (Kampala), 4 May 2005. It is probably no coincidence that Kayumba Nyamwasa suddenly decided to leave for New Delhi at the moment of Karegeya's arrest.

[137] Well-placed sources in Kigali indicated that, during a meeting held on November 28 to discuss this security lapse, Kagame was furious and severely reprimanded the director general of the NSS, Lieutenant Colonel Emmanuel Ndahiro, despite their being close.

[138] "Museveni Is on the Ropes and Rwanda Has to Pay", *The New Times*, 6 May 2005.

[139] "Ubuhamya bwa Abdul Ruzibiza", Brennäsen (Norway), 14 March 2004. He later published a book: A.J. Ruzibiza, *Rwanda. L'histoire secrète*, Paris, Editions du Panama, 2005.

[140] A. Ruyenzi, "J'accuse le général-major Paul Kagame d'être un criminel", Norway, 5 July 2004.

2001 and made similar allegations. The substance of their accusations is discussed later. These defections caused a great deal of nervousness, and showed strong intra-Tutsi tensions.[141] This was particularly understandable in the case of officers such as Kayumba Nyamwasa, Karegeya, and Rudasingwa, who occupied senior functions at the very core of the power structure. They had knowledge of the regime's darkest secrets and had themselves been involved in its crimes. Particularly after Karegeya's departure into exile, rumours about purges and impending coups d'état widely circulated, at such a point that the army had to deny them on several occasions and Kagame felt the need to assure that there were no "cliques" within the RPF.[142] According to *Umuseso*, in January 2009 a reported coup attempt, unconfirmed by official sources, led to the arrest of eleven RDF members and the dismissal or suspension of other senior officers.[143]

Things came to a head in 2010. When Kayumba Nyamwasa was in the country for the annual ambassadors' meeting, he feared arrest, a fear enhanced by the way he was grilled by the RPF's general secretary,[144] as well as by the fact that no officials showed up at the burial of his mother. On February 26, he left clandestinely for Uganda, from where he sought asylum in South Africa. A government communiqué announced his dismissal as ambassador and declared that he was sought for having committed crimes that were, however, not specified.[145] The defection of Kayumba Nyamwasa caused a great deal of nervousness in circles of power. The high functions he exercised made him privy to the regime's secrets, and his name figured on the lists of personalities sought by French and Spanish justice; it was feared that he might spill the beans in highly embarrassing files for the

---

[141] This feeling was well rendered by a text that circulated on the internet at the end of May 2005: P. Katabirora, "Batutsi twirinde kugwa mu mutego", which translates as "Dear Tutsi brothers, beware not to fall in the trap" (of division).

[142] See, for instance, "No Cliques in RPF – Kagame", *The New Times*, 26 May 2007.

[143] *Umuseso*, No. 327, 12–18 January 2009, quoted by D. Beswick, "The Role of the Military in Rwanda: Current Dynamics and Future Prospects", in M. Campioni, P. Noack (Eds.), *Rwanda Fast Forward*, p. 254.

[144] General Secretary François Ngarambe justified his questioning Kayumba Nyamwasa as follows: "Why should he (Kayumba Nyamwasa) question my asking him to give a report to RPF on duties he was assigned to by the nation? (. . .) It is the RPF that made Kayumba an Ambassador, it is the RPF that made it possible for him to become a General" ("Ruling party has the right to summon officials – SG", *The New Times*, 5 March 2010). Ngarambe thus acknowledged the confusion between the party and the state.

[145] On this affair, see "Gov't Searching for Fugitive Gen. Kayumba Nyamwasa", Kigali, RNA, 26 February 2010; "Breaking News: Rwanda Fugitive General in South Africa", Kampala, 256news.com, 2 March 2010; "Kayumba Nyamwasa: Rwanda's Sadistic General", *The Uganda Record* (Kampala), 2 March 2010.

RPF, particularly those related to war crimes and the attack against the airplane of President Habyarimana (see the following discussion). His departure while under surveillance also raised the issue of complicity in the security services,[146] always a delicate problem in Rwanda's securocracy. Verhoeven notes that the regime's security core was "electrified" by the Kayumba-Karegeya challenge and that the "Who's next?" question was on everybody's mind.[147] Contrary to Karegeya, who adopted a very low profile after going into exile, Kayumba Nyamwasa attacked Kagame virulently. In an interview with the VOA on March 3, he stated that "the regime in Kigali is descending in total dictatorship" and that he had "no faith in the judiciary, no faith in the government institutions." He later accused Kagame of abuses, for instance, the purchase of luxury jets[148] and the exorbitant costs made for his numerous trips abroad, the property of the building that houses the Rwandan high commission in London, the construction of his residence at Lake Muhazi, the RPF's control of the national economy and so on.[149]

The regime immediately set out to construct files against Karegeya and Kayumba Nyamwasa. Between September 2009 and May 2010, grenade attacks in Kigali and elsewhere caused several dead and many injured. An attack on February 19, 2010, was at first attributed by the police to "interahamwe criminals" and the FDLR,[150] but after Kayumba Nyamwasa went into exile, the general prosecutor stated that he and Karegeya were behind the attacks.[151] Kagame even claimed that there might be a link between both scenarios,[152] a claim that was to be made concrete later on (see the following discussion), while assuring once again that a coup d'état was impossible.[153] The regime also divulged the "dark side" of Kayumba Nyamwasa: according to the spokesperson of the army, the RDF had long been concerned "with Kayumba's nepotism, intrigues,

---

[146] "Kagame Attacks Security Apparatus over Gen. Nyamwasa", Kigali, RNA, 3 March 2010.

[147] H. Verhoeven, "Nurturing Democracy", p. 275.

[148] On which the South African press reported in February ("Rwanda Splurges on Luxury Jets", *Sunday Times* [Johannesburg], 14 February 2010), a story denied by the Rwandan government on February 20.

[149] "Gen. Nyamwasa Responds to Kagame", *Sunday Monitor* (Kampala), 30 May 2010.

[150] "'Interahamwe' Accused by Gov't of Grenade Blasts", Kigali, RNA, 20 February 2010.

[151] "Kayumba, Karegeya behind Terror Attacks – Prosecution", *The New Times*, 3 March 2010.

[152] "Kagame Attacks Security Apparatus".

[153] "'Personne ne peut faire un coup d'Etat' au Rwanda, selon Kagame", Kigali, AFP, 3 March 2010.

divisionism and primitive accumulation of wealth, among others" and assured that "Kayumba and his fellow errands are losers and they will remain losers in their treacherous game."[154] Rwanda demanded the extradition of both officers, but South African president Jacob Zuma indicated that his country was "going to be guided by what governs the world in regards to refugee status."[155]

In early May 2010, a Ugandan site almost prophetically quoted a former officer of the RDF exiled in Europe, who stated that he received the order to assassinate Kayumba Nyamwasa in March 2008, and he revealed the names of seventeen officers murdered on Kagame's orders.[156] On June 19, 2010, Kayumba was severely injured in an attempt against his life in Johannesburg. In a hypocritical statement, the Rwandan foreign minister said she was "shocked" by the news: "The Government of Rwanda does not condone violence, and we wish the family strength and serenity."[157] A couple of days later, the assassins attempted to finish off Kayumba Nyamwasa in his hospital bed.[158] Suspects were arrested, and on July 1 the South African authorities stated, without mentioning Rwanda, that "security operatives" involved in the shooting came from a "country with which we have good and strong diplomatic relations."[159] In early August, Pretoria recalled its high commissioner "for consultations," and he had not returned to Kigali at the time of this writing.[160]

---

[154] "Kayumba Nyamwasa: A Victim of his Own Making", *The New Times*, 8 March 2010.

[155] "Zuma Explains Why Rwanda Officers Won't Return", *Sunday Monitor* (Kampala), 28 March 2010.

[156] "Rwanda Officer Reveals How He Was Sent to Assassinate Gen. Kayumba" (http://www.freeuganda.org/article103-Paul-Kagame-s-Brutality, visited on 2 May 2010).

[157] "Kayumba Wounded in S. African Gun Attack", *The Sunday Times* (Kigali), 20 June 2010. As a matter of fact, Kagame nearly claimed the assassination of opponents abroad during a speech in Gatsibo on 5 August 2010: "When these criminals declare war on Rwanda (. . .), we will kill them. They won't even realise who struck them. (. . .) When we strike, we make victims. People should not forget our past. If they forget, they will bear the consequences" (translated from Kinyarwanda).

[158] "Rwandan Murder Accused Denied Bail", *The Star* (Johannesburg), 16 September 2010.

[159] "Foreign 'Security Operatives' Involved in Gen. Nyamwasa Shooting", Kigali, RNA, 1st July 2010.

[160] Apart from the bilateral relations with South Africa, the Kayumba affair made another victim in the person of the Rwandan envoy to Pretoria. Ignatius Kamali Karegyesa was brutally relieved from his function on March 7, 2011, when he was in Rwanda for a diplomats' retreat (just as happened to Kayumba Nyamwasa a year earlier). Although he was officially sanctioned because of "indiscipline," the real reason for his sacking appears to have been the way he handled the Kayumba Nyamwasa affair. According to persons present at the meeting, Kagame publicly slapped Karegyesa in the face ("Triste printemps rwandais", *Le Monde*, 5 May 2011).

The regime was caught red-handed when tapes leaked on the Internet disclosed telephone conversations of General Jack Nziza and Colonel Dan Munyuza with Rwandan agents, discussing the murder of Kayumba Nyamwasa and Karegeya in a very concrete fashion (including moneys to be paid to the hit men and the use of poison).[161]

This is the place to open a parenthetical discussion on the way in which the regime did not shy away from political killings abroad. The cases of Lizinde and Sendashonga were mentioned earlier. Those considered a threat, Hutu and Tutsi alike, were physically eliminated. Jon Swain listed eight persons assassinated by the intelligence services only because of their knowledge of the RPF's role in the downing of former President Habyarimana's plane[162]; scores of others were killed because "they knew."[163] Assassinations did not spare RPA officers, as soon as their loyalty was in doubt. Ruzibiza described the physical elimination of over twenty military, in addition to several foreigners working in Rwanda who were suspected of having leaked information on RPF abuse (cf. Chapter 4).[164] Strong indications point at the role of Rwanda in the killing of DRC president Laurent Kabila in Kinshasa (January 2001).[165] In April 2011 MI5 warned the Rwandan high commissioner in London that the intimidation of supposed opponents in the United Kingdom needed to stop.[166] The plea was not heeded, and threats took on more radical forms. The following month, Scotland Yard formally warned two British of Rwandan origin: "Reliable intelligence states that the Rwandan Government poses an immediate threat to your life. The threat could come in any form. (...) Conventional and unconventional means may be

---

[161] See, for example, http://youtu.be/405DiSsx6ZU; http://youtu.be/WMwkcyFMpto; http://youtu.be/sNIf76WBaGw. The authenticity of these tapes has never been challenged by the regime. When I confronted a senior advisor to Kagame with these facts, all I got was an embarrassed silence.

[162] J. Swain, "The Riddle of the Rwandan Assassin's Trail", *The Sunday Times*, 4 April 2004.

[163] This is the title of a documentary film on the murder in Nairobi of Seth Sendashonga (cf. supra): J. Elie, *Celui qui savait*, Montreal, Alter-Ciné, 2001.

[164] A. J. Ruzibiza, *Rwanda, l'histoire secrète*, pp. 420–441.

[165] See "Un ex agente de Ruanda implica a su Gobierno en el asesinato de Kabila", *El País*, 21 December 2008; "Murder in Kinshasa", film by Arnaud Zajtman on Al Jazeera, 28 October 2011. In an interview with RFI on January 26, 2012, a former Congolese justice minister stated that "it is absolutely clear" that Kigali was implicated in the plot and that "the Americans were not far away" (interview with Christophe Boisbouvier, RFI, 26 January 2012). Sources in the Rwandan intelligence apparatus have confirmed to this author that Kigali masterminded the assassination.

[166] "Rwandan Wedding Guest Told to Stop Harassing Dissidents in UK", *The Independent* (London), 29 April 2011.

used."[167] The press picked up the story[168] and suggested U.K.-Rwanda relations should be revised.[169] In February 2012, the Swedish authorities ordered the second councilor of the Rwandan embassy to leave the country within forty-eight hours for "activities incompatible with his diplomatic status." This expulsion occurred while Jean-Bosco Gasasira, a former journalist of *Umuvugizi* had "disappeared." After the diplomat had left, Gasasira resurfaced and explained that he had had to go into hiding because Rwandan services were "after him."[170] David Himbara, a former advisor to Kagame who fled the country in 2010, claimed to have been the victim of attempted abduction by Rwandan agents and had been warned by intelligence officials in South Africa, where he sought asylum, that he was on a Rwandan government hit list.[171]

The most dangerous place to live for suspected opponents was Kampala where Rwandan agents were very active threatening and even physically assaulting them. On November 30, 2011, Charles Ingabire, editor of the online publication *Inyenyeri News* very critical of the regime, was shot and killed in a Kampala neighborhood, after having been attacked two months earlier and receiving telephone death threats warning him to stop writing articles critical of the Rwandan government.[172] There were strong indications that Rwandan operatives were involved: Leon Mageshi, said to coordinate espionage activities in Kampala, was suspected to have organized the assassination.[173] Other dissidents living in Kampala, too, were threatened and harassed, and former Kagame bodyguards who had fled to

---

[167] "Threats to Life Warning Notice", 12 May 2011.

[168] "British Police Warn Rwandan Dissidents of Threat", *The New York Times*, 19 May 2011; "Rwandan Assassin 'Sent to Kill Dissidents in UK'", *The Independent* (London), 20 May 2011; "Rwandan Exiles Warned of Assassination Threat by London Police", *The Guardian* (London), 20 May 2011.

[169] "UK 'Should Review Relations with Rwanda'", *The Independent* (London), 21 May 2011.

[170] "Rwandan Journalist Emerges after Month in Hiding", Nairobi, AFP, 17 February 2012.

[171] "Britain's Aid to Rwanda Is Funding a 'Repressive Regime' Says Former Kagame Official", *The Daily Telegraph*, 24 November 2012.

[172] Human Rights Watch, *Uganda/Rwanda: Investigate Journalist's Murder. Ugandan Government Should Ensure Safety of Rwandan Exiles*, New York, 6 December 2011.

[173] "Rwandan journalist Charles Ingabire of Inyenyeri News Killed in Kampala", *Rwandinfo*, 2 December 2011. Kagame rejected the allegations and claimed that Rwandan authorities had unearthed evidence showing that Ingabire had stolen money from an organization helping orphans which he had headed before fleeing to Uganda. "We have many cases like this in Rwanda of people committing crimes and claiming political persecution," Kagame said ("Kagame Denies Any Link to Kampala Journalist Murder", Kampala, AFP, 12 December 2011).

Kampala lived in constant fear of being killed by the regime's death squads.[174]

Kagame's mouthpiece *The New Times* even openly justified the elimination of dissidents abroad. An op-ed appeared in the issue of May 4, 2011, under the title "Osama bin Laden's Lesson for Local Terrorists," in which the author wrote, "In Rwanda we have our own criminals and terrorists sheltering in foreign countries. What has happened to Osama bin Laden should serve as notice to them that they cannot hide forever. Justice, *in whatever form*, will catch up with them" (emphasis added). The article went on to list a number of opponents by name who "will soon find out that the jungles of foreign countries and villas in upmarket areas of foreign capitals are not very safe. They can run and hide, but will run out of options and their actions will catch up with them." By labeling dissidents as "criminals and terrorists," the regime thus gave itself a license to kill.[175] Just two weeks later, Ugandan journalist Andrew Mwenda, who is in the pay of the Kigali regime (cf. the following discussion), justified (and, in a sense, admitted) these practices: "I do not put it past the Rwandan government to try to kill those it considers dangerous to its security. All governments, democratic or otherwise do. (...) [S]tates kill to promote their interests; if Kagame tried it, it would not be an aberration by a 'delusional despot.'"[176] The boldness with which the regime engages in violent operations against opponents abroad is quite astonishing and illustrative of its feeling of impunity. And so is the fact that it continues doing so even after having been caught red-handed on several occasions.

Kayumba Nyamwasa's departure was not the end of trouble inside the army. On April 19, 2010, Generals Karenzi Karake and Muhire were arrested, despite the fact that the latter was appointed chief of staff of the reserve forces barely a week earlier. Observers linked these arrests to recent rumors of an impending coup d'état and to the Kayumba Nyamwasa incident, but Muhire was officially accused of corruption and abuse of office and Karenzi Karake of "immoral conduct." The army spokesperson stated

---

[174] "'Kagame Is a Killer.' Defectors Tell of Life on Run from Rwandan Assassins", *The Times* (London), 8 October 2012.

[175] Admittedly, it merely followed the example given by the United States in killing Osama bin Laden. One may suppose that other regimes across the world wonder why, if the Americans have given themselves a license to kill, they should not do likewise.

[176] "Rwanda and Prejudices towards Africa", *The New Times*, 28 May 2011. Kagame himself came close to admitting the attempt on Kayumba Nyamwasa's life when he told *Time*: "I you have somebody out there saying 'I wanted to carry out a coup', and later on he is shot, maybe he deserves it" (A. Perry, "Q&A: Rwandan President Paul Kagame", *Time*, 14 September 2012).

that the two generals were not suspected of involvement in the grenade incidents and that there was no link with the Kayumba Nyamwasa affair.[177] The next day, retired-colonel-turned-businessman Dodo was arrested for "abuse of office and corruption" while attempting to flee to Uganda. It is, of course, not certain that all these affairs were linked, or that they had a political connotation. However, the fact that three generals fled or were arrested in just one-and-a-half month's time suggested unrest within the security apparatus, and thus at the core of power. Tensions again surfaced in January 2012, when Lieutenant General Fred Ibingira, Brigadier Generals Richard Rutatina and Wilson Gumusiriza, and Colonel Dan Munyuza were placed under house arrest, alledgedly for being engaged in illegal business deals in the DRC.[178] Events such as these instilled fear in the officer corps who wondered who would be next. The possibility of revolt within the army was for Kagame a greater threat than the activities of political parties that, as seen earlier, were much easier to control or of diaspora organizations.

The "renegades" translated their opposition to Kagame into political action. In August 2010, Kayumba Nyamwasa, Patrick Karegeya, Theogene Rudasingwa, and Gerald Gahima published a document called *Rwanda Briefing*. As the authors earlier occupied important functions in the RPF and the state apparatus,[179] this was the strongest challenge the regime faced from within. The *Rwanda Briefing* contained a long diatribe against the regime; accused it of having put in place a totalitarian dictatorship based on terror, of grave human rights violations, of corruption and nepotism, of having committed numerous political assassinations; and – quite a remarkable accusation coming from four Tutsi – of having marginalized and excluded the Hutu. The regime immediately counter attacked by accusing the authors of crimes and abuse of office when they were in function.[180] An extensive campaign of character assassination was

---

[177] "Arrested officers not Linked to Renegade General – RDF", *The New Times*, 22 April 2010.

[178] "Arrested Rwandan Generals Led Anti-smuggling Drive", Kigali, Reuters, 19 January 2012.

[179] Kayumba Nyamwasa had been chief of army staff, head of the NSS, and ambassador; Patrick Karegeya was the former head of the ESO; Theogene Rudasingwa had been the RPF general secretary, ambassador, and chief of staff of the president's office; Gerald Gahima was the former general prosecutor and vice-president of the Supreme Court.

[180] Some of these accusations may well be justified, but it is interesting to note that they were only made after the four became open dissidents. It is useful to recall here that *Umuseso* was seized in January 2004 after it made similar accusations against two of the "renegades" (cf. supra).

launched.[181] At the same time a judicial file was opened, and on November 15, 2010, the four were indicted for attempting against state security, menacing the authority of the state, ethnic divisionism, slander, and forming a terrorist group. The four "categorically" rejected the accusations as "false and malicious, the latest in the regime's campaign of terror, denial, deception, and attempts at tarnishing the image of those who dare speak the truth about the situation in Rwanda and the authoritarian character of the regime."[182] On January 14, 2011, Kayumba Nyamwasa and Rudasingwa were sentenced to twenty-four years in prison, whereas Karegeya and Gahima received twenty-year sentences.[183] Rwanda launched arrest and extradition warrants through Interpol.

In the meantime, the four were among the main founders of a new political movement, the Rwanda National Congress (RNC), created on December 12, 2010. After again denouncing the misdeeds of the regime, the founders proclaimed their vision for a new Rwanda: "Rwanda will be a united, democratic, and prosperous nation inhabited by free citizens with harmonious and safe communities who will live together in peace, dignity and mutual respect, regardless of ethnic or other differences, within a democracy governed according to universal principles of human rights and the rule of law."[184] The RNC set out to forge alliances with other opposition movements abroad, and even inside Rwanda. In addition, and

[181] It would be fastidious to mention all the attacks. Their gist is well summarized in the conclusion of a text published at the end of October 2010 by General Richard Rutatina, defense and security advisor to Kagame, and army spokesman Jill Rutaremara, under the title *Response to Allegations by Four Renegades*: "Four renegades in the persons of Kayumba, Karegeya, Rudasingwa and Gahima have hurled wild, unsubstantiated and malicious allegations against the Government of Rwanda and the person of the Head of State. The authors' background is tainted with a criminal record and they have failed to live up to the high standards of accountability espoused by the government of Rwanda under the leadership of President Kagame. They lack the moral authority and credibility that would qualify them to criticize, let alone challenge, what the Government of Rwanda, her President and the people of Rwanda have achieved. They should therefore be treated with the utmost contempt that they deserve" (text published on http://www.mykagame.com/spip.php?article750).

[182] "Statement on Criminal Charges Instituted by the Government of Rwanda against the Authors of 'Rwanda Briefing'", Washington, DC, 17 November 2010.

[183] Retribution also hit dissidents' family members. In March 2012, the government canceled the passports of twenty-five family members of the "renegades" and some other recent dissidents. In July 2012, Kayumba Nyamwasa's brother Lieutenant Colonel Rugigana Ngabo was found guilty by the Military High Court of conspiring to threaten state security and inciting violence and was sentenced to nine years in prison (on the irregularities surrounding this case see Amnesty International, *Rwanda: Shrouded in Secrecy. Illegal Detention and Torture by Military Intelligence*, London, October 2012, pp. 23–24).

[184] Rwanda National Congress, *Rwanda: Pathway to Peaceful Change. Declaration of Core Values, Goals and an Agenda for a New Rwanda*, December 2010.

potentially more threateningly, some RNC leaders seemed to establish contacts with armed groups opposed to Kagame in the region, particularly in the DRC and Uganda.[185] As a matter of fact, the regime and the four "renegades" had each other in a hold. For the regime, it was easy to criticize them for "opportunism," as they had occupied high office in the past, but it could not challenge them on the role they played in eliminating the opposition (Gahima), war crimes committed in 1997–1998 (Kayumba Nyamwasa; see Chapter 4), or the killing of opponents such as Lizinde and Sendashonga abroad (Karegeya), because it could not admit these facts. The "renegades" are the most serious threat to Kagame, because they share his background and belief in "force as transformational in politics" and know the regime and its security detail so well.[186] The fact that they remain well connected to military circles inside the country and in Uganda only makes the threat more salient.

The departure into exile, arrests and condemnation, and even murder of Tutsi increasingly confirmed that power rather than ethnic belonging became the main dividing factor. This is another continuity with the previous regime that did not hesitate to eliminate Hutu considered a threat, both before and during the genocide.

CONCLUSION

The regime cordoned off political space and eliminated sources of dissent from the day it seized power, but it did so gradually. After physically neutralizing those individuals seen as a threat by killing or jailing them, or by forcing them into exile, it finished eliminating the political opposition in 2003 and what was left of civil society in 2004. Although it maintained some procedural aspects of democracy through deeply flawed elections, it established full physical, political, administrative, and judicial control over the country's territory and its population. The piecemeal implementation of this authoritarian project, coupled with a technocratic style of governance, allowed to secure the tolerance of the international community that hoped "things would get better." But things could not go better, as the RPF cannot open up space. The RPF's experience, the knowledge it has of its narrow base, and its narrative of the role it played as the savior of Rwanda

---

[185] Elements pointing in that direction can be found in United Nations, Security Council, *Letter Dated 26 October 2010 from the Group of Experts on the Democratic Republic of the Congo Addressed to the Chair of the Security Council Committee Established Pursuant to Resolution 1533 (2004)*, S/2010/596, 29 November 2010.

[186] H. Verhoeven, "Nurturing Democracy", p. 276.

does not allow sharing and inclusion, let alone competition. Verhoeven notes that its self-perception "will continue to clash with ideas of compromise, relativism and empathy that are integral parts of democracy."[187]

A report commissioned by U.S. AFRICOM, the military side of Rwanda's most important political sponsor, expressed a great deal of concern in 2011. In its overview, it noted that "the country's apparent stability masks deep-rooted tensions, unresolved resentments, and an authoritarian government that is unwilling to countenance criticism or open political debate."[188] It went on, saying, "In the coming decade, the greatest vulnerability that Rwanda will confront is the unyielding nature of the ruling RPF and its inability – or unwillingness – to allow and manage genuine political competition and debate." It pointedly observed that "[c]riticism of the country's leadership is met with a level of outrage and vehemence that belie the RPF's seeming confidence in its near-universal popularity among Rwandans."[189] Among the greatest vulnerabilities Rwanda would confront in the coming decade, it noted "the unyielding nature and occasionally brutal tactics of the RPF. (...) The government's absolute suppression of dissent ultimately adds to its own fragility and thus makes even a gradual opening of political space increasingly difficult."[190] The report sounded a firm warning: "Rwanda's well-wishers should not ignore troubling signs of increasing inflexibility and potential fragility. Although the country is currently calm and orderly, its stability could be put at risk by political repression, a narrowing of the ruling party's base, and a failure to address deep-seated grievances openly and equitably."[191] These are exactly the points made in this book, and these fears echo those expressed by many analysts since the RPF seized power.

Coercion was not the only instrument on which the RPF based its power. As will be seen later, it also attempted to build legitimacy by improving economic and social indicators, by promoting a narrative of reconciliation, by engineering modernity in the framework of a well-articulated development ideology, and by ensuring physical security. These were ways to win over people, both at home and in the international community, but the legitimacy the RPF sought to achieve was to a large extent artificial and imposed. Indeed, there is a large gap between the discourse and the policies of the regime and popular concerns and expectations. This gap is addressed in Chapters 6 and 7.

[187] *Idem*, p. 271.
[188] Center for Strategic & International Studies, *Rwanda. Assessing Risks*, p. 1.
[189] *Idem*, p. 2.
[190] *Idem*, p. 14.
[191] *Idem*, p. 3.

4

Human Rights – A Dismal Record

This chapter only discusses large-scale violations of the right to life. Other human rights, such as political rights, freedoms of the press and association, and personal freedom were discussed earlier, whereas the right to justice is addressed in Chapter 8. Three episodes of widespread RPF/RPA abuse are analyzed here: mass killings inside Rwanda from the period of the genocide to 1996, the extermination of Hutu refugees in Zaire/DRC in late 1996 and early 1997, and the killing of civilians during the insurgency of 1997–1998, particularly in northwestern Rwanda. The regime's record is truly appalling. It has committed massive human rights abuse in an organized and systematic fashion. Crimes against humanity, war crimes, and possibly genocide (in Zaire/DRC) have gone unpunished and have only slightly dented Kagame's international standing. However, these crimes are well documented and were known at the time they were committed, which means that the international community in general, and the regime's main sponsors in particular (the United States, the United Kingdom, and the EU), carry a heavy responsibility in their repeated occurrence. Yet they are a strong and lasting testimony to the true nature of the regime of Paul Kagame who, judged by the number of his victims and by the nature of the crimes committed, is probably the worst war criminal in office today.

RWANDA, 1994–1996

The human rights record of the RPF/RPA has been dismal from day one. In 1992, Africa Watch found that the RPF had been responsible for grave human rights violations since the beginning of the war.[1] Even though its work in RPF-held territory was sabotaged, in early 1993 an international commission of enquiry reported summary executions, pillaging and forced deportations.[2] RPA defector Ruzibiza too listed a number of massacres committed by the RPA before 1994.[3] Tens of thousands of civilians were massacred by the RPF after the resumption of the war, most of them between April and September 1994. In a number of cases, witnesses from within the RPA interviewed by the Office of the Prosecutor (OTP) of the ICTR declared that Kagame himself ordered some of the killings.[4] Although it was documented from early on, this massive abuse was covered by an international conspiracy of silence.[5]

While the Hutu extremists were openly conducting a massive genocide against the Tutsi, the RPF was also engaged in large-scale killings that were, however, hidden from the public eye. During the first days of the fighting in April 1994, the RPA contingent in Kigali killed dozens of Hutu civilian elites and their families.[6] These killings were selectively operated

[1] Africa Watch, *Rwanda: Talking Peace and Waging War. Human Rights since the October 1990 Invasion*, New York, 27 February 1992.

[2] Fédération internationale des droits de l'homme, Africa Watch, Union interafricaine des droits de l'homme et des peuples, Centre international des droits de la personne et du développement démocratique, *Rapport de la commission internationale d'enquête sur les violations des droits de l'homme au Rwanda depuis le 1er octobre 1990*, March 1993, pp. 66–75.

[3] See, for example, A.J. Ruzibiza, *Rwanda. L'histoire secrète*, Paris, Editions du Panama, pp. 123–124, 133, 137, 150, 186 (where the practice of *kwitaba imana*, see the following, could already be seen), 190–192, 196, 209, 222.

[4] As a few examples show, "[t]he instruction for killings in and around the stadium in Gitarama in June 1994 came directly from Paul Kagame" (witness interview, 29 March 2002, ICTR ref R0000148); on a number of occasions during which Colonel James Kabarebe oversaw civilian killings, "he got his instructions directly from Kagame" (witness interview, 10 May 2002, ICTR ref R0000144); Kagame directly ordered the killing of the clergy at Gakurazo (witness interview, 9 February 2002, ICTR ref R0000233). Investigations by the Spanish Audiencia Nacional offer other examples, as well as finding that, on or around May 12, 1994, Kagame personally killed between thirty and forty unarmed civilians using a 12.70 millimeter gun (Audiencia Nacional, Juzgado central de instrucción numero cuarto, 6 February 2008, p. 136).

[5] However, two pieces of investigative journalism uncovered massive abuse by the RPF: S. Smith, "Rwanda: enquête sur la terreur tutsie. Plus de 100.000 Hutus auraient été tués depuis avril 1994," *Libération*, 27 February 1996; N. Gordon, "Return to Hell," *The Sunday Times* (London), 21 April 1996. Earlier, I coauthored S. Desouter, F. Reyntjens, *Rwanda. Les violations des droits de l'homme par le FPR/APR. Plaidoyer pour une enquête approfondie*, Institute of Development Policy and Management, Working Paper, Antwerp, June 1995.

[6] A list of 121 persons killed by the RPA in Kigali sector Remera alone on April 7, 8, and 9 is on file with the author.

with the use of lists. On May 17, when the RPF was firmly in control of Kibungo prefecture, a sitrep (situation report) of Refugees International stated that the RPF was engaged in large-scale killings of civilians. For instance, "[a]t Rusumo commune, sector Kigarama, the RPF came and called for a 'peace meeting.'[7] Those who did not participate voluntarily were forced to the meeting. At the school people were tied together, three by three – men/women/children – and stabbed. The bodies were put on trucks and thrown into the Kagera river." In other sectors of Rusumo, "the RPF comes at 05h00 waiting for villagers to open their doors. The villagers are caught and taken away to the river by trucks. No one has returned." The sitrep quoted an IRC (International Rescue Committee) staff member: "Someone really needs to do something about all of the killings and torture on the other side [of the Tanzanian border]. Each day there are more and more bodies in the river and most of them without their heads; the count is between 20 and 30 each 30 minutes."[8] UNHCR made similar observations. It reported that the RPA assembled people and killed them and that many, "alive with hands and feet bound" were thrown into the Kagera River.[9] After fleeing the country, Col. Théoneste Lizinde, MP for the RPF, listed a number of large-scale killings by the RPA.[10] Some of these killings were claimed to be on the direct order of Kagame.[11] Documenting mass killings and other abuses from April through July,[12] Des Forges noted that "[c]ertain kinds of RPF abuses occurred so often and in such similar ways that they must have been directed by officers at a high level of

[7] The convening of "meetings" purportedly aimed at providing information or support was a widely used ploy to get people together. Once assembled, the population was indiscriminately killed by the RPA. This practice was so widespread that people equated *kwitaba inama* (be called to a meeting) to *kwitaba imana* (be called to God).

[8] Refugees International, "Rwandan Refugees in Tanzania," Sitrep #10, 17 May 1994.

[9] "Le HCR accuse le FPR de poursuivre massacres et tortures au Rwanda," Geneva (UN), AP, 17 May 1994. Ruzibiza (*Rwanda. L'histoire secrète*, pp. 259–328) lists a number of massacres committed by the RPA during the genocide. These findings lent credence to the claim that bodies that ended up in Lake Victoria were those of Tutsi victims of the genocide, but also those of Hutu slaughtered by the RPA.

[10] T. Lizinde, *Déclaration. Rwanda: la tragédie*, Brussels (in fact: Kinshasa), 1 May 1996.

[11] "On 21 April 1994, when the commander of a unit based in Zoko (Buyoga-Byumba) asked what to do with Hutu refugees fleeing the fighting (...), General-Major Paul Kagame ordered to liquidate them in the following terms : 'Fagia wale washenzi': eliminate these imbecils'" (*idem*, p. 5).

[12] A. Des Forges, *Leave None to Tell the Story. Genocide in Rwanda*, New York and Paris, Human Rights Watch-Fédération internationale des ligues des droits de l'homme, 1999, pp. 702–723.

responsibility. It is likely that these patterns of abuse were known to and tolerated by the highest levels of command of the RPF forces."[13]

Organized mass killings continued after the war ended. A mere ten days after the RPF took full control of Kigali in July 1994, General Dallaire's intelligence officer reported that "the RPF was running two interrogation centres in Kigali and that summary executions were being conducted all day long."[14] Former RPA members interviewed by the OTP of the ICTR mentioned large-scale killings of Hutu. Many were assembled in military installations in Kigali, from where they were taken to Gabiro and Bigogwe camps to be killed; in a number of cases, the victims' bodies were incinerated. One of the witnesses stated that he did not know how many were killed, but that just in Bigogwe, "for the whole month of November 1994, three or four trucks filled with prisoners would arrive every day or second/third day." He added that "[i]t was understood that if there were no Hutus from our side present, we would kill everybody on site [*sic*]."[15] Human Rights Watch documented massacres in Kivumu, Butare, Save, Rango, Kayenzi, Masango and other places were over a thousand people were killed.[16] Ruzibiza too mentions a large number of killings after the RPF took power, including of its own people not considered reliable.[17] Although making similar observations about mass killings, abductions, and "disappearances" by the RPA, Amnesty International noted that "the RPA closely monitored and controlled movements of foreigners in areas under its control. (...) This ensured that (...) very limited information about abuses by the RPA could be gathered or made public by independent observers."[18] The RPF's information management is addressed in Chapter 7. Hutu ministers were aware of the killings; however, they probably underestimated their scale.[19] Interior minister Sendashonga

[13] *Idem*, p. 692. The reference to Kagame himself is only thinly veiled.

[14] R. Dallaire, *Shake Hands with the Devil. The Failure of Humanity in Rwanda*, Toronto, Random House Canada, 2003, p. 469.

[15] Witness interview, 28 March 2002, ICTR ref R0000299–302; Witness interview, 18 May 2002, ICTR ref R0000280–283.

[16] Human Rights Watch, *The Aftermath of Genocide in Rwanda*, New York, September 1994. Data were updated and complemented in Human Rights Watch, *A New Catastrophe?*, New York, September 1994.

[17] A.J. Ruzibiza, *Rwanda. L'histoire secrète*, pp. 150, 158, 334–346, 420–428.

[18] Amnesty International, *Reports of Killings and Abductions by the Rwandese Patriotic Front April –August 1994*, London, October 1994.

[19] After fleeing the country, the then chief of the intelligence service, Sixbert Musangamfura, estimated that the RPF/RPA killed over 300,000 people until July 1995 (S. Musangamfura, *J'accuse le FPR de crimes de génocide des populations d'ethnie hutu, de purification ethnique et appelle á une enquête internationale urgente"*, Nairobi, 8 December 1995).

sent hundreds of memos to Kagame, to no avail. The Kibeho massacre was the proverbial straw that broke the "government of national union" (cf. supra). Sources from within the RPF later confirmed the widespread nature of the abuse.[20]

Despite the secrecy and the way in which the RPA limited access to the scenes of atrocities, information did surface. A UNHCR team led by Robert Gersony conducted research in August and early September 1994, by visiting refugee camps and more than a quarter of Rwanda's *communes* and by interviewing over 300 persons. He found that

> significant areas of Butare Prefecture, Kibungo Prefecture, and the southern and eastern areas of Kigali Prefecture have been – and in some cases were reported to remain as of early September – the scene of systematic and sustained killing and persecution of their civilian Hutu populations by the RPA. (...) Large-scale indiscriminate killings of men, women, children, including the sick and the elderly, were consistently reported.[21]

"[A]n unmistakable pattern of systematic RPA conduct of such actions is the unavoidable conclusion of the team's interviews."[22] Those actions included mass killings at meetings, house-to-house killings, pursuit of hidden populations, and killings of asylum seekers and of returnees.[23] The killings targeted Hutu indiscriminately: "No vetting process or attempt to establish the complicity of the victims in the April 1994 massacres of the Tutsi was reported."[24] The team estimated that, between May and July and just for the areas mentioned earlier, between 15,000 and 30,000 persons were killed in this way by the RPA.[25] Although the

---

[20] A.J. Ruzibiza, *Rwanda. L'histoire secrète*; A. Ruyenzi, "Major-General Paul Kagame behind the Shooting Down of Late Habyarimana's Plane: An Eye Witness Testimony," Norway, 5 July 2004; A. Furuma, "Open Letter to H.E. Paul Kagame, Reference: RPF/ RPA Performance in the Last Ten Years," 23 January 2001. I have received several personal communications by (former) RPA officers to that effect.

[21] "Prospects for Early Repatriation of Rwandan Refugees Currently in Burundi, Tanzania and Zaire. Summary of UNHCR Presentation before Commission of Experts," Geneva, 10 October 1994, p. 4.

[22] *Idem*, p. 6.

[23] *Idem*, pp. 4–7. These recurring practices were confirmed by an NGO team that conducted interviews with injured Rwandans in Jomba hospital (Zaire): "Rapport de visite des blessés par le FPR, hospitalisés à l'hôpital Bugusa/Jomba et Rwanguba," Goma, 11 August 1994. Also see J. Balzar, "Rwanda's New Leaders Accused of Harassing Refugees: Africa: Aid Official Says Actions Don't Match Words of Conciliation. New Exodus to Zaire Is Feared," *The Los Angeles Times*, 16 August 1994; R. Bonner, "Mass Killings by Rwandan Rebels Are Reported," *The New York Times*, 5 September 1994.

[24] "Prospects", p. 8.

[25] Ibid.

Gersony report did not exist officially,[26] some of its observations leaked in the press.[27] More importantly, the United States, due to become a major support of the new regime, was fully aware of the facts. An information memorandum of the State Department issued in September 1994 under the title "New Human Rights Abuses in Rwanda" reported on a debriefing by members of the UNHCR team on September 17. Summarizing the contents of the Gersony report, it added that "[t]he UNHCR team speculated that the purpose of the killing was a campaign of ethnic cleansing intended to clear certain areas in the south of Rwanda for Tutsi habitation. The killings also served to reduce the population of Hutu males and discouraged refugees from returning to claim their lands."[28] Although the term was not used, this description comes close to the definition of the genocide convention. The document stated that UN secretary general Boutros Ghali "plans to brief the Security Council and subsequently make the gist of the UNHCR report public."[29]

None of this happened, and the report was effectively suppressed. How this came about was later explained by the Rwandan minister of foreign affairs at the time, Jean-Marie Vianney Ndagijimana. On September 19, 1994, the report was shown to him by Kofi Annan, who was the UN deputy general secretary in charge of the Department of Peacekeeping Affairs, in the presence of Gersony. Annan told Ndagijimana that if the Rwandan government did not take measures to end the systematic massacre of Hutu, it would be accused of genocide itself. The next day, Ndagijimana received U.S. undersecretary for global affairs Timothy Wirth, who was equally severe. In early October, President Bizimungu, accompanied by Ndagijimana, visited Washington and New York. Bizimungu issued a flat and virulent denial, and accused the United Nations of having "commanded a biased and hasty inquiry, with the sole aim of damaging the image of the government of national union."

---

[26] "The Gersony Report Does Not Exist": A. Des Forges, *Leave None to Tell the Story*, pp. 728–732. Also see G. Prunier, *Africa's World War. Congo, the Rwandan Genocide, and the Making of a Continental Catastrophe*, Oxford, Oxford University Press, pp. 15–17. UN military officers and relief workers were forbidden to discuss the report (D. Lorch, "Rwandan Rulers Warn Against Violence," *The New York Times*, 2 October 1994).

[27] "Un rapport américain accable le nouveau régime de Kigali. Des milliers de Hutus massacrés au Rwanda," *Libération*, 1–2 October 1994.

[28] "New Human Rights Abuses in Rwanda," Information Memorandum from (Assistant Secretary of State for African Affairs) George E. Moose to the Secretary of State. The copy in my possession of this document is not dated, but – based on the contents – it was written between September 17 and 19, 1994.

[29] *Idem.*

Vice-President Kagame lashed out at the UNHCR and warned to "beware of foreigners who preach ethnic divisions."[30] We shall see later that aggressive denial became the hallmark of Rwandan government positions when faced with criticism. Although USAID director Brian Atwood reiterated his government's concerns and threatened to "review US cooperation with our country, in light of the massive violations of human rights documented in the Gersony report," a meeting with Moose ended on a note of understanding. Moose told Bizimungu, "We will help you. But help us to help you," thus making the Rwandans understand that if the killings stopped, the Gersony findings would be shelved.[31] According to Des Forges, the United Nations decided to suppress the Gersony findings, "not just in the interests of the recently established Rwandan government but also to avoid further discredit to itself. The U.S., and perhaps other member states, concurred in this decision, largely to avoid weakening the new Rwandan government."[32] With hindsight, the suppression of the Gersony report was the start of a consistent pattern of internationally sanctioned acceptance of the RPF's crimes (see Chapters 5 and 8).

Later in 1994, UN special rapporteur René Degni-Ségui found cases of summary executions, massacres, and forced disappearances and noted that "in addition to the mass graves for which the RPA is responsible we therefore have all those for which the militia and the Rwandese Armed Forces are responsible, so that it is now difficult to tell them apart."[33] In December 1994, a UN commission of experts concluded

on the basis of ample evidence that individuals from both sides to the armed conflict in Rwanda during the period from 6 April 1994 to 15 July 1994 perpetrated serious breaches of international humanitarian law [and] that ample evidence indicates that individuals from both sides to the armed conflict perpetrated crimes against humanity in Rwanda in the period mentioned above.[34]

[30] D. Lorch, "Rwandan Rulers Warn".

[31] J.M.V. Ndagijimana, *Paul Kagame a sacrifié les Tutsi*, Orléans, Editions La Pagaie, 2009, pp. 134–138. Five days after that meeting, Ndagijimana resigned in protest over the regime's human rights abuse.

[32] A. Des Forges, *Leave None to Tell the Story*, p. 726.

[33] United Nations, Economic and Social Council, Commission on Human Rights, *Report on the Situation of Human Rights in Rwanda Submitted by Mr. René Degni-Ségui, Special Rapporteur of the Commission on Human Rights, under Paragraph 20 of Resolution S-3/1 of 25 May 1994*, E/CN.4/1995/70, 11 November 1994, para. 40.

[34] United Nations, Security Council, *Final Report of the Commission of Experts Established Pursuant to Security Council Resolution 935 (1994)*, S/1994/1405, 9 December 1994, para. 181–182.

The commission remained "disturbed by ongoing violence committed by some RPF soldiers and recommends that investigation of violations of international humanitarian law and of human rights law attributed to the Rwandese Patriotic Front be continued by the [ICTR] Prosecutor."[35] For reasons discussed later, no such thing happened: the ICTR became an instrument of victor's justice, and the RPF got away unpunished. Together with international tolerance, impunity was to herald massive human rights abuse in the years to come, in both Rwanda and Zaire/DRC.

Mass killings abated as a result of the warnings made by the United States based on the Gersony report, but individual killings and disappearances continued. As seen earlier, the highly publicized Kibeho massacre in April 1995 was to deal a final blow to the "government of national unity."[36] Kibeho was one of the large IDP camps that were a leftover of the Safe Humanitarian Zone put in place under the French Opération Turquoise. Although a UN Integrated Operations Centre (IOC) successfully repatriated close to 100,000 IDPs between October 1994 and January 1995, the resumption of the killings by the RPA after the Geneva Roundtable discouraged people from returning home, and many repatriated IDPs even returned to the camps. The government nevertheless wanted to clear the camps, seen as havens of *génocidaires*. On April 17, 1995, the *préfet* of Butare decreed the closure of all camps in his préfecture. The next day, the RPA moved in on Kibeho camp, and dozens of people were killed. Worse was to come on April 22, when the RPA, using guns, RPGs and mortars, opened fire on the crowd. Although the RPA buried many bodies during the night, on April 23, Australian medics of UNAMIR counted more than four thousand dead when they were prevented by the RPA to continue counting.[37] An on-site report mentioned "a column of RPA soldiers marching down the hill from the church, whistling and singing." It also pointed at manipulation: the government claimed that the fact

---

[35] *Idem*, para. 186.

[36] On the Kibeho massacre, see J. Pottier, *Re-imaging Rwanda. Conflict, Survival and Disinformation in the Late Twentieth Century*, Cambridge, Cambridge University Press, 2002, pp. 160–170; A.J. Ruzibiza, *Rwanda. L'histoire secrète*, pp. 369–384; C. Vidal, "Des humanitaires témoins de l'histoire," *Les Temps Modernes*, 627 (2004), pp. 92–107. The most comprehensive account is offered in S.T. Kleine-Ahlbrandt, *The Protection Gap in the International Protection of Internally Displaced Persons: the Case of Rwanda*, Geneva, Graduate Institute of International Studies, 2006.

[37] Two Australian medics "had already counted about 4,000 dead and 650 wounded when they were stopped halfway along the road. The RPA had forced them to stop when they realised what was going on" (T. Pickard, *Combat Medic. An Australian's Eyewitness Account of the Kibeho Massacre*, Wavel Heights, Big Sky Publishing, 2008, p. 81).

that some victims suffered machete wounds was proof that "interahamwe" started the hostilities, but "during the night the soldiers had been shooting and had forced displaced to wound and kill other displaced by machete, threatening them that they would be shot themselves if they would not obey."[38] An Australian medic present believed that "if Australians had not been there as witnesses to the massacre, the RPA would have killed every single person in the camp."[39]

When Interior minister Seth Sendashonga came to the site on the morning of April 23, he was refused access by the army. President Bizimungu arrived in the afternoon, and he was told by the military that the number of killed was about 300, an estimate he did not question. The official position was that "casualty estimates (. . .) stand at about 300. (. . .) The cause of the incident which resulted in the deaths of so many was traced to the criminal gangs in the camps who were determined to make the [repatriation] process fail."[40] Human Rights Watch and FIDH observed that "[i]n those areas where the UN personnel were permitted access, they established a detailed count of 2,000 dead and an estimated total of 4,050,"[41] but – in what Pottier has called a "masterclass in surreal diplomacy"[42] – the government set the figure at 338. In addition to the thousands killed at the Kibeho site, Prunier estimates that at least 20,000 more "disappeared" after the massacre, between the camp and their homes.[43]

---

[38] Médecins sans frontières, *Report on Events in Kibeho Camp, April 1995*, Kigali, 16 May 1995, p. 9.

[39] P. Jordan, "Witness to Genocide – A Personal Account of the 1995 Kibeho Massacre," reprint from the *Australian Army Journal* (www.anzacday.org.au/history/peacekeeping/anecdotes/kibeho.html). This feeling was confirmed by an Australian commander who told his men that "there was absolutely no doubt if we had not been at Kibeho the whole camp of around 100,000 people probably would have been slaughtered and the world would have been none the wiser" (T. Pickard, *Combat Medic*, p. 114).

[40] Ministère de la Réhabilitation et de l'Intégration sociale, *Closure of Displaced People's Camps in Gikongoro*, Kigali, 25 April 1995, quoted by G. Prunier, *Africa's World War*, p. 41.

[41] Human Rights Watch/Africa, Fédération internationale des ligues des droits de l'homme, *Communiqué*, 24 April 1995. The text referred to the hasty burial of victims by the RPA, thus making a precise count impossible: "RPA soldiers quickly buried corpses during the night of April 22–23, and in the early morning of April 23. Soldiers also threw corpses into latrines." An Australian eyewitness recounted that "[t]he RPA was quietly retrieving the dead and burying them in mass graves. We believed it was to lower the body count, and they had been at it since the night before" (T. Pickard, *Combat Medic*, p. 84).

[42] J. Pottier, *Re-imagining Rwanda*, p. 160.

[43] G. Prunier, *Africa's World War*, p. 41–42. On the Butare-Runyinya road, an MSF nurse witnessed 10,000 to 15,000 people pass by. "Many of them had bullet wounds, and were beaten up with sticks. (. . .) Sometimes they had to walk through a corridor of stone-throwing people" (Médecins sans frontières, *Report on Events*, p. 16).

Scores of others were killed when other IDP camps were cleared after Kibeho.[44]

The aftermath was to confirm the sense of impunity prevalent among radicals in the government. Sendashonga asked for an independent international commission of inquiry into the massacre, but Kagame aggressively refuted the idea. Instead, on April 27 President Bizimungu announced the establishment of his own "independent international inquiry." The commission consisted of ten members from several countries (including Rwanda, represented by RPF lawyer Christine Umutoni), as well as the United Nations and the Organisation of African Unity (OAU), with terms of reference drawn up by the Rwandan government. A mere fourteen pages long, the report (which mostly relied on RPA witnesses) essentially toed the government line: the IDP camps were a threat to national security, Kibeho was becoming a "criminals' sanctuary" and "something had to be done," and the RPA "responded" to attacks by IDPs. Although the "reactions" by the RPA were "disproportionate and, therefore, violative of international law," the report explained them on technical grounds, such as deficiencies in communication systems and equipment. The conclusion: "[T]he tragedy of Kibeho neither resulted from a planned action by Rwandan authorities to kill a certain group of people, nor was it an accident that could not have been prevented."[45] The commission was unable to establish a dead count, although it felt that "it is apparent that the numbers are more than those formally counted in Kibeho camp."[46] The report was, of course, well received by the government, but two members of the commission themselves had some misgivings. One felt that the conclusions did "not contain half of what we found," whereas another criticized the lack of area expertise among members and the censorship inflicted.[47] Although welcoming the fact that an inquiry was held, Amnesty International expressed disappointment at the report, which "failed to satisfy the strict international standards for such inquiries (...) and to make adequate recommendations to prevent further human rights violations in Rwanda."[48] The EU froze its direct aid to

---

[44] "60.000 déplacés disparus au Rwanda," *Libération*, 23 June 1995.

[45] *Report of the Independent International Commission of Inquiry on the Events at Kibeho, April 1995*, Kigali, 18 May 1995, p. 12.

[46] *Idem*, p. 10.

[47] J. Pottier, *Re-imagining Rwanda*, p. 168.

[48] Amnesty International, *Rwanda: Mixed Reaction to Publication of Kibeho Killings Inquiry*, AFR 47/11/95, London, 1995.

Rwanda for some time,[49] but the United Kingdom and the United States did not protest and accepted Kigali's official version of the events. Pottier notes that "[a]lready, the two governments were indicating that they had relinquished the right to an independent view on matters Rwandan."[50] With Kibeho and since, "the British and US press (and many humanitarian workers) came to follow the 'politically correct' view that Rwanda's problems were best understood as resulting exclusively from international indifference," which resulted in "the loss of the outsider's right to an independent opinion on politics in Rwanda."[51] The hard-liners in the Rwandan regime were to remember the lesson of Kibeho very well. They realized that playing hardball toward a pliant international community works, and they replayed Kibeho one-and-a-half years later, this time in Zaire, at an infinitely larger scale.

In the meantime, human rights abuse inside Rwanda continued. Having fled the country in April 1995, Kigali prosecutor François-Xavier Nsanzuwera held a press conference in Brussels on May 11. In the published document he denounced the disappearances, massive arrests, and the interference in the justice system by the RPF.[52] Interestingly, his draft text was more outspoken and complete than the version he delivered. Referring to a "reign of terror," he listed summary executions and disappearances, massive and arbitrary arrests, the "hunt" against judicial staff, and the resurgence of death squads, among others.[53] On April 7, another human rights activist who left Rwanda in early 1995 produced a document in which he outlined summary executions and disappearances, the detention of scores of people in military installations, the persecution of Hutu, the abuse committed by RPF cadres, and the interference of the RPA in the judicial and administrative systems.[54] In June 1995, the UN special

---

[49] The Belgian reaction was severe. On April 25, Minister of Foreign Affairs Erik Derycke summoned the Rwandan chargé d'affaires to express Belgium's "very firm condemnation (...) of the brutal behaviour of the Rwandan army which has led to many innocent victims." Pending the findings of an inquiry and the identification and punishment of those guilty for the massacre, Belgium suspended its bilateral aid ("Communiqué de presse," Brussels, 25 April 1995). Despite this strong language, aid was quietly resumed after the publication of the report of the "independent international commission."

[50] J. Pottier, *Re-imagining Rwanda*, p. 166.

[51] *Idem*, p. 107.

[52] "Rwanda: Et si demain il y avait un autre génocide," press release, Brussels, 11 May 1995.

[53] RPF sympathizers, including a Belgian professor of international law, threatened Nsanzuwera the day before the press conference and made him tune down his statement (manuscript of the draft on file with this author).

[54] J. Matata, "Rapport succint sur la situation des Droits de l'Homme au Rwanda," letter to Vice-President Kagame and to the chairman of the RPF, Brussels, 7 April 1995.

rapporteur regretted that "[v]iolations of the right to life, which had decreased somewhat and given way to arbitrary arrests and detentions, are now unfortunately on the increase again, taking the form of summary executions, massacres, and abductions and enforced disappearances."[55] More than half a year later, Degni-Ségui did not notice any improvement in the situation.[56] Not just Rwandans, but foreigners who witnessed killings and were suspected of informing international opinion, were targeted: among the victims of RPA killings were Canadian priest Claude Simard on October 17, 1994; three Spanish volunteers of the NGO Médicos del mundo on January 19, 1997; Canadian priest Guy Pinard on February 2, 1997; Spanish priest Joaquim Vallmajó on April 26, 1997; Belgian school director Griet Bosmans on April 27, 1997; Croatian priest Curic Vjecko on October 31, 1998; and Spanish priest Isidro Uzcudun Pouso on June 10, 2000.

The UN Human Rights Field Operation in Rwanda (UNHRFOR) continued to observe killings of civilians, in some cases dozens, in 1996, such as in Kabaya and Satinsyi in April. More than a hundred were killed in late July.[57] During the month of August alone, UNHRFOR received reports of the killings of 284 persons in seventy separate incidents.[58] Amnesty International claimed that "[b]etween April and July especially, violence directed against unarmed civilians, including women, the elderly, children and even babies, intensified, claiming more than 650 lives."[59] Most of these incidents occurred in the regions bordering Zaire, from where an increasing number of attacks and infiltrations were launched by former FAR and interahamwe who committed atrocities too, particularly against genocide survivors. These actions paused after the RPA invaded Zaire in September 1996 (see the following discussion), but they developed into a major insurgency in 1997. Killings during that episode are discussed later in this chapter.

[55] United Nations, Economic and Social Council, Commission on Human Rights, *Report on the Situation of Human Rights in Rwanda Submitted by Mr. René Degni-Ségui, Special Rapporteur, under Paragraph 20 of resolution S-3/1 of 25 May 1994*, E/CN.4/1996/7, 28 June 1995, para. 97. Likewise, in July 1995 the UN Integrated Operations Centre (IOC) in Kigali mentioned "increased reports of disappearances of former IDPs from home communes" ("Humanitarian Situation in Rwanda," 19 July 1995).

[56] United Nations, Economic and Social Council, Commission on Human Rights, *Report on the Situation of Human Rights in Rwanda Submitted by Mr. René Degni-Ségui, Special Rapporteur, under Paragraph 20 of Resolution S-3/1 of 25 May 1994*, E/CN.4/1996/68, 29 January 1996.

[57] "UN Workers Say over 100 killed in Rwanda Operation," Nairobi, Reuters, 25 July 1996.

[58] UNHRFOR, *Update on the Human Rights Situation during August 1996*, Kigali, n.d.

[59] Amnesty International, *Rwanda: Sharp Increase in Killings Could Plunge Rwanda Back into a Cycle of Violence*, London, 12 August 1996.

ZAIRE/DRC, 1996–1997

During 1995 and 1996, armed elements in the refugee camps across the border in Zaire conducted raids in the préfectures of Gisenyi, Ruhengeri, Kibuye and Cyangugu. In addition to this constant threat, the Rwandan government had intelligence showing that operations at a wider scale, and possibly an all-out invasion were being prepared. On several occasions, Kagame asked members of the international community to do something about this situation, failing which he would have to "break the abscess" himself. Hiding behind the AFDL "rebellion" engineered in Kigali, Rwanda attacked the refugee camps in September 1996.[60] Many thousands of refugees were killed in and around the camps; hundreds of thousands were, in part forcibly, in part voluntarily repatriated to Rwanda; and hundreds of thousands more fled westward, where they became the victims of a relentless pursuit by the RPA.

Despite the many obstacles put in its way by Laurent Kabila's regime after the AFDL seized power in Kinshasa, a UN investigative team managed to produce a report on these massacres, which Secretary General Kofi Annan submitted to the Security Council on June 29, 1998. The report concluded that the RPA had committed large-scale war crimes and crimes against humanity. It went further by suggesting that genocide might have occurred. However, this needed additional investigation: "The systematic massacre of those [Hutu refugees] remaining in Zaire was an abhorrent crime against humanity, but the underlying rationale for the decision is material to whether these killings constituted genocide, that is, a decision to eliminate, in part, the Hutu ethnic group."[61] A mapping exercise conducted on behalf of the UN High Commission for Human Rights, published in 2010, confirmed and detailed a long list of atrocities uncovered earlier by UN panels, national and international NGOs, and investigative journalists. It concluded that the vast majority of the 617 listed incidents were to be classified as war crimes and crimes against humanity. On the issue of genocide, it noted that "[s]everal incidents listed in this report, if investigated and judicially proven, point to circumstances and facts from which a court could infer the intention to destroy the Hutu ethnic group in the DRC in part, if these were established beyond all reasonable

---

[60] For details see G. Prunier, *Africa's World War*, pp. 113–125; F. Reyntjens, *The Great African War*, pp. 45–58.

[61] United Nations, Security Council, *Report of the Investigative Team Charged with Investigating Serious Violations of Human Rights and International Humanitarian Law in the Democratic Republic of Congo*, S/1998/581, 29 June 1998, para. 96.

doubt."[62] These reports, along with other extensive documentation, outlined a number of consistent patterns and practices by the RPA, which are briefly summarized in the following paragraphs.[63]

The RPA systematically shelled numerous camps in South and North Kivu, where massacres were also committed with light weapons. Thousands of refugees, most of them unarmed civilians, were killed. These attacks continued and intensified as the refugees moved westward. The largest massacres occurred between Shabunda and Kingulube, at Shanji, Walikale, Tingi-Tingi, Kasese and Biaro, and finally between Boende and Mbandaka. The report of a UN joint mission referred to information it received concerning 134 sites where atrocities had been committed.[64] At the end of May 1997, when the AFDL had taken control of the whole country, the UNHCR found that 246,000 refugees were "unaccounted for." On July 8, 1997, the acting UN High Commissioner for Human Rights (UNCHR) stated that "about 200,000 Hutu refugees could well have been massacred." After detailed calculations, Emizet arrives at a death toll of about 233,000.[65]

It would be fastidious to describe or even simply enumerate the many massive and focused killings. However, the nature and the extent of this tragedy can be illustrated with two examples. In mid-March 1997, survivors from massacres in the area of Tingi-Tingi, who numbered approximately 135,000, set up camp near the villages of Biaro and Kasese on the rail line between Ubundu and Kisangani. Around mid-April, journalists and humanitarian agencies were denied access beyond km 42 of the rail

[62] United Nations, Office of the High Commissioner for Human Rights, *Democratic Republic of the Congo, 1993–2003. Report of the Mapping Exercise Documenting the Most Serious Violations of Human Rights and International Humanitarian Law Committed within the Territory of the Democratic Republic of the Congo between March 1993 and June 2003*, Geneva, August 2010, para. 31.

[63] Facts described here are not individually referenced, as they appear in several sources and because this would create a needless accumulation of footnotes. A full list of sources for these events can be found in F. Reyntjens, *The Great African War*, pp. 287–90. Also see J.K. Stearns, *Dancing in the Glory of Monsters. The Collapse of the Congo and the Great War of Africa*, New York, Public Affairs, 2011, pp. 127–141; F. Reyntjens, R. Lemarchand, "Mass Murder in Eastern Congo, 1996–1997," in R. Lemarchand (Ed.), *Forgotten Genocides. Oblivion, Denial, and Memory*, Philadelphia, University of Pennsylvania Press, 2011, pp. 20–36.

[64] United Nations, Economic and Social Council, Commission on Human Rights, *Report of the Joint Mission Charged with Investigating Allegations of Massacres and Other Human Rights Violations Occurring in Eastern Zaire (Now Democratic Republic of the Congo) since September 1996*, A/51/942, 2 July 1997.

[65] K. Emizet, "The Massacre of Refugees in Congo: A Case of UN Peacekeeping Failure and International Law," *Journal of Modern African Studies*, 38:2 (2000), pp. 173–179.

line from Kisangani. The refugees were then out of reach of assistance or protection. On April 17, between 200 and 400 "search and destroy" elements of the RPA landed in Kisangani and were dispatched to the south and then, across the river, were deployed to the camps.[66] Between April 21 and 25, the camps were attacked by RPA and AFDL military. The number of victims probably exceeded 10,000; 2,500 of them were children in a severe state of malnutrition. When humanitarian assistance finally arrived, soldiers escorted the starving, sick, and exhausted survivors to Ubundu, eighty kilometers to the south, an area in turn declared a no-go zone. Reporters later visiting Biaro heard the sound of a digging machine requisitioned a week earlier by the rebels, but they were prevented from proceeding any further, supposedly for reasons of security. Congolese soldiers and civilians said there was an "open air incinerator." A Belgian entrepreneur running a logging operation in the area confirmed this information to this author. A soldier told a photographer working for Associated Press that "there is much work to do, digging up the bodies and burning them. When the UN eventually comes to investigate, there will be no evidence."[67]

The second example is a sequel to the first. About 45,000 survivors of the Kasese-Biaro carnage continued their trek westward. The RPA/AFDL elements chasing them made a detour to cut off the refugees at Boende. A phased massacre then began between Boende and Mbandaka. Thousands were killed in Boende, on the road to Mbandaka, and, finally, in Mbandaka itself. The Mbandaka massacres are particularly incriminating for the RPA/AFDL, because the killings took place in front of numerous local residents who were profoundly shocked by the cruelties committed against inoffensive civilians. The cross-checking of sources suggests that the number of victims in southern Equateur is about 15,000.

As early as November 26, 1996, in a communiqué concerning a massacre in Chimanga, Amnesty International mentioned the separation of men and women and children by AFDL forces, after which the men were killed.

---

[66] It is interesting to note that this RPA "cleansing team" arrived just two days after a visit to Kasese and Biaro by Dr. Ephraïm Kabayija, advisor in the Rwandan president's office and chairperson of a commission for the repatriation and reintegration of refugees. He was invited by the UNHCR, which wished to convince the Rwandan government to accept refugee repatriation by air rather than overland. Kabayija was thus able to exactly identify the refugees' location. If he transmitted their whereabouts to the RPA, then he played the same role as "facilitators" did elsewhere in eastern Zaire (see the following discussion). Kabayija subsequently became a minister in the Rwandan government, and he is currently a provincial governor.

[67] "Kabila's Soldier Shows Mass Graves," Kisangani, AP, 22 May 1997.

In his report of January 28, 1997, UN special rapporteur Roberto Garretón found that "many witnesses (...) underline the habit of the AFDL to separate men from women and children. The fate of the latter is generally known, but no news is heard from the former." According to UN sources, RPA's "Commander Jackson" admitted that it was his job to kill Hutu refugees, adding that all the male refugees were members of the interahamwe militia responsible for the 1994 genocide of the Tutsi.[68] Médecins sans frontières (MSF) found that by March and April 1997, these gender distinctions were no longer made: women and children were exterminated too. A commander confirmed to MSF that "all those who are in the forest are considered to be the enemy."[69] Indeed it is striking that the massacres became more widespread and systematic at the time of the Biaro-Kasese episode. It is likely that at this moment the Rwandan authorities decided that repatriation was no longer a viable option, because an insurrection inside the country had started to expand, particularly in the northwest (see the following discussion). Kigali realized that the civil war had been re-imported with the returnees in the autumn of 1996. The only avenue remaining then became pure and simple extermination.

On a number of occasions, AFDL forces and their Rwandan allies made it impossible to get humanitarian aid to starving, exhausted, and sick refugees, either by blocking access to them or by relocating them out of reach of assistance. As early as November 1996, humanitarian agencies were denied access to the area around Goma, which was declared a military zone. A similar decision was taken in Bukavu, where access was made impossible beyond a thirty-kilometer radius around the town; even within that radius, freedom of movement was severely restricted.[70] During a press conference at the United Nations in November 1996, Secretary General Boutros-Ghali claimed that "two years ago, the international community was confronted with the genocide of the Tutsi by weapons. Today we are faced with the genocide of the Hutu by starvation."[71] Six

---

[68] J. Pomfret, "Congo Leader Bars Helping U.N. Probes," *The Washington Post*, 19 June 1997.

[69] Médecins sans frontières, *Forced Flight: A Brutal Strategy of Elimination in Eastern Zaire*, 16 May 1997, p. 7.

[70] This technique is similar to the one used by the RPF in Rwanda in 1994: on many occasions the areas where the RPA committed massacres were declared "military zones" with prohibited access (S. Desouter, F. Reyntjens, *Rwanda: Les violations des droits de l'homme*).

[71] Quoted in Organisation of African Unity, International Panel of Eminent Personalities, *Rwanda: The Preventable Genocide*, Addis Ababa, 2000, p. 212.

months later, his successor Kofi Annan accused the rebels of organizing a "slow extermination" of the refugees in the Kisangani area.[72]

Humanitarian aid was also used as bait. After humanitarian organizations had located the whereabouts of refugee concentrations, the AFDL/RPA would then declare the area a military zone with prohibited access. When the humanitarian agencies were eventually allowed back in, the refugees had disappeared. This strategy used so-called "facilitators", designated by the AFDL, who were supposedly in charge of liaison with the aid organizations, but who, in reality, directed the "rebel" forces to the refugee concentrations. In April, Rwandan refugees and village chiefs in South Kivu asked the UNHCR and the International Committee of the Red Cross (ICRC) to end the search for refugees, because they feared that these operations exposed both the refugees and certain Zairian groups to attacks by AFDL and RPA troops. In mid-May 1997, the ICRC decided to stop accepting the use of facilitators.

In most cases, the massacres were committed by the RPA, and perhaps by their Congolese Tutsi allies, but much less so by the AFDL per se. Kabila's aim was the overthrow of Mobutu, and he had no particular interest in the extermination of the Rwandan refugees, or at least the unarmed elements among them. An RPA colonel, interviewed in Goma by John Pomfret of the *Washington Post*, candidly admitted that the military campaign in Zaire had a dual objective: to take revenge against the Hutu and to ensure the security of Rwanda. A Tutsi official in the Congolese ministry of the interior told the same reporter that the Rwandan troops and their Congolese allies had been given authorization to attack the Hutu refugees, provided that they contributed to the overthrow of Mobutu.[73]

The operations of the RPA in the Kisangani and Boende-Mbandaka regions clearly targeted the refugees who became the object of an extermination project.[74] Many sources mentioned military who spoke Kinyarwanda and/or who wore uniforms donated to the RPA by Germany. Names of Rwandan officers were cited, but the fact that they used their (real or fake) first names renders their identification difficult. However, it is possible to establish that the following at least were

---

[72] "United Nations Warns of Problems in Repatriating Refugees," New York (UN), IPS, 28 April 1997.

[73] J. Pomfret, "Massacres Became a Weapon in Congo's Civil War," *The Washington Post*, 11 June 1997.

[74] Stearns (*Dancing in the Glory*, pp. 138–139) shows the systematic and organized nature of the killings.

implicated: James Kabarebe, currently the Rwandan minister of defense; Godfrey Kabanda; and Jackson Nkurunziza (alias Jack Nziza), nicknamed "The Exterminator."[75] Congolese General Gaston Munyango, officially the AFDL regional commander, had no real power and was an impotent witness to the atrocities committed by his allies.[76]

The DRC filed a case against Rwanda before the International Court of Justice, but as a result of Rwanda's refusing its jurisdiction, it could not entertain the merits of the case. The court held, however, that "[w]hether or not States have accepted the jurisdiction of the Court, they are required to fulfil their obligations under the United Nations Charter and the other rules of international law, including international humanitarian and human rights law, and they remain responsible for acts attributable to them which are contrary to international law."[77] In a joint separate opinion, five judges expressed their outrage:

It is a matter for serious concern that at the beginning of the twenty-first century it is still for States to choose whether they consent to the Court adjudicating claims that they have committed genocide. It must be regarded as a very grave matter that a State should be in a position to shield from international judicial scrutiny any claim that might be made against it concerning genocide. A State so doing shows the world scant confidence that it would never, ever, commit genocide, one of the greatest crimes known.[78]

Although this was a serious moral warning, Rwanda escaped formal judicial condemnation. It was to gain impunity again at the ICTR (see Chapter 8).

RWANDA, 1997–1998

As a result of the massive repatriation, part voluntary and part forced, of hundreds of thousands of Hutu refugees from Zaire in late 1996, and of rapidly mounting resentment caused by the occupation of eastern Zaire by the Rwandan army, the RPA faced an increasing insurgency within

---

[75] Human Rights Watch, *Democratic Republic of Congo: What Kabila Is Hiding. Civilian Killings and Impunity in Congo*, New York, October 1997; C. McGreal, "Digging up Congo's Killing Fields," *Weekly Mail and Guardian*, 25 July 1997.

[76] J. Pomfret, "Massacres".

[77] International Court of Justice, Case concerning armed activities on the territory of the Congo (*Democratic Republic of the Congo v. Rwanda*), Judgment of 3 February 2006, para. 127.

[78] *Idem*, joint separate opinion of Judges Higgins, Kooymans, Elaraby, Owada and Simma, para. 25.

Rwanda from early 1997, in the northwest in particular. In brutal counter-insurgency operations, the RPA killed tens of thousands of people. According to Amnesty International, at least 6,000 persons, mostly unarmed civilians, were killed between January and August 1997, mainly by the RPA; according to the report, the real number was undoubtedly much higher, because numerous massacres were not reported.[79] These facts were implicitly acknowledged by the regime, when, refuting observations made by UNHRFOR, presidential adviser Claude Dusaidi claimed that "if civilians had been killed, they were accomplices, persons who sympathized with these armed men."[80] Ironically, this language is reminiscent of that used by the former regime in 1994 when seeking to justify the persecution of the *"ibiyitso"* (accomplices) of the RPF, a coded expression referring to the Tutsi.

The killings were on the increase in the second half of 1997, especially after October. In a new report, Amnesty International observed that "during the months of October, November and the beginning of December, Amnesty International received almost daily reports of slaughters of unarmed civilians in Rwanda, namely extra-judicial executions conducted by soldiers of the RPA and deliberate and arbitrary slaughters by armed opposition groups."[81] Adding up available data that were often incomplete and imprecise, the death toll for the period October 1997 to January 1998 was close to 10,000 victims at the hands of the RPA and several hundred at the hands of the rebels. Those figures do not include a particularly gruesome incident in October 1997, when the RPA killed thousands of civilians hiding in natural caves in Nyakinama. The UNHRFOR was denied access to the site. Moreover, there was no news about large populations groups, in particular in the subprefecture of Kabaya, the highly populated region of origin of former President Habyarimana, where, in January 1998, Belgian public television VRT filmed hills and town centers completely void of their populations. The high number of casualties can in part be explained by the use of indiscriminate weapons, in particular recently acquired MI24 helicopters and T55 tanks. The civilians faced a murderous dilemma: if suspected of assisting the rebels, they were killed by the RPA; if they refused to

---

[79] Amnesty International, *Rwanda: Ending the Silence*, London, 25 September 1997.
[80] Nairobi, AFP, 8 August 1997.
[81] Amnesty International, *Rwanda: Civilians Trapped in Armed Conflict. 'The Dead Can no Longer Be Counted'*, London, 19 December 1997. Also see L. Lindholt, H.-O. Sano, *Rwanda 1997: An Analysis of Human Rights and Politics*, Copenhagen, The Danish Centre for Human Rights, September 1998, pp. 13–25.

collaborate with the rebels, they became their target. This was made clear by the warnings given to the population: on December 21, 1997, Prime Minister Rwigema declared that "whoever acts in connivance with them (the rebels) will suffer a fate similar to theirs."[82] During a visit to Nkuli (Ruhengeri) at the beginning of 1998, Kagame made similar statements, seeking in some way to justify the massacres of civilians.[83]

So the regime responded the way it did after Kibeho and the killings in Zaire/Congo, namely, by admitting "raw facts" (such as "civilians were caught in cross-fire") or shifting responsibility to the armed opposition while denying the victimhood of innocent people ("genocide perpetrators, criminal elements and their sympathisers were the targets").[84] Amnesty International found that, while the government attributed the majority of human rights abuses to "infiltrators," members of the Armée pour la liberation du Rwanda (ALIR) operating from the DRC, most killings were carried out by the RPA.[85] Likewise, the OAU panel of eminent personalities found that "RPF forces made little or no attempt to spare civilian lives; and it appears that they killed more unarmed civilians than the rebels."[86] Against the regime's minimization of the death toll among civilians and the lack of interest by the international community for information provided by human rights organizations, Verpoorten provides robust data on the impact of the army's counterinsurgency campaign in the northwest. She finds a large and significant high-high excess mortality cluster in Gisenyi, which can only be explained by the RPA's killing of civilians during 1997–1998.[87]

Some grave incidents were surrounded by an air of manipulation that was reinforced by the relative inaccessibility of the theater of events and by the absence on the ground of impartial international observers. The intimidation and even killing of foreigners led to their leaving these

---

[82] Kigali, AFP, 21 December 1997.

[83] For more on the insurgency in the Northwest and its humanitarian fallout, see U.S. Committee for Refugees, *Life after Death: Suspicion and Reintegration in Post-Genocide Rwanda*, Washington, DC, February 1998, pp. 18–25.

[84] T. Eide, "Violence, denial and fear in post-genocide Rwanda," in A. Suhrke, M. Berdal (Eds.), *The Peace In Between. Post-war Violence and Peacebuilding*, London, Routledge, 2012, p. 270.

[85] Amnesty International, *Rwanda. Gacaca: A Question of Justice*, London, December 2002, p. 18.

[86] Organisation of African Unity, International Panel of Eminent Personalities, *Rwanda*, para. 22.40.

[87] M. Verpoorten, "Detecting Hidden Violence: The Spatial Distribution of Excess Mortality in Rwanda," *Political Geography*, 31 (2012), pp. 44–56. Of course, Verpoorten does not blame all excess deaths on the RPA, because ALIR too killed civilians.

areas.[88] On January 19, 1997, three Spanish workers, who had witnessed a massacre, were killed by the RPA,[89] after several priests too had been eliminated; others followed (cf. supra). The absence of witnesses allowed crimes to be committed far from the eyes of the international community and to sow confusion. A dramatic instance occurred on December 11, 1997, when a refugee camp of Congolese Tutsi at Mudende was attacked. According to the Rwandan government, the RPA contingent was overrun by "rebels" who were defeated by troops sent in reinforcement. Depending on the source, the death toll among the refugees was between 300 (Rwandan government) and 1,500 (Congolese government). Many facts point at manipulation by the RPA. The RPA reinforcement that came from Gisenyi (a twenty-minute drive from Mudende) arrived so late that, according to survivors, the killings of refugees lasted for hours. According to the UNHCR, the fighting did not cause one single killed or wounded among the RPA or the assailants.[90] The contradictions between the stories of the survivors and the declarations of the Rwandan government suggested at best that the RPA did not actively protect the refugees and at worst that it stage-managed this incident itself, which came in handy the day before the arrival in Kigali of U.S. secretary of state Madeleine Albright. Having been taken severely to task less than a week earlier by the UN High Commissioner for Human Rights, the regime indeed had every interest in portraying itself as a victim. These doubts were shared by the United States. State Department spokesperson James Rubin stated that "there was a marked failure by the RPA to adequately defend the refugees (...). The reasons for this failure by the RPA remain uncertain but point to the local commander's actions."[91] The doubts surrounding the Mudende massacre were reinforced by a little known fact. On December 16, the Congolese ambassador to the United Nations asked the Security Council to set up a commission of inquiry into the events. When asked about its position, Rwanda stated that the incident had been investigated twice,[92] and that another inquiry was not necessary. As a

---

[88] The annual political report for 1997 of the Belgian embassy noted that "the authorities do not want the presence of foreign witnesses."

[89] This was one of the incidents that led to the indictment of RPA elements by the Spanish National Tribunal (Juzgado central de instrucción Numero 4, Audiencia Nacional, Sumario 3/2008-D, Auto, 6 February 2008). Also see A.J. Ruzibiza, *Rwanda. L'histoire secrète*, pp. 429–431.

[90] UNHCR, "Briefing Notes", Geneva, 12 December 1997.

[91] "Rwanda Massacre Branded Genocide by Administration," London, AP, 18 December 1997.

[92] These "inquiries" were those of UNHRFOR and U.S. ambassador for war crimes David Scheffer. Both were very summary and did not lead to any firm or definitive conclusions.

result, the DRC asked informally that the item be removed from the council's agenda. Had it been confident about the outcome, it would have been in Rwanda's best interest to allow a thorough investigation.

A similar example of manipulation as a result of the absence of external observation occurred in July 1998, when dozens of people were killed in Tare, some thirty-five kilometers North of Kigali. Although the government claimed that so-called *interahamwe* were responsible for the attack, a version that was relayed by the AFP in a dispatch on July 13 without questions asked, eyewitnesses later stated that elements of the RPA committed the massacre.[93] During the same period, people disappeared at a large scale: in the northwest in particular, but also in Kigali and elsewhere, thousands of people were rounded up.[94] Some disappeared without leaving a trace, others were detained in *cachots*, military camps, and even containers; others still were forcibly enrolled to fight in the DRC.[95] For instance, in early December 1998, dozens of people were picked up in the Nyakabanda neighborhood of Kigali and taken to the former UNAMIR base in Remera, where many were held in containers; those who died from suffocation were buried in a nearby mass grave.[96] Those particularly targeted in Kigali were people from Gisenyi and Ruhengeri préfectures, suspected of sympathizing with the rebellion.

THE SITUATION AFTER 1998

The human rights situation improved in 1999–2000, particularly in the sphere of the most important right, that to life. RPA attacks on the population decreased in intensity and violence as a result of a combination of factors, in particular the forcible regrouping of the inhabitants of the northwestern region, the gradual shift from sheer repression to sensitization, and the Rwandan army operations in the Congo, where they attacked and destabilized the rear bases of the ALIR rebellion. However, these strategies gave rise to new forms of human rights abuse. Hundreds of

---

[93] Human Rights Watch, *World Report 1999*. This was later confirmed by A.J. Ruzibiza, *Rwanda. L'histoire secrète*, pp. 414–415.

[94] Among the 11,000 Rwandans that fled to Tanzania between January and June 1998, many said that the disappearances were the reason for their flight (Human Rights Watch, *World Report 1999*).

[95] A report observed the forced recruitment by the RPA of thousands of children: Coalition to Stop the Use of Child Soldiers, *The Use of Children as Soldiers in Africa*, April 1999, p. 58.

[96] Other examples can be found in Centre de lutte contre l'impunité et l'injustice au Rwanda, *Rwanda: Les enlèvements de civils s'intensifient à Kigali*, 19 February 1999.

thousands of people rounded up in the préfectures of Gisenyi and Ruhengeri were forcibly settled in regroupment camps during 1999; these displacements were usually against the people's wishes, and the sanitary situation in these sites was deplorable.[97] At the end of 1998, 342,000 people were displaced in Gisenyi prefecture, of whom 31 percent were in camps; the number was 224,000 for Ruhengeri (86 percent in camps). At the end of 1999, numerous lawsuits about landed property had not been settled, and only 60 percent of the arable land in the prefecture of Ruhengeri was effectively farmed, which explained in part the high rates of malnutrition in this very fertile region.[98] The "villagization" policy (*imidugudu*) is discussed later.

Paradoxically, one of the firmest international sponsors of the regime was also the one expressing the strongest criticism of its human rights record, through the U.S. State Department's *Country Reports on Human Rights Practices*. In the one dealing with 2005, it observed that "the government's human rights record remains poor," and it deplored many cases of arbitrary arrest and detention of persons "either after they expressed viewpoints unacceptable to the government or because of their membership in religious organizations," as well as the interference of the executive branch in the judicial system and the numerous restrictions on the freedoms of the press, expression, assembly, and association. The State Department was also concerned about the fact that, in practice, the *gacaca* courts did not function honestly and failed to achieve their dual objective of justice and reconciliation (also see infra).[99] Although noting some improvements, the report on 2006 made similar observations.[100] The Rwandan reaction to these criticisms is discussed later. The irritation of the U.S. ally also expressed itself in the fact that the United States mentioned seven countries that were not to be included in the new UN Human Rights Council, because "their own records make them unfit to sit in judgment of others," and Washington wanted "to keep some of the worst offenders off." Rwanda was included in the list of seven, along

---

[97] Republic of Rwanda, *Etude sur les conditions de vie des déplacés vivant dans les camps du Nord-Ouest du Rwanda*, Kigali, March 1999.

[98] In this connection, see Human Rights Watch, *World Report 2000*, New York, 2000, entry on Rwanda; U.S. Department of State, *1999 Country Reports on Human Rights Practices*, entry on Rwanda.

[99] U.S. Department of State, *Country Reports on Human Rights Practices*, 8 March 2006.

[100] U.S. Department of State, *Country Reports on Human Rights Practices*, 6 March 2007.

with Sudan, Liberia, the DRC, the Ivory Coast, Somalia, and Sierra Leone.[101]

When examining Rwanda's periodic report in March 2009, the UN Human Rights Committee summarized its observations in no uncertain terms.[102] Although lauding Rwanda for the abolition of the death penalty and for the representation of women in its Parliament, the UNHRC expressed concern over a wide variety of points. Among other issues it mentioned "reported cases of enforced disappearances and summary or arbitrary executions in Rwanda and (...) the impunity apparently enjoyed by the police forces responsible for such violations" (para. 12),[103] "the large number of persons, including women and children, reported to have been killed from 1994 onwards in the course of operations of the Rwandan Patriotic Army, and at the limited number of cases reported to have resulted in prosecution and punishment by the Rwandan courts" (para. 13), the replacement of the death penalty "by life imprisonment in solitary confinement" (para. 14), the "appalling prison conditions" (para. 15), the arrest of "persons belonging to vulnerable groups, such as street children, beggars and sex workers, on the grounds of vagrancy" (para. 16), the fact that "the *gacaca* system of justice does not operate in accordance with the basic rules to the rights to a fair trial, particularly with regard to the impartiality of judges and protection of rights of the accused" (para. 17), "reports that journalists who have criticised the Government are currently subjected to intimidation by the State party authorities and that some have been charged with 'divisionism'" (para. 20), and "reported obstacles to the registration and freedom of action of human rights NGOs and opposition political parties" (para. 21).

These observations were serious, but they could have been made about any banal dictatorship in Africa. But Rwanda is no banal dictatorship, and the Human Rights Committee failed to see that the regime had years ago achieved a stage at which visible repression was no longer necessary, at least until forms of domestic opposition resurfaced in 2009–2010. Indeed, political and social political spaces were closed off, and political competition was nonexistent or manipulated; massacres, disappearances, and

---

[101] "US Tries to Exclude Some from U.N. Group," Washington, AP, 31 August 2005.

[102] United Nations, General Assembly, Official Records, *Report of the Human Rights Committee*, Volume I, A/64/40 (Vol. I), 2009.

[103] In a later report, Amnesty International documented a systematic pattern of unlawful detention, torture and other forms of ill-treatment and enforced disappearances, mostly of civilians, at the hands of the DMI (Amnesty International, *Rwanda: Shrouded in Secrecy*).

intimidation forced Rwandans into submission or silence, and those bold enough to express dissident opinions were very rare; the uncertainty created by the criminalization of "divisionism" and "genocide ideology" further contributed to a widely shared sense of conformism. Terror had succeeded in consolidating political control, and widespread physical violence was replaced by more subtle forms of repression. Eide notes that the violence had sent a clear message: "The denial of state-sponsored violence in Rwanda and Zaire/DRC not only showed what RPA soldiers were capable of doing, but also that they could get away with it. Impunity hence manifests itself as another central characteristic of the Rwandan 'victor's peace.'"[104]

CONCLUSION

Subscribing to the view that the RPF had been guilty of very serious human rights abuse over the years, a panel put in place by the OAU felt that

[f]ailure to allow independent investigations has caused the RPF to forfeit much of its moral capital. At the very least, the refusal by the Kigali government to allow independent investigations of alleged human rights violations seems to us a major strategic error; in return for retaining control of the flow of information – especially potentially embarrassing news – it is seriously sacrificing its own credibility.[105]

This is true, but the criticism was directed at the wrong party. Rwanda got away with its practice of denial because the international community shied away from demanding and, if needed, imposing accountability.

Answering a question about the lack of response to RPA abuse in the DRC, a British diplomat told Jason Stearns that "we had invested so much in rebuilding Rwanda – did we want to give that all up on the basis of rumors?"[106] Against the background of Rwanda's application for membership of the Commonwealth, the Commonwealth Human Rights Initiative (CHRI) advised that, on account of the state of governance and human rights, "Rwanda does not (...) qualify for admission."[107] Among its recommendations, the report noted that it "has made it clear that Rwanda does not satisfy the test of

---

[104] T. Eide, "Violence, Denial and Fear," p. 270.

[105] Organisation of African Unity, International Panel of Eminent Personalities, *Rwanda*, para. 22.37.

[106] J. Stearns, F. Borello, "Bad Karma. Accountability for Rwandan Crimes in the Congo," in S. Straus, L. Waldorf (Eds.), *Remaking Rwanda*, p. 161.

[107] Commonwealth Human Rights Initiative, *Rwanda's Application for Membership of the Commonwealth: Report and Recommendations of the Commonwealth Human Rights Initiative*, Delhi, August 2009, p. 47.

Commonwealth values. There are considerable doubts about the commitment of the current regime to human rights and democracy. It has not hesitated to use violence at home or abroad when it has suited it."[108] The CHRI suggested having Rwanda's application reviewed by an independent commission before taking a decision, adding that "[u]nless this is done, there is a danger that the Commonwealth could slide into debased standards, and lose its attraction to the people of the Commonwealth – and the reputation of the organisation."[109] Its concerns materialized when Rwanda was admitted on November 29, 2009, without awkward questions asked, and with the backing of major members such as the United Kingdom, Canada, Australia, and India. As will be seen in Chapters 5 and 8, with the support of some of its powerful international sponsors, the RPF escaped accountability for some of the worst violations of international humanitarian law committed during the late twentieth century.

[108] *Idem*, p. 49.
[109] *Idem*.

$$5$$

Dealing with the World and the Region

Since the RPF came to power in July 1994, keeping or getting outside observers out has been a constant concern. Already at the end of 1995, thirty-eight international NGOs had been expelled, and the activities of eighteen others had been suspended, their assets frozen and their equipment impounded. In June 1997, the government, through a large-scale diplomatic offensive, succeeded in having the mandate of UN special rapporteur René Degni-Ségui terminated, as his reports had become a nuisance. He was replaced by a special representative whose mandate and interest in criticizing the regime over its human rights record was much more limited.[1] The UNHRFOR was next in line. On December 7, 1997, the UN High Commissioner for Human Rights, Mary Robinson, previously considered a friend of the "New Rwanda" (she visited the country on a couple of occasions when she was president of Ireland), issued a communiqué condemning the absence of a reconciliation policy and the practice of serious human rights violations. The spokesperson for the Rwandan presidency immediately responded by vehemently and categorically denying Robertson's observations and accusing her of being

---

[1] In 2000, Special Representative Michel Moussali found that the Rwandan leaders "are seen to be totally dedicated to the welfare of the country, close to the people of Rwanda and attentive to their needs" (United Nations, General Assembly, *Report of the Special Representative of the Commission on Human Rights on the Situation of Human Rights in Rwanda*, A/55/269, 4 August 2000, p. 9). Human rights violations were systematically watered down, and the image painted by Moussali did not tally with that of most observers inside and outside the country. At the end of March 2001, Moussali requested that his mandate should not be extended "for personal reasons."

influenced "by informants whose aims are to mislead international opinion on the situation of Rwanda." The following year the government refused to allow UNHRFOR to continue monitoring the human rights situation and sought to limit its activities to mere technical assistance. Robinson decided that such a truncated mandate was unacceptable, and she closed the operation at the end of July 1998. The mission's spokesperson had been expelled on May 9, and on the departure of one of the members of the operation on July 24, his laptop, disks, and papers were confiscated at the airport. In April 2001, a round of efficient lobbying ensured the support of the African group in the UN Commission for Human Rights for striking Rwanda off the agenda (by a majority of twenty-eight votes against nineteen and nine abstentions), thus putting an end to formal international concerns about human rights in Rwanda. The EU and Canada strongly objected, and the latter got the routine treatment in return: the Rwandan delegate accused Canada of "harbouring many *génocidaires*."[2] The resolution presented by Kenya in the name of the African group expressed "its appreciation for the Government of Rwanda for the progress made in restoring the rule of law and the actions taken to consolidate peace and stability and to promote national unity and reconciliation." Despite multiple signs to the contrary, both domestically and in the DRC, Rwanda was thus declared a "normal" country no longer deserving the attention of the international community.

Other external meddlers were from the press or academia. In 1997 alone, two journalists and one researcher were declared persona non grata. French scholar Gérard Prunier was violently taken to task after the publication of a critical but on the whole appropriate analysis.[3] The director of the official information office lashed out against Prunier, "who claims to be an academic," who presents "a pseudo analysis of Rwandan society," and who is no less than "indirectly responsible for the 1994 genocide."[4] On February 9, Reuters correspondent Christian Jennings was expelled, apparently for having written two days earlier that, during a press conference, (then vice-president) Kagame had asserted that "Rwanda has the right to divert a part of international aid to contribute to the internal war against Hutu extremists."[5] On November 28, Stephen

[2] Geneva, AFP, 20 April 2001.
[3] G. Prunier, *Rwanda: The Social, Political and Economic Situation in June 1997*, Writenet (UK), July 1997.
[4] W. Rutayisire, "Gérald [sic] Prunier: A Eulogy for Genocide", Kigali, 24 October 1997.
[5] Kigali, Reuters, 7 February 1997.

Smith of the French daily *Libération* was in turn declared undesirable. The chargé d'affaires at the Rwandan embassy in Paris explained that "Smith only has himself to blame, given the horrors he has written about the country."[6] After the Belgian daily *Le Soir*, in its issue of September 8, 2000, criticized the operations of the Rwandan army in the DRC, the Rwandan ambassador in Brussels reacted furiously. Referring to "frenetic anti-Tutsi racism," he claimed that "this sickening phantasmagoria which *Le Soir* unleashes on its readers recalls the worst literature of the worst periods of racism." In a direct attack on the author of the article, Colette Braeckman, he suggested she was in the pay of the DRC: "Kinshasa owns more diamonds than Rwanda. It can buy the hearts of many journalists; Rwanda cannot even afford fidelity."[7] As seen earlier, the Belgian priest and journalist Guy Theunis was arrested at Kigali airport in September 2005 and was indicted for incitement to genocide, for having translated and republished articles of the radical paper *Kangura* in a press review published before the genocide by *Dialogue*, of which Theunis was one of the editors. In August 2008, the Rwandan minister of information accused the BBC and the VOA to "destroy the unity of Rwandans" and announced that the government had "the capacity and the right" to suspend their broadcasts "if the situation doesn't change."[8] We saw earlier that, on April 25, 2009, the government banned the Kinyarwanda service of the BBC. After having listened to a preview of a forthcoming program of *Imvo n'Imvano*, the minister claimed that it contained "most outrageous statements," including a claim by an interviewee that a number of dead bodies that ended up in Lake Victoria in 1994 were those of people killed by the RPF.[9]

The award-winning film *Hotel Rwanda* was very well received in Kigali on its release in 2005, and President Kagame and most ministers were present in the packed national stadium when it was premièred. But after Paul Rusesabagina (who inspired the main character played by Don

---

[6] RSF/IFEX, *Communiqué*, Toronto, 2 December 1997. In "Rwanda: enquête sur la terreur tutsie", published in *Libération* on 27 February 1996 (cf. supra), Smith had documented crimes against humanity and war crimes committed by the RPF.

[7] Communiqué by the Rwandan Embassy, 11 September 2000. The last sentence referred to the fact that Braeckman used to be considered a "friend of the New Rwanda"; in 1995, she received a plaque in the same embassy in recognition of her support.

[8] "La BBC et la VOA accusées par Kigali de 'détruire l'unité des Rwandais'", Kigali, AFP, 19 August 2008.

[9] Although this claim was true, it was fundamentally opposed to the RPF's "truth" (see Chapter 7 on the issue of truth construction).

Cheadle) started criticizing the regime,[10] the RPF embarked on a campaign of character assassination. Rusesabagina was suddenly accused of genocide denial and even of complicity in the genocide, and the movie became a "revisionist falsehood."[11] At a forum organized in Chicago in September 2007 by the Rev. Jesse Jackson and Rusesabagina, along with former U.S. ambassadors to Rwanda and to Burundi, were accused by the Rwandan ambassador in Washington, D.C., James Kimonyo, who had invited himself to the venue, of being involved in arms trafficking with a view to attacking Rwanda.[12] On March 19, 2008, Ibuka chairperson Théodore Simburudali accused a number of foreign observers of genocide denial. Among those targeted were former U.S. congresswoman Cynthia McKinney, former UN representative in Rwanda Roger Booh-Booh, writers Robin Philpot and Pierre Péan, and Spanish judge Andreu Merelles. Simburudali asked to "prevent these individuals that hide behind free speech in their countries to deny the massacres," adding that "any country that gives a platform to such people who deny the genocide cannot be separated from the views these people express."[13] What those who stood accused had generally done was to challenge the official story of the genocide. Deguine understandably wondered whether it was "still allowed to talk about Rwanda."[14]

DEALING WITH CRITICAL VOICES

Criticism routinely met with strongly worded rebuttals. Reports about human rights abuse were always received in the same terms. A few examples must suffice. After reports were almost simultaneously released by Amnesty International[15] and Human Rights Watch[16] in April 2000, the

---

[10] In addition to lecturing and writing critical texts, he published a book that became a *New York Times* best seller: P. Rusesabagina (with T. Zoellner), *An Ordinary Man. An Autobiography*, New York, Penguin Books, 2006.

[11] A. Ndahiro, P. Rutazibwa, *Hotel Rwanda or the Tutsi genocide as seen by Hollywood*, Paris, L'Harmattan, 2008. Ndahiro is an adviser to President Kagame and Rutazibwa is an RPF ideologue. A survey of the character assassination of Rusesabagina can be found in L. Waldorf, "Revisiting Hotel Rwanda: Genocide Ideology, Reconciliation, and Rescuers", *Journal of Genocide Research*, 11:1 (2009), pp. 114–118.

[12] "U.S. Ambassadors Accused of Dealing Arms", COA News, 15 September 2007.

[13] "Rwanda: Genocide Survivors Accuse U.S. Politician, UN Diplomat of Negationism," Kigali, RNA, 19 March 2008.

[14] H. Deguine, "Peut-on encore parler du Rwanda?", *Médias*, Spring 2008, No. 16, pp. 70–74.

[15] Amnesty International, *The Troubled Course of Justice*, London, 26 April 2000.

[16] Human Rights Watch, *Rwanda. The Search for Security and Human Rights Abuses*, New York, April 2000.

Rwandan ministry of foreign affairs claimed that this was part of a "political strategy" of opponents acting "under the cover of international human rights organisations."[17] The Human Rights Watch report was described as "very mean-spirited, grossly prejudiced and shallowly researched," and the organization was accused of "consciously waging a war of lies and defamation against the Rwandan government of national unity"; the report was a "patent and shameless attempt to interfere in the internal politics of Rwanda and an immoral attempt to enhance the political agendas of certain opponents." Barely a month later, a report by Human Rights Watch accusing the Rwandan army of massacring civilians and practicing rape at a large scale in the DRC[18] was said to be "malicious, baseless and biased" by the government spokesperson Joseph Bideri: "These are not human rights reports, but just political documents (...) These documents are authored by one Dr Alison Des Forges who wants to slander the Rwandan government in the face of the donor community."[19] Almost a decade later Des Forges, Human Rights Watch senior advisor for Africa, was declared persona non grata.[20] Human Rights Watch's May 2001 report *Uprooting the Rural Poor in Rwanda* was said to be "baseless and full of lies," and Human Rights Watch stood accused of disseminating "a propaganda that undermines human rights by promoting ethnic division among Rwandans." A month later, a report by Amnesty International on the human toll of the Rwandan occupation of eastern DRC[21] was characterized as "outright bias, lack of objectivity and outright lies." Amnesty's observations were "clearly unsubstantiated" and "a reflection of the longstanding antipathy that AI has demonstrated towards Rwanda." Using its "genocide credit" (cf. infra) to exploit the suffering of the victims for political ends, the government claimed that

---

[17] Kigali, PANA, 29 April 2000.

[18] *Eastern Congo Ravaged. Killing Civilians and Silencing Protest*, New York, May 2000.

[19] *The Monitor* (Kampala), 13 May 2000. Interestingly, during a visit to Kigali the U.K. minister for overseas development cooperation Clare Short made exactly the same accusations on Rwandan television.

[20] After having been refused access a first time at a land border crossing with Burundi in early September 2008, Des Forges landed on Kigali airport on December 3, 2008, to attend an international conference on judicial assistance, but was prevented from leaving the plane and forced to return to Brussels. General Prosecutor Ngoga later justified the measure by stating that "HRW's interference only benefited the *génocidaires*" ("HRW Chief Meets Government Officials", *The Sunday Times* [Kigali], 22 March 2009).

[21] *Democratic Republic of Congo. Rwandese-controlled East: Devastating Human Toll*, London, 19 June 2001.

Amnesty International's accusations were "an insupportable insult to the memory of the more than a million victims of the 1994 genocide."[22] Accusations of intimidation and fraud related to the 2003 elections gave rise to new angry statements. In a communiqué of May 11, 2003, of the Foreign Ministry, a Human Rights Watch report[23] was said to attempt to "sabotage the process of political normalisation (and) to counter the sending of aid." On May 13, the Rwandan (governmental) National Commission for Human Rights was "surprised by the lightness of the information (that) only aims at stirring up confusion in the minds of the Rwandans." Reacting to a report by Amnesty International,[24] the government wondered "whether AI's sources are not those who still harbour the philosophy of *génocidaires*" and failed to "understand the motive behind the baseless and malicious allegations contained in (the) report," adding that "AI, since 1994, has been relentless in rubbishing the efforts of the Rwandan government."[25]

Criticism from other sources received a similar treatment. Without addressing the substance of a report by the International Crisis Group,[26] the government accused the organization of waging an "anti-Rwanda misinformation campaign" and claimed that two of its researchers were working as "agents of the French government, whose hostile position towards Rwanda has never been a secret."[27] When Rwanda fell forty places in the 2006 ranking of Transparency International, which measures the degree of corruption, Kagame stated that "as far as we are concerned, this NGO is under influence of circles that are hostile to us (...). Transparency has ridiculed and discredited itself in this affair."[28] Reports by official multilateral bodies fared no better. In July 2000, an International Panel of Eminent Persons (IPEP) entrusted by the OAU to

---

[22] Government of Rwanda, "Response to the Amnesty International Report, Democratic Republic of Congo. Rwandese-controlled East: Devastating Human Toll", Kigali, n.d. (2001).

[23] Human Rights Watch, *Preparing for Elections: Tightening Control in the Name of Unity*, New York, May 2003.

[24] Amnesty International, *Rwanda: Run-up to Presidential Elections Marred by Threats and Harassment*, London, 22 August 2003.

[25] Government of Rwanda, "Response to Amnesty International's Report on Rwanda's Forthcoming Elections", Kigali, n.d. (2003).

[26] International Crisis Group, *Rwanda at the End of the Transition: A Necessary Political Liberalisation*, Nairobi and Brussels, 13 November 2002.

[27] Kigali, AFP, 17 November 2002.

[28] *Jeune Afrique-L'Intelligent*, No. 2404, 4 February 2007.

investigate the genocide published its report,[29] which contained a brief section highly critical of the RPF, accused of having committed large-scale massacres before, during, and after the genocide. In a press statement, President Kagame accused the IPEP of bias and of a lack of independence, and he claimed it had heavily relied on the "revisionist literature" of Gérard Prunier and this author.[30] Interestingly, President Kagame stated that "[w]here the investigation has remained within the mandate and terms of reference given by the OAU, the report has been relevant, informative and shows originality in its investigation," but he criticized the report where, in his view, it went "outside the mandate and terms of reference"[31], that is, where it mentioned RPF abuse, although nothing in its mandate prevented the IPEP from doing so. After an EU observer mission criticized aspects of the August 2003 presidential election, the chairperson of the National Election Commission claimed that the mission was "inspired by a spirit of bias, lacks the slightest objectivity, and simply wants to defend the interest of [opposition] candidate Faustin Twagiramungu."[32] When the report on Rwanda from the African Peer Review Mechanism (APRM) congratulated the country on a number of issues but was also critical on themes of political governance, Kagame lashed out at the experts: "People who made the peer review report were experts who studied in the best universities in the world. We gave them access to all the information they wanted, but I was so surprised when they came up with allegations that Rwanda has no political space"; he added that "[p]robably they don't understand the meaning of political space. Because if they knew, Rwanda would be an example."[33] As Rwanda was seeking admission to the Commonwealth, the NGO Commonwealth Human Rights Initiative (CHRI) published a critical report recommending that the international body should postpone its decision until Rwanda met Commonwealth standards.[34] *The New Times* published

---

[29] Organisation of African Unity, International Panel of Eminent Personalities to Investigate the 1994 Genocide in Rwanda and the Surrounding Events, *Rwanda: The Preventable Genocide*, Addis Ababa, 7 July 2000.

[30] We were part of the editorial committee for the report; the Rwandan government unsuccessfully attempted to have us excluded.

[31] "Rwandan Government Protests against New Report on the Genocide", *Africa Online*, 24 August 2000.

[32] "Présidentielle: le Rwanda mécontent des critiques européennes sur le scrutin", Kigali, AFP, 28 August 2003.

[33] "Enough Political Space – Kagame", *The New Times*, 27 January 2006.

[34] Commonwealth Human Rights Initiative, *Rwanda's Application for Membership of the Commonwealth: Report and Recommendations of the Commonwealth Human Rights Initiative*, Delhi, August 2009.

a scathing editorial very insulting for the main author of the report, Kenyan professor Yash Ghai. The report was said to be "without substance," and Ghai was lectured: "All you have to do is smear a whole nation and then waddle off."[35]

Critical voices from academia too are intimidated and treated with contempt. Several scholars have described the difficulties and even the anguish that accompany field research in Rwanda. Begley tells about pervasive control and threats by officials and about how fear became a recurring theme throughout her research, for both herself and her participants and translators.[36] Sommers recounts how the experience of another researcher, whose assistants were detained and who was given twenty-four hours to leave the country, had an impact on his own work.[37] The need to be careful extended to the writing of his initial draft: "I had internalized the restrictive environment within which I had carried out the field research in Rwanda. (…) I wrote the draft anticipating government criticism." More surprisingly, other foreign researchers and international agency officials did not criticize the Rwandan government for having shut down the previous research effort. The fault lay with the researcher who "had done things that researchers cannot do in Rwanda."[38] Davenport and Stam recalled,

Halfway into our presentation [at a conference in Kigali in November 2003], a military man in a green uniform stood up and interrupted. The Minister of Internal Affairs, he announced, took great exception to our findings. We were told that our passport numbers had been documented, that we were expected to leave the country the next day and that we would not be welcomed back into Rwanda – ever. Abruptly, our presentation was over, as was, it seemed, our fieldwork in Rwanda.[39]

The experience of Susan Thomson, who was told that her research was "against national unity and reconciliation" and "not the kind of research

---

[35] "The Boo-Boys Should Just Give it a Rest", *The New Times*, 21 July 2009; a diatribe of a similar nature can be found in "Prof. Ghai, You Missed a lot on Rwanda", *The New Times*, 9 October 2009.

[36] L. Begley, "The Other Side of Fieldwork: Experiences and Challenges of Conducting Research in the Border Area of Rwanda/Eastern Congo", *Anthropology Matters*, 11:2 (2009), pp. 1–11.

[37] One example is the following: "Was the same Rwandan man reading a thin Rwandan newspaper in three consecutive restaurants where I held meetings one afternoon in Kigali spying on me (when I asked the waitress in the third restaurant to offer him a beer for me, the man abruptly left)?" (M. Sommers, *Stuck. Rwandan Youth and the Struggle for Adulthood*, Athens, GA, and London, University of Georgia Press, 2012, p. 51).

[38] M. Sommers, *Stuck*, pp. 41–42.

[39] C. Davenport, A.C. Stam, "What Really Happened in Rwanda?," Miller-McCune Research Essay, 6 October 2009.

the government needed,"[40] had her passport confiscated and was sent to a
"re-education camp," is presented in Chapter 7.

A document signed by some fifty Rwanda researchers worldwide who
advocated the prosecution before the ICTR of RPF suspects (see
Chapter 8) provoked an angry reaction. The authors were "an alliance
of strange bed fellows found in the western academia, those who have
worked for the previous Genocide regime, including known negationists of
the Genocide against the Tutsi."[41] Quite strikingly, the U.K. ambassador
to Rwanda Nicholas Cannon strongly endorsed the regime's rejection of
criticism, such like that of the CHRI and Human Rights Watch. He called
the claims "unfair" and "unfounded, misplaced," and stated that the
authors of the CRHI report "have quite a limited experience of
Rwanda." Cannon went so far as to claim that, just prior to her death in
February 2009, Human Rights Watch's Alison Des Forges expressed support for Rwanda joining the Commonwealth,[42] a claim immediately
denied by Human Rights Watch.[43]

When the committee in charge of attributing the Mo Ibrahim Prize for
good governance in Africa decided not to propose a laureate for 2009,
Kagame took this personally. He stated that he was well placed to win the
award but that the Mo Ibrahim Foundation was "among the country's
possible detractors."[44] The government accused the authors of the *Mo
Ibrahim Index on Good Governance*, in which Rwanda was poorly
ranked, of "deliberately ignoring locally conducted but credible studies
before ranking the country."[45] Around the same time, *The Economist*
published an article on Sino-African relations in which it was said that
"Mr Kagame is sensitive to growing Western criticism of his increasingly
autocratic ways, so he too may start looking east."[46] The information
minister's reaction was swift: "Neither Paul Kagame nor China aided and

---

[40] S. Thomson, "Reeducation for Reconciliation. Participant Observations on Ingando," in
S. Straus, L. Waldorf (Eds.), *Remaking Rwanda. State Building and Human Rights after
Mass Violence*, Madison, The University of Wisconsin Press, 2011, p. 331.

[41] "'Group of Academics' or Have the HRW Genocide Negationists Come Out Clear?," *The
New Times*, 11 June 2009.

[42] "British Envoy Defends Kigali against Fierce Criticism", Kigali, RNA, 18 November 2009.

[43] Human Rights Watch, "Rwanda: None So Blind as Those That Will Not See", 26
November 2009.

[44] "Kagame Attacks Mo Ibrahim, Accuses West of 'Polluting Africa'", Kigali, RNA, 12
October 2009. Actually, Kagame could not be "well placed" for the prize, which is
awarded to former heads of state or government.

[45] "Mo Ibrahim Index Misleading – Gov't", *The New Times*, 13 October 2009.

[46] "Don't Worry about Killing People", *The Economist*, 15 October 2009.

abetted a genocidal regime in Rwanda: unfortunately, I cannot say the same for a number of Western countries."[47]

Criticism from allies was not received any better. The 2005 U.S. Department of State's *Country Reports on Human Rights Practices* met with an acerbic rebuttal. The report was said to be "riddled with inaccuracies and inconsistencies," and most of its observations were simply denied. Thus, "[t]here are no political detainees in Rwanda"; the accusation that political freedoms were limited was "a subjective opinion unsupported by evidence"; "Government considers the charge that Tutsis, particularly English speaking Tutsis, are favored contemptible and unworthy to be dignified with a reply," etc.[48] The United Nations was treated in much the same vein. When a report discussed in the Security Council[49] documented Rwanda's continuing support for the DRC rebel group CNDP, the government responded in its usual style, denouncing "the dangerous inaccuracies and outright lies" contained in the report, whose objectives were "malicious" and which was replete with accusations "resulting from hearsay, perceptions and stereotypes." As always, it was the others' fault: the United Nations and the international community "have failed to neutralise the persistent threat" posed by the FDLR, and they should "boldly acknowledge and confront their own failures and weaknesses."[50] Once again exploiting the "genocide credit," the minister of information claimed that the report was "a continuous ploy by powerful countries to disregard the truth when it comes to Rwanda [and] to hide their guilt after they abandoned Rwandans during the genocide."[51]

This incomplete yet tedious survey shows the systematic nature of the regime's reaction to criticism formulated by outside sources. Not one expression of concern was accepted, nor did the RPF engage in dialogue with critical voices. Quite the contrary, it vehemently denounced them, accused them of acting in bad faith, practiced character assassination, and systematically avoided debate. This heavy-handed approach was applied

---

[47] L. Mushikiwabo, "Rwanda: East-West Rumblings – What About Country's Burden of Choice?", *The New Times*, 20 October 2009.

[48] "Rwanda Response to the 2005 State Department Country Reports on Human Rights Practices, Released by the Bureau of Democracy, Human Rights and Labor on March 8, 2006", s.l. (Kigali), s.d. (2006).

[49] United Nations, Security Council, *Final Report of the Group of Experts on the Democratic Republic of the Congo*, S/2008/773, 12 December 2008.

[50] "Statement by the Government of Rwanda on the Report of the UN Group of Experts on the Democratic Republic of the Congo", Kigali, 15 December 2008.

[51] "UN Report 'Part of West Conspiracy against Rwanda'", Kigali, RNA, 15 December 2008.

to all: journalists, academics, international civil society, the United Nations, the OAU and bilateral partners, and human rights organizations.[52] To a large extent, this aggressive way of responding paid off, as many were intimidated enough to either keep silent or tune down criticism.

TACKLING THE WORLD

Rwanda is a small, landlocked, and extremely dependent country without much of a real economy. On average during the post-1994 period, it relied on international aid for about 25 percent of its GDP and for more than 50 percent of its budget. And yet, since 1994 it has tackled the rest of the world as if it were a global superpower. Its assertiveness has been based on three pillars: the genocide credit, a strong army, and – after 2000 – its decent bureaucratic governance. This defiance of the international community started from the early days of the new regime. Although Tutsi were being massively killed in April 1994, the RPF told foreign troops to leave the country within forty-eight hours. Failing this, they would be considered enemy combatants and engaged. Kagame told Dallaire that "[t]hose that were to die are already dead. If an intervention force is sent to Rwanda, we will fight it. Let us solve the problems of the Rwandans. The force is to protect the criminals in power."[53] During discussions about the redeployment of UNAMIR, three weeks into the genocide, this was the official RPF position: "The time for U.N. intervention is long past. The genocide is almost completed. (...) Consequently, the Rwandese Patriotic Front

---

[52] This aggressive stance did not diminish over time, quite the contrary, as a sample of reactions in 2011 shows. On foreign media, see "Is it Time to Turn our Back on Foreign Media?," *The Sunday Times*, 29 May 2011; J.P. Kimonyo, "It Is High Time Africans Came to their Senses on Democratization," *The New Times*, 14 December 2011. On human rights organisations, see "Africa Should Divorce Self-made World Policemen," *The New Times*, 4 June 2011; "Genocide Fugitives Shielded by Rights Groups – Ngoga," *The New Times*, 28 September 2011; "Double Standards by Rights Groups Promotes Impunity", *The New Times*, 29 September 2011. Kagame himself stated that Human Rights Watch and Amnesty International should "get lost": "I don't give a damn what they say or what they do" ("Rwanda President Kagame Says International Rights Groups Should 'Get Lost'", Kigali, Bloomberg, 23 June 2011). On international scholars, see "When Foreign 'Experts' Author our History", *The New Times*, 12 May 2011; "Mark Naftalin: Is there Another Rwanda in Your Part of the World Led by Another Paul Kagame?", *The New Times*, 18 July 2011; "Susan Thomson Distorts Rwanda's Reconciliation Story", *The New Times*, 30 July 2011; "Research Should Be about the Truth", *The New Times*, 6 August 2011; "Rwandans Impatient to Move On, Have no Time for Liars", *The New Times*, 20 December 2011.

[53] R. Dallaire, *Shake Hands with the Devil. The failure of Humanity in Rwanda*, Toronto, Random House Canada, 2003, p. 342.

hereby declares that it is categorically opposed to the proposed U.N. intervention force and will not under any circumstances cooperate in its setting up and operation." The statement also contained the line that was to be that of the RPF until today: "The international community was fore warned but did not find it possible or necessary to take any measures to prevent [the] massacres. (. . .) It has (. . .) fallen upon us to rescue many Rwandans from [the] atrocities. (. . .) The international community stood by and helplessly watched while hundreds of thousands of innocent citizens perished."[54] After UNAMIR 2 was eventually deployed, the RPF made its life as difficult as possible.[55] A report of the UN secretary-general noted that

[a]crymonious criticism of the international community in general, and UNAMIR in particular, has also continued unabated (. . .). [T]he Rwandese Patriotic Army has continued to deny UNAMIR access to parts of the country, has searched and seized UNAMIR vehicles and other equipment and has participated in anti-UNAMIR demonstrations. (. . .) There have been continuing difficulties over troop rotations, with UNAMIR personnel being delayed or denied entry at Kigali airport.[56]

This assertive behavior was to set the trend toward a compliant international community.

A major conflict with the international community expressed itself through constant wrangling with the ICTR. Rwanda, which in 1994 happened to be a nonpermanent member of the UN Security Council, voted against the resolution establishing the ICTR because, among other reasons, its statute did not provide for the death penalty, its seat was not located in Kigali, and its competence *ratione temporis* covered the whole of 1994, that is, including the period after the RPF seized power.[57] More

---

[54] Rwandese Patriotic Front, "Statement by the Political Bureau of the Rwandese Patriotic Front on the Proposed Deployment of a U.N. Intervention Force in Rwanda," New York, 30 April 1994, signed by Gerald Gahima and Claude Dusaidi. At that moment, hundreds of thousands of Tutsi were still alive, and the genocide was far from "completed." We have seen earlier that the RPF did not do much to "rescue many Rwandans from the atrocities."

[55] Force commander General Dallaire recalled that "the Americans put obstacle after obstacle in our way, with the British playing a coy supporting role. (. . .) If I had been a suspicious soul, I could have drawn a link between the obstructive American position and the RPF's refusal to accept a sizeable UNAMIR 2" (R.Dallaire, *Shake hands*, p. 364).

[56] United Nations, Security Council, *Report of the Secretary-General on the United Nations Assistance Mission to Rwanda*, S/1995/457, 4 June 1995, para. 7–8.

[57] During the debate in the Security Council, Rwanda raised seven reasons for its opposition to the resolution (Security Council, 3453rd meeting, 8 November 1994, S/PV.3453, pp. 13–16). On the obstacles the new Rwandan regime put on the road towards creating the ICTR, see D. Scheffer, *All the Missing Souls. A Personal History of the War Crimes*

fundamentally, the regime disliked a process it could not control: "it has no sympathy for the international community's desire to reaffirm its morality. Rather, it cares about the establishment of its own power, stability and control."[58] The main cause for the troubled relations with the ICTR lay in the Rwandan attempts to – successfully – impose the vision of victors' justice on the institution.

On November 3, 1999, the ICTR Appeals Chamber rejected the indictment of genocide suspect Jean-Bosco Barayagwiza on procedural grounds and ordered his immediate release. The reaction of Kigali was furious. The cabinet "vehemently contested the decision" and argued that "[t]he Rwandan people cannot tolerate this decision, which was the result of complete incompetence by the prosecution." If the Appeals Chamber did not reconsider its decision, the government "would take other measures."[59] Rwanda suspended its cooperation with the ICTR and increased the pressure by refusing a visa to Prosecutor Del Ponte and by preventing witnesses from testifying in Arusha.[60] When she argued the case for review before the appeals chamber, Del Ponte acknowledged the role played by political pressure: "Justice as dispensed by this Tribunal was paralysed. (. . .) Due account has to be taken of the fact that, whether we like it or not, our ability to continue proceedings and investigations depends on the goodwill of the government of Rwanda."[61] Using her mother tongue, she claimed that, in case the decision was not reviewed, *"possiamo*

Tribunals, Princeton, NJ, and Oxford, Princeton University Press, 2012, pp. 80–84. Revealingly, during the negotiations the RPF proposed a competence *ratione temporis* from April 6 to July 15, 1994, which meant that "[t]hey obviously were prepared to sacrifice the genocide planning period prior to April 6 in order to avoid liability for themselves after July 15" (*idem*, p. 81). China abstained in light of Rwanda's opposition, and feared that "[w]ithout [such] cooperation and support from the Rwanda Government, it will be difficult for the Tribunal to perform its duties in an effective manner" (Security Council, 3453rd meeting, 8 November 1994, S/PV.3453, p. 11). This was indeed to prove one of the ICTR's major weaknesses. During a meeting of the Security Council on 22 February 1995, Rwanda again made things clear: "The Government of Rwanda [...] wishes to cooperate to the extent that cooperation is possible and to the extent that the interests of the Rwandan people [read: the RPF] are not put at risk" (Security Council, 3502nd meeting, 22 February 1995, S/PV.3502, p. 2).

[58] P. Uvin, C. Mironko, "Western and Local Approaches to Justice in Rwanda," *Global Governance*, 9:219 (2003), p. 221.

[59] Hirondelle News Agency, "Rwanda Slams Decisions to Free Jean-Bosco Barayagwiza," Arusha, 6 November 1999.

[60] Hirondelle News Agency, "ICTR Prosecutor to Ask for Review of Appeal Court Decision, as Rwanda Refuses Her a Visa," Arusha, 22 November 1999.

[61] Hirondelle News Agency, "UN Prosecutor Says Appeals Court Decision on Barayagwiza Violated Victims' Rights," Arusha, 22 February 2000.

chiudere la baracca" ("we can close the shop").[62] Although the "new facts" needed to ground its decision were flimsy, the Appeals Chamber duly revised its earlier ruling on March 31, 2000.[63] The Barayagwiza affair was just the first of a long series of generally successful attempts by Kigali to interfere in the international judicial process, just as it did domestically (cf. Chapter 8), and Del Ponte herself was to be the main victim.[64]

In early 2002, the most influential survivors' association, Ibuka, over which the government had established control in 2000 (cf. supra), called on survivors to boycott the ICTR. The relations between the government and the Tribunal got worse when Del Ponte announced on April 4, 2002, that she hoped to issue the first indictments against RPF suspects before the end of the year. She complained about the lack of cooperation on the part of Rwanda and added that President Kagame did not honor his promises; as a result, the Office of the Prosecutor was forced to conduct its investigations into massacres by the RPF outside of Rwanda.[65] A few days later, ten prosecution witnesses refused to travel to Arusha, thus forcing the prosecutor to strike them off the witness list. Although the reason given for this refusal to cooperate was the treatment of witnesses, the prosecutor stated that "the true reason is to be found elsewhere. (...) We have good reasons to believe that powerful elements within Rwanda strongly oppose

[62] T. Cruvellier, *Le Tribunal des vaincus. Un Nuremberg pour le Rwanda?*, Paris, Calmann-Lévy, 2006, p. 174.

[63] Although the Appeals Chamber insisted that "the Tribunal is an independent judicial body, whose decisions are exclusively based on justice and law and if a government for some reason decided not to cooperate with the Tribunal, it would seize the Security Council" (Jean-Bosco Barayagwiza c/Le Procureur, Arrêt [Demande du Procureur en révision ou réexamen], 31 March 2000, ICTR-97–19-AR72), it left most observers skeptical. According to Schabas, "[i]n view of the lamentable reasoning in the (...) decision, the judges' insistence that Rwanda's pledge not to cooperate with the Tribunal – a threat echoed by the prosecutor at the February 20 hearing on the review motion – had no bearing in their deliberations was, and remains, unconvincing" (W. Schabas, "Barayagwiza v. Prosecutor [Decision, and Decision [Prosecutor's Request for Review or Reconsideration]]," *American Journal of International Law*, 94 (2000), pp. 570–571). Luc Côté, a former member of the OTP, concurred: "This political-judicial saga will darken the history of the ICTR, leaving a perception of a certain lack of independence" (L. Côté, "Le Tribunal Pénal International pour le Rwanda : Un tribunal dans la tourmente", in F. Reyntjens, S. Marysse (Eds.), *Dix ans de transitions conflictuelles. L'Afrique des grands lacs. Annuaire 2005–2006*, Paris, L'Harmattan, 2006, p. 428).

[64] On the Barayagwiza affair see K.C. Moghalu, *Rwanda's Genocide. The Politics of Global Justice*, New York-Houndmills, Palgrave MacMillan, 2005, pp. 101–123; J. Meierhenrich, *Lawfare. Gacaca Jurisdictions in Rwanda*, forthcoming with Cambridge University Press.

[65] C. McGreal, "Genocide Tribunal Ready to Indict First Tutsis: Rwanda Is Blocking Investigations of Former Rebels Despite Pledges, Prosecutor Says", *The Guardian*, 5 April 2002.

the investigation (...) of crimes allegedly committed by members of the RPF in 1994."[66] In her report of July 24, 2002, to the UN Security Council, Del Ponte denounced the lack of cooperation by the Rwandan authorities. On the same day, Rwandan prosecutor general Gérald Gahima questioned the usefulness of the ICTR and rejected any idea to prosecute RPF suspects: the RPA saved the nation and any attempt to indict one of its officers would be tantamount to an attack against the nation's unity.[67] Quite simply, RPF crimes were "a black box that no one dares open."[68]

By the end of 2002, the Rwandan government had decided that Del Ponte had to go, and it increased the pressure. In late November, it announced that Del Ponte "has lost the moral authority to prosecute cases linked to the genocide"[69] and on December 12 asked that she be removed. Open warfare now started. Reacting to the Rwandan criticism that she was "politicising" her office, Del Ponte called this "an unjustified and baseless accusation. It was ridiculous and petty. They should give the real reasons since everyone knows them. What's more, they did share them with me privately during our meetings."[70] Indeed, she later recalled that during a conversation with Kagame at the end of 2002, he told her, "as if he was giving an order," to limit herself to the genocide and to leave it to his government to deal with the soldiers: "Your work creates political problems for me and will destabilise the country."[71] As the press relayed contradicting information that the OTP signed a U.S. brokered agreement with the Rwandan government renouncing to further investigate RPF abuse,[72] Del Ponte's spokesperson stated on July 1, 2003, that the investigations continued and that "the Prosecutor cannot conclude any

[66] Hirondelle News Agency, "UN Prosecutor Rallies UK Support", Arusha, 3 December 2002.

[67] "Rwanda Questions Usefulness of UN Genocide Court", New York (UN), Reuters, 24 July 2002.

[68] Unattributable interview in S. Brown, "The Rule of Law and the Hidden Politics of Transitional Justice in Rwanda", in C. Lehka Sriram, O. Martin-Ortega, J. Herman (Eds.), *Peacebuilding and Rule of Law in Africa. Just Peace?*, Abingdon, Routledge, 2011, p. 188.

[69] Gouvernement du Rwanda, *Communiqué de presse*, Kigali, 21 November 2002.

[70] "Exclusive Interview with Carla Del Ponte", Arusha, Hirondelle News Agency, 19 December 2002.

[71] Interview in *La Repubblica*, 12 September 2003.

[72] At the time, the United States, under the stewardship of Pierre-Richard Prosper, formerly of the OTP who had become the U.S. ambassador-at-large for war crimes issues, was indeed busy burying the "special investigations." A deal made in May 2003 included that RPF suspects were not to be tried by the ICTR, but that Rwanda would take care of them. Del Ponte refused the deal, and domestic prosecutions never materialised, except for one whitewash trial in 2008 (see Chapter 8).

agreement with any government whatsoever, in contradiction to its mandate."[73] A few weeks later, the OTP claimed that Rwanda was exercising discreet pressures on the UN Security Council not to renew Del Ponte's mandate, which was due to expire in September. Her spokesperson stated that "the objective is to prevent the Prosecutor to investigate crimes possibly committed by members of the RPA."[74] On July 29, the UN general secretary, with the support of Kigali's allies the United States and the United Kingdom, proposed to maintain Del Ponte as prosecutor of the International Criminal Tribunal for the Former Yugoslavia (ICTY), but to appoint a separate prosecutor for the ICTR. Apart from the fact that this move appeared to shield Rwanda, it also made sense in managerial terms, as the running of both OTPs (ICTY and ICTR) by the same prosecutor based in The Hague had created many problems in the past, and left the OTP of the ICTR as something of an orphan. Rwanda immediately supported the proposal and urged the Security Council to adopt it.[75] Without surprise, the Security Council endorsed the proposal, and Rwanda finally got rid of Del Ponte.[76] Her successor, Gambian judge Hassan Bubacar Jallow, abandoned the investigations against RPF/RPA suspects (also, see the following discussion and Chapter 8).[77]

Another major clash with the United Nations occurred with regard to a mapping exercise on serious violations of human rights and international humanitarian law in the DRC conducted on behalf of the High Commission on Human Rights. Like other countries concerned, Rwanda received the draft report in June 2010. In a letter of August 8 to Secretary General Ban Ki-moon, Foreign Minister Louise Mushikiwabo claimed that the report was "not only fatally flawed but an embarrassment to the United Nations." She denounced "errors and omissions," "the Team's reliance on

---

[73] Fondation Hirondelle, "Le TPIR n'a pas renoncé à poursuivre les membres de l'APR, selon un porte-parole," Arusha, 1 July 2003.

[74] "Le Rwanda veut écarter Mme Del Ponte de son poste de procureur (porte-parole)," The Hague, AFP, 24 July 2003.

[75] Fondation Hirondelle, "Kigali soutient la nomination d'un procureur distinct pour le TPIR," Arusha, 29 July 2003.

[76] Del Ponte's spokesperson detailed this shameful saga in F. Hartmann, *Paix et châtiment: Les guerres secrètes de la politique et de la justice internationales*, Paris, Flammarion, 2007, pp. 262–277. Del Ponte confirmed the manoeuvring of Rwanda, but did not detail the circumstances of her removal (C. Del Ponte, *La caccia. Io e i criminali di guerre*, Milan, Feltrinelli, 2008).

[77] More details on the "axing" of Del Ponte can be found in K.C. Moghalu, *Rwanda's Genocide*, pp. 125–151. Moghalu argues that both institutional (improving the management of the OTP) and political (shielding the RPF) reasons came into play: "a case of two simultaneous truths" (p. 137).

the work of certain NGOs," and the use of "the lowest evidentiary stand-ard to investigate claims." The letter's conclusion was very threatening: "attempts to take action on this report – either through its release or leaks to the media – will force us to withdraw from Rwanda's various commitments to the United Nations, especially in the area of peacekeeping." This obviously referred to the 3,500-strong Rwandan contingent in Darfur. Probably because of fears that this blackmail might work, the report was leaked to the press. On August 27, *Le Monde* published large extracts that were particularly damning for Rwanda, said to have committed war crimes, crimes against humanity, and possibly genocide.[78]

The reaction of Kigali was furious. In its habitual style, the government called the text "malicious, offensive and ridiculous." "The report is a dangerous and irresponsible document that under the guise of human rights can only achieve instability in the Great Lakes Region and under-mine ongoing efforts to stabilize the region," an invocation of the classical stability versus accountability argument. As on other occasions, it was the others' fault: "It is immoral and unacceptable that the United Nations, an organization that failed outright to prevent genocide in Rwanda and the subsequent refugee crisis (...), now accuses the army that stopped the genocide of committing atrocities in the Democratic Republic of Congo."[79] Echoing her letter of August 8, Mushikiwabo announced that Rwandan troops were on standby to be pulled out of UN operations if the report were published.[80] Faced with this attempt at blackmail, Ban Ki-moon traveled to Kigali to save both the report and the Rwandan con-tingent in Sudan by ensuring that the states pinpointed in the report were to have the opportunity to submit their observations before the official pub-lication.[81] According to UN sources, Rwanda accepted not to withdraw its troops in case the report were published; in exchange, the UN would not immediately refer the report for judicial treatment.[82]

---

[78] "Afrique: l'ONU ne veut pas laisser impunis dix ans de massacres en RDC"; "Une longue série d'obstacles à la justice et à la vérité," *Le Monde*, 27 August 2010.

[79] "Statement by the Government of Rwanda on leaked draft UN report on DRC," Kigali, 27 August 2010.

[80] "Peacekeepers on Standby for Pull Out – Mushikiwabo," *The New Times*, 1 September 2010.

[81] One cannot fail to note the absurdity of the secretary general's genuflection: rather than deciding to withdraw an army that was strongly suspected of massive human rights abuse, he was begging to maintain that very army to protect human rights in Darfur.

[82] "Dispute Over U.N. Report Evokes Rwandan Déjà Vu," *The New York Times*, 30 September 2010.

In order to avoid publication, the regime then embarked on a campaign aimed at discrediting the report. It went at great lengths, even by having victims of RPA massacres say that the report was but a web of lies. Four female Hutu MPs who lived in the refugee camps in the DRC until late 1996 were led to declare that "[n]o Hutu civilians were murdered by RPA" in Kibumba and Mugunga, where, however, everyone knew massacres had occurred and were well documented. MP Fortunate Nyiramadirida who lived at Mugunga camp stated, "There were no civilians who died at the hands of RPA. Those are manipulative fabrications. Look, I am a Hutu, a wife of an ex-FAR officer, why didn't they kill me when they had a chance to do so?"[83] What these victims of RPA abuse were forced to declare was part of the structural violence so prevalent in Rwanda. Against all evidence, General Rwarakabije, former FAR and "integrated" FDLR officer, stated that "[W]hat they say in the report is not what I saw."[84] In the meantime, just as it did to combat the application of universal jurisdiction in third countries (see Chapter 8), Rwanda tried to rally the support of the African Union.[85] On the eve of publication, the government reminded that this "flawed and dangerous" report could threaten regional stability.[86]

The report came out on October 1, 2010.[87] The reaction of Kigali was foreseeable. The report "is flawed and disregards the facts"; it was claimed to be "manipulation, contradiction, omissions and overall flawed methodology," "a blueprint for revisionism," "a desperate plan to assassinate the truth and run away from responsibility," and so on.[88] The substance of the report was briefly discussed in Chapter 4, and I argue in Chapter 8 that it is possibly the last opportunity to break with victor's justice in the Great Lakes region.

The regime reacted in a similar vein when the UN Group of Experts accused Rwanda of supporting a new rebellion in the DRC in 2012 (see the

---

[83] "MPs who Lived in DRC Camps Dismiss UN Report," *The New Times*, 4 September 2010.

[84] "Gen. Rwarakabije Slams UN report," *The New Times*, 8 September 2010.

[85] "African Union to Protest UN 'Genocide' Report in New York," Kigali, RNA, 19 September 2010.

[86] "UN DRC Report Threatens Regional Security," *The New Times*, 1st October 2010.

[87] United Nations, High Commissioner for Human Rights, *Democratic Republic of the Congo, 1993–2003. Report of the Mapping Exercise Documenting the Most Serious Violations of Human Rights and International Humanitarian Law Committed within the Territory of the Democratic Republic of the Congo between March 1993 and June 2003*, Geneva, August 2010.

[88] "Premier Makuza Slams UN Report," *The New Times*, 2 October 2010; "The UN Mapping Exercise Report Will not Deter Rwanda's Progress," *The New Times*, 4 October 2010; "Researcher Dismisses UN report," *The New Times*, 5 October 2010.

following discussion). As often shifting the blame to others, Kagame stated that "this recent problem was created by the international community, our partners and because they don't listen. (. . .) They are so arrogant that they don't listen."[89] In its response to the report, the government claimed that "the release of the addendum served as the latest act of a carefully orchestrated media and political strategy to cast Rwanda as the villain."[90]

Apart from the United Nations, the regime also engaged in open warfare with other international players, sometimes even with its own backers. Particularly from 2002 on, Kagame became increasingly irritated by criticism, while feeling limited in his response by Rwanda's dependency on aid. In August 2002, he insisted that "Rwandans must stop being dependent" of the international community whose attitude "that compounds our problems emerge from indifference, ignorance and malice." This came just after the United States blocked a disbursement for Rwanda's Poverty Reduction and Growth Facility (PRGF) with the IMF. Without specifically mentioning Washington, Kagame stated that "there may be abuse by some board members of these institutions [IMF, World Bank]" and he complained about the "injustices perpetuated by some of the big powers."[91] A month later, Belgium was lectured in less diplomatic terms, after Foreign Minister Louis Michel told a newspaper that "the exceptional situation (of Rwanda) as a result of the 1994 genocide should not be eternally translated in lack of democracy." Rwandan government spokesperson Joseph Bideri reacted, saying, "Rwanda has nothing to learn about democracy from Louis Michel or Belgium (. . .). Democracy is proceeding in Rwanda, fortunately without the contribution of Belgium (. . .). If Mr. Michel is in search of colonies, Rwanda should be the last of his centres of interest."[92] The message got across very well. A year later, Michel was the only foreign official to applaud the electoral exercise of 2003, although according to all independent sources it was grossly flawed (cf. supra). On August 26, 2003, he stated that he was "confident that the vote is the premise of a new democratic era in the country's history." After

---

[89] Republic of Rwanda, "Speech by H.E. Paul Kagame, President of the Republic of Rwanda, at the Inauguration of the Senior Command and Staff College and Course," Nyakinama, 23 July 2012.

[90] Republic of Rwanda, Ministry of Foreign Affairs and Cooperation, *Rwanda's response to the allegations contained in the addendum to the UN Group of Experts interim report,* Kigali, 27 July 2012, p. 1.

[91] Speech at the opening of the Rwanda National Security Workshop with Civil Society, Kigali, 8 August 2002.

[92] Kigali, AFP, 11 September 2002.

the elections, he disavowed the EU election observers (about whom he wondered whether they "know the precise context" and who "render judgments that are sometimes a bit fast") and explained that "these elections have yielded results that without the slightest doubt cannot be contested."[93]

Showing a great deal of nervousness about external pressures to open up political space, Kagame echoed Robert Mugabe when demanding that the donors let developing countries determine their own future: "What is political space? What is the standard and who sets the standards?."[94] His assertiveness was, however, tempered by opportunism. He accused ministers and other top government officials of "being arrogant when dealing with donors instead of expressing the kind of humility necessary to convince development partners that Rwandans badly need their money." He then tipped the officials on how to deal with donors:

When I meet them I humble myself and make sure the language I use reflects my true economic needs. Calling them sirs when I have to is not a problem. (. . .) Yes, some of them might think that you are a fool, but by the time they realize you are not, you have already got what you wanted from them. And since they will have given it willingly, they will not feel hard-done by you.[95]

In a widely commented speech at a genocide commemoration on April 7, 2007, he took to task religious faiths, local associations, and the international community, which "needs to confess and plead guilty." "Some of its members" – clearly not just the usual culprit France – "have played an important role in the genocide." At the same occasion he regretted "that we have not had enough time to deal with those people who have escaped": this reference to refugees and IDPs was particularly shocking, as he pronounced these words in Murambi, close to the site of the Kibeho massacre of April 1995.

Kagame's unease about international criticism and the country's dependency on aid led him to develop an increasingly radical discourse. In December 2008 he stated that "[w]e (. . .) must find an immediate

---

93 Kigali, AFP, 9 October 2003. Michel, an MEP by then, was a guest of honor at the celebrations of the RPF's silver jubilee in December 2012.
94 "I Never Wanted to be President – Kagame," *The New Times*, 18 January 2006. He did of course not mention the fact that foreign aid accounted for 50 percent of the national budget and that this aid allowed to pay him a monthly salary of €15,000, in addition to numerous material advantages (Presidential Decree Nr. 52/01, 12 October 2006).
95 "Kagame Attacks Cabinet Ministers", *The New Times*, 14 February 2006.

solution to handouts" and "come out of the reliance on foreign aid."[96] He developed a strongly nationalist language in his end of year speech, in which he accusing the West of blocking "our development out of vested interest to keep us backward."[97] In March 2009, Kagame invited the Zambian economist Dambisa Moyo who just published a book highly critical of international aid,[98] to hear from her how Rwanda could become self-sufficient. He detailed his thoughts in an op-ed published in the *Financial Times* of London,[99] writing that the central question was when to put an end to aid and how to do so. In mid-2012, when some donors suspended part of their aid after the publication by the UN group of experts of a report on Rwandan involvement in support of a new rebellion in the DRC (see the following discussion), the government launched the Agaciro Development Fund[100] aimed at generating domestic finance for development. Although the aim of self-reliance is appealing, Rwanda is, however, in no position to embark on such a course, and Kagame understood the fragility of his position very well. After an article appeared in the *New Times* of May 26, 2009, under the title "Shun Aid, Kagame Tells Youths," Kagame's office was quick in pointing out that the article "confused Rwandans and the world on President Kagame's views on development and the necessary role of aid in that process." He was opposed to "bad aid," but "fully appreciates the role of good aid."[101] Next to nationalist rhetoric, another way of countering external criticism was the claim that Rwandans know best what is good for them.[102] Although, according to extensive field research,[103] many Rwandans do not share his position, Kagame portrayed himself as the spokesperson for his people. Thus, rebutting criticism of the genocide ideology law, he stated that "nobody has the right to undermine what happens in Rwanda": "We've lived this

---

[96] "Kagame Tells Government Departments 'Aid Must Stop'", Kigali, RNA, 18 December 2008.

[97] "Kagame Tells Nation to Beware of Foreign Exploitation", Kigali, RNA, 31 December 2008.

[98] D. Moyo, *Dead Aid. Why Aid Is not Working and How there Is a Better Way for Africa*, New York, Farrar, Straus and Giroux, 2009.

[99] P. Kagame, "Africa Has to Find its own Road to Prosperity", *The Financial Times*, 7 May 2009.

[100] *Agaciro* is Kinyarwanda for "dignity." The first information available suggests that many contributions are compulsory, thus turning the *Agaciro* fund into a taxation system, just like contributions made to the RPF.

[101] "Shun (Bad) Aid Dependency," *The New Times*, 28 May 2009.

[102] "We Know What Is Best for Us, Kagame Says," *The New Times*, 13 February 2010.

[103] Well summarized in S. Straus, L. Waldorf (Eds.), *Remaking Rwanda*. Also see Chapter 7 in this book.

life. We've lived the consequences. So, we understand it better than anyone from anywhere else."[104] In his April 2010 genocide commemoration speech, he expressed "contempt" for those criticizing him, called his opponents "hooligans," and again claimed to speak for all Rwandans: "who can tell us what is good for us and what is bad for us? – We know it already."[105]

Donors' suggestions that Rwanda should engage in negotiations with the (armed) opposition met with robust reactions. In early 1998, the Japanese ambassador encouraged the government to "forget hatred, distrust and pride," so that "the fighting may cease and negotiations may begin." The response was like lightning. On 29 January, Minister of Foreign Affairs Anastase Gasana stated that he was "surprised to hear the ambassador of a country friendly towards Rwanda (...) request negotiations with criminal groups, which should be brought before the courts," adding that "given the historical heritage of Japan, it is regrettable that Mr. Shinsuke proposes negotiations with the forces of genocide."[106] Four days after this diatribe, the Japanese government announced that "it did not speak out in favour of a negotiation between Rwanda and the rebels"; it had been a "misunderstanding."[107] When in April 2008 Belgian foreign minister Karel De Gucht advocated a dialogue with the FDLR, the reaction was equally furious. Foreign Minister Museminali stated that "this declaration by a Belgian official is scandalous (...) and of a nature that could feed another diplomatic scandal,"[108] probably a reference to the severing of relations with France in late 2006 (cf. infra).

Even close allies sometimes got a rough ride. After the U.S. ambassador criticized the government's election year abuses, particularly the April 2003 disappearances, government officials retaliated by refusing to meet with her and other embassy staff.[109] In early 2004, the U.K.'s DFID scrapped its civil society program, because it required the office to "actively pursue human rights," something that was "too confrontational."[110]

---

[104] "Angry Paul Kagame Says Criticism of Rwandan Genocide Law Is 'Nonsense'," Kigali, RNA, 5 April 2010.

[105] Speech by H.E. Paul Kagame, President of the Republic of Rwanda, at the 16th commemoration of the genocide against the Tutsi, 7 April 2010.

[106] Kigali, AFP, 29 January 1998.

[107] Kigali, AFP, 4 February 1998.

[108] "Rwanda: Kigali critique la proposition belge de médiation avec les FDLR," Kigali, Panapress, 30 April 2008.

[109] Front Line Rwanda, *Disappearances, Arrests, Threats, Intimidation of Human Rights Defenders 2001–2004*, Dublin, 2005, p. 102.

[110] *Idem*, p. 105.

After the EU expressed concern about the way in which Liprodhor was eliminated (cf. supra), stating that "individuals were publically accused on the basis of insufficiently checked information,"[111] Minister of Regional Cooperation Protais Musoni called the EU declaration "a kind of unacceptable intimidation."[112]

Analyses by international donor agencies that did not fit the government discourse were aggressively suppressed. A costly multicountry study launched by the World Bank in 2005 sought to collect data on determinants of movements out of poverty; it included observations of participatory decision making at local and national levels. Six months into the study, the Rwandan security forces seized at least half the data because "genocide ideology" was present in the study's design and content, and Rwandan and foreign researchers were questioned by the police. The World Bank was forced to destroy all data and to abandon the research project altogether.[113] In August 2007, the UNDP published its National Human Development Report on Rwanda.[114] As it contained a number of observations critical of government policy, the report was rejected by the cabinet, which asked the minister of Finance and Economic Planning James Musoni to refute it officially. Musoni was, however, the chairperson of the steering committee that oversaw the drafting, and he signed the foreword to the report. He claimed that he only saw a draft and blamed "the inaccuracies (...) on additional interpretations by the author." About the Swedish main author and a Rwandan university lecturer involved in the process, Musoni added, "We have blacklisted them and won't associate them in any business."[115] The UNDP was forced to issue a five-page "Addendum-Corrigendum," which contained twenty-eight points on which "inaccuracies" were put right. When in May 2006, the World Food Programme stated that almost 300,000 Rwandans needed urgent humanitarian assistance due to famine, the government strongly dismissed the assessment, describing it as "mere fabrication, opportunistic and serving selfish interests. (...) WFP's claims are just politics intended to achieve

---

[111] Kigali, Hirondelle News Agency, 8 October 2004.

[112] Kigali, IRIN, 12 October 2004.

[113] For more details on this saga, see B. Ingelaere, "Do We Understand Life after Genocide? Center and Periphery in the Construction of Knowledge in Postgenocide Rwanda," *African Studies Review*, 53:1 (2010), pp. 49–50. It is interesting to note that the World Bank did not encounter similar problems in the other countries involved in the study, although some of them (Afghanistan, China) were far from perfect democracies.

[114] UNDP, *Turning Vision 2020 into Reality. From Recovery to Sustainable Human Development*, Kigali, 2007.

[115] "I Never Read UN Report before Launch – Musoni", *The New Times*, 24 August 2007.

nothing but to destroy the country. (...) They are just looking for assistance on our behalf to keep them operating in the country."[116] A few days later, the world march against hunger, organized worldwide by the WFP, was cancelled in Kigali "for unclear reasons."[117]

COUNTERING FRENCH AND SPANISH JUDICIAL MOVES

The most intense conflict was with France, an ally of the former regime that the RPF claimed to have been actively involved in the genocide. Rwandan accusations remained vague, and the dispute was diffuse until on March 10, 2004, *Le Monde* published elements from a French judicial inquiry into the downing of President Habyarimana's plane, an attack that triggered the genocide. As the investigation pointed an accusing finger at the RPF and even Kagame in person, the reaction was swift. Minister of Foreign Affairs Charles Murigande issued a "categorical denial" and announced the line of defence Rwanda was to systematically adopt: "These allegations must be placed in a certain context: everyone knows well the role France has played in the Rwandan genocide. (...) It is France which has trained the genocidal army and the militias that have committed genocide."[118] In an interview with Radio France Internationale (RFI) on March 16, Kagame damaged relations further by stating that France had offered weapons and training to those guilty of genocide.[119] During the tenth genocide commemoration ceremony in Kigali on April 7, he denounced the "shameful attitude" of the international community and lashed out again at France: "[The French] have knowingly trained and armed the soldiers and militiamen who were about to commit genocide, and they knew that they were going to commit genocide." Directly addressing the French vice-minister of foreign affairs who was present at the ceremony, Kagame said that the French "have the audacity to stay here without apologising."[120]

---

[116] "Hunger: Government Refutes WFP claims," *The New Times*, 14 May 2006. Interestingly, during the same period, the Burundian government recognized the problem in a region that straddles both countries, and requested international assistance for famine victims ("Nkurunziza Urges Burundians to Assist Famine Victims", Bujumbura, PANA, 20 February 2006).

[117] "Report d'une manifestation du PAM à Kigali contre la faim", Kigali, PANA, 22 May 2006.

[118] Brussels, AFP, 10 March 2004.

[119] Kigali, Reuters, 16 March 2004.

[120] "France Blamed as Rwanda marks genocide date", *The Guardian*, 8 April 2004.

When, in November 2006, French judge Bruguière issued arrest warrants against nine Rwandan officers suspected of having been involved in the attack against the presidential plane, Kigali immediately broke off diplomatic relations with France and opened two backfires in the form of so-called independent commissions of inquiry. The report of the first, known as the "Mucyo Commission,"[121] which was made public on August 5, 2008, "found" that France had been actively engaged in the genocide, both before and while it took place. As the name of the commission "entrusted with the task of collecting evidence of the implication of the French state" showed, it had a clear mission that it did not, however, accomplish in a convincing fashion. France stood accused of military assistance to the old regime, direct participation in combat, training of interahamwe militia, and assistance to the putting in place of "civilian self-defence," violence and ethnic segregation at roadblocks, sexual aggressions and rape, conducting Opération Turquoise,[122] and collaboration with those responsible for the genocide after their departure in exile. Even before the report was published, Kagame announced that French leaders could be prosecuted for crimes committed in Rwanda. The Mucyo report asked the government "to reserve itself the right to lay complaints against the French state" and "to support any action (...) of victims who wish to bring cases for the prejudice caused by actions of the French state and/or its agents in Rwanda." On November 12, 2008, in the wake of the arrest of Rose Kabuye (see the following discussion), Kagame confirmed that "our judges (...) can issue arrest warrants against people (...) in France," and the office of the Rwandan general prosecutor indicated that indictments against twenty-three of the thirty-three French political and military officials mentioned in the report "are being finalised, and arrest warrants may be issued at any moment."[123] They never materialized.

The Mucyo report was problematic for several reasons. Very selective in the use of sources and citations, it avoided mentioning any responsibility of the RPF in the events leading up to the genocide. It quoted many witnesses, but it was not possible to ascertain under which conditions they were interviewed, while it was, of course, impossible to cross-examine them.

---

[121] République du Rwanda, Commission nationale indépendante chargée de rassembler les preuves montrant l'implication de l'Etat français dans le génocide perpétré au Rwanda en 1994, *Rapport final*, Kigali, 15 November 2007.

[122] During which members of the French military alledgedly did not only allow the exfiltration of genocide leaders, but also were accused of direct or indirect participation in the killings of Tutsi, torture, rape, and pillage.

[123] "Le Rwanda menace de faire arrêter des Français," *Le Monde*, 12 November 2008.

Certain data were unlikely, to say the least; for instance, Tutsi were thrown out of helicopters above Nyungwe forest, but later told their story to the commission. At least one document (on page 295 of the report) was a crude fake. A letter allegedly sent on June 2, 1998, by Colonel Gilles Bonsang, the commander of the military camp of Caylus, mentioned payments and supplies made to ALIR, a predecessor of the FDLR; ex-FAR; and inter-ahamwe. However, by June 1998 Bonsang had left Caylus for almost a year; the 7th RIMA (Régiment d'infanterie de Marine), which Bonsang supposedly commanded, had been disbanded years earlier; Bonsang was a lieutenant colonel rather than a colonel; the letter was signed at the order of General Germanos (presented as the "Chief of Staff of the Special Forces," while he was at the time head of the military office at the defense ministry), but Bonsang never worked under his direct orders (in addition, the letter mentions Yves Germanos, but the general's first name is Raymond). Neither the substance nor the form of the letter resists internal examination. The member of the Mucyo commission contacted by this author on the fake document responded by an embarrassed silence. French genocide specialist Jacques Sémelin, who cannot be suspected of aversion toward the RPF, concluded that "the aim of the report is political: give Rwanda the basis for a legal attack against the French leaders at the time [of the genocide], in order to counter the procedure of judge Bruguière against RPF officials."[124]

The second report, produced by the "Mutsinzi Committee," was delivered to the government on April 20, 2009, but published only on January 11, 2010.[125] It attempted to show that the presidential plane was not taken down by the RPF as claimed by Judge Bruguière, but by Hutu extremists close to Habyarimana. The report raised a number of important questions. The committee claimed to be "independent," but all its members were from the RPF, which thus were judge and party at the same time. This was clear from the first pages, and it was confirmed throughout the report, as the "inquiry" went in one direction, that of the Hutu extremists, whereas facts pointing in the direction of the RPF were systematically ignored. The committee claimed to have interviewed hundreds of witnesses, but their creditworthiness was limited. Among those identified, dozens were

---

[124] J. Sémelin, "Génocide, un discutable rapport rwandais," *Le Monde*, 18 August 2008.

[125] Republic of Rwanda, Independent Committee of experts charged with investigation into the crash on 06/04/1994 of Falcon 50 Aeroplane, registration number 9XR-NN, *Report of the Investigation into the Causes and Circumstances of and Responsibility for the Attack of 06/04/1994 against the Falcon 50 Rwandan Presidential Aeroplane, Registration Number 9XR-NN*, Kigali, 20 April 2009.

members of the former government army FAR: interrogated while being convicted or detained, or fearing arrest, they were fully aware of what those in power wished them to say. The committee used a number of documents, including from Belgian judicial files, in a selective and at times dishonest way, making witnesses say the opposite of what they actually declared. The report also quoted British UNAMIR officer Sean Moorhouse as stating that "the Rwandan president's aeroplane had been shot down by three whites with the help of the Presidential Guard and that the shots from weapons which brought down the aeroplane were fired from the Kanombe military camp."[126] Moorhouse was also claimed to have established that the FAR possessed surface-to-air missiles, but he told this author that he could not have made these statements because there was no evidence and that he explained this to the members of the Mutsinzi committee.[127] Many other examples in the report show serious methodological flaws: the committee first presented unproven hypotheses and even forthright untruths as facts, and the accumulation of those "facts" then allowed to discover a "truth." The conclusion the committee arrived at was not credibly based on the data that emerged from the inquiry, and the fraudulent way in which the report was drafted rather reinforced the suspicion that the RPF had committed the attack.[128]

In the meantime, the regime played hardball with regard to the French judicial inquiry. Rose Kabuye, the chief of protocol at the president's office, was one of the officers against whom an arrest warrant was issued. Knowing that she would be arrested, she was sent on a mission to Germany, where she was duly apprehended on November 9, 2008,[129] and transferred to Paris. After she was indicted and set free under

---

[126] *Idem*, p. 165.

[127] E-mail Sean Moorhouse to Filip Reyntjens, 15 April 2011: "[I]t was not possible to say with any certainty who had shot down the aircraft or from where."

[128] For a critical analysis see F. Reyntjens, *A Fake Inquiry on a Major Event. Analysis of the Mutsinzi Report on the 6th April 1994 Attack on the Rwandan President's Aeroplane*, IOB Working Paper 2010-7 Antwerp, 2010. In this context, it is also interesting to note that in July 2011 President Museveni travelled to Rwanda for the first time by plane. "Officials in Rwanda believe, and their counterparts in Uganda confirm, that the President had always been afraid that Rwandan officials could easily shoot his plane out of the skies" (A. Mwenda, "Burying the hatchet," *The Independent* (Kampala), 14 July 2012). It does not require a great deal of bad faith to suppose that Museveni knew what Kagame had done to his predecessor, particularly because the missiles used to down Habyarimana's plane came from Ugandan stocks.

[129] The Rwandan government immediately retaliated by expelling the German ambassador in Kigali and by recalling the Rwandan ambassador in Berlin. However, Germany had not done anything but to act upon a European arrest warrant.

conditions, she (and Rwandan intelligence) gained access to the Bruguière file, which came in handy at the time the Mutsinzi report was being drafted.[130] The paradoxical outcome of this saga was that France and Rwanda restored diplomatic relations. There were now two "truths" on the attack, that of the Bruguière inquiry[131] and that of the Mutzinsi report. Both pointed at suspects, albeit different ones, and found that a crime had been committed. The natural way to deal with such a situation would be to have a contradictory debate in a court of law. Wishing to normalize their relations, both Rwanda and France, however, sacrificed the need for justice to considerations of political expediency.

Besides the ICTR and France, Spain also was attacked over a delicate judicial file. After on February 6, 2008, Spanish judge Andreu Merelles issued arrest warrants against forty officers of the RDF over both the killing of Spanish nationals and crimes against humanity committed in Rwanda and the DRC, the reaction was swift and furious. In a communiqué dated February 9, 2008, the Foreign Ministry stated that Andreu Merelles based his decision on information provided by "well-known detractors of Rwanda," without specifying who these were. "[H]is so-called judicial file is full of hate and racist language, genocide denial and absolute falsehoods [and] an unacceptable attempt to rewrite and confuse history for political expediency."[132] On the same day, Justice Minister Karugarama stated that this "racist and negationist document (. . .) should be treated with the contempt it deserves" and that it was "the result of coordinated efforts between negative forces and genocide suspects still at large, bent on destabilising the country,"[133] again without offering any

---

[130] According to Guichaoua, the whole scenario of Kabuye's arrest, the Rwandan access to the case file, and – eventually – the burial of the entire affair was set up by French and Rwandan officials in late October 2008 (A. Guichaoua, *Rwanda: de la guerre au génocide. Les politiques criminelles au Rwanda (1990–1994)*, Paris, La Découverte, 2010, pp. 288–290).

[131] The release, in January 2012, of a technical report on the attack did not really challenge Bruguière's findings. Although claimed by the advocates of the indicted Rwandan officers, the Rwandan government, and many in the French press to demonstrate the innocence of the RPA, it did neither accuse nor exonerate any suspect. On the manipulation of information after the technical report came out, see C. Vidal, "Sur un emballement médiatique. L'attentat du 6 avril 1994 contre le président Habyarimana: comment la presse française a fait dire à un rapport d'expertise ce qu'il ne disait pas," in F. Reyntjens, S. Vandeginste, M. Verpoorten (Eds.), *L'Afrique des grands lacs. Annuaire 2011–2012*, Paris, L'Harmattan, 2012, pp. 337–349.

[132] Republic of Rwanda, Ministry of Foreign Affairs and Cooperation, *Rwanda Government Reaction to the Spanish Judge Indictments*, Kigali, 9 February 2008.

[133] "Karugarama Accuses Judge of Snubbing International Law," *The New Times*, 9 February 2008.

specification. Parliament followed suit: accusing Andreu Merelles of "judicial terrorism," it urged the government to prosecute him for "negationism."[134] Kagame too did not mince his words. Denouncing the "arrogance" of the Spanish judge, he said that "[i]f I met him, I would tell him to go to hell."[135] During his speech at the genocide commemoration in Nyamata on April 7, 2008, he again used the genocide as a tool for countering criticism: Judges Bruguière and Andreu Merelles "are nothing but vagabonds [and] the games [they] play are a mockery of the one million people who were killed during the genocide."[136]

The Rwandan government fought the French and Spanish procedures in several ways, in particular by seeking African support against what it called "the abuse of universal jurisdiction." On May 16, 2008, the Pan-African Parliament condemned the indictments as a violation of the sovereignty of an AU member state. In early July 2008, the African heads of state and of government, meeting in Sharm el-Sheikh, denounced the "abuses of the principle of universal competence [that could] endanger international law, order and security." After Rose Kabuye was arrested, the AU commission recalled the resolution of Sharm el-Sheikh and formally asked that the question of the "abuse of the principle of universal jurisdiction" be put on the agenda of the Africa-EU ministerial troika scheduled for November 2008. At their ordinary meeting in February 2009, the AU heads of state and of government reiterated their position and regretted the launching of an arrest warrant against Kabuye, "thus creating tension between the AU and the EU." These positions created a serious problem for international justice, as the African leaders suggested that only Africans could judge other Africans, a suggestion made explicit in the July 2008 declaration: "The political nature and abuse of the principle of universal jurisdiction by judges from some non-African States against African leaders, particularly Rwanda, is a clear violation of the sovereignty and territorial integrity of these states."[137] In addition, Rwanda (probably deliberately) created confusion with regard to the French judicial enquiry, as the competence of France was

---

[134] "Sue Spanish Judge, Parties Urge Government," *The New Times*, 25 February 2008.

[135] "Rwanda's Kagame Blasts Spanish Genocide Indictments", Kigali, Reuters, 1 April 2008.

[136] "Commemoration of the 14th Anniversary of Tutsi Genocide", *The New Times*, 8 April 2008.

[137] The AU reiterated its stand as a "syndicate of heads of state" in 2009 with regard to the prosecution launched at the ICC (International Criminal Court) against Sudanese president Al-Bashir. It called on the UN Security Council to suspend the process and directed member states to withold cooperation in the arrest of Al-Bashir (Decision of the Meeting of African State Parties to the Rome Statute of the ICC, Press Release, 14 July 2009).

not based on the principle of universal jurisdiction but on the fact that three of the victims of the plane attack were French citizens. Interestingly, in cases where genocide suspects were judged in third countries based on universal jurisdiction laws, Rwanda was the first to applaud. In February 2009, the Rwandan government exhorted the international community to extradite or judge, based on universal jurisdiction, genocide suspects living abroad, but it would not have that same principle applied to itself.

A REGIONAL POWERHOUSE

While it tackled the international community aggressively, Rwanda developed into a regional powerhouse. It twice invaded Zaire/DRC, where it supported proxy rebel movements and committed massive war crimes and crimes against humanity, and it came close to waging a full war with its former ally Uganda.[138] Despite being a small and poor country, Rwanda developed an extraordinary degree of military, political, and economic control over its huge (but weak) western neighbor, and it shamelessly lied about its involvement. In January 1997, when Belgium stated publicly what everyone knew, namely, that thousands of Rwandan soldiers were deployed in Zaire, presidential advisor Claude Dusaidi reacted, saying, "I believe that Belgium has gone senile (...). It looks like they don't know where the borders are, nor do they distinguish between Zairians and Rwandans."[139] Many more denials were aggressively issued, but they sounded very hollow after Kagame himself unveiled the public secret in an interview with the *Washington Post* after the first war. Claiming regional leadership, he said that "the Rwandan Government planned and directed the rebellion," that "Rwandan forces participated in the capture of at least four cities" and that "Rwanda provided training and arms for the (rebel) forces even before the campaign to overthrow Marshal Mobutu began last October." Kagame added that it would have been "more suitable if Congolese rebels had done most of the fighting," but they were not "fully prepared to carry it out alone."[140] Rwanda again

---

[138] For details, see G. Prunier, *Africa's World War. Congo, the Rwandan Genocide, and the Making of a Continental Catastrophe*, Oxford, Oxford University Press; F. Reyntjens, *The Great African War. Congo and Regional Geopolitics, 1996–2006*, New York, Cambridge University Press, 2009; J.K. Stearns, *Dancing in the Glory of Monsters. The Collapse of the Congo and the Great War of Africa*, New York, Public Affairs, 2011.

[139] Nairobi, AFP, 29 January 1997.

[140] J. Pomfret, "Defence Minister Says Arms, Troops Supplied for Anti-Mobutu Drive," *The Washington Post*, 9 July 1997.

intervened in 1998 and continues doing so up to the present day. Its constant denials in the face of overwhelming evidence eventually irritated even its best friends (see the following discussion).

Rwanda's regional ambitions were made explicit early on. During a meeting in Brussels, RPF general secretary Denis Polisi stated in mid-1997 that Rwanda had become a "master piece" and that "henceforth nothing can be done [in the region] without passing by Rwanda," adding that "Rwanda has just solved the problem of Zaire and is getting ready to solve other problems in the region."[141] One of the RPF's ideologues, Privat Rutazibwa, referring to the nickname "soldiers without borders" given to the RPA by the Congolese, wrote that "the freedom fighters should have no borders, as long as there are still retrograde ideologies and oppressive regimes on this continent," and he underlined "the stabilising role of the new Rwanda throughout the region."[142] He published these lines just weeks after Rwanda invaded the DRC a second time, while Kigali again denied its presence there. What was seen as hegemonic ambitions inspired fear in neighbouring countries. On August 28, 2001, Ugandan president Museveni wrote a letter to the U.K. secretary of state for international development Clare Short, asking for the authorization to increase defense spending, because "we have no doubts that Rwanda is planning aggression against us either using proxies or, even, directly." Referring to the size of the Rwandan army, he added that "[i]t is possible this level of manpower gives the arrogance to think that they can interfere in the internal affairs of Uganda."[143] The arrogance that so infuriated Museveni explains the condescending and humiliating way in which the then RPA chief of staff and current minister of defense James Kabarebe described Congolese president Joseph Kabila:

Joseph has always found it very difficult to adapt himself to the life of a soldier. This was clear during the exchange of fire. He didn't know what to do. I have taught him everything. (. . .) [Laurent] Kabila insisted [that Kabarebe became Chief of Staff of the Congolese army], arguing that his son Joseph did not have a sufficient background. (. . .) While Laurent-Désiré Kabila was a cheater, his son is timid. He is

[141] Meeting of Polisi with the Rwandan community, Brussels, 15 June 1997 (based on notes taken by two persons present).

[142] P. Rutazibwa, "Crises des Grands Lacs: la solution viendra du Rwanda", Kigali, ARI/RNA, No. 104, 20–26 August 1998. This was an astonishing statement, as the Rwandan regime itself was oppressive and thoroughly destabilized the region.

[143] B. Leloup, "Les rébellions congolaises et leurs parrains dans l'ordre politique régional", in F. Reyntjens, S. Marysse (Eds.), *L'Afrique des grands lacs. Annuaire 2001–2002*, Paris, L'Harmattan, 2002, pp. 83–84.

incapable of looking people in their face. I have never seen in him the slightest ability to command.[144]

This insulting "assessment" was made publicly about the head of state of a neighboring country.

The Rwandan presence in the DRC continued well after it officially withdrew its troops in application of an accord signed in Pretoria on July 30, 2002, between the DRC and Rwanda, as shown by the unpublished part of a UN panel's report of October 2003.[145] At the request of the panel this section was to remain confidential and not be circulated beyond the members of the Security Council, because it "contains highly sensitive information on actors involved in exploiting the natural resources of the DRC, their role in perpetuating the conflict as well as details on the connection between illegal exploitation and illicit trade of small arms and light weapons."[146] The findings showed an ongoing presence of the Rwandan army in the DRC. It had, the panel found, continued shipping arms and ammunition to the Kivus and Ituri, provided training, exercised command, supported North Kivu governor Serufuli's militia, and manipulated ex-FAR/Interahamwe by infiltrating RDF officers into them. The "Rwanda Network" was considered by the panel "to be the most serious threat to the Congolese Government of National Unity. The main actor in this network is the Rwandan security apparatus, whose objective is to maintain Rwandan presence in, and control of, the Kivus and possibly Ituri."[147]

Rwandan support for dissident forces went on throughout 2004, while the DRC was engaged in its delicate and fragile political transition. A later UN panel was concerned that "the territory of Rwanda continues to be used for recruitment, infiltration and destabilisation purposes,"[148] and it observed a "residual presence" of the RDF in North Kivu.[149] A report released at the end of 2008 "found evidence that the Rwandan authorities

---

[144] *Jeune Afrique/L'Intelligent*, no. 2155–2156, 29 April–12 May 2002, quoted by B. Leloup, "Les rébellions congolaises", pp. 95–96.

[145] United Nations, Security Council, *Final Report of the Panel of Experts on the Illegal Exploitation of Natural Resources and Other Forms of Wealth of the Democratic Republic of the Congo*, S/2003/1027, 23 October 2003.

[146] Letter dated 20 October 2003 from Mahmoud Kassem, chairman of the Panel, to UN secretary general Kofi Annan.

[147] Para. 2 of the unpublished Section V of United Nations Security Council, *Final Report of the Panel of Experts*

[148] United Nations, Security Council, *Report of the Group of Experts on the Democratic Republic of the Congo*, S/2005/30, 25 January 2005, para. 185.

[149] *Idem*, para. 199–200.

have been complicit in the recruitment of soldiers, including children, have facilitated the supply of military equipment, and have sent officers and units from the RDF to the Democratic Republic of the Congo in support of CNDP [rebel movement]."[150] The report documented supplies of uniforms and ammunition, financial support, and military backing during operations.[151] As a result, the Netherlands and Sweden, considered "friends of the New Rwanda," suspended part of their budget support, and influential voices in the United Kingdom suggested that Rwanda's main bilateral donor should follow suit.[152] A year later, the UN group of experts found that the leader of the CNDP general Laurent Nkunda, although arrested by Rwanda and placed under house arrest, continued to have meetings with associates and supporters in Kigali.[153] Another Congolese rebel group, the mainly Banyamulenge Forces républicaines fédéralistes (FRF), continued to have significant regional support bases in Rwanda (and Burundi).[154]

Although it had been caught red-handed on several occasions and major donors issued serious warnings, Rwanda again took the risk of destabilizing North Kivu in the spring of 2012.[155] Several reports[156] showed that it supplied weapons, ammunition, and recruits to a new rebel movement, the M23, an offspring from the CNDP. They documented direct RDF interventions into Congolese territory to reinforce M23, as well as support to other mutinies and secessionist politicians in eastern DRC. The group of

[150] United Nations, Security Council, *Final Report of the Group of Experts*, para. 61.

[151] *Idem*, para. 61–68.

[152] Thus Richard Dowden, the director of the Royal Africa Society, published an op-ed in *The Independent* (London) of December 15, 2008, under the title "Britain should cease its one-sided support for Rwanda".

[153] United Nations, Security Council, *Final Report of the Group of Experts on the Democratic Republic of the Congo*, S/2009/603, 23 November 2009, paras 189–190.

[154] *Idem*, para. 236.

[155] Even before Rwandan support for a new rebellion became known, Kigali anticipated. A revealing op-ed in the regime's daily claimed that "the attempt to arrest General Bosco Ntaganda and haul him before the ICC are merely skirmishes before swooping on their real target – Rwanda and its leaders" ("Gen. Ntaganda Is Only a Pawn in a Wider Game", *The New Times*, 8 May 2012). Clearly, the regime feared that its new intervention was likely to be uncovered.

[156] An internal MONUSCO document leaked to the press in May 2012; Human Rights Watch, *DR Congo: Rwanda Should Stop Aiding War Crimes Suspect. Congolese Renegade General Bosco Ntaganda Receives Recruits and Weapons from Rwanda*, Goma, 4 June 2012; United Nations, Security Council, *Addendum to the Interim Report of the Group of Experts on the Democratic Republic of the Congo (S/2012/ 348) concerning Violations of the Arms Embargo and Sanctions Regime by the Government of Rwanda*, S/2012/348/Add.1, 27 June 2012.

experts charged Rwanda with violating the UN-imposed assets freeze and travel ban through supporting sanctioned individuals. Rwanda again flatly denied the charges.[157] Even its staunchest allies had now had it. After the release of the group of experts' report, the U.S. State Department declared that it was "deeply concerned about the report's findings that Rwanda is implicated in the provision of support to Congolese rebel groups." It had "asked Rwanda to halt and prevent the provision of such support from its territory."[158] The United States, the United Kingdom, the Netherlands, Germany, and Sweden suspended aid payments, and the head of the U.S. War Crimes Office, Ambassador Stephen Rapp, suggested that Rwandan leaders might be accountable under international criminal law for aiding and abetting a group committing war crimes.[159] At a summit held on August 18, 2012, the Southern African Development Community (SADC), of which the DRC is a member, noted that rebel groups operated "with assistance of Rwanda, and urged the latter to cease immediately its interference that constitutes a threat to peace and stability, not only of the DRC, but also of the SADC Region."[160] SADC intervened on the DRC's side in 1998 and suggested it might do so again. Despite these strong warnings, Rwanda continued to actively support M23, as noted in an unpublished letter of the group of experts[161] and a new report of Human Rights Watch.[162] In the meantime, it waged a campaign of character assassination against Steve Hege, the coordinator of the group of experts,

---

[157] Just two examples among the many angry denials: Foreign Minister Mushikiwabo described the internal MONUSCO memo as "categorically false and dangerous rumours" ("Gov't Slams UN Report on DRC", *The New Times*, 29 May 2012); in an interview with *Metro*, Kagame stated, "We simply cannot support a rebellion outside our border" ("Exclusive Interview: Paul Kagame, President of Rwanda," *Metro*, 29 August 2012). This is quite a strange claim, because Rwanda admitted having supported Congolese rebellions in 1996 and 1998.

[158] U.S. Department of State, "Findings of the Group of Experts," Press Statement, 30 June 2012.

[159] "Rwanda's Paul Kagame Warned He May Be Charged with Aiding War Crimes", *The Guardian*, 25 July 2012.

[160] "Final Communiqué of the 32nd summit of SADC Heads of State and Government", Maputo, 18 August 2012, para. 13.1.

[161] United Nations, Security Council, Letter dated 7 August 2012 from the Coordinator of the Group of Experts on the DRC addressed to the Acting Chair of the Committee, S/AC.43/2012/COMM.32, 8 August 2012. This letter was said to be "leaked," but it was actually obtained by the Rwandan government through the hacking of the e-mail account of the group's coordinator.

[162] Human Rights Watch, *DR Congo: M23 Rebels Committing War Crimes. Rwandan Officials Should Immediately Halt All Support or Face Sanctions*, Goma, 11 September 2012.

claiming he was "anti-Rwanda" and a sympathizer of the FDLR.[163] Rwandan pressure failed to prevent the publication of the group of experts' final report, which detailed Rwandan involvement in a precise and convincing fashion[164] and even showed that Rwandan officials, including Minister of Defense General James Kabarebe and RDF chief of staff General Charles Kayonga, exercised overall command and strategic planning for M23.[165]

Although Rwandan leaders could face justice for crimes committed by proxies, Tim Reid has observed that the invasions of the DRC and the gross violations of human rights that accompanied them occurred at a time of considerable Western support for Rwanda (and Uganda). Major donors were aware of the crimes committed by the beneficiaries of their aid. Reid calculated that, if Rwanda's military operations in the DRC were viewed as an investment, they had an estimated return of 188 percent to 317 percent. Yet Rwanda was hailed as a model of economic development and offered unconditional aid during the period of its greatest appropriation of resources in the DRC. Reid argued that, when they knowingly give aid to countries that engage in wars of aggression, war crimes, crimes against humanity, and possibly genocide, donors bear a legal responsibility and should at least exercise prior due diligence.[166]

CONCLUSION

Attack is the best defense: this has been the regime's leading attitude toward the world and the region. Even moderately formulated criticism

---

[163] Among many examples, see "Are the UN Experts Credible?," *The New Times*, 4 August 2012, where it is pointed out that "Hege's views portray him as a sympathiser for genocide perpetrators and an apologist of the crime of genocide. (...) [H]e's a genocide revionist to say the least." In October 2012 Foreign Minister Mushikiwabo claimed that "[a] sympathizer or, more accurately, apologist of genocide perpetrators has been put in a position to sit in judgment of the victims, the Rwandan people" ("Exclusive Interview: Louise Mushikiwabo, Rwandan Foreign Minister", *Metro*, 16 October 2012).

[164] Rwanda's most important bilateral donor, the United Kingdom, judged "the overall body of evidence of Rwandan involvement with M23 in the DRC to be credible and compelling" (Foreign and Commonwealth Office, "UN Group of Experts Report on the Democratic Republic of Congo," 22 November 2012). On 30 November, the United Kingdom halted £21 million in aid payments to Rwanda.

[165] United Nations, Security Council, *Letter Dated 12 October 2012 from the Group of Experts on the Democratic Republic of the Congo Addressed to the Chair of the Security Council Committee Established Pursuant to Resolution 1533 (2004) concerning the Democratic Republic of the Congo, S/2012/843*, 15 November 2012.

[166] T. Reid, "Killing Them Softly: Has Foreign Aid to Rwanda and Uganda Contributed to the Humanitarian Tragedy in the DRC?," *African Policy Journal*, 1 (2006), pp. 74–94.

by international partners, among them some of the main donors, was treated furiously and with disdain. Manipulation and deceit were shamelessly used. It was a risky but successful tactic, because it contributed to ensuring the international community's tolerance for the regime's behavior. Aggressive statements, the rallying of support, and sheer blackmail were also instrumental in averting a grave danger, that of prosecutions of RPF/RPA suspects for international crimes, and thus in imposing victors' justice, just like that applied domestically (see Chapter 8). Contrary to what the "friends of the New Rwanda" thought, this tolerance did not earn them respect in Kigali. Quite the opposite, what they got was contempt: "[T]he continual humiliation of the international community subsequent to the 1994 genocide, a humiliation made infinitely worse with Kibeho, contributed to the international community turning into a servile instrument at the beck and call of the Rwandan authorities."[167] "For people caught red-handed, whether petty thieves or members of the international community, Rwandans can only feel contempt. Such people have lost face, must not be taken seriously and can be lied to."[168] This point must be underscored. Rwanda's aggressive behavior, both verbal and physical, was a show of contempt and expressed a feeling of superiority, which in turn weakened the international community even further. Every time someone admitted to something (such as UN secretary general Kofi Annan,[169] President Clinton, or the Belgian prime minister going to Kigali and apologizing for "having done nothing in 1994"), they were "caught red-handed," thus allowing Kigali to gain further ground.[170] This element of Rwandan culture also explains why the regime, just like ordinary Rwandans, never admits any wrongdoing, even if the evidence flies in the face.[171]

---

[167] J. Pottier, *Re-imagining Rwanda. Conflict, Survival and Disinformation in the Late Twentieth Century*, Cambridge, Cambridge University Press, 2002, p. 156.

[168] *Idem*, p. 155.

[169] During a visit to Kigali in May 1998, Annan did not apologize, but rather extolled the UN's achievements. He was then shrugged by the Rwandan president and vice-president who did not show up at a reception offered by them in Annan's honor. However, a year later Annan publicly recognized the UN's failure during the genocide (this episode is described in C.M. Waugh, *Paul Kagame and Rwanda. Power, Genocide and the Rwandan Patriotic Front*, Jefferson, NC, McFarland & Company, 2004, pp. 115–118).

[170] As the French refused to apologize (although Sarkozy came close during his visit to Kigali in February 2010), the Rwandans had to try and "catch them in the act" themselves (cf. the Mucyo report discussed earlier).

[171] This became abundantly clear again in 2012, when the regime denied any involvement with M23 in the DRC, although no one, even its closest allies, believed it.

Although the genocide credit, the narrative of difference, and decent bureaucratic governance shielded this very aid-dependent country from conditionalities, the donor community sometimes expressed concern and even discontent with regime behavior, particularly with regard to Rwanda's interference in the DRC[172], as well as with some internal policies, such as *imidugudu* and *gacaca* (see the following discussion). The great political issues, such as human rights, the democratic deficit, and rising inequality were not really addressed. Admittedly, the aid community was faced with enormous difficulties and donor assessments differed considerably on

basic matters such as the current dynamics of the Rwandan conflict, the nature and intentions of the government, the weight of the past in explaining the present, or the nature of current ethnic, social and economic trends in society. As a result, even if donors have had the same broad aims, they are unable to agree on priorities and policies.[173]

Contradictions also affected individual donors internally, and particularly the most important bilateral one, the United Kingdom. Marriage found quite a gap between "what DFID says" and "what DFID does" in Rwanda. For instance, "DFID's bilateral support accommodated the Rwandan government's dislike of NGOs,"[174] "DFID funded the government alongside unofficial acceptance that it had no sway over Kagame's interests in Congo,"[175] and "DFID's discourse cut out political analysis and implied no accountability."[176] Her conclusion is severe: "DFID defines the morality (...), and uses the positive terminology to credit and legitimise its activity. (...) Meanwhile (...) a poverty focus was abandoned and rights and impartiality were not prioritised, still less fulfilled, by the new humanitarianism."[177] In a submission that focused on the human rights dimension of DFID's strategy, Human Rights Watch reached similar conclusions. DFID often presented an overly optimistic picture of the situation in Rwanda, and "its apparent lack of attention to the human

---

[172] Particularly since 2004, the principle seems to be that the regime must refrain from causing regional instability and that in exchange it can more or less do as it pleases domestically.

[173] P. Uvin, "Difficult Choices in the New Post-conflict Agenda: The International Community in Rwanda after the Genocide," *Third World Quarterly*, 22:2 (2001), p. 178.

[174] Z. Marriage, "Defining Morality: DFID and the Great Lakes", *Third World Quarterly*, 27:3 (2006), p. 481.

[175] *Idem*, p. 484.

[176] *Idem*, ibid.

[177] *Idem*, p. 489.

rights situation has encouraged the Rwandan government to believe that respect for human rights and good governance matter little to its largest donor."[178] Although it formally adheres to "evidence-based policies," in the case of Rwanda "it appears that DFID has sometimes been willing to discard evidence relating to human rights abuses, with the result that the evidence on which it has based its policies has been selective and incomplete."[179]

Around the same time, Beswick argued that "UK attempts to promote state building by supporting a 'developmental' elite in Rwanda have negatively impacted prospects for long-term peace building."[180] Indeed the U.K.'s faith in Rwanda's leadership is in part based on "unarticulated and poorly evidenced assumptions about the motivations of the RPF."[181] Her conclusion: "Through silence, inaction and reducing its potential tools for influencing the Rwandan government, the UK has effectively minimised its ability to support the positive trajectory it seeks to promote."[182] This is exactly the claim made against France with regard to its relations with the pre-genocide regime. However, the United Kingdom and other "friends of the new Rwanda" assumed they operated on a clean slate, not hindered by much historical background: both Marriage and Beswick point to the fact that the United Kingdom had little prior involvement and limited knowledge of Rwanda before the genocide.[183] Indeed, countries such as the United Kingom and the Netherlands,[184] and the United States to a lesser extent, discovered Rwanda through the lens of genocide, and it was easy to draw them into the simple stories (such as good guys versus bad guys) proposed by the RPF. This explains the

---

[178] Human Rights Watch, "Human Rights Watch Submission to International Development Committee (IDC)", May 2011, p. 2.

[179] *Idem*, p. 7.

[180] D. Beswick, "Aiding State Building and Sacrificing Peace Building? The Rwanda-UK relationship 1994–2011", *Third World Quarterly*, 32:10 (2011), p. 1911.

[181] *Idem*, p. 1921.

[182] *Idem*, p. 1927.

[183] Scholars such as Pottier and Browne suggest that "since 1994, the RPF has actively encouraged relationships with states that had little prior involvement in Rwanda" (D. Beswick, "Aiding State Building", p. 1918). Hayman also notes that "[o]fficials accept how little knowledge the UK government really had of the situation (. . .), speaking of their 'enormous naivety' and 'complete ignorance'" (R. Hayman, "Abandoned Orphan, Wayward Child: The United Kingdom and Belgium in Rwanda since 1994," *Journal of Eastern African Studies*, 4:2 [2010], p. 347).

[184] The establishment of a strong aid relationship was, at least in part, the consequence of a personal commitment towards Rwanda by ministers of international development, Clare Short in the the United Kingdom and Jan Pronk in the Netherlands.

difference in approach between the "new" and the "old" donors such as Belgium, Germany, and Switzerland, who were much more cautious.[185]

From the lack of consistency between and within donors, aid flows remained constant and high in per-capita terms, and the regime by and large maintained its policies and practices. This it could afford, because the incoherent attitudes of the international community offered a great deal of political space for Kigali. Zorbas concluded that "the government of Rwanda can largely continue to define and pursue its own preferred development strategy, which does not fundamentally improve the lot of the poor and vulnerable nor does it alter the conditions of structural violence."[186] Brown reached a similar conclusion: "Western donors (...) are complicit to the institutionalization of authoritarian rule and help undermine the same long-term goals that they profess to support."[187] Although showing understanding for the desire to maintain stability, Silva-Leander warned that "[t]he longer Rwanda and its partners put off necessary democratic reforms for fear of upsetting the delicate balance that has been achieved after the war, the greater the risk of a violent backlash in the future."[188] I can only agree with these worrying assessments.

---

[185] However, during recent years, positions have tended to get closer together (R. Hayman, "Abandoned Orphan", pp. 351–353).

[186] E. Zorbas, "Aid Dependence", pp. 114–115.

[187] S. Brown, "The Rule of Law", p. 179.

[188] S. Silva-Leander, "On the Danger and Necessity of Democratisation: Trade-offs between Short-term Stability and Long-term Peace in Post-genocide Rwanda", *Third World Quarterly*, 29:8 (2008), p. 1602.

6

Engineering a New Society

Although I said in the introduction why I do not dwell on the Rwandan "success story," this is the place to note a number of achievements of good bureaucratic/technocratic governance. Having inherited a country that was destroyed in human and, to a lesser extent, material terms, the regime achieved strong recovery, especially after 2000. However, the growth path was less impressive than usually claimed. Indeed, the economy nearly halved in 1994, and during the next years, GDP climbed back to its "natural" level: in 1993 GDP/capita stood at US$287 (constant 2000 U.S. dollars); it fell to US$152 in 1994, but reached US$209 (+37 percent) in 1995. If 1994 is taken as the reference year, the growth was obviously impressive, as it stood at an average of around 8 percent per year until 2008. However, the average annual growth from 1995 to 2008 amounted to 4.5 percent, which was in line with figures seen elsewhere in sub-Sahara Africa. Growth consolidated in the latter half of the 2000s and averaged around a robust 8 percent. It is likely that a number of Millennium Development Goals will be achieved. Progress on social indicators was strong. Infant and maternal mortality dropped considerably (but infant malnutrition increased); the decrease in malaria mortality rates was spectacular; by 2010, nearly all Rwandans were covered by health insurance (*mutuelles de santé*)[1]; literacy and school enrollment rates strongly

---

[1] Despite it being internationally hailed as a model, the sustainability of the system is under stress. In mid-2011, contributions were increased from RWF 1,000 to RWF 7,000, 3,000 and 2,000 depending on income categories. For a family of six in the second category, this

163

increased, particularly in secondary and higher education.[2] The country is safe and clean, and Kigali in particular experienced a building boom. Civil servants are at their desk, and petty corruption is actively combated. In the World Bank's *Doing Business* ranking, Rwanda was the top performer for 2010, rising from rank 143 to 67 on the ease-of-doing-business rankings.

Booth and Golooba-Mutebi argue that Rwanda thanks the dynamic nature of its modern economy to what they call "developmental patrimonialism." Contrary to the rent seeking in many African countries, where elites pursue policies that are market constraining and antidevelopment, Rwanda is characterized by "ruling elites [acquiring] an interest in and a capacity for managing rents in a centralised way with a view to enhancing their incomes in the long run rather than maximising them in the short run."[3] Booth and Golooba-Mutebi see three main sources of primary accumulation in Rwanda: wartime contributions by RPF supporters, excess profits from unregulated and untaxed mineral trading out of the DRC, and monopoly profits earned in domestic protected business.[4] I would add aid, which accounted for almost half the budget and over 20 percent of GDP. Rent extraction was centralized through the operation of a fully owned company of the RPF/RPA, Tri-Star Investments (and its subsidiary Rwanda Metals for wartime minerals from the DRC), currently registered as Crystal Ventures Ltd. Later on, the army created its own investment arm under the form of Horizon Group, whereas the government brokered the creation by RPF private supporters of an investment consortium known as the Rwanda Investment Group (RIG).[5] Although both groups do appear to adhere to the tenets of "developmental patrimonialism," they are not without "neo-patrimonial" characteristics: Professor Nshuti Manasseh, a presidential advisor and strong defender of the "RPF faith" is group chairperson of Crystal Ventures, and the front man of Kagame's private business interests, Hatari Sekoko, is a major shareholder in RIG. In addition, Booth and Golooba-Mutebi fail to

---

meant an annual disbursement of RWF 18,000 (roughly US$30), in addition to a 10 percent charge for each intervention. For many people, this became unbearable and made them resort to traditional medicine or self-medication ("Rwanda. En dépit des mutuelles, ils ne peuvent pas se faire soigner", *Syfia Grands Lacs*, 6 July 2012).

[2] More data can be found in A. Ansoms, D. Rostagno, J. Van Damme, "*Vision 2020 à mi-parcours: l'envers du decor*", in S. Marysse, F. Reyntjens, S. Vandeginste (Eds.), *L'Afrique des grands lacs. Annuaire 2010–2011*, Paris, L'Harmattan, 2011, pp. 261–280.

[3] D. Booth, F. Golooba-Mutebi, *Developmental Patrimonialism? The Case for Rwanda*, APPP Working Paper No. 16, London, ODI, March 2011.p. 3.

[4] *Idem*, p. 7.

[5] *Idem*, pp. 12–21.

address the question how the rents were acquired. To the extent they come from the illegal exploitation of resources in the DRC, one must wonder whether a regime can be "developmental" if it underdevelops its neighbors. One of the flaws of analyses like these is that they disregard the wider politics, both domestically and regionally.

Nilgün Gökgür casts another eye on the performances of Rwanda's business sector. While ostensibly committed to privatization, the government actually increased its presence in the economy, and enterprises with close (direct or indirect) ties with the RPF benefited from all sorts of preferential treatment. In an opaque, weblike business environment, the fiscal risks of the state are considerable: in 2010, among seventeen enterprises in which the government had full or majority stake, only two paid out dividend; among fourteen enterprises in which it had a minority shareholding, none paid out dividend. Although their truly private nature is doubtful, Crystal Ventures, Horizon, and the RIG constituted more than half of the ten registered domestic investors between 2006 and 2010. In order to create more transparency and limit fiscal risks, Gökgür recommended that the Ministry of Finance and Economic Planning exert its ownership functions vis-à-vis the public enterprises.[6] After Gökgür handed in her inception report, her consultancy contract was suddenly terminated. She lifted a veil of a business environment in which public interests and those of powerful private players are interwoven in a complex and opaque web, and thus threatened the image of progress. In a later paper, Gökgür detailed and deepened her findings, showing that the "party-statals" received advantages unavailable to other economic operators, whereas neither their productivity nor the employment they generate is convincing. She argued that elite capture led to inefficient resource allocation from scarce budgetary means channeled to the party-statals.[7] A report quoted earlier expressed similar concerns: "The RPF's inner circle has pervasive influence within the Kigali business sector, with a lucrative and extensive portfolio that includes aviation, banking, agriculture, telecommunications, energy, construction, real estate, communication, and manufacturing," adding that "there are few oversight mechanisms to regulate or make public the RPF's vast investment portfolio or revenues."[8]

---

[6] N. Gökgür, *Formulating a Broad-based Private Sector Development Strategy, Inception Report*, 20 June 2011.

[7] N. Gökgür, *Rwanda's Ruling Party-owned Business Enterprises: Do They Enchance or Impede Development?*, IOB Discussion Paper 2012.03, Antwerp, 2012.

[8] Center for Strategic & International Studies, *Rwanda. Assessing Risks to Stability*, Washington, DC, June 2011, p. 16.

A REGIME WITH A MISSION

The RPF embarked on a formidable project of political, economic, social, and cultural engineering which is truly astonishing for such a small and intrinsically poor country. This ambitious project aimed at radically changing the domestic scene, but it also applied to the region and the world. Domestically it involved bold experiments in transitional justice, land tenure and agriculture, reeducation, the spiriting away of ethnic identity, the construction of truth, spatial reorganization (under the form of both villagization and the redrawing/renaming of territory), the instauration of pervasive control, and much more. As seen earlier, internationally it included the imposition of extraordinary political, military, and economic control over the DRC, as well as taking hostage the international community. Straus and Waldorf compared the RPF's top-down reconstruction to those brought about by the French revolutionaries or by Kemal Atatürk,[9] although one must have doubts about whether the ultimate outcome will have the same positive effects in Rwanda as it did in Turkey. The modernization drive was extremely fast,[10] especially after 2000, and for most Rwandans it was too fast: when the Rwandan government wants something, it wants it immediately, and it sets close and clear deadlines. Although we will see that the rural world was strongly affected by change, the modernization went at two speeds, further compounding the urban-rural rift.

An internal text quoted earlier, dating from before the RPF came to power, stated that "[t]he majority of the Rwandans have neither democratic culture nor the will to change. (...) Very few of them are really progressive, whence the need for the Front to approach this conservative population and bring to it the message of change."[11] Eight years later, when the RPF was solidly in power, Aloysia Inyumba, an influential leader of the party, expressed the opinion that "the ordinary citizens are like babies. They will need to be completely educated if we want to move

---

[9] S. Straus, L. Waldorf, "Introduction. Seeing Like a Post-Conflict State", in S. Straus, L. Waldorf, *Remaking Rwanda. State Building and Human Rights after Mass Violence*, Madison, The University of Wisconsin Press, 2011, p. 4.

[10] Purdekova describes the predominant government conception of development as a "fast-paced, forward-bound transformation" (A. Purdekova, "Civic Education and Social Transformation in Post-Genocide Rwanda: Forging the Perfect Development Subjects", in M. Campioni, P. Noack (Eds.), *Rwanda Fast Forward. Social, Economic, Military and Reconciliation Prospects*, Houndmills, Palgrave Macmillan, 2012, p. 192).

[11] FPR, "L'environnement actuel actuel et à venir de l'organisation", n.d. (early 1994), p. 10.

towards democracy."[12] Explaining the rationale behind the genocide ideology law, general prosecutor Martin Ngoga stated in 2010 that "[t]here is a population that we continue to educate but is not educated enough to the extent that they will not be manipulated again."[13] These statements summarize the RPF's long-standing dual attitude toward its citizens: disdain and distrust on the one hand, the belief that man is makeable on the other. The attitude that Sommers found towards the youth extended to the entire population: young people must be "guided, shaped, led, influenced, directed, and persuaded. An equally strong theme among officials is the steady resistance of youth to accepting their instructions, orders, guidelines, remedies, and advice."[14]

The way in which the RPF looked on Rwandans, and the Hutu in particular, can be understood in light of its entire history. Prunier notes that during the war, the RPF never had to face the problems of relations with the local populations, as it "ruled over an eerily empty landscape."[15] Its ignorance of daily life gave it the "flavour of an alien body," upon which its Hutu "fellow citizens" looked as an army of occupation.[16]

Since it came to power, the RPF has aimed at producing a new Rwanda and a new Rwandan. This belief in engineering became particularly prominent after 2000. It went from the prohibition of the use of polyethylene bags, an environment-friendly measure probably unique in the world, to the mass consecration of marriages according to state law. This chapter looks at some of these bold and dramatic projects, and tries to understand the consequences of these ambitious projects for the country's future stability.

Vision 2020 epitomises the Rwandan elites' ambitions. Released in 2000, it aims to "transform Rwanda's economy into a middle income country (per capita income of about 900 USD per year, from 290 USD today)" through a radical modernization process, including in the agricultural sector where the vast majority of the population makes its

---

[12] J. Corduwener, "Wederopbouw in Rwanda, met ijzeren hand" ("Reconstruction in Rwanda, with an Iron Fist"), *NRC-Handelsblad*, 27 March 2002.

[13] Quoted in L. Waldorf, "Instrumentalizing Genocide.The RPF's Campaign against 'Genocide Ideology'", in S. Straus, L. Waldorf (Eds.), *Remaking Rwanda*, p. 58.

[14] M. Sommers, *Stuck. Rwandan Youth and the Struggle for Adulthood*, Atlanta, GA, and London, University of Georgia Press, 2011, p. 81.

[15] G. Prunier, "The Rwandan Patriotic Front", in C. Clapham (Ed.), *African Guerrillas*, Oxford, James Currey, 1998, p. 131.

[16] *Idem*, p. 133.

"living."[17] Although *Vision 2020* makes sense on paper, it has effects that are not anticipated by planners sitting at their desks in Kigali. This is not surprising, given the vast divide separating the small urban elites and the rural population. Indeed, the almost overnight replacement of one elite by another has profoundly altered relations, and led to the virtual disappearance of the personalized links that existed between rulers and peasants and between towns and hills before 1994.[18] Holvoet and Rombouts found that this distance even affects NGOs. The umbrella organizations the government prefers to talk to "tend to be located in Kigali, and increasingly become alienated from the poor in rural areas."[19] Ansoms noted that "[t]he current Rwandan elite is mostly Tutsi, urban-based and often from outside Rwanda, while the Rwandan peasantry is mostly Hutu, rural-based and born in the country."[20] As a district official sent to the countryside by the Ministry of Agriculture told her: "I do not like to look at poor people and deal with them. In fact, when I worked in the ministry, I did not have to look at the poor."[21] The elites feel

---

[17] Republic of Rwanda, Ministry of Finance and Economic Planning, *Rwanda Vision 2020*, Kigali, July 2000. The following "pillars" were identified to achieve this goal:

- Reconstruction of the nation and its social capital anchored on good governance, underpinned by a capable state;
- Transformation of agriculture into a productive, high value, market oriented sector, with forward linkages to other sectors;
- Development of an efficiënt private sector spearheaded by competitiveness and entrepreneurship;
- Comprehensive human resources development, encompassing education, health, and ICT skills, aimed at public sector, private sector and civil society. To be integrated with demographic, health and gender issues;
- Infrastructural development, entailing improved transport links, energy and water supplies and ICT networks;
- Promotion of regional economic integration and cooperation (pp. 3–4).

[18] I remember visiting government ministers or senior civil servants "*chez eux,*" on their hill of origin where they often spent their weekends in a (generally quite modest) house. Local people, including barefoot peasants would walk in and out to share an *urwagwa* (sorghum beer), which allowed the *big men* to maintain kinship and neighborhood links and to have a feel of ordinary people's lives and concerns. This does not mean to say that the former elites effectively pursued pro-peasant policies, but they did have a feel of the countryside that current elites lack. On the largely semantic nature of the previous regime's pro-peasant discourse see P. Verwimp, "Development Ideology, the Peasantry and Genocide: Rwanda Represented in Habyarimana's Speeches", *Journal of Genocide Research*, 2:3 (2000), pp. 325–361.

[19] N. Holvoet, H. Rombouts, "The Challenge of Monitoring and Evaluation under the New Aid Modalities: Experiences from Rwanda", *Journal of Modern African Studies*, 46:4 (2008), p. 590.

[20] A. Ansoms, "Re-engineering Rural Society: The Visions and Ambitions of the Rwandan Elite", *African Affairs* 108:431 (2009), p. 308.

[21] *Idem*, p. 307.

that poverty and underperformance in rural Rwanda can be tackled, because they are not the consequence of institutional constraints but of a "wrong mentality" among the peasants. Thus, the *Strategic Plan for Agricultural Transformation* refers to the problem of peasants' ignorance and resistance to modernization.[22] Ansoms observed that "[e]ven official policy documents refer to the ignorance of peasants and their resistance to new productivity-enhancing measures that go beyond their traditional subsistence farming logic. In its most blatant form, this conviction reduces the problem of rural poverty to one of bad mentality."[23]

MODERNIZING RWANDA AND THE RWANDANS

The modernization drive resulted in ever-increasing demands on ordinary people. Children are not allowed to enter school if they do not wear shoes and uniforms, and access to health centres and hospitals is prohibited to barefoot people.[24] Rural populations are confronted with ever mounting cumbersome and costly obligations: the construction of latrines, the use of impregnated mosquito nets, the wearing of clean clothes after work on the fields, the joining of health associations and so on; compliance with those duties is enforced through fines.[25] Every Rwandan aged sixteen or older even needs to buy a card to participate in the compulsory community work *umuganda* or in *gacaca* proceedings. People thus pay 100 RWF to fulfill obligations that keep them away from their fields; those without a card are fined and barred from access to municipal services.[26] The card of a health association is equally needed: without it, access to markets is refused.[27] All these constraints are accompanied by a great deal of bureaucratic hassle: thus, for instance, is an "authorisation to seek administrative documents,"

---

[22] Government of Rwanda, *Strategic Plan for Agricultural Transformation*, pp. 6–17, quoted by A. Ansoms, "Re-engineering Rural Society", p. 298.

[23] A. Ansoms, "Striving for Growth, Bypassing the Poor? A Critical Review of Rwanda's Rural Sector Policies", *Journal of Modern African Studies* 46:1 (2008), p. 27.

[24] "Les Rwandais ne veulent pas qu'on fasse leur bien malgré eux", *Syfia Rwanda*, 10 November 2006.

[25] "Rwanda: la propreté à marche forcée", *Syfia Rwanda*, 7 July 2006. Ingelaere lists twenty-nine obligations or prohibitions for which peasants can be fined, for example, "religious groups praying at night," "refusal to make use of a 'modern cooking stove,'" "house without closed toilet," or "consumption of beers in cabarets or at home with a straw" (based on a letter from a district mayor, June 2006) (B. Ingelaere, "Do We Understand Life after Genocide?Center and Periphery in the Construction of Knowledge in Post genocide Rwanda", *African Studies Review*, 53:1 [2010], p. 52).

[26] *Umuseso*, No. 276, 3–10 February 2007.

[27] "Locked Out of Market over Mutuelle Cards", *The New Times*, 28 February 2007.

signed by several local officeholders, necessary to obtain an identity card or
the many other indispensible forms and documents. All this needs, of
course, to be paid for: "Even those who need a declaration of indigence
are forced to first pay certain taxes."[28] The so-called performance contracts (*imihigo*) signed between the government and the local districts were
extended to the level of households, that were expected to present a list of
objectives to be attained, and whose implementation is to be regularly
evaluated.[29] *Imihigo* thus led to deeper permeation of society by the state
and represented openings for increased coercion. Indeed, it incorporated
households into the administrative hierarchy and led to increasing
demands on ordinary citizens.[30] All this happened in a situation of disconnection between center and periphery. Ingelaere noted that "an ambitious and internally coherent national ideology and vision is translated to
the local level where measures are taken by coercion irrespective of 'real-
world' considerations."[31] In a similar vein, Ansoms notes "a profound
mismatch between the Rwandan elite's ambitions and the rural realities on
the ground."[32] It should however be noted that enforcement of all these
measures is not complete and that much depends on local political dynamics and local officials' flexibility or lack thereof.

The urban poor also are not spared by the regime's engineering mission.
Thousands of residents of poor neighbourhoods in Kigali were expelled
from their houses, which were demolished to make place for residential
developments. They were "resettled" far from the city centre in areas
without power, running water or schools, and they faced the cost of
daily transport into town.[33] In April 2007, it was announced that hundreds of other households were to make place for a free trade zone and a
100-hectare amusement park.[34] A month later, very ambitious plans for
the construction of a "New Kigali" were laid out, with the consequences

---

[28] "Les tracasseries de la décentralisation", *Syfia Grands Lacs*, December 2006.

[29] "Performance Contracts to be Signed at the Household Level", *The New Times*, 19
November 2007. However, in practice this is far from generally applied.

[30] A. Purdekova, "'Even If I Am not Here, There Are so Many Eyes': Surveillence and State
Reach in Rwanda", *Journal of Modern African Studies*, 49:3 (2011), pp. 484–485.

[31] B. Ingelaere, *Living the Transition. A Bottom-Up Perspective on Rwanda's Political
Transition*, IOB, Discussion Paper 2007–6, Antwerp, 2007, p. 36.

[32] A. Ansoms, "Rwanda's Post-genocide Economic Reconstruction. The Mismatch between
Elite Ambitions and Rural Realities", in S. Straus, L. Waldorf (Eds.), *Remaking Rwanda*,
p. 248.

[33] "Rwanda: le coût social d'une politique de modernisation menée au détriment des pau-
vres", Kigali, IRIN, 15 September 2006.

[34] "Rwanda: Kigali Gets $25 Million Amusement Park", *East African Business Week*, 16
April 2007.

one can imagine for the less well-off.[35] The old Kigali central market was razed to make place for a new commercial center, thus destroying the livelihood of hundreds of small vendors. In July 2006, the Infrastructure Minister announced that the use of mud bricks was prohibited for construction work in Kigali. The ministry was to build cheap housing for those unable to afford a modern house; "cheap" was specified as an amount not more than 1 million RWF (about US$1,800), a fortune for poor people in poor neighborhoods.

As has been the case in other African countries, the showcase Kigali was cleansed at the occasion of increasingly frequent summit conferences. Street children, beggars, vendors and other poorly dressed people were rounded up and locked up in Gikondo prison. In Rwanda, these things tend to be done more thoroughly than elsewhere. In April 2010, the *New York Times* carried a story about the rounding up of nearly 900 "vagrants," including dozens of children, who were sent to Iwawa Island in Lake Kivu without trial or court appearance.[36] Hardly a year later, the government got its act together. Although in 2010 Iwawa was described as an Alcatraz and children complained about the harsh conditions and the fact that their parents were unaware of their whereabouts, the "Youth Rehabilitation and Vocational Skills Development Centre" was now hailed as an "example to other African countries" by a visiting group of Dutch youth,[37] and Iwawa students spread the official discourse.[38] Measures in the countryside too were radical. Traditional brick and tile making was banned in 2006, thus making house construction nearly unaffordable for the rural poor.[39] During the spring of 2011 thatched houses known as *Nyakatsi* were forcibly destroyed, leaving many poor people without shelter. Other obligations, such as the wearing of shoes or the need "to be clean," meant, in Ansoms' words, that people were "prohibited to appear poor. This cosmetic upgrading of rural life only hides the true extent of poverty and inequality in the countryside."[40]

---

[35] "Rwanda Dreams of New Kigali City", *The New Times*, 29 May 2007.

[36] "Rwanda Pursues Dissenters and the Homeless", *The New York Times*, 30 April 2010.

[37] "Dutch Youth Impressed by Iwawa Rehab Centre", *Sunday Times* (Kigali), 3 April 2011.

[38] "Our Lives Have Been Transformed – Iwawa Students", *The New Times*, 4 April 2011. In light of the distance between the public and the hidden transcript (cf. Chapter 7), statements such as these made by Rwandans need to be interpreted with caution.

[39] Sommers (*Stuck*, pp. 115–139) describes the consequences of these constraints for young males and their impossibility to attain adulthood.

[40] A. Ansoms, "Rwanda's Post-genocide Economic Reconstruction", p. 247.

The government's radical, fast, and imposed engineering program has generally had dramatic consequences. Examples abound, of which the villagization program, known as Imidugudu, was a very ambitious piece of social engineering, particularly in a country without a tradition of grouped settlement. In line with government policies in other fields, the program "was a blueprint policy for the whole country, disregarding local diversity, implemented in a top-down fashion and with little space for popular participation."[41] Sommers called the collective effect of the policy "breathtaking: the Rwandan state is in the process of forcibly changing the residence of nearly all of its citizens."[42] Initially launched in December 1996 to tackle the problem of land scarcity and to make more efficient use of public services, it was also a way to ensure compliance with government orders: according to officials, the patterns of dispersed housing made it difficult to "persuade" the population to follow directives.[43] Although the program was based on doubtful assumptions from the beginning, among others because similar attempts had generally failed elsewhere in East Africa,[44] it became messier as other motives intervened. It was first redesigned to cater for the needs of new caseload refugees returning from Zaire at the end of 1996 and beginning of 1997, many whose land and houses had been occupied by old caseload refugees. In 1997–1998, during the insurgency in the northwest discussed earlier, the program was again redesigned as a security measure: after residents had been forcibly regrouped in large camps, they were later moved to new settlements rather than allowed to return to their original homes. Despite the many ambiguities, the program was supported by several UN agencies, the UNHCR in particular, and international NGOs who justified their involvement on account of "emergency,"[45] although it is the government's intention to regroup the entire population, including those living in decent houses.

---

[41] D. Hilhorst, M. van Leeuwen, "Emergency and Development: The Case of *Imidugudu*, Villagization in Rwanda", *Journal of Refugee Studies*, 13:3 (2000), p. 265.

[42] M. Sommers, *Stuck*, p. 26.

[43] A. Des Forges, "Land in Rwanda: Winnowing out the Chaff", in F. Reyntjens, S. Marysse (Eds.), *L'Afrique des grands lacs. Annuaire 2005–2006*, Paris, L'Harmattan, 2006, p. 361.

[44] M. van Leeuwen, "Rwanda's Imidugudu programme and earlier experiments with villagisation and resettlement in East Africa", *Journal of Modern African Studies*, 39: 4 (2001), p. 623.

[45] D. Hilhorst, M. van Leeuwen, "Emergency and Development", p. 268. The UNHCR consistently spoke of "shelter" program instead of "settlement" or "housing" (*idem*, p. 271).

Over the years, hundreds of thousands were expelled from their land and houses (which in many cases they were forced to destroy themselves), more often than not without receiving the promised compensation. The Global IDP Project found that none of the residents had enough land and that as a consequence, many suffered from lack of food and resources to pay educational and medical expenses. None of the *imidugudu* visited during Sommers' research had the promised amenities with the exception of shared water taps in some villages.[46] As was the case elsewhere in Rwanda, some of the land was taken over by military officers, and a number of residents had to seek day labor on the land they used to own.[47] Des Forges's conclusion is an indictment of this attempt of engineering change through *imidugudu*: "Rwandan authorities put forward the villagisation policy as a way to improve the lives of ordinary Rwandans, but the perceptions of many residents of these settlements is that they are poorer now than they were before they moved."[48] Van Leeuwen observed that, faced with worries expressed by some donors, the Rwandan government discarded them, claiming that the Rwandan program was radically different from failed experiences elsewhere. The agencies accepted this "narrative of difference," and van Leeuwen shows how through a series of assumptions the doubts were silenced and the narrative was upheld. He finds that, for the external players involved, "ambiguous assumptions formed a reasonable basis for accepting the narrative and going ahead with its implementation."[49] Rwandan key decision makers too were ill informed. Newbury notes that "since [they] are returnees from exile and therefore relative newcomers to Rwanda, many had never lived in Rwanda – at least not as farmers – and therefore they could be guided in their planning unencumbered by the realities on the ground."[50] It is therefore not surprising that Newbury concludes that the *imidugudu* policy "has failed in three key respects: (1) it quickly became coercive (. . .); (2) it reduced economic security and quality of life; and (3) it increased social tensions, particularly along ethnic lines."[51]

---

[46] M. Sommers, *Stuck*, p. 25.

[47] Global IDP Project, *Ensuring Durable Solutions for Rwanda's Displaced People: A Chapter Closed too Early*, 8 July 2005 (www.internal-displacement.org).

[48] A. Des Forges, "Land in Rwanda", p. 363.

[49] M. van Leeuwen, "Rwanda's Imidugudu programme", p. 635.

[50] C. Newbury, "High Modernism at the Ground Level. The *Imidugudu* Policy in Rwanda", in S. Straus and L. Waldorf (Eds), *Remaking Rwanda*, p. 229.

[51] *Idem*, p. 235. More on the disastrous consequences of *imidugudu*, as well as of urban resettlement policies, for the vast majority of Rwandans can be found in M. Sommers, *Stuck*, pp. 25–30.

Overall, Guichaoua summarized the effects of the modernization drive on rural communities as follows:

The main result of the new agronomic order imposed without dialogue with the producers is up to now the maintaining of widespread misery, situations of chronic regional famine and the accelerated production of radically pauperised landless farmers. Thus, technocratic and/or security-based decisions are imposed on top of the brutality of social relations, thus disrupting the last links with the peasant order.[52]

There even is an effect of modernization on the dead, as the way in which the regime organizes the memorialization of the genocide is contrary to burial rites in Rwandan culture.[53]

LAND AND AGRICULTURAL POLICY

In a country where over 80 percent of the population is mainly engaged in subsistence farming, land and agricultural policies are crucial. After a process that started in 1997; that was dominated by technocrats of the Rwandan government, the FAO, and the World Bank[54]; and during which mere lip service was paid to the consultation of peasants, a land law was adopted in 2005. A Swisspeace report noted that the capacity of civil society to influence government policies was very limited. "Consultations" were held *a posteriori* and called a farce by a farmers' NGO representative. The report concluded that "in the end the new land policy and law remained an achievement of the Rwandan government, not of the Rwandan population, whose needs are much too often said to have been neglected to a large extent."[55] Although Newbury noted that "[i]n such a highly charged political terrain, Rwanda's leaders might have been expected to take a gradual-ist, consultative approach to changing land policy,"[56] the law operates

---

[52] A. Guichaoua, "Transition politique à la rwandaise: d'un totalitarisme à l'autre", *Eins-Entwicklungspolitik Nord-Süd*, 2007, No. 5.

[53] J. Meierhenrich, "Topographies of Remembering and Forgetting. The Transformation of *Lieux de Mémoire* in Rwanda", in S. Straus, L. Waldorf (Eds.), *Remaking Rwanda*, p. 290.

[54] Pottier notes that "donor-driven environmental narratives highlight particular elements while obscuring others, and result in one-sided recommendations" (J. Pottier, "Land Reform for Peace?Rwanda's 2005 Land law in Context", *Journal of Agrarian Change* 6:4 [2006], p. 520).

[55] K. Wyss, *A Thousand Hills for 9 Million People. Land Reform in Rwanda: Restoration of Feudal Order or Genuine Transformation?*, Swisspeace Working Paper 1/2006, March 2006, p. 25.

[56] C. Newbury, "High Modernism", p. 224.

a radical and sudden break with the past, aiming at creating a private land market (through a system of registration of private tenure) and at enlarging holdings (through a system of consolidation). In a country where the average cultivated land holding per household is around 0.6 hectare, the law provides for a minimal holding of 1 hectare, but the upper ceiling of 50 hectares foreseen by the 2002 PRSP was abandoned. The 2004 National Land Policy even mentioned the need to "protect the rights of absentee landlords," while noting "the increasing hold of the urban elite over rural land." This change may be quite telling, as "some politically connected individuals have acquired, over the last few years, land holdings of 50 ha or more for coffee and cattle production."[57] Concerns raised over the law included the "Latin-Americanization" of property, the fact that the state remained the owner of all land, the lack of consultation, the bias in favor of the rich, including military officers and high officials, and the nontransparent nature of the land commissions.[58] Equally telling about the regime's vision on the modernization of land use was the signing, in October 2009, of a deal allowing the South Korean biodiesel producer Eco-fuel to exploit 10,000 hectares of land in the eastern province.[59] This concession was granted in a country experiencing the highest population pressure in Africa.

At the beginning of 2008, Kagame proceeded to a strongly publicized redistribution of land. However, the conditions were far from transparent: there were no known rules on who was to abandon which surface or on who benefited from the exercise. A presidential land commission functioned in an unaccountable and nontransparent way, without its guidelines or decisions made publicly available.[60] Its chairperson, General Fred Ibingira, was himself a major absentee landlord. Above all, the "redistribution exercise" revealed to what extent the regime notables – army officers, politicians, business people – had been able to accumulate large land holdings in a brief time. The compilation of data from three articles in *The New Times* offers an (incomplete) view of widespread absentee

---

[57] H. Musahara, C. Huggins, "Land Reform, Land Scarcity and Post Conflict Reconstruction. A Case Study of Rwanda", *Eco-Conflicts*, 3:3 (2004), p. 3.

[58] Front Line Rwanda, *Disappearances, Arrests, Threats, Intimidation of Human Rights Defenders, 2001–2004*, Dublin, 2005, p. 60.

[59] "Korean Firm Given 10,000 Hectares of Land for Biodiesel", Kigali, RNA, 28 October 2009.

[60] On this commission, see C. Huggins, "The Presidential Land Commission. Undermining Land Law Reform", in S. Straus and L. Waldorf (Eds), *Remaking Rwanda*, pp. 252–265.

landlordism.[61] The following RPF-linked people owned 100 hectares of land or more: Alfred Nkubiri (508 ha), Patrick Ngoga (384 ha), Edgard Rwangabwoba (380 ha), General Major Fred Ibingira (320 ha), Lieutenant General Kayumba Nyamwasa (207 ha), Colonel Aloys Muganga (199 ha), James Kimonyo (176 ha), Lieutenant General Charles Muhire (119 ha), and Théoneste Mutsindashyaka (105 ha). The question, of course, arises how people who arrived in Rwanda in 1994 were able to amass such large holdings in a country experiencing an acute land shortage. Kagame himself offered a hint when explaining how he acquired his forty-three-hectare Ntebe Farm on the shores of Lake Muhazi: he acknowledged that he did not buy it, but he "formally applied to Minagri [Ministry of Agriculture] requesting for that land and they granted it to me."[62] Huggins concludes that these practices and the way in which the presidential commission functioned "cast serious doubt on Rwanda's commitment to following the laws and procedures for registering land claims and thus improving security of land tenure."[63]

Although the World Bank stresses the importance of smallholders in a green revolution for sub-Sahara Africa, the Rwandan government favors larger land holdings, and therefore the number of people dependent on agriculture must dramatically decrease. However, it has no clear vision of the employment alternatives of the population to be driven out of agriculture.[64] As land consolidation is not likely to increase productivity, rather the opposite, this policy risks provoking major conflicts, particularly in the Rwandan context. In a conflict vulnerability assessment for USAID, a team of consultants feared that "Rwanda could be on a collision course between the state's need to achieve economic growth and individual household needs for livelihood security. (…) [The new land policy] could increase inequality and exacerbate class divisions, which if politicised, could lead to conflict." Worse still, "[i]f the dispossessed subsistence farmers are mostly Hutu and the commercial farmers are mostly the Ugandan Tutsi elite, there is a risk of recreating the ethnically-based, patron-client relations that characterised the Tutsi monarchy and colonial period."[65] Likewise, Uvin

---

61 "Share Resources, Kagame Tells Rwandans", *The New Times*, 26 January 2008; "Land Re-distribution Exercise Resumes this Week", *The New Times*, 29 January 2008; "Kagame Winds up Land Re-distribution Launch", *The New Times*, 31 January 2008.

62 "Kagame Clears Air on Ntebe Country House", *The New Times*, 12 September 2007.

63 C. Huggins, "The Presidential Land Commission", p. 260.

64 A. Ansoms, "Re-engineering Rural Society", p. 301.

65 Management Systems International, *Rwanda Conflict Vulnerability Assessment*, October 2002, quoted in Front Line Rwanda, *Disappearances, Arrests*, pp. 58–59.

notes that the regime's engineering "has led to a dramatic rise in income inequality, mainly between the city and the countryside, which de facto means between Tutsi and Hutu. This may be politically very dangerous, and it may well be one of the reasons the RPF intends to maintain tight control over all the reigns of power."[66]

Pottier also pointed out that implementing the land law will amount to an endorsement of widening class differences, reinforced by the "ethnicisation of landlessness."[67] He sees "the appropriation of large plots by powerful new elites (...). [They], including senior government and military officials, are acquiring land for the purpose of speculation rather than agricultural production."[68] In short, Tutsi absentee landlords are seen grabbing the land of Hutu peasants. This was the view of many interviewees in Nakivale settlement who told how they had tried to reclaim their land and failed. Many stories recounted that army officers are on their land, and that they had been intimidated until they had fled.[69] Begley found that, although land and other issues were often based on the search for personal gain, "many Hutu gave them an ethnic interpretation."[70] Needless to say that, given Rwanda's history of ethnic relations, this is causing grave danger, the more so because, Pottier suggests, "the scene is set for a (modified) return to the patron-client politics that have dominated the political economy for a number of centuries."[71] But maybe that is the idea: Ansoms noted that "so-called pro-poor policies can introduce or reinforce institutional barriers for many, while facilitating access and enhancing opportunities for the few."[72] Likewise, Wyss suggested "the possibility that the Rwandan authorities may take advantage of restructuring the agrarian sector in order to pursue their own particular interests"[73] and found ground for the "suspicion that the upcoming land reform is more likely to benefit the rich and powerful than the rural poor."[74] The spectacular rise of inequality underscores that evolution: Rwanda evolved

[66] P. Uvin, "Structural Causes, Development Co-operation and Conflict Prevention in Burundi and Rwanda", *Conflict, Security & Development*, 10:1 (2010), p. 172.

[67] J. Pottier, "Land Reform for Peace?", p. 533.

[68] *Idem*, p. 511.

[69] *A Dangerous Impasse*, p. 32.

[70] L. Begley, "'Resolved to Fight the Ideology of Genocide and all of Its Manifestations': The Rwandan Patriotic Front, Violence and Ethnic Marginalisation in Post-genocide Rwanda and Eastern Congo", DPhil thesis, University of Sussex, 2011, p. 95.

[71] J. Pottier, "Land Reform for Peace?", p. 533.

[72] A. Ansoms, "Striving for Growth", p. 25.

[73] K. Wyss, *A Thousand Hills for 9 Million People*, p. 6.

[74] *Idem*, p. 32.

from a low-inequality country (Gini coefficient of 0.289 in 1985) to a high-inequality one (Gini coefficient of 0.451 in 2000, rising to 0.510 in 2006, "which has put Rwanda among the top 15 percent of most unequal countries in the world"[75]). Although the UNDP claimed that, by 2011, the Gini coefficient had risen to 0.531, making Rwanda the eleventh highest-inequality country worldwide,[76] a national survey published in February 2012 however suggested a marked decrease in both poverty and inequality. These figures are discussed later in this chapter.

Agricultural policies also attempted to engineer modernity from above. In the framework of its "Green Revolution," from 2006 the government started to impose the growing of cash crops. Each province was to plant species supposedly best suited to the region, and this selection of crops was to be accompanied by changes in techniques and modes of cultivation. It was also decreed that all crops were to be planted in rows and that other species, such as beans, would no longer be tolerated in banana fields. In order to force the peasants to respect these new rules, agricultural technicians and local authorities paid site visits, sometimes with radical consequences. In Musanze, local authorities ordered peasants to destroy all crops other than maize, selected in that region for the current cultural season. In Ngoma district, peasants were forced to cut hundreds of hectares of banana trees and to plant coffee instead.[77] In September 2006, the mayor of Muhanga ordered the population to cut all banana trees and replace them with flowers or pineapple. A BBC story about this radical intervention forced the authorities to backtrack, and Muhanga's banana trees were eventually saved, but measures such as these showed how the government totally ignored the situation of the peasants for whom bananas are a vital source of physical and social survival.[78] The authoritarian transformation of agriculture included a mass rollout of commercial seeds, imported fertilizers, and pesticides. Since the inception in 2007 of the Crop Intensification Programme (CIP), agricultural production rose by

---

[75] UNDP, *Turning Vision 2020 into Reality. From Recovery to Sustainable Human Development*, Kigali, 2007, p. 17. This evolution had started before the RPF took power, but it has dramatically accelerated since.

[76] UNDP, *Human Development Report 2011*, p. 137. *Vision 2020* aimed at a Gini coefficient of 0.350 by 2020, down from 0.451 in 2000.

[77] "Cultiver pour vendre et non pour se nourrir", *Syfia Grands Lacs/Rwanda*, 15 November 2007.

[78] M.-F. Cros, "Rwanda. Développement: de gré ou de force?", *La Libre Belgique*, 5 October 2006.

about 14 percent per annum,[79] but success came with a price. In CIP-participating cooperatives, agricultural diversity plummeted while, conversely, the proportion of land occupied by maize rose from 48 percent to 89 percent. The price of staple foods on the local markets increased by 24 percent from 2006 to 2008. Imported hybrid seeds imposed on the farmers are expensive and cannot be saved and replanted. Farmers thus became dependent on a complex supply chain for seeds they once produced themselves.[80]

These hardest hit by such measures of rural engineering were the poorest peasants who suffered from famine and malnutrition as a result of compulsory mono-cropping. Although Kagame said that he failed to understand "why in these days an adult can suffer from kwashiorkor,"[81] peasants blamed government policies: "During the last season, we were forced to grow maize only, and we have harvested nothing because of the severe draught (...). If we were allowed to grow several crops at the same time, we would be able to save at least part of our yield."[82] These radical changes imposed from above understandably worried the peasants, who feared for their food security: "If we don't find the market we hoped for after growing maize, we risk starvation, and we will be unable to reimburse our credits," said one farmer, whereas another was even more pessimistic: "Before producing, we will die of hunger."[83] At the very moment a report of Action Aid Rwanda found that a quarter of Rwandans were hungry,[84] the agriculture and livestock minister stated that "the food situation in the country is more stable than it has been in many years."[85]

Land and agricultural policies were phrased in technical terms: security of tenure, effective exploitation, plot consolidation, optimal management, and productivity. Gready noted that "[u]nderlying these somewhat neutral sounding phrases is a more radical, and risky, vision

[79] M. Milz, *The Authoritarian Face of the "Green Revolution": Rwanda Capitulates to Agribusiness*, 8 août 2011.

[80] *Idem.*

[81] "Rwanda: la malnutrition ronge les campagnes", *Syfia Grands Lacs*, 14 May 2009.

[82] *Idem.*

[83] "Cultiver pour vendre et non pour se nourrir", *Syfia Grands Lacs/Rwanda*, 15 November 2007.

[84] "Rwanda: un quart des Rwandais ont faim", *Syfia Grands Lacs*, 15 October 2009. UNICEF's assessment was not more optimistic: "More than half of the children in the country are not having normal growth due to malnutriation – placing Rwanda among the 10 countries most affected globally" ("More than 50% of Children in Rwanda Are Stunted –UNICEF", Kigali, RNA, 13 November 2009).

[85] "Country Is Food Secure – Kalibata", *The New Times*, 19 October 2009; "Rwanda Is Malnutrition Free – Sezibera", *The New Times*, 29 October 2009.

of a privatized, market-driven, modernized and mechanized agricultural sector."[86] Ansoms summarizes the elite's engineering mission within the rural setting as follows:

> First, policy makers aim to transform the agricultural sector into a professionalised motor for economic growth, with little scope left for traditional smallholder agriculture. Second, policy makers seek to upgrade rural life by inserting "modern" techniques and strategies into local realities, while hiding the extent of poverty and inequality. Finally, they hope to transform Rwanda into a target-driven society from the highest to the lowest level. Taken together, these three social engineering ambitions amount to a top-down developmentalist agenda with a central role for the state as the engineer that shapes and reshapes the rural environment.[87]

FIGURES

As said earlier, a survey released in February 2012 found a national reduction of poverty by 11.8 percent between 2005/2006 and 2010/2011; absolute poverty fell from 35.8 percent to 24.1 percent during the same period. The national Gini coefficient came down from 0.522 in 2005/2006 to 0.490 in 2010/2011.[88] These are impressive figures, and they are striking particularly as far as inequality is concerned, as they show a sudden reversal in a strong trend, a trend that was also found in local-level qualitative research during the years preceding the survey. Among the "initial explanations" of the findings, the report lists a reduction in average household size, an important increase in wage income from nonfarm jobs (however, the researchers do not know in which areas these jobs have been created), an increase in transfers, an increase in agricultural production, and an increased commercialization of agriculture.[89] However, the survey offers a snapshot. Thus, agricultural production was a lot better in 2010 than in 2005, a factor that is very significant in a society in which the peasant mode of production is still overwhelmingly present. The data will therefore need to be confirmed or invalidated over the coming years, particularly as the survey results were not matched by subjective feelings on the ground.

---

[86] P. Gready, "'You're Either with Us or against Us': Civil Society and Policymaking in Post-genocide Rwanda", *African Affairs*, 109:437 (2010), p. 647.

[87] A. Ansoms, "Re-engineering Rural Society", p. 292.

[88] Republic of Rwanda, National Institute of Statistics of Rwanda, *The Evolution of Poverty in Rwanda from 2000 to 2011. Results from the Household Surveys (EICV)*, Kigali, February 2012.

[89] *Idem*, p. 28.

Thus, Ansoms and Rostagno found that a comparison of "sentiments" in six rural villages during fieldwork in 2007 and 2011 revealed a worrying rise in feelings of frustration and anger. Living conditions were said to be worse in 2011 than in 2007.[90] Ansoms also found that almost 300,000 youth or more than 13 percent of the population between fifteen and twenty-four years of age in 2005/2006 were missing in the 2010/2011 survey. This may be due to youngsters being unable to build a house set up a household in the "kitchen" of their parents, who no longer consider them part of their household, a phenomenon also observed by Sommers.[91] Ansoms estimated that at least 6 percent of the existing households were not included in the survey sample, which resulted in a significant under-estimation of poverty and thus inequality in 2010/2011.[92] What the publication of the survey achieved though, was a widespread feeling among donor agencies that the Rwandan "model" was working and that, maybe, a degree of authoritarianism was a price worth to be paid for socioeconomic progress,[93] a point underscored by Sommers: "To see Rwanda in positive terms, it appears that one must be comfortable with, and deem necessary for now, the government's authoritarianism."[94]

As a consequence of their need for success stories and their reluctance to question the regime's narrative, donors have embraced the results of the national survey without asking questions about its validity. However, the fact that the government has tampered with data in the past should inspire some caution. For instance, Sommers raised serious questions about the statistics on the HIV/AIDS infection rate, which, in a 2003, official

---

[90] A. Ansoms, D. Rostagno, "Rwanda's *Vision 2020* Halfway Through: What the Eye Does Not See", *Review of African Political Economy*, 39:133 (2012), p. 442.

[91] M. Sommers, *Stuck*, p. 130.

[92] A. Ansoms, *So Where Has the Youth Gone? An Anomaly in the EICV Dataset*, unpublished note, 15 March 2012.

[93] This feeling could be reinforced by research showing that the introduction of new infrastructure in the Rwandan coffee sector, under the form of cooperatives and private washing stations, is correlated with reconciliation between Hutu and Tutsi (J.M. Tobias, K.C. Boudreaux, "Entrepreneurship and Conflict Reduction in the Post-genocide Rwandan Coffee Industry", *Journal of Small Business and Entrepreneurship*, 24:2, pp. 217–242). However, a fundamental flaw of this research is that it does not include a control group made up of coffee farmers not involved in the new infrastructure. As the authors themselves acknowledge, their findings might point towards a false positive, where the observed reconciliation is unrelated to coffee industry changes (*idem*, p. 238).

[94] M. Sommers, *Stuck*, p. 20. In a similar vein, Hayman suggests that "donors are more willing to engage with the developmental side of the Rwandan government than penalise it for its misdemeanours" (R. Hayman, "Abandoned Orphan Wayward Child, the United Kingdom and Belguim in Rwanda since 1994", *Journal of Eastern African Studies*, 4:2 [2010], p. 354).

estimate stood at 13 percent but was reported in 2005 to be a mere 3 percent, a drop that cannot be explained, except by the fact that the design of the 2005 survey included only what the authors considered "ordinary households" in their sample. For other reasons too, the survey appeared to "contain a self-selecting sample."[95] Not one of Sommers's respondents suggested that the AIDS situation facing urban youth in Kigali was anything but serious, and no one predicted that it might improve,[96] whereas the 2005 national survey set HIV prevalence among the youth in Kigali at just 3.4 percent.

National data based on the aggregation of local data too might be unreliable, due to the way in which local level officials are constrained by performance contracts (*imihigo*) to reach certain targets. Sommers found strong indications that local officials kept information that challenged performance objectives to themselves. A sector official explained that the reports he and others send "up" the government chain highlighted achievements that supported government objectives, but did not relay information that conflicted with them.[97] The partial information that higher government levels receive invites distorted and overly positive assessments of actual realities.[98] Civil servants who worked in the Ministries of Agriculture (Minagri) and of Finance and Economic Planning (Minecofin) confirmed to this author that data on, for example, agricultural production provided by local authorities tended to be unreliable and overly optimistic.[99] This might be the explanation of a fact that the Rwandan health minister noticed only in 2008: "We do not know why, but for many years our measuring charts were simply wrong. Those children shown as fine were often malnourished, those as malnourished were acutely malnourished, and so on."[100] Bad reporting "from below" may well have an impact on other aggregate figures, such as GDP.[101] As

[95] M. Sommers, *Stuck*, pp. 34–35.
[96] *Idem*, p. 180.
[97] *Idem*, p. 87.
[98] *Idem*, p. 88.
[99] One civil servant told this author that when he raised the issue of the unreliability of local data, he was shrugged off by his superiors and barred from further accessing figures.
[100] "Malnutrition: The Scourge of Rwanda's children", *The Observer*, 19 February 2012. A U.S. medical doctor who worked in Rwanda noted that Rwandan leaders "are obsessed with the outward perception of their performance (...). The Rwandan government doctors statistics on health indicators to impress their donors" (V. DeGennaro, "Global Doc: Safe Distance", *Notre Dame Magazine*, 12 December 2012).
[101] A former civil servant who was part of a Minagri supervision team realized that local survey data on agricultural production were forged and that, in some cases, enumerators

shown earlier, the government has lied about other subjects, such as its involvement in the DRC, and has organized electoral fraud, systematically tampering with poll data. These examples suggest that the Rwandan "success story" might well be less evidence based than is usually admitted.

CONCLUSION

Scott found "a pernicious combination of four elements in (...) large-scale forms of social engineering that ended in disaster": the administrative ordering of nature and society; a high-modernist ideology that believes it is possible to rationally redesign human nature and social relations; an authoritarian government that is "willing and able to use the full weight of its coercive power to bring these high-modernist designs into being"; and "a prostrate civil society that lacks the capacity to resist these plans."[102] This is the combination of elements prevailing in post-genocide Rwanda.

Despite experiences elsewhere, the regime believes that it is possible to legislate unity and modernity into existence, to create a new Rwanda and a new Rwandan. This belief is informed by paternalism and disdain for ordinary Rwandans, who do not understand what is good for them and who need to be educated. The disconnection between Kigali and the rest of the country is reinforced by the fact that the elites are urban and dominated by Tutsi coming from the diaspora, whereas most Rwandans are rural, Hutu, and born inside Rwanda. This artificial imposition of a world vision unlinked to the daily experience and struggle of most people, together with the trauma of dealing with the past of genocide, has rapidly and profoundly altered an ancient peasant order, with potentially tragic consequences.

Some of these engineering efforts have been studied here. They are both top-down and aimed at control. They are also heavy-handed, radical, and immediate, and they are informed by a strong sense of entitlement among RPF elites who firmly believe – both in their engineering efforts and their politics more generally – that they have it right and that those who criticize them have it wrong. Land and agricultural policies are part of a wider modernization drive, but they also marginalize and disable small peasants while offering institutional opportunities to commercial farmers and absentee landlords well connected to those in

did not fill out questionnaires in the field. When he and some of his colleagues raised that issue, nothing was done about it (personal communication).

[102] J.C. Scott, *Seeing Like a State: How Certain Schemes to Improve the Human Condition Have Failed*, New Haven CT, Yale University Press, 1998, pp. 4–5.

power,[103] strongly increasing inequality in the process. These policies may make good sense on paper, but – particularly in the Rwandan context – they contribute to the exacerbation of the structural violence so prevalent today. Through their support for land reform and other risky policies, aid agencies such as DFID and USAID, which saw Rwanda as an interesting laboratory of engineering, have unwillingly contributed to this structural violence. As shown by Uvin with regard to pre-1994 Rwanda, this is a potent breeding ground for renewed actual violence.[104]

As will be seen later, the engineering does not, however, go unchallenged. In an authoritarian environment, forms of resistance are kept as invisible as possible, and they sometimes take the form of popular modes of political action.[105] Thomson finds subtle, indirect, and nonconfrontational acts that make life more sustainable under strong and centralised state power.[106] Strategies include staying on the sidelines, irreverent compliance,[107] and withdrawn muteness,[108] all ways of concealing or revealing political opinions,[109] whereas those in power believe they get away with their oppressive behavior. In a sense, the RPF behaves similar to an occupying force, and it is seen as such by many Rwandans, who resist in a way reminiscent of the situation in occupied France during World War II.

[103] Cf. the case of General Fred Ibingira mentioned earlier.

[104] P. Uvin, *Aiding Violence: The development enterprise in Rwanda*, West Hartford, CT, Kumarian Press, 1998.

[105] This notion has been developed in France by Jean-François Bayart, Achille Mbembe, and other advocates of *"la politique par le bas"* (politics from below) who insist on the capacity to react of the oppressed. These popular modes take on hidden and subtle forms such as mockery, body language, sabotage, ambiguity, evasive behavior, petty crime, and violence (see J.-F. Bayart, A. Mbembe, C. Toulabor, *La politique par le bas en Afrique noire. Contribution à une problématique de la démocratie*, Paris, Karthala, 1992). These insights are akin to Scott's hidden transcripts discussed in the next chapter.

[106] S. Thomson, "Whispering Truth to Power: The Everyday Resistance of Rwandan Peasants to Post-genocide Reconciliation", *African Affairs*, 110:440 (2011), pp. 446–447. For a survey of forms of everyday resistance (including playing dumb, which even further reinforced the elites' conviction that Rwandans are not political beings and need to be educated), see S. Thomson, *Resisting Reconciliation: State Power and Everyday Life in Post-genocide Rwanda*, PhD thesis, Dalhousie University, pp. 213–227.

[107] Begley offers a nice instance. A voter stormed into a polling station shouting, "Show me where to vote for the RPF. I am here to vote for the RPF." He explained his behavior as follows: "The elections are all the same. (...) I don't want any more problems with them, so I stood in front of everyone and asked them where do I vote for the RPF" (L. Begley, "Resolved to Fight", p. 135). What he did in reality was make a mockery of the vote in such a way that he could not be sanctioned because he observed the rules imposed by the public transcript.

[108] S. Thomson, "Whispering Truth", pp. 448–455.

[109] *Idem*, p. 456.

A report quoted earlier points at the contradiction between good technocratic and flawed political governance, as the latter may defeat the former. Noting the limits of authoritarian-led development, it considered three factors, two of which are relevant here. First, demands for political change are likely to outstrip the stabilizing effects of economic growth, "particularly (…) if economic benefits are perceived as skewed toward a particular segment of the population."[110] Second, the authoritarian nature of political life may stifle healthy competition and the kind of entrepreneurial culture and risk taking that drive the economy. In addition, the top-down social engineering approaches have met with costly failure elsewhere, but "[t]he Rwandan government has pressed forward, despite considerable observer and donor scepticism and mounting evidence that such policies may ultimately prove deeply unpopular and counterproductive."[111]

This concern is underscored by the paradoxical results of research into the visions and ambitions of youth in Rwanda and Burundi. The strong reach of the Rwandan state and its pervasive social engineering was found to coexist with and to reinforce a risk-averse and quietly resistant population, whereas in Burundi, a weak and easily subverted state coexists with a more dynamic and flexible population. "In Rwanda, a great many youth seem despondent and disillusioned. In Burundi, youth face many of the same challenges as in Rwanda, yet many Burundian youth believe that the future holds promise if they can work hard, remain flexible, and have some luck."[112] Sommers and Uvin find this unexpected outcome in many fields, such as attaining manhood, belief in education and internal migration as ways out, and prospects of social mobility. For instance, in Rwanda, where much has been invested in education, the vast majority of youth (strikingly even more in urban than in rural areas) do not consider education or training as a component of their future because "it is impossible to change your situation."[113] In contrast, 85 percent of those interviewed in Burundi, where the educational sector is much less developed, spontaneously brought up education as the single most important means of improving their lives. According to Sommers, "Rwanda faces the imminent prospect of producing almost an entire generation of failed adults."[114] He found

---

[110] Center for Strategic & International Studies, *Rwanda. Assessing Risks*, p. 15.
[111] *Idem*, p. 16.
[112] M. Sommers, P. Uvin, *Youth in Rwanda and Burundi. Contrasting Visions*, Special Report 293, Washington, DC, United States Institute of Peace, October 2011, p. 9.
[113] *Idem*, p. 5.
[114] M. Sommers, *Stuck*, p. 193.

high levels of frustration, anxiety, destitution, and lack of perspective among both rural and urban youth. His research made it clear that many if not most poor youth quietly resist a great deal of what their government wants them to do: join associations, attend youth meetings, participate in *umuganda*, avoid working in the informal sector, build houses exclusively in *imidugudu*, and so on.[115] These findings are dramatic, and they confirm the invisible side effects of the stifling ambitions by the Rwandan state to engineer people's lives.

[115] *Idem*, p. 201.

7

Managing Information, Imposing the Truth

"A NEW WAY OF DOING THINGS"

The regime has been extremely successful in projecting an image of morality, vision, and success. Indeed, already during the civil war the RPF realized that battles are fought in the media as much as, if not more than, on the ground. Well prepared and managing public opinion in a very professional vein, it succeeded with surprising ease to have a dual simple message penetrate the international media: on one hand, its invasion from Uganda wanted to rid Rwanda of a corrupt, regionalist, discriminatory, and totalitarian regime; on the other, the RPF was going to put into place democracy, harmony between ethnic groups and regions, social justice, and a healthy and rigorous management of public affairs. It portrayed itself as a liberation movement, the "good guys." Although nothing supported this claim, it was hardly contested by anyone except the handful of Rwanda old hands.[1] By successfully demonizing the Habyarimana regime and pointing at its indisputable faults, it secured the support of influential but ill-informed political circles abroad and of some NGOs, human rights organizations, and press outlets influenced by RPF supporters. This was achieved by using efficient diaspora networks,[2] by creating relays in

---

[1] For instance through a forty-five-page memorandum published by a number of Belgian NGOs in the wake of the invasion: COOPIBO, FOS, NCOS, Vredeseilanden, *Le Rwanda. Et maintenant?*, 7 November 1990.

[2] One example among many are the activities of a Comité pour le respect des droits de l'homme et la démocratie au Rwanda (CRDDR) created in Brussels in November 1990, just after the RPF's invasion. It was very active in denouncing the human rights violations of the Habyarimana regime, but remained systematically silent about RPF abuse. As soon as the

international media and political circles, by using the right discourse, and through the inclusion of some Hutu who had fallen out with the Habyarimana regime.

This has remained the RPF's strategy ever since, as was shown in a 2009 lobbying plan at the cost of US$50,000 per month.[3] The goals included "[to]build a strong and sustained image campaign communicating the successes of Rwanda with key stakeholders in the political and financial elite communities (...) [and] offset the negative and factually incorrect information of those parties with vested interests in mis-portraying Rwanda's advancements." With regard to the latter, "the campaign will help insure [to] negate the misinformation being pedalled by expats, NGOs and others with a vested interest in creating an image of Rwanda as a failed state." The "strategic roadmap" included "[to] develop a believable narrative," "establishing an influencer network," "seeding the story," and "erecting a perimeter" (destined to "blunt the online impact of our opposition by initiating a wall of defence debunking their accusations"). BTP Advisers, another public relations firm, created an Internet "attack site" for the government. It targeted people who "over-criticised" over "who did what in the genocide."[4] As a matter of fact, the RPF did not need the services of an expensive lobbying firm, as it had been doing this itself very effectively for many years, often by using relays in its pay.

The involvement in disinformation of African Rights, an organization that split from Human Rights Watch/Africa, started just months before the RPF seized power. In May 1994, it reported that "there is absolutely no evidence that the RPF is responsible for large scale indiscriminate killings of civilians."[5] Although this could be seen at the time as a statement due to lack of information, the organization persevered. Even in the revised

RPF seized power, the CRDDR ceased to function. Its leader, Gasana Ndoba, later became president of the (governmental) National Human Rights Commission. Not only Rwandan sympathizers of the RPF were active in this propaganda war, but Europeans (often married to Tutsi) also contributed, and they do so up to the present day. Some information on these networks can be found in P. Péan, *Noires fureurs, blancs menteurs. Rwanda 1990–1994*, Paris, Mille etunenuits, 2005; and in C. Onana, *Les secrets de la justice internationale. Enquêtes truquées sur le génocide rwandais*, Paris, Editions Duboiris, 2005, pp. 330–361. In July 2010, a number of foreigners received a medal "for their individual role in the liberation struggle." Among them were Roger Winter, Jean-Paul Gouteux, Jean Carbonare, and Jean Gol who had all supported the RPF's cause.

[3] "Master Service Agreement by and between Government of Rwanda and W2 Group, Inc.", 11 September 2009.

[4] "Rwanda: How Dare You Accuse our Client of Genocide", *The Independent* (London), 7 December 2011.

[5] African Rights, *Rwanda. Who Is Killing; Who Is Dying; What Is to Be Done*, May 1994.

edition of its monumental *Rwanda. Death, Despair and Defiance* published in August 1995,[6] the conclusion of African Rights on RPF abuse was that "no convincing evidence has yet been produced to show that the RPF has a policy of systematic violence against civilians," and it went on: "The RPF has one enormous credit to its name. It succeeded in inflicting a decisive military defeat on a genocidal regime, and thereby halting the mass killings of civilians (...). In doing so it was fulfilling its fundamental moral and legal obligation under international law."[7] This, of course, echoed the RPF line. It later appeared that the closeness of African Rights to the regime was not just intellectual. In letters of June 6 and 23, 2008, Jean de Dieu Mucyo, the executive secretary of the National Commission for the Fight against Genocide, referred to an amount of more than US$100,000 that the government owed African Rights for the drafting of a report.[8] Money changed hands at other occasions too. The way in which one of the best Ugandan journalists, Andrew Mwenda, incensed Kagame for years intrigued many, but things became clearer when it appeared that he received a payment of US$200,000 from the Rwandan government for "advertising." The money was paid "confidentially" from a classified account.[9] In September 2011, Mwenda was appointed a member of Kagame's Presidential Advisory Council, a network of Rwandan and international personalities lobbying in support of the regime.

An early *"chef d'oeuvre* of obfuscation"[10] was written by *New Yorker* journalist Philip Gourevitch.[11] Well written, it became a Bible of sorts, particularly in the United States, and it has probably had more influence

---

6   This was at the time of the severe government crisis precisely against the background of massive human rights abuse by the RPA; cf. Chapter 1.

7   African Rights, *Rwanda. Death, Despair and Defiance*, London, August 1995, p. 1087. This report also announced that "[t]he human rights record of the RPF and the new government will be the focus of future African Rights investigations" (p. 1075). However, no such investigations were carried out (at least, no results of such investigations were published).

8   African Rights' Rakiya Omaar did "consultancy" for other Rwandan government bodies too. In a report (African Rights, *The Leadership of Rwandan Armed Groups Abroad with a Focus on the FDLR and RUD/Urunana*, December 2008), Omaar presented herself as a "consultant to the Rwandan Demobilisation and Reintegration Commission."

9   "Rwanda Pays Mwenda through Classified Account", 256newsonline, 19 March 2011 (http://www.256newsonline.com). A copy of the payment order was reproduced in the article, and Mwenda did not deny the story.

10 J. Pottier, *Re-imagining Rwanda. Conflict, Survival and Disinformation in the Late Twentieth Century*, Cambridge, Cambridge University Press, 2002, p. 169.

11 P. Gourevitch, *We Wish to Inform You that Tomorrow We Will Be Killed with our Families*, New York, Farrar, Straus and Giroux, 1998.

than most of the thoroughly researched academic writing. However, the book was weak on historical background, contained dozens of factual errors, did not offer any new insights into the genocide, and – above all – was a thinly veiled apology for the RPF whose crimes were either not mentioned or explained away. Interestingly, when Gourevitch interviewed regime people such as Kagame, he took what they stated at face value without wondering whether what they claimed was true (e.g., chapter 14), but when talking to opponents, he added comments tending to discredit what they had to say (e.g., chapter 17). Ten years later, although the nature of the regime had become very clear (which was perhaps not the case for beginners such as Gourevitch in 1997), another journalist published a glowing hagiography of Kagame, who was said to be "the man of the hour in modern Africa. The eyes of all who hope for a better Africa are upon him."[12]

With regard to the massacres by the RPA of refugees in Zaire in 1996–1997 (cf. Chapter 4), Nik Gowing has shown the importance of information management by the Rwandan regime. Without false modesty, Kagame stated that "[w]e used communication and information warfare better than anyone. We have found a new way of doing things."[13] One technique, first used in Rwanda and later in Zaire, was the "closure of the conflict scene": Kagame confirmed that "the aim was to let them (the NGOs and the press) continue their work, but deny them what would be dangerous to us."[14] A reporter noted in 1994 that "[j]ournalists are required to travel with armed escorts in rebel-controlled territory and are closely monitored."[15] This was also the experience of an international commission of inquiry that visited the RPF-held area in early 1993.[16] Intimidation was another tool: "Kagame does not like NGOs, so he

---

[12] S. Kinzer, *A Thousand Hills: Rwanda's Rebirth and the Man who Dreamed It*, Hoboken, NJ, John Wiley and Sons, 2008, p. 337. We have seen that Kinzer has since changed his mind about Kagame.

[13] N. Gowing, "New Challenges and Problems for Information Management in Complex Emergencies: Ominous Lessons from the Great Lakes and Eastern Zaire in Late 1996 and Early 1997", paper presented at Dispatches from Disaster Zones conference, Oxford, 28 May 1998, p. 4.

[14] *Idem*, p. 15.

[15] D. Lorch, "Rwanda Rebels: Army of Exiles Fights for a Home", *New York Times*, 9 June 1994.

[16] Fédération internationale des ligues des droits de l'homme, Africa Watch, Union interafricaine des droits de l'homme et des peuples, Centre international des droits de la personne et du développement démocratique, *Rapport de la commission internationale d'enquête sur les violations des droits de l'homme au Rwanda depuis le 1ᵉʳ octobre 1990*, March 1993, p. 70.

paralysed them completely and terrorised them. If he did not like what they did with information, he kicked them out."[17] Likewise, journalists "knew the Rwandan government could make life unpleasant."[18] Fear was reinforced by a practice of encouraging leaks and monitoring communications. Thus, "one particular NGO partial to the Rwandan government" would fax sit-reps directly to Kagame's office.[19] A humanitarian agent indicated that "if the Save the Children person in Bukavu radioed that he had refugees (...), then those refugees would be under threat because networks were bugged."[20] Not content with remaining silent about RPF crimes, some reporters became "RPF groupies," ready to excuse what they did wrong: one of them recognized that "journalists and NGOs were in bed with the RPF."[21] At any rate, the choice was simple: "The RPA's line was that you are either with the RPA or against them."[22]

Pottier notes that Kagame's information strategy was "built around denial."[23] It actually amounted to shameless lying, such as on Rwanda's involvement in and plunder of the DRC, its human rights record, electoral fraud, and political murder abroad.[24] The RPF's routine was "simple but effective: ban outsiders from the battle zone; delay and frustrate their movements; deny any 'rumour' of military excesses; withhold information; apply moral argument by shaming the international community."[25] Even during the months that the RPF was just establishing its control, it was remarkably successful in restricting access by foreigners to areas where it was "cleaning up":

The RPF established close control over foreigners working or travelling in areas under its authority. Information and liaison officers worked hard at shaping the ideas of outsiders while persons employed by foreigners were ordered to report on their activities and conversations. Ordinarily journalists and aid workers were allowed to travel in RPF territory only in the company of officially designated "guides" who sought to ensure that they travel just to approved areas, usually via

---

[17] N. Gowing, "New Challenges", p. 22.

[18] *Idem*, p. 36.

[19] *Idem*, p. 47.

[20] *Idem*, p. 50.

[21] *Idem*, p. 41.

[22] *Idem*, p. 62. Cf. P. Gready, "'You're Either with Us or against Us': Civil society and Policy Making in Post-genocide Rwanda", *African Affairs*, 109:437 (2010), pp. 637–657.

[23] J. Pottier, *Re-imagining Rwanda*, p. 55.

[24] Eventually, this habit of lying irritated even the RPF's closest international allies in 2012, when the regime again denied the light of the sun about its involvement in the DRC (cf. Chapter 5).

[25] J. Pottier, *Re-imagining Rwanda*, p. 58.

the main roads. The RPF closed whole regions to UNAMIR and other foreign observers for weeks at a time.[26]

This kind of manipulation was facilitated by the genocide credit the regime astutely maintained and exploited to escape condemnation. The constant reference to the genocide served several purposes: justifying Tutsi dominance (without saying so), keeping alive the fear of Hutu revenge,[27] maintaining the support of many Tutsi, and keeping the international community at bay. It became a powerful ideological weapon that allowed the RPF to acquire and maintain victim status and to enjoy impunity for its own crimes. Pottier observed that "[T]hose who represent the victims of genocide are not to be challenged."[28] A diplomat interviewed by *Le Monde* in New York acknowledged that "any action undertaken against the regime in Kigali is always perceived as offering moral support to those guilty of genocide; it is true that the Rwandan regime is benefiting from this ambivalence, and we know it."[29] The regime too knew: Minister Patrick Mazimhaka stated that "we were [diplomatically] stronger because nobody could argue against us,"whereas a U.S. diplomat admitted that "the Americans were terribly manipulated by this government and now we are almost held hostage by it."[30] A donor representative quoted by Zorbas remarked that there is "an element of 'we know better' and 'you have no moral authority.' And it is hard to disagree with them."[31]

The reluctance to speak out extended to international donor agencies, quite a remarkable fact in light of Rwanda's profound aid dependence. Sommers quotes a Kigali-based donor official who described how troubling information about particular economic and service sectors had to be "sanitized" or framed in a positive way before it could be shared with government officials. Others mentioned performing this kind of

[26] A. Des Forges, *Leave None to Tell the Story. Genocide in Rwanda*, New York and Paris Human Rights Watch-Fédération internationale des ligues des droits de l'homme, 1999, p. 723.

[27] Indeed, referring to "Tutsi Power," Mamdani notes that not only the genocide of the past but also preventing one in the future was part of the RPF's argument: "The moral certainty about preventing another genocide imparts a moral justification to the pursuit of power with impunity" (M. Mamdani, *When Victims Become Killers. Colonialism, Nativism, and the Genocide in Rwanda*, Princeton, NJ, Princeton University Press, 2001, p. 271).

[28] J. Pottier, *Re-imagining Rwanda*, p. 176.

[29] *Le Monde*, 26 October 1996.

[30] *Washington Post*, 14 July 1998.

[31] E. Zorbas, "Aid Dependence and Policy Independence. Explaining the Rwandan Paradox", in S. Straus, L. Waldorf (Eds.), *Remaking Rwanda. State Building and Human Rights after Mass Violence*, Madison, The University of Wisconsin Press, 2011, p. 108.

self-censorship, "which essentially sounded like providing a positive spin on troubling information."[32] Another aid official candidly stated, "You toe the party [RPF] line here. If you don't, you're out. No one wants to look bad before their bosses. So you pretend that everything's OK."[33] Sommers was also told that international agencies might alter or simply not release reports that might upset Rwandan officials.[34]

However, a panel put in place by the OAU was not fooled: The RPF

are masters of shrewd communication strategies. RPF leaders have long understood that they begin with the benefit of the doubt, based on a combination of guilt and sympathy from the world at large. Guilt for failing to prevent the genocide and sympathy for the RPF as the government of the victims help explain why the international community, bolstered by like-minded journalists and NGOs, has often been ready to believe the RPF version that most human rights violations have been perpetrated by the genocidaires. (...) [C]ritics of the government are simply dismissed as genocide sympathisers –a technique that puts a chill on legitimate dissent.[35]

In 2001, Claudine Vidal analysed the use made of the annual genocide commemorations for propaganda purposes: "The ceremonies organised by the regime reveal an inevitable relation of power, first because they capture the silent words of the victims, giving them a meaning determined by current goals, and second because they take over the private mourning of the survivors and transform it into a collective mourning in the name of considerations that are not theirs."[36] She concluded that "at every commemoration, those in power have instrumentalised the representation of the genocide in the context of the political conflicts at the time."[37] In a similar vein, Burnet found that "Kagame mobilized the bodies of victims as part of his indictment of the international community" at the national ceremony held in 2001 in Kibungo prefecture.[38] Likewise, Meierhenrich contends that "notably some Tutsi elites who returned from exile (...)

---

[32] M. Sommers, *Stuck. Rwandan Youth and the Struggle for Adulthood*, Athens, GA, and London, University of Georgia Press, 2012, p. 20.

[33] *Idem*, p. 21.

[34] *Idem*, p. 50.

[35] Organisation of African Unity, International Panel of Eminent Personalities to Investigate the 1994 Genocide in Rwanda and the Surrounding Events, *Rwanda: The Preventable Genocide*, Addis Ababa, 7 July 2000, § 22.36.

[36] C. Vidal, "Les commémorations du génocide au Rwanda", *Les Temps Modernes*, No. 613 (2001), p. 44.

[37] *Idem*, p. 45.

[38] J.E. Burnet, "Whose Genocide? Whose Truth?", in A.L. Hinton, K.L. O'Neill (Eds.) *Genocide, Truth, Memory, and Representation*, Durham, NC, and London, Duke University Press, 2009, p. 96.

conceive of memorialisation as a means to an end, the marketing of genocide to the international community."[39] Johan Pottier translated this observation into the arena of the regime's dealing with the outside world. The RPF, "as Rwanda's post-genocide spiritual guardian, displays exceptional skill at converting international feelings of guilt and ineptitude into admissions that the Front deserves to have the monopoly on knowledge construction."[40] The regime "convinced the world that they – and they alone – had the right to know and determine what was going on in those parts of the Great Lakes region they now controlled," and they achieved this through a strategy based on the "concept of morality, guilt and punishment."[41]

Besides its moral high ground, the regime also succeeded in having its flawless narrative swallowed by the donor community because of its decent technocratic governance, with competent and even charming élites articulating an intelligent discourse, exactly the one the international community wished to hear. Rwanda is seen as "a serious place run by serious people."[42] The regime's rhetoric, neatly in line with modern development thinking as articulated in the 2005 Paris Principles, is liked by donors who see the RPF as "hardworking, professional, ambitious," "enlightened and progressive," "active and dynamic."[43] All this is even true. And yet, behind this façade is a regime that has ruthlessly killed hundreds of thousands of its own citizens and that has practiced political murder at a large scale. I referred in Chapter 3 to behind-the-curtain views reminiscent of Nero's Rome offered by a former Speaker of Parliament, a former minister, and a former chief of army staff.

THE TRUTH

Alternative readings of the RPF's record needed to be avoided. Although the Arusha peace accord provided for the setting up of an international commission of inquiry (on which the RPF insisted before its military victory), it never materialized because it would in all likelihood have challenged the RPF's

---

[39] J. Meierhenrich, "Topographies of Remembering and Forgetting. The Transformation of Lieux de Mémoire in Rwanda", in S. Straus, L. Waldorf (Eds.), *Remaking Rwanda*, p. 284.
[40] J. Pottier, *Re-imagining Rwanda*, p. 203.
[41] *Idem*, p. 151.
[42] M. Sommers, *Stuck*, p. 15.
[43] E. Zorbas, "Aid Dependence", p. 108.

narrative. The "international community" never insisted, and abandoned the "power over memory"[44] to the regime.

The monopoly of truth the regime successfully gained extended not just to Rwanda's visions and analyses of current affairs, for instance, its democratic credentials, its human rights record, or its involvement in the DRC, but also to history more generally. In summary, this official history claims that precolonial Rwanda had been for centuries a unified, harmonious and peaceful society and that, inspired by the so-called Hamitic Hypothesis,[45] ethnicity was introduced by the Belgian administration and the Catholic Church in the context of a divide and rule policy, and they did so in an artificial fashion, by basing ethnic identity on the possession of cattle.[46] The RPF put an end to the genocide[47] that resulted from divisive politics, and restored peace and harmony.[48] Organizations that claimed to be independent of the government proposed a similar reading,

[44] J. Meierhenrich, "Topographies", p. 285.

[45] E.R. Sanders, "The Hamitic Hypothesis: Its Origin and Function in Time Perspective", *Journal of African History*, 10:4 (1969), pp. 521–532.

[46] The narrative of the Rwandan government, but also of many academic writers (e.g., P. Clark, *The Gacaca Courts, Post-genocide Justice and Reconciliation in Rwanda. Justice without Lawyers*, Cambridge, Cambridge University Press, 2010, p.17) almost invariably contains a reference to the ten-cow myth, which claims that, at the Belgian census of the early 1930s, those possessing at least ten heads of cattle were considered Tutsi, thus showing the artificial nature of the categorization. This claim is never accompanied by a source (except a source without a source). As common with myths, this is factually untrue, for at least two reasons. First, René Bourgeois, who was a young *administrateur de territoire* in these days and who participated in the census, told this writer that the categorization was based on what heads of households themselves declared as their ethnicity, and not on their possession of cattle (interview with R. Bourgeois, Brussels, 19 October 1981). Second, there were simply not enough cows to make this possible, even if one were to assume that not a single Tutsi had more than ten cows and that no Hutu possessed a single head of cattle (both these assumptions are wrong). In 1949, the first year for which I found reliable data, there were about 591,000 cows and about 62,000 Tutsi *hommes adultes valides* (HAV).

[47] However, we have seen earlier that the RPF's main objective during April-June 1994 was not to halt the genocide but to win the war. Dallaire realized that "Kagame wanted all of the country, not parts of it. I came to believe he didn't want the situation to stabilise until he had won" (R. Dallaire, *Shake Hands with the Devil. The Failure of Humanity in Rwanda*, Toronto, Random House Canada, 2003, p. 438). Dallaire also wondered "[w]ho exactly had been pulling [Kagame's] strings throughout the campaign? I found myself thinking such dire thoughts on whether the campaign and the genocide had been orchestrated to clear the way for Rwanda's return to the pre-1959 status quo in which Tutsis had called all the shots. Had the Hutu extremists been bigger dupes than I?" (*idem*, p. 476).

[48] This presentation can be found in many statements and documents; see, for example, Republic of Rwanda, Office of the President, *The Unity of Rwandans: Before the Colonial Period and under Colonial Rule, under the First Republic*, Kigali, August 1999; Republic of Rwanda, Office of the President of the Republic, *Report on the Reflection Meetings Held in the Office of the President of the Republic from May 1998 to March 1999*, Kigali, August 1999; Republic

though sometimes phrased in a more subtle fashion. For instance, whereas a 2003 report of the Institute of Research and Dialogue for Peace (IRDP) pleaded in favor of a research effort to elucidate disputed questions of Rwanda's history,[49] three years later the IRDP proposed a reading that was perfectly in line with the RPF's narrative.[50] This narrative is coherent and articulated in a systematic fashion. Pottier notes "the pervasiveness and power of clustered narratives that simplify reality to make the post-genocide government of Rwanda and its practices intelligible, rational and legitimate in the eyes of the world."[51]

However, a leading historian of Rwanda, Jan Vansina,[52] finds "a whole set of false propositions and assertions"[53] in this narrative. "The linguistic and cultural unity of the country today did not exist in the seventeenth century and Rwanda is not a 'natural' nation. (...) Rwanda really became a nation in the twentieth century"[54]; "Formerly, neither abundance nor order flourished in the country and it is false to think that everyone was happy with their station in life and all lived in peace under the shepherd's staff of wise kings"[55]; "The reasons for the elaboration of such erroneous propositions are evident. (...) there is the projection of a nostalgic utopia into the past, a past that contrasts with a painful present."[56] Miller too finds that "[t]he problem (...) is that the narrative is – from a scholarly perspective – inaccurate. (...) The effects of these particularised versions are both to suppress discussion in the population and to perform a certain narrative for the internationals who involve themselves with Rwanda."[57]

of Rwanda, National Unity and Reconciliation Commission, *The Rwandan Conflict: Origin, Development, Exit Strategies*, Kigali, 2004; Courses taught in *ingando* reproduced in PRI, *From Camp to Hill, the Reintegration of Released Prisoners*, May 2004, pp. 83–112. For a summary of the government's reading of history, see S. Buckley-Zistel, "Nation, Narration, Unification? The Politics of History Teaching after the Rwandan Genocide", *Journal of Genocide Research*, 11:1 (2009), pp. 33–38.

[49] IRDP, *Reconstruire une paix durable au Rwanda: La parole au peuple*, Kigali, 2003.

[50] IRDP, *La démocratie au Rwanda*, Kigali, n.d. (2006), pp. 56–79.

[51] J. Pottier, *Re-imagining Rwanda*, p. 47.

[52] The IRDP does not think highly of Vansina: "The social and ethnic political reading of history is not that of Rwandans, but results from domination and imperialism, *n'en déplaise à* certain authors such as Jan Vansina who pretend that this already existed before colonial days" (IRDP, *La démocratie*, p. 21). Not a single source is offered to substantiate that claim.

[53] J. Vansina, *Antecedents to Modern Rwanda. The Nyiginya Kingdom*, Madison, University of Wisconsin Press, 2004, pp. 197–198.

[54] *Idem*, p. 198.

[55] *Idem*.

[56] *Idem*, p. 199.

[57] Z. Miller, *Constructing Sustainable Reconciliation: Land, Power and Transitional Justice in Post-genocide Rwanda*, Cape Town, Institute for Justice and Reconciliation, 2007, p. 46.

The evocation of an Eden-like past is also practical, as it allows the RPF to legitimize actions in the name of "tradition," even if such tradition does not exist.[58] *Gacaca, ingando, imihigo, itorero, ubudehe, umuganda,* and other concepts with a positive "traditional" overtone were helpful in allowing the RPF to sell its story.

If history did not suit the regime, a new history needed to be constructed. Even the constitution was called in to protect the truth. An amendment of August 13, 2008, added the words "against the Tutsi" after "genocide" in article 51, thus attempting to outlaw the proponents of a "double genocide." During a scholarly debate in Kigali in 2004 about the nature of the genocide, one academic expert mentioned the value of different "truths." A high-ranking official in the audience immediately demanded the floor to insist: "There is only one truth and we know it."[59] This was made clear by Kagame too: "Those who have divergent interpretations of how and why the genocide occurred are revisionists and/ or proponents of the theory of double genocide. This, as we know, is another phase of genocide."[60] The stated aim of an "international conference" held in Kigali in July 2008 was "on the one hand, to observe the failure of the human and social sciences that have led to genocide,[61] on the other, the resourcing of the human and social sciences thanks to the efforts of the Rwandans." The meeting called for "a new methodology, a new literature, *a new history.*"[62]

When the "truth" is put forward, it is presented as that of "the Rwandans" or "the Rwandan people" serving as proxies for the RPF.[63] The regime even succeeded in penetrating international academic

---

[58] On the use of tradition to legitimize contemporary political projects, see E. Hobsbawn, T. Ranger (Eds.), *The Invention of Tradition*, Cambridge, Cambridge University Press, 1983.

[59] Human Rights Watch, *Law and Reality. Progress in Judicial Reform in Rwanda*, New York, 24 July 2008, p. 36. This is the line held at all levels. Thus, Begley recalls a U.S. tourist in the Kigali Memorial Centre asking his guide "What's the Hutu side of the story?", to which the guide replied "This is what happened" (L. Begley, "Resolved to Fight", p. 115).

[60] P. Kagame, "Preface", in P. Clark, Z.D. Kaufman (Eds.), *After Genocide. Transitional Justice, Post-conflict Reconstruction and Reconciliation in Rwanda and Beyond*, London, Hurst, 2008, p. xxii.

[61] Note that researchers (supposedly those who do not adhere to the RPF's truth) are thus made responsible for the genocide.

[62] "Rwanda: Apprendre de l'expérience du génocide rwandais", Kigali, ARI, 23 July 2008 (emphasis added).

[63] Interestingly, while the RPF claims to speak in the name of all Rwandans or to articulate their view, this population is considered immature and in need of education and enlightenment (cf. supra).

publishing to settle scores with critical scholars. A book published in 2008 contained a six-page-long preface[64] in which President Kagame was not only allowed to put forward his regime's view on Rwanda's past, present, and future, but also to propose a strongly worded rebuttal of a chapter written by Lemarchand in that very book. Lemarchand was said to be "mistaken," "simplistic," and "wrong"; "The revisionists must receive justice for their crimes against historical truth and the affront of their fraudulent narratives." The single truth even applied to children and to matters other than general history. When, at a 2007 National Summit for Children and Young People, children reported that parents were selling their children as slaves to other households, they were criticized by ministers and told slavery did not exist in Rwanda.[65] As a matter of fact, regime behavior reinforced a long-standing, strong desire among Rwandans for certainty. The Berkeley history curriculum project mentioned earlier was confronted with teachers expressing a strong need for "truth" about any narratives that entered the classroom.[66]

One particular aspect of imposing the truth served a very concrete project. The RPF vigorously denied the reality of ethnicity, a denial that was an essential element of the hegemonic strategies of a small Tutsi elite. The claim that "there are no Hutu and Tutsi, but only Banyarwanda" allowed to hide domination by Tutsi. So the "myth" of ethnic difference must be erased, and Mgbako found that reeducation regarding the ethnicity question is at the heart of the *ingando* program,[67] which is the only place where history is currently taught.[68] Purdekova notes that the discursive frame of the "de-ethnicisation" project "merely obscures the top-down dissemination, tightly policed boundaries and authoritarian nature of the discourse."[69] The link with authoritarianism is obvious, as the top-down imposition of this project is not matched by attempts at involving people in the construction of their state and their history. "Rwandanness" is thus a "fictive ethnicity" instituted by the

---

[64] P. Kagame, "Preface", pp. xxi–xxvi.

[65] K. Pells, "Building a Rwanda 'Fit for Children'", in S. Straus, L. Waldorf (Eds.), *Remaking Rwanda*, p. 81.

[66] S. Warshauer Freedman et al., "Teaching History in Post-genocide Rwanda", in S. Straus, L. Waldorf (Eds.), *Remaking Rwanda*, p. 307.

[67] C. Mgbako, "*Ingando* Solidarity Camps: Reconciliation and Political Indoctrination in Post-genocide Rwanda", *Harvard Human Rights Journal*, 18 (2005), p. 218.

[68] A survey of what is taught at *ingando* and in memorial sites can be found in L. Begley, "Resolved to Fight", pp. 112–120.

[69] A. Purdekova, *Repatriation and Reconciliation in Divided Societies: The Case of Rwanda's "Ingando"*, RSC Working Paper No. 43, Oxford, January 2008, p. 3.

state.[70] However, unity, reconciliation, and truth are not shared, but decreed (see also the discussion on *gacaca* in Chapter 8), and moreover they are imposed by a minority.[71] So the RPF attempts to fabricate unity without reconciliation, and without allowing a national, public space where this issue can be addressed.[72] Quite to the contrary, the message is "reconcile or die."[73]

Under these circumstances it is not surprising that genocide commemorations have different meanings for different groups. Although the adhesion to the official view is imposed, "for a minority of those assisting, a victory and the return to the country are remembered; another group acknowledges defeat in order to avoid accusations; yet for another group, namely the Tutsi survivors, the meanings are ambiguous."[74] What Zorbas calls the RPF's "Healing Truth" on reconciliation is based on two pillars (the backward-looking one attributes guilt for the genocide, the forward-looking one seeks to prevent genocide in the future) that generate significant resentment and resistance.[75] With regard to this top-down approach, Desrosiers and Thomson find a remarkable continuity between pre- and post-genocide Rwanda. The image of "benevolent leadership" projected by both Habyarimana and Kagame served to establish strict norms of order and obedience.[76] The current regime is aware of the impact of previous governments on ethnicization, and hence of its own potential to de-ethnicize.[77]

[70] S. Buckley-Zistel, "Dividing and Uniting: The Use of Citizenship Discourses in Conflict and Reconciliation in Rwanda", *Global Society*, 20:1 (2006), p. 108.

[71] A Hutu female participant told Thomson that "[s]ome [Tutsi] survivors have said that I should be kicked out of [a women's cooperative] because I'm not respecting the rules of reconciliation". She was told "her truth is not good enough" (S. Thomson, *Resisting Reconciliation*, p. 164).

[72] S. Buckley-Zistel, "Dividing and Uniting", p. 112.

[73] B. Oomen, "Donor-driven Justice and its Discontents: The Case of Rwanda", *Development and Change*, 36:5 (2005), p. 905.

[74] D. de Lame, "Deuil, commémoration, justice dans les contextes rwandais et belge. Otages existentiels et enjeux politiques", *Politique Africaine*, No. 92, December 2003, p. 47.

[75] E. Zorbas, "What Does Reconciliation after Genocide Mean? Public Transcripts and Hidden Transcripts in Post-genocide Rwanda", *Journal of Genocide Research*, 11:1 (2009), p. 128.

[76] M.-E. Desrosiers, S. Thomson, "Rhetorical Legacies of Leadership: Projections of 'Benevolent Leadership' in Pre- and Post-genocide Rwanda", *Journal of Modern African Studies*, 49:3 (2011), pp. 429–453.

[77] S. Buckley-Zistel, "Dividing and Uniting", p. 108.

FAILED DE-ETHNICIZATION

Despite all the regime's efforts, studies that have focused on identity suggest, however, that "ethnicity remains a central factor for Rwandan social identity," that "today (ethnic) group identity is meaningful (arguably even more than before the genocide)," and that "the Hutu/Tutsi distinctions are more rigid than ever."[78] Ingelaere goes on noting that "[a]s much as the former regime was overtly vested in the idea of Hutu supremacy, these state contemporary practices perpetuate in a much more tacit fashion what they are supposedly eradicating – Hutu and Tutsi subcultures or awareness. It signals an increased ethnicization."[79] A reporter of the *New York Times* found that, in the National University, "ethnicity remains an inescapable part of growing up for the young people," and that the government "so far succeeded only in burying ethnic tensions just beneath the surface": "So the students live in a surreal world of imposed silence, never talking about the only thing always on their minds: each other."[80] It is interesting to note that researchers working in the field have no difficulty in ethnically labeling their participant samples, despite the prohibition of using ethnic categories. "Tutsi" have been replaced by categories such as victims, survivors, English speakers, and old caseload, whereas "Hutu" are perpetrators, (former) prisoners, French speakers, and new caseload. Paradoxically, although officially denied, ethnic identity was thus indirectly reintroduced, and an ethnic hierarchy (victims are better than perpetrators) was established.[81] This is why it is so important for the RPF that it should not be seen as a perpetrator of crimes, hence its attempts to shield its own suspects, and that no Hutu "saviours" are found. In this respect, Eltringham notes that it is implied that the only "moderate" (i.e., not guilty) Hutu are those who are dead,[82] which leaves only Hutu perpetrators. This collectivization of guilt and victimhood is addressed more fully in Chapter 8.

---

[78] B. Ingelaere, "Peasants, Power and Ethnicity: A Bottom-up Perspective on Rwanda's Political Transition", *African Affairs*, 109:435 (2010), p. 275, with further references to studies on identity.

[79] *Idem*, p. 291.

[80] J. Kron, "For Rwandan Students, Ethnic Tensions Lurk", *The New York Times*, 16 May 2010.

[81] T. Eide, "Violence, Denial and Fear in Post-genocide Rwanda", in A. Suhrke, M. Berdal (Eds.), *The Peace In Between. Post-war Violence and Peacebuilding*, London, Routledge, 2012, p. 272.

[82] N. Eltringham, *Accounting for Horror: Post-genocide Debates in Rwanda*, London, Pluto Press, 2004, p. 75.

When, in the past, Hutu were a majority in public institutions, this was called "ethnic domination"; however, now that Tutsi are a majority, this has become "meritocracy." The prohibition of discussing ethnicity is a way to hide the RPF's own ethnic discrimination. Indeed, although obviously denying this, the regime operates in ethnic terms, as evidenced by some telling facts. We have seen earlier that about two thirds of the most important officeholders in the country are Tutsi, while they are about 10 percent of the population. Ruzibiza confirmed the distrust the RPF displayed towards Hutu. Even those collaborating with the RPF

were simple instruments to whom we could give a few jobs in the leadership of the country in case of our victory, because they helped us. (...) We felt that, while certain of these Hutu had political problems with their regime, that did not mean they decided to love Tutsi and honestly help them in their liberation struggle. The only Hutu personality we saw as irreproachable was Seth Sendashonga.[83]

Many examples show that, despite its "anti-ethnic" discourse, the regime thinks in strongly ethnic terms. A U.S. embassy cable mentioned earlier revealed that "[s]ome senior Tutsi officials privately assert that the Tutsi population (...) is growing as a percentage of the population," adding that "there is no statistical analysis to support this."[84] A member of an INGO targeted by the government observed the contradiction in the accusations against his organization: "On one hand you can't talk about ethnic groups, everyone is Rwandan, but then an organisation can be raked over the coals for not hiring Tutsi."[85] A parliamentary report noted that Liprodhor "never gives an employment contract to a Tutsi" and found that the mayor of Kanama district "refused to hire Tutsi."[86] After, during the proceedings of the 2004 parliamentary commission, the

---

[83] A.J. Ruzibiza, *Rwanda. L'histoire secrète*, Paris, Editions du Panama, 2005, p. 65. This attitude toward Hutu was confirmed to this author by several (former) members of the RPF.

[84] "Ethnicity in Rwanda – Who Governs the Country", US Embassy Kigali, Ref. Kigali 480, 5 August 2008, available through WikiLeaks (http://wikileaks.org/cable/2008/08/08KIGALI525.html). Of course, no statistical analysis could support such a claim, because it would be illegal to construct such statistics. Had the senior officials been Hutu claiming that "Hutu were growing (or decreasing) as a percentage of the population," they would in all likelihood be prosecuted for "divisionism."

[85] Front Line Rwanda, *Disappearances, Arrests, Threats, Intimidation of Human rights Defenders, 2001–2004*, Dublin, 2005, p. 90.

[86] République du Rwanda, Chambre des députés, *Rapport de la Commission parlementaire ad hoc créée en date du 20 janvier 2004 chargée d'examiner les tueries perpétrées dans la province de Gikongoro, l'idéologie génocidaire et ceux qui la propagent partout au Rwanda*, 30 June 2004.

Forum des organisations rurales (FOR) was accused of employing only Hutu, it replied that "there is no mention of ethnic groups in FOR's staff files. One would then ask oneself (how) did the Parliament (learn) the ethnic element attributed to FOR. It would be better if the process used by the Parliament in identifying ethnic groups be announced to the public."[87] Former agriculture minister Habamenshi recalled that he was summoned by Kagame "to explain to him how Hutu think."[88] In 1998, Kagame told U.S. ambassador Gribbin that Rwanda "felt honor bound to support (the Banyamulenge mutiny in the DRC) on grounds of ethnic solidarity."[89] Former bodyguards accused Kagame of running the country along ethnic lines: "All of the soldiers in his bodyguard were Tutsi. If you married a Hutu woman, you were kicked out."[90] After the RPF's victory, the exiled former Speaker of Parliament Joseph Sebarenzi, a Tutsi genocide survivor himself, realized that "the tables were turned and Hutu felt the same lack of security we Tutsi had felt for so many years."[91]

Another illustration of persistent ethnic bias, Ibuka does not provide assistance to Tutsi women married to Hutu.[92] Rombouts found that the government encouraged victim competition and incomprehension on both sides by recognizing Tutsi genocide victims and refusing recognition to Hutu victims of RPF crimes while at the same time proclaiming a reconciled and united Rwanda where there is no room for different ethnic groups.[93] Research among refugees in Uganda found that many Hutu feel that ethnicity is used as a basis for repression. Despite official rhetoric on the end of ethnicity and on "Rwandanness," "it is clear from the perspective of those reluctant to return home that the question of ethnicity has remained profoundly polarised in Rwanda. Ongoing repression on the basis of ethnicity continues to feed localised ethnic divisions and create further polarisation."[94] Many examples of the regime practising ethnic

---

[87] Quoted in Front Line Rwanda, *Disappearances, Arrests*, p. 63.

[88] P. Habamenshi, *Rwanda. Where Souls Turn to Dust*, p. 75.

[89] R.E. Gribbin, *In the Aftermath of Genocide. The U.S. Role in Rwanda*, New York, iUniverse, 2005, p. 280.

[90] "'Kagame Is a Killer.' Defectors Tell of Life on Run from Rwandan Assassins", *The Times* (London), 8 October 2012.

[91] J. Sebarenzi, *God Sleeps in Rwanda*, p. 82.

[92] Human Rights Watch, *Rwanda. Justice Compromised. The Legacy of Rwanda's Community-based Gacaca Courts*, New York, May 2011, p. 82.

[93] H. Rombouts, *Victim Organisations and the Politics of Reparation: a case study on Rwanda*, Antwerp-Oxford, Intersentia, 2004, p. 356.

[94] *A Dangerous Impasse: Rwandan Refugees in Uganda*, Citizenship and Displacement in the Great Lakes Region, Working Paper No. 4, June 2010, p. 2.

discrimination despite its rhetoric are given by Begley who notes that "many Hutu complained that they were often excluded from employment and other public resources by some Tutsi and the government." One informant stated that "the government says that everyone has the same identity, but when it comes to getting better jobs or benefits, the better identity is Tutsi."[95] This even leads Hutu to not consider themselves Rwandans: Begley noted several expressions by Hutu such as "If I were a Rwandan, I would have a job."[96] Symbolic changes contributed to the feeling of exclusion that so frustrates many Hutu. So the introduction of new national symbols (flag, anthem, and seal) in 2001 was interpreted by Thomson's participants as "designed for those who returned after the war" and an effort to "remind those like me (released prisoner) that Rwanda no longer belongs to us (Hutu)."[97] All sorts of discrimination against Hutu also occur in the private sphere, but they are not tackled by a government that preaches reconciliation.[98]

Hidden too by a de-ethnicized dominant script is that many nonofficial Tutsi not only find it in their interest to subscribe to the RPF's vision of ethnicity, but also to treat Hutu with disdain. Although this is invisible to outsiders, many Hutu realize this very well, and it fuels their frustration and anger. In particular, old caseload returnees consider the RPF as their army, "and thus they shared the victors' attitude of many RPF soldiers."[99] The fact that this army is expected to protect them against renewed Hutu-led violence understandably contributes to this hidden ethnic solidarity. Although ethnicity is no longer recognized officially, Burnet notes that it continues playing a role in the policing of identity. Thus, during the insurgency in the northwestern prefectures in 1997–1999, Hutu faced

---

[95] L. Begley, "Resolved to Fight," p. 156.

[96] For instance *idem*, p. 154.

[97] S. Thomson, *Resisting Reconciliation*, p. 176.

[98] A Rwandan acquaintance told Waldorf that one of the luxury hotels in Kigali excluded Hutu from its swimming pool. Waldorf adds that this may actually not be true, but that it shows that Rwandans have ethnic grievances (L. Waldorf "Revisiting Hotel Rwanda: Genocide Ideology, Reconciliation, and Rescuers", *Journal of Genocide Research*, 11:1 [2009], p. 130). A Hutu acquaintance of mine, who looks like a Tutsi (his mother was Tutsi), told me how he was struck by the fact that Hutu would adopt a subdued attitude when passing him in the streets of Kigali. Stories showing that ethnic distrust remains widespread abound, and they sometimes give rise to interesting strategies of resistance. During a group interview, Zorbas' participants said the following: "You go into a *cabaret* (local bar) and you hear someone ask 'do you have a piece of paper?' Asking for paper is a signal that a Tutsi has just come in and that they should change the topic of conversation" (E. Zorbas, "What Does Reconciliation", p. 130).

[99] J.E. Burnet, "Whose Genocide?, p. 83.

increased scrutiny during identity checks, and those who "looked Hutu" or were from the northwest were frequently questioned extensively and sometimes arrested or forced into military service.[100]

An issue that may have a major impact in the future is that of access to (higher) education. In the absence of official statistics, it is difficult to clearly establish ethnic bias in this field, but some of the available indications are revealing. The Fund for Support to Genocide Survivors (known under its French acronym Fonds d'assistance aux rescapés du genocide – FARG) announced in 2010 that more than 17,000 genocide survivors graduated from university in the last twelve years through its sponsorship. At that time, FARG sponsored almost 5,000 students in institutions of higher learning.[101] All those students were Tutsi, as only Tutsi are recognized as survivors. The available figures show that almost 12,000 students graduated from National University in the ten-year period from 2001 to 2011, whereas the figures for other universities are unknown, but they are certainly smaller.[102] In addition, other Tutsi besides survivors are enrolled at universities. These figures suggest that a majority of university students are Tutsi. Parliament wanted to go even further, as it "instructed the government to ensure that every survivor who graduates from the high school joins university."[103] In 2006, secondary school enrollment stood at 179,153; during that same year, FARG beneficiaries totaled 47,371, that is, more than 26 percent, again in addition to Tutsi not supported by the FARG. Such a situation obviously creates a strong overrepresentation of Tutsi in elite-creation, thus engendering a pre-1988 Burundi-like situation with all the consequences seen in that country.[104] At any rate, this is the perception that was created: many of those interviewed among poor, rural Hutu families viewed the availability of FARG funding to Tutsi genocide survivors as a form of institutionalized ethnic preference.[105] So, in the eyes of many Rwandans, the ethnic amnesia[106] preached by the regime only

---

[100] *Idem*, pp. 86–87.

[101] "17,000 Genocide Survivors Complete University", *The New Times*, 13 April 2010.

[102] An October 2011 survey by the National Council for Higher Education showed 40,830 graduates in all higher learning institutions from 2001 to 2010, but this figure included many nonuniversity institutions.

[103] "Genocide Issues Dominate Parliament Retreat", *The New Times*, 20 January 2010.

[104] When, from 1988, place was made for Hutu in Burundian politics, the civil service, the judiciary and other sectors of public life, it was (and still is today) very difficult to attract persons with sufficient education, and professional standards declined as a consequence.

[105] J.E. Burnet, "Whose Genocide?", p. 94.

[106] Term coined by R. Lemarchand, "Burundi: The Politics of Ethnic Amnesia", in Helen Fein (Ed.), *Genocide Watch*, New Haven, Yale University Press, 1992, pp. 70–86.

serves to thinly veil the fact that rule by a minority of the majority ethnic group was replaced by rule by a minority of the minority ethnic group.

IMPOSING THE MODEL

All means are good to communicate and transmit the "Truth": laws on divisionism and genocide ideology, reeducation, the use of lobbying firms, and even the memory of the dead. Meierhenrich found that one of the intended consequences of memorialization at the genocide memorial sites is "to disable comprehension." They "service privileged memory, that is, memory that is officially sanctioned because it is in accordance with the post-genocidal raison d'état."[107] He concluded that memorialization serves, more often than not, the purpose of underpinning authoritarian rule rather than of honoring the victims of the genocide.[108] Guyer concurs: the "spectacle of skulls and bones" contributes "neither to clearer understanding of the genocide nor to the restoration of powers of mind in the face of violence."[109] Brandstetter finds that the memorial practices are radically new symbolic settings, far apart from the way in which Rwandan culture remembers the dead. "Kigali Memorial Centre seems to highlight the cosmopolitanism of the ruling elite in Kigali and its familiarity with globalised practices of commemoration. The emphasis on modernity also guarantees an easy accessibility for international visitors."[110] In addition, "memorials and commemorations could drive Rwandans to identify themselves as either 'Hutu' or 'Tutsi', thereby reducing complex and overlapping individual identities to a simple model of ethnic antagonism."[111] Burnet writes that "[t]hrough this nationalized mourning the RPF regime promotes a particular version of national history and a narrative about the genocide that promotes the polarizing ethnicized discourse and symbolic pairing of victim and perpetrator."[112] Under those circumstances, the scientific writing and teaching of history becomes impossible.[113] As the Berkeley curriculum project found out, "[w]hen one identity group has

---

[107] J. Meierhenrich, "Topographies", p. 288.

[108] *Idem*, p. 292.

[109] S. Guyer, "Rwanda's Bones", *Boundary 2*, 36:2 (1996), quoted by A.-M. Brandstetter, *Contested Pasts: The Politics of Remembrance in Post-Genocide Rwanda*, Ortelius Lecture at the University of Antwerp, Wassenaar, NIAS, 2010, p. 10.

[110] M.-A. Brandstetter, *Contested Pasts*, p. 12.

[111] *Idem*, pp. 17–18.

[112] J.E. Burnet, "Whose Genocide?", p. 95.

[113] On the régime's steering of history teaching, see S. Buckley-Zistel, "Nation, Narration, Unification?", pp. 41–44.

power and others are subject to that group's policies and practices, history reform becomes an almost impossible task." In fact, "teaching a critical approach to history may be fundamentally at odds with the political effort to re-create the nation as a new, imagined community."[114]

There is a great deal of continuity in this way of dealing with history and the truth. The use of words, the art of speaking, and the semantic strategy so prevalent in precolonial Rwanda have remained powerful political tools. Perhaps unwittingly, a parliamentary commission lucidly wrote that

[p]eople who speak the truth are called "indiscreet" and are called after the name of the Minister of Local Government "Bazivamo," which refers to someone giving away his own secrets. But, in order to fool those who are not from the region [Gisenyi], they use the first name of the Minister and say that those betraying their own secrets are called "Christophe."[115]

Foreigners may be fooled,[116] but Rwandans know the link between power and truth very well: Ingelaere's respondents said that "[the origins and context of the genocide] are already known and that the current government is taking care of the general 'Truth' (with capital T) about the past."[117]

Apart from the legal means mentioned earlier, one way of imposing the truth domestically is the National Unity and Reconciliation Commission (NURC) and the *ingando* or solidarity camps it organises. Established by an act of Parliament in March 1999 and entrusted by article 178 of the Constitution with a number of tasks, NURC is one of the keepers of the regime's orthodoxy. On its creation, it took over the *ingando* program that was originally run by the Ministry of Youth, Culture and Sports. *Ingando* has two main target groups: released prisoners who need to be "reeducated" and youth (students more specifically) who are taught the RPF's values. Just as with *gacaca* (see Chapter 8), the government claims that *ingando* is an updated version of a Rwandan tradition, but it is in reality a

---

[114] S. Warshauer Freedman et al., "Teaching History", p. 309.

[115] République du Rwanda, Chambre des députés, *Rapport de la Commission parlementaire ad hoc.*

[116] A former police officer who was asked to assess the effectiveness of reforms in the justice system told Human Rights Watch, "You can't understand. You see what's on paper but you don't know the truth. (...) You foreigners are easily tricked" (Human Rights Watch, *Law and Reality*, p. 44).

[117] B. Ingelaere, *"Does the Truth Pass across the Fire without Burning?".Transitional Justice and its Discontents in Rwanda's Gacaca Courts*, IOB Discussion Paper 2007-7, Antwerp, 2007, p. 29. Also see B. Ingelaere, "'Does the Truth Pass Across the Fire Without Burning?' Locating the short circuit in Rwanda's Gacaca courts", *Journal of Modern African Studies*, 47:4 (2009), pp. 520–523.

modern political creation: "the RPF has an interest in 'inventing traditions' that legitimise current forms of social control or practice. Additionally, the government's appeal to culture may be an attempt to deemphasise the political utility of *ingando* as a mechanism of pro-RPF ideological indoctrination."[118] Indeed, interviews conducted by Mgbako revealed that political indoctrination is a dominant part of the *ingando* experience. However, particularly with regard to released *génocidaires*, just like *gacaca* it is also an instrument for the victimization of Hutu. Mgbako notes that "the assignment of collective guilt for the genocide to all Hutu (...) undermines the recognition and prosecution of genocide."[119] Van Hoyweghen sees *ingando* as just one way of socially engineering the entire country. University students were urged in an *ingando* opening session "to choose their side and work with or against the government."[120] Rather than being, as the government claims, an updated version of a Rwandan tradition, *ingando* is "a modern RPF political creation that serves to consolidate RPF power."[121] It is not a forum for discussion or exchange, even less of contestation, but of the reproduction of the government script, as indicated in notes of participants that, at places, read like a catechism (question-answer).[122]

So the image the regime wishes to project does not correspond to reality. Purdekova describes how images of peace are created, for instance in so-called reconciliation villages where visits for foreigners include presentations by perpetrators and victims and testimonies how they now live together in happiness. She finds that "the image of unity and reconciliation is more important than actual unity and reconciliation."[123] That the Rwandans are not fooled shows in the experience of Susan Thomson, a

---

[118] C. Mgbako, "*Ingando* Solidarity Camps", p. 208.

[119] *Idem*, p. 223.

[120] S. Van Hoyweghen, "The Urgency of Land and Agrarian Reform in Rwanda", *African Affairs*, 98:392 (1999), p. 366.

[121] C. Mgbako, "*Ingando* Solidarity Camps", p. 208. Pudekova notes that "[r]econciliatory activities claimed to be based in tradition (...) spring up primarily from the 'factory' of NURC and are partly financed by international donors" (A. Purdekova, *Repatriation and Reconciliation*, p. 19).

[122] For instance, the question: "How did the genocide come about?";the answer: "The policies of the colonizers, based on ethnic discrimination, created dissension, jealousy and hate within Rwandan society. Etc." (PRI, *From Camp to Hill*, p. 96).

[123] A. Purdekova, "Civil Education and Social Transformation in Post-genocide Rwanda: Forging the Perfect Development Subjects", in M. Campioni, P. Noack (Eds.), *Rwanda Fast Forward. Social, Economic Military and Reconciliation Prospects*, Houndmills, Palgrave Macmillan, 2012, p. 205.

Canadian scholar whom the Rwandan government sent to an *ingando* camp to undergo "reeducation." Her conclusion:

> The graduates of these *ingando* camps that I met do not believe in the national unity of the re-imagined past or in the reconciliation of a re-engineered future. Rather, they see the camps and their ideological discourse as efforts to exercise social control over adult Hutu men. Instead of being re-educated, these graduates merely learned new forms of "ritualised dissimulation" and strategic compliance.[124]

In the same vein, Zorbas's respondents proposed a hidden transcript of the RPF's "Healing Truth" that is very different from the public version, although there is also overlap between both transcripts.[125] Many researchers have had the same experience as that recounted by Eide, namely, that informants changed their story when realising they were free to speak out: they then engaged in "conversations that under current laws could be considered illegal."[126] Begley is just one of the researchers who on several occasions heard participants saying one thing with other persons present and the opposite in private. For instance, a respondent stated that "[t]here is reconciliation. We all have the same opportunities (...), there is peace and security." Later he wanted to meet her again, "as there were things he could not say in front of other people." He then stated that "unity and reconciliation do not exist in Rwanda."[127] In her focus groups, Burnet frequently heard various versions of the "official response": "the vast majority of respondents were very careful to stick to this official, idyllic version (...). In many cases, in more private contexts, the very same respondents would recount an entirely different version."[128]

This makes so-called opinion surveys so unreliable. A good example is offered by a *Rwanda Reconciliation Barometer* produced on behalf of the NURC. On one hand, it candidly "perceived some challenges in eliciting forthright responses from research participants,"[129] noted that local leaders' presence on field "may have influenced both the data collection process and the research findings," that "citizens were generally reluctant to

---

[124] S. Thomson, "Reeducation for Reconciliation: Participant observations on Ingando", in S. Straus, L. Waldorf (Eds.), *Remaking Rwanda*, p. 338.

[125] E. Zorbas, "What Does Reconciliation", pp. 138–142.

[126] T. Eide, "Violence, Denial and Fear", p. 273.

[127] L. Begley, "Resolved to Fight", p. 162.

[128] J.E. Burnet, "The Injustice of Local Justice: Truth, Reconciliation, and Revenge in Rwanda", *Genocide Studies and Prevention*, 3:2 (2008), pp. 180–181.

[129] Republic of Rwanda, National Unity and Reconciliation Commission, *Rwanda Reconciliation Barometer*, Kigali, October 2010, p. 29.

participate in interviews related to very sensitive topics,"[130] and that "many research participants told fieldworkers that referring to ethnic groups, such as Hutu, Tutsi or Twa, is 'currently forbidden' by the government."[131] However, on the other hand, this sense of caution did not prevent the study from finding, for example, that "95.2% [of the respondents] indicated that national reconciliation was going in the right direction. A further 91.7% of respondents also indicated that democratic governance was going in the right direction."[132]

In other words, although the RPF may well believe that its metanarrative of the past, the present and the future is successfully imposed, counternarratives continue to exist.[133] As they are clandestine, not only can they not be seen, but they may even be more radical than the one the regime wants to eradicate, particularly as real or imagined victimization along ethnic lines reinforces the feelings of belonging to a group. Not only does this strengthen the "ethnic logic," but it also effectively continues the conflict through discursive means,[134] which could pave the way for new physical confrontation.

As in other areas of the RPF's attempts at engineering, devising a "truth" and imposing it need not therefore lead to the outcome the regime propagates publicly. Janine Clark finds that the government's national unity and reconciliation policy is "critically flawed," as it "relies upon a negation of ethnic differences and, hence, does not allow for an open and honest engagement with the past."[135] Hintjens arrives at a similar conclusion: "[W]hilst public expression of political identities has been largely 'de-racialised', this has been done in a very top-down and authoritarian manner. The result has prevented the emergence from below of potentially more complex forms of political identification, which could form the basis for more inclusive forms of Rwandan citizenship in future."[136] Clark's and Hintjens's observations hold true if the regime's publicly stated aims are taken for granted. However, just like other forms of engineering, the real

---

[130] *Idem*, p. 30.

[131] *Idem*, p. 31.

[132] *Idem*, p. 51.

[133] A number of studies show this to be the case. On the meaning(s) of reconciliation, see E. Zorbas, "What Does Reconciliation Mean?".

[134] L. McLean Hilker "Young Rwandans' Narratives of the Past (and Present)", in S. Straus, L. Waldorf (Eds.), *Remaking Rwanda*, p. 327. Eide refers to the emergence of "discursive communities of fear" (T. Eide, "Violence, Denial and Fear...", p. 278).

[135] J.N. Clark, "National Unity and Reconciliation in Rwanda: A Flawed Approach?", *Journal of Contemporary African Studies*, 28:2 (2010), p. 138.

[136] H. Hintjens, "Post-genocide Identity Politics in Rwanda", *Ethnicities*, 8:1 (2008), p. 6.

agenda behind disseminating the "truth" may well be consolidating control rather than achieving reconciliation.

CONCLUSION

Early on, Sibomana said that

Rwandans realize perfectly well that there is a significant discrepancy between what they see with their own eyes every day and what they hear through the official media or private newspapers, which support the government line. They can see they are not being told the truth. Once again, we have fallen into an era of suspicion and speculation, which is so favourable to dissemination of the worst kind of propaganda.[137]

Rwanda is by no means the only place and historical circumstance in which the construction of truth is the privilege of those in power, or where the power to say what counts as true is an issue of contemporary politics. However, in today's Rwanda the use of the instruments of knowledge construction has an extraordinary impact on the relations of those in power with both their own citizens and the outside world. Toward the latter, this allowed the regime to have its own narrative accepted and to silence the challenges to that narrative. Pottier notes that the "rewriting project, a high priority in Kigali, has benefited from the empathy and services not only of journalists unfamiliar with the region, but also of newcomer academics, diplomats and aid workers."[138] Domestically, one truth was imposed, at least in its public expression. When interviewing

[137] A. Sibomana, *Gardons espoir pour le Rwanda. Entretiens avec Laure Guilbert et Hervé Deguine*, Paris, Desclée de Brouwer, 1997. The quote is from the translation in English: A. Sibomana, *Hope for Rwanda: Conversations with Laure Guibert and Hervé Deguine*, London – Sterling VA, Pluto Press, 1999, p. 144, quoted by L. Waldorf, "Censorship and Propaganda in Post-genocide Rwanda", in A. Thompson (Ed.), *The Media and the Rwanda Genocide*, London, Pluto Press; Kampala, Fountain publishers, 2007, p. 404.

[138] J. Pottier, *Re-imagining Rwanda*, p. 53. In a chapter titled "For Beginners, by Beginners: Knowledge Construction under the Rwandese Patriotic Front," Pottier shows how the RPF, to help popularise its preferred vision of history, secured the support of sympathetic journalists and aid workers uninformed about the region, and academic scriptwriters without research experience in Rwanda" (*idem*, p. 109). He mentions the award-winning *Season of Blood: A Rwandan Journey* (Harmondsworth, Penguin Books, 1996) of the BBC's Fergal Keane as an example of the nurturing of the RPF's narrative and of how "the pressures of war journalism – ignorance about the place, strict deadlines, trauma and empathy – may combine to produce and legitimate a seductively simplistic, distorted version of history as we know it; a version deemed 'politically correct.' Ignorant about Rwandan society and history, ignorant too about the quality of scholarly research since the end of colonialism, Keane was game for the interpretation of his RFP guides" (J. Pottier, *Re-imagining Rwanda*, p. 64).

ingando participants, Mgbako was struck by "responses that seemed like recitations of what they had heard during *ingando* lessons."[139]

However, James Scott has shown that, besides the public transcript of the powerful, the powerless – in this case most Hutu and many Tutsi – develop a hidden transcript.[140] This insurgent reading of history is invisible, yet very present in people's minds and private exchanges, as shown in much field research referred to in this book. If *ingando* is the only place where "history" is officially taught, other narratives are inevitably transmitted in households and whispered conversations, where they take the form of a counterhistory that is invisible though radical – in the opposite sense of the one decreed by the regime. Wishing this "other history" away and indeed criminalizing it only contributes to frustration and anger.

The eclipse of ethnicity may even run counter to Rwanda's international obligations. The UN independent expert on minority issues finds that "[t]he right of individuals to freely identify themselves as belonging to an ethnic, religious or linguistic group is (...) well-established in international law. (...) Domestic law (...) should recognize such rights and ensure that no individual or group suffers from any disadvantage or discriminatory treatment on the basis of their freely chosen identity."[141] In addition, "the Government's policy of non-recognition of ethnic groups restricts opportunities for individuals and communities to formally lodge complaints regarding discrimination and to pursue such complaints."[142]

[139] C. Mgbako, "*Ingando* Solidarity Camps", p. 214.
[140] J.C. Scott, *Domination and the Arts of Resistance. Hidden Transcripts*, New Haven CT, Yale University Press, 1992.
[141] United Nations, General Assembly, Human Rights Council, *Report of the Independent Expert on Minority Issues, Gay McDougall*, A/HRC/19/56/ Add.1, 28 November 2011, p. 6.
[142] *Idem*, p. 12.

8

The Politics of Justice

After genocide and massive crimes against humanity and war crimes, clearly some form of justice was going to be needed, because more than 1 million people were unlawfully killed by a huge number of perpetrators. But "justice" sounds more neutral than it is: paraphrasing von Clausewitz's most famous aphorism ("War is the continuation of politics by other means"), one could say that "lawfare," though less conspicuous than warfare, can be the continuation of war by other means.[1] This chapter does not study the technicalities of transitional justice in Rwanda,[2] but rather address its politics in three realms: domestic Rwandan justice, *gacaca* in particular, the International Criminal Tribunal for Rwanda (ICTR), and the application of universal jurisdiction in third countries. A major thread in these three realms is that victor's justice has been meted out.

---

[1] See the forthcoming book by J. Meierhenrich, *Lawfare. Gacaca Jurisdictions in Rwanda*, Cambridge University Press.

[2] Among the avalanche of publications on transitional justice in Rwanda, see M.A. Drumbl, "Punishment, Postgenocide: From Guilt to Shame to Civis in Rwanda," *New York University Law Review*, 75:5 (2000), pp. 1221–1326; W.A. Schabas, "Justice, Democracy, and Impunity in Post-genocide Rwanda: Searching for Solutions to Impossible Problems", *Criminal Law Forum*, 7:3 (1996), pp. 523–560; W.A. Schabas, "Genocide Trials and *Gacaca* Courts", *Journal of International Criminal Justice*, 3:4 (2005), pp. 879–895; L. Waldorf, "Mass Justice for Mass Atrocity: Rethinking Local Justice as Transitional Justice", *Temple Law Review*, 79:1 (2006), pp. 1–88. An uninspiring analysis of diverse judicial responses can be found in N.A. Jones, *The Courts of Genocide. Politics and the Rule of Law in Rwanda and Arusha*, Abingdon, Routledge, 2010. This is mainly a legal/formal survey of data, based on sources that are not critical, and with little empirical and political analysis.

DOMESTIC CONVENTIONAL JUSTICE

During the years immediately following the genocide, Rwanda was confronted with a drastically reduced justice system: material assets were destroyed, and most judges, prosecutors, and support staff were dead, detained, or in exile. On the demand side, close to 100,000 people were detained by the end of 1996.[3] Most arrests were made by military, local RPF cadres (*abakada*), or other persons without proper authority, and most detainees had no case file. The release of prisoners against whom there were no indications of guilt was made impossible: the case of Judge Gratien Ruhorahoza, who was arrested by military and "disappeared" after having ordered the release of several dozen prisoners in October 1994, served as a strong warning. The conditions of detention were appalling, and several thousands of detainees died in prisons[4]; the situation was even worse in communal lockups (*cachots*), *gendarmerie* brigades, and even containers, where the number of victims can only be guessed. Uvin estimated in the early 2000s that "[c]urrently, more people die in prison every year than are judged."[5] In addition to living in overcrowding and poor sanitary and nutritional conditions, detainees were ill treated and tortured.

Unlike what happened in certain other "post-conflict" situations, the RPF was in a position where it could impose its view on how to deal with the past. It did not have to seek compromise. Even so, the challenge was daunting: the justice system was in shatters, the scale and gravity of the crimes were gigantic, and the number of victims and perpetrators was enormous. Even the most affluent society would not know how to deal with this legacy, and Ian Martin (former secretary-general of Amnesty International and head of the UNHRFOR in 1995–1996) referred to the

---

[3] According to the ICRC, about 59,000 persons were held in prisons and about 33,000 in other holding facilities such as municipal lockups. The ICRC was able to visit these locations, and the figures did not include persons detained in military facilities and illegal and unknown places of detention.

[4] On "living" conditions in jails, see C. Tertsakian, *Le Château. The Lives of Prisoners in Rwanda*, London, Arves, 2008.

[5] P. Uvin, "Difficult Choices in the New Post-conflict Agenda: The International Community in Rwanda after the Genocide", *Third World Quarterly*, 22:2 (2001), p. 182. This did not seem to worry the authorities too much. Asked about suspects who died in custody, presidential adviser Claude Dusaidi stated that "if they are dead, why should anyone care? They are killers" ("Rwandan Suspects Die in Custody", Kigali, AP, 23 January 1997).

"impossibility of justice,"[6] whereas Bill Schabas spoke of "solutions to impossible problems."[7] The regime's approach was almost exclusively judicial, whereas Vandeginste showed the inherent limitations of such an approach: dealing with the past in a context such as that of Rwanda "cannot solely be a judicial issue; it is a political challenge and a challenge for society as a whole."[8] However, as will be seen, the approach was only overtly judicial, whereas in reality it was very political, with justice becoming a major instrument for the consolidation of the RPF's grip on power and the protection of its narrative. This was quite understandable in light of the fact that the past was not the past, that Rwanda was not a post-conflict state, and that gross human rights abuse continued after the new regime seized power.

The government's initial position was threefold: justice was to be retributive, it was to be national, and it was to be meted out by the ordinary courts. Full accountability was claimed to be what Rwandans wanted. Schabas stated that "Rwandans have consistently rejected any compromise with full accountability, insisting upon criminal prosecution for all alleged perpetrators."[9] Unless Schabas means "the government" when referring to "Rwandans," one wonders where this assumption comes from, as he did not conduct any research on what "Rwandans" felt, and as no such data were available. Despite its resolve, at first the regime did not however appear very interested in getting the justice system going.[10] In July 1995, it refused a loan of foreign judges, deeming it to be "unconstitutional and a breach of the sovereignty of the Rwandese people."[11] Indeed, not much happened until the government convened an international conference from October

---

[6] I. Martin, "Hard Choices after Genocide: Human Rights and Political Failures in Rwanda", in J. Moore (Ed.), *Hard Choices: Moral Dilemmas in Humanitarian Intervention*, Lanham, MD, Rowman & Littlefield, 1998, p. 157.

[7] W.A. Schabas, "Justice, Democracy".

[8] S. Vandeginste, "Rwanda: Dealing with Genocide and Crimes against Humanity in the Context of Armed Conflict and Failed Political Transition", in N. Biggar (Ed.), *Burying the Past. Making Peace and Doing Justice after Civil Conflict*, Washington, DC, Georgetown University Press, 2001, p. 223.

[9] W.A. Schabas, "Genocide Trials", p. 880.

[10] This remained a constant feature. While the regime was successful in many other, particularly economic, fields, it displayed a marked lack of interest in the quality of legislation and of justice, except in areas of immediate political interest. Lack of interest may have played a role, but also the fact that those active in the legal sector were mainly Hutu who held office before 1994 and Tutsi returnees from Zaire/DRC and Burundi who did not belong to the "core" of the regime made up of returnees from Uganda.

[11] G. Prunier, *Africa's World War. Congo, the Rwandan Genocide, and the Making of a Continental Catastrophe*, Oxford, Oford University Press, 2002, p. 12.

31 to November 4, 1995. The meeting recommended the setting up of new mechanisms, including specialized chambers of the existing courts, a classification scheme to separate different types of offenders, and a scheme aimed at encouraging suspects to confess to their crimes.[12] These recommendations found their way into legislation during 1996. Organic law No. 8/96 of 30 August 1996 "on the organisation of prosecutions for offences constitutive of the crime of genocide or of crimes against humanity committed since October 1st, 1990" was the first law that provided for the division of suspects in four categories.[13] Although they were quite vague and open to a great deal of interpretation, these categories were to have an important impact on both penalties and the possibility to enter a guilty plea.

In application of the law, the general prosecutor published a first list of category 1 suspects in the *Official Gazette* on November 30, 1996.[14] In a number of cases, this list and the later updates appeared more as an instrument of political intimidation than as a judicial instrument. The case of Léonidas Rusatira was telling. A former FAR general "reintegrated" in the RPA at the beginning of 1995, he fled Rwanda in November 1995 and went into exile in Brussels, from where he issued positions critical of the regime. Denouncing "the purely political nature" of his inclusion in the list, Rusatira claimed that "the system used in Kigali wants, while downplaying the genocide into an inexhaustible source of political exploitation, to finish off all attempts at contestation by using all available means to force into silence all opinion leaders and to eliminate potential interlocutors."[15] This opinion was shared by former justice minister Faustin Nteziryayo, who (after going into exile in early 1999) wrote that "the drafting of this list has served the political agenda aimed at eliminating personalities of the old regime considered as political opponents or other persons with some influence within civil society, rather than the advancement of prosecutions by allowing to identify the real perpetrators of the Rwandan tragedy."[16] In the same logic but in the opposite

---

[12] W.A. Schabas, "Genocide Trials", p. 884.

[13] Category 1 included the planners and organizers, those occupying positions of authority, the most-renowned killers, and those having committed acts of sexual torture. Category 2 grouped those guilty of homicide and their accomplices. Those having caused other grave bodily harms were placed in category 3, whereas category 4 contained those having committed offences against property.

[14] This first list contained 1946 names. Some of the persons mentioned were dead, others appeared on the list more than once, and some were identified with their first name only.

[15] Letter addressed on 8 February 2000 by L. Rusatira to General Prosecutor G. Gahima.

[16] F. Nteziryayo, "Enlisement du système judiciaire et dérive des droits humains au Rwanda", *Dialogue*, 213 (November-December 1999), p. 6.

sense, the name of Boniface Rucagu (against whom there were serious indications of involvement in the genocide), who by then served the regime as governor of Ruhengeri, disappeared from the list.

The law created special chambers in the courts of first instance and the military courts that were to be exclusively competent to deal with the offences covered by this legislation. Appeal possibilities were much more limited than those in the ordinary criminal justice system, as it was made possible only on questions of law or "flagrant factual errors." This was a classical criminal justice approach, dealing with individual suspects in a retributive fashion, as well as aiming – at least in principle – to judge every suspect. As Rwanda refused offers of assistance of foreign judges and prosecutors, and given the poor state of its judicial system, these were ambitious objectives.

Technically speaking, most if not all persons detained were illegally held, as procedures for arrest and detention on remand were not (and, of course, could not be, given the enormous number of prisoners) respected. Before the start of trial procedures, law No. 9/96 of 8 September 1996 "on temporary modifications of the code of criminal procedure" purported to retroactively regularize arrests and detentions of the past, and considerably limited suspects' protection in the future as well.[17] Even the regularization of tens of thousands of case files turned out to be an impossible task for police officers and prosecutors. Other laws adopted in 1996 concerned the organization of the Supreme Court, the High Council of the Judiciary (*Conseil supérieur de la magistrature*) and the Bar. This flurry of legislation on judicial matters was a clear indication of the government's will to finally get trials underway.

Despite resignations, arrests, "disappearances" and assassinations of judicial staff, mainly Hutu who were in office before 1994 and who stayed or returned after the RPF's takeover, by the end of 1996 staff again reached, indeed surpassed pre-genocide levels: in December 1996 there were 699 judges against 661 before the genocide and 145 prosecutors against 83.[18] There were thus no good reasons why judicial activities should not fully resume, and yet they did not. Rather a purely administrative measure at the level of prosecutors' offices, put in place by an "instruction" of the minister

---

[17] As the Constitutional Court declared a previous attempt to suspend safeguards of the Code of Criminal Procedure unconstitutional in 1995, the government packed the court which allowed to pass the amendment in September 1996 (see F. Nteziryayo, "Enlisement", p. 5).

[18] S. Vandeginste, "Poursuite des présumés responsables du génocide et des massacres politiques devant les juridictions rwandaises", in S. Marysse, F. Reyntjens (Eds.), *L'Afrique des grands lacs. Annuaire 1996–1997*, Paris, L'Harmattan, 1997, p. 110.

of justice, was supposed to address the overpopulation of prisons. "Sorting commissions" (*commissions de triage*), composed of representatives of the police, the army, the intelligence service, and the prosecutor's office were to propose the liberation of vulnerable groups and of persons without substantial case files. However, during 1996 fewer than 300 were set free under this scheme, and a number of them were rearrested afterward. This was due in large part to the fact that the representatives of the security services generally opposed the release of detainees regardless of information contained in their files,[19] which confirmed that military and intelligence forces continued to dominate the judicial system. When the sorting commissions stopped functioning at the end of 1996, they had not contributed much to solving the problem, despite having received funding to the tune of US$1.9 million from the Netherlands.[20] Later on, after the sorting commissions had ceased functioning, the government ordered the provisional release of tens of thousands of suspects, because they had no case files, were elderly or ill, had confessed, or had served their maximum sentence in pretrial detention.[21]

Another mechanism that was supposed to accelerate procedures was the possibility for suspects, under the organic law of August 30, 1996, to enter a guilty plea under a so-called Confessions and Guilty Plea Procedure. Although this allowed for a considerable reduction of sentences for suspects in categories 2 through 4, the program failed to convince most detainees. Many suspects who were innocent or who considered themselves as such did not want to admit guilt, whereas in many cases those tempted by the offer were discouraged or threatened by other inmates who had every interest to hide behind as large a number of detainees as possible. The practice of *"ceceka"* ("keep silent," an implicit agreement that Hutu do not testify against other Hutu) (cf. infra) was already visible inside the prisons. Rather than diminishing, the number of detainees increased: by early 1998, around 130,000 people were held in prisons and other places of detention in life threatening conditions.[22] Nevertheless,

---

[19] Amnesty International, *Rwanda. Gacaca: A Question of Justice*, London, December 2002, p. 19.

[20] S. Vandeginste, "Poursuite des présumés responsables", pp. 110–112.

[21] An overview of these attempts to reduce the prison population can be found in L. Waldorf, "Mass Justice for Mass Atrocity", pp. 42–43.

[22] According to government figures, several thousands of detainees died during 1998 as a result of AIDS, malnutrition, dysentery and typhus. During the month of November 1998 alone, 400 prisoners died of typhus in Rilima prison (Kigali, Reuters, 30 January 1999).

more than 20,000 confessions were registered by early 2000[23], but this did not lead to a corresponding increase in the number of trials.

Trials at last started at the end of December 1996. When the first judgments were pronounced in January 1997, they raised grave concerns about the rights of defense, the treatment of suspects and witnesses, and the presumption of innocence.[24] By March 1998, a mere 330 persons had been judged: at that rate, it would take over four centuries to try all suspects, particularly as the number of those arrested exceeded that of those brought before the courts. According to a report by UN Human Rights Commission Special Representative Michel Moussali, by early 2000 about 2,406 suspects had been tried, of whom 14.4 percent were sentenced to death, 30 percent to life imprisonment, 34 percent to jail sentences of between one and twenty years; 19 percent were acquitted.[25] At the end of 2003, slightly fewer than 10,000 persons had been tried, but sentences showed a distinct, and positive, evolution: 3 percent death penalties, 16 percent life sentences, and 27 percent acquittals.[26] Bill Schabas painted a rosy picture of the judicial process: "the judgments provide a reassuring portrait of a judicial system hard at work, contending with the rights of the accused, conflicting evidence and legal questions, and attempting to come to a fair result."[27] However, his assessment was based on a highly selective set of case law published by Avocats sans frontières,[28] which, according to the introduction to the first volume, aimed at "identifying the most interesting decisions" and which was far from representative, but instead wanted to promote good practice. Other assessments were distinctly critical. Referring to many sources, Waldorf disagreed with Schabas: "In fact, the quality of justice in trials has been poor due to inadequate defence representation, lack of resources, and especially political interference."[29] Amnesty International noted continuing corruption, inefficiency, and

---

[23] W.A. Schabas, "Genocide Trials", p. 887.

[24] See, for example, Amnesty International, *Rwanda. Unfair Trials: Justice Denied*, London, April 1997.

[25] United Nations, Economic and Social Council, Commission on Human Rights, *Report on the Situation of Human Rights in Rwanda Submitted by the Special Representative, Mr. Michel Moussali, Pursuant to Commission Resolution 1999/20*, E/CN.4/2000/41, 10 February 2000, para. 136.

[26] Liprodhor, *Problématique des informations et témoignages devant les juridictions Gacaca*, Kigali, 2006, quoted by J. Meierhenrich, *Lawfare*.

[27] W.A. Schabas, "Genocide Trials", p. 889.

[28] Avocats sans frontières, *Recueil de jurisprudence. Contentieux du génocide et des massacres au Rwanda*, 5 vols., Brussels, 2004–2005.

[29] L. Waldorf, "Mass Justice", pp. 45–46.

government interference in the judiciary, and found evidence for this in the disappearance, intimidation, suspension, removal, arrest, or exile of a number of leading members of the judiciary.[30]

Although he found that "[t]here is much to applaud in this process,"[31] Moussali noted the "paralysis in the justice sector."[32] The impasse showed in the fact that the law of September 8, 1996, which retroactively regularized the remand files until December 31, 1997, was renewed by a law of December 26, 1997, in order to prolong the detentions until December 31, 1999. Indeed, these successive extensions meant that those arrested in 1994 were to remain in prison for six years and more without having been produced before a judge. Avocats sans frontières, which ran a field office in Rwanda, expressed concern that this was a dangerous precedent, because nothing would prevent a renewal of the remand regularizations at the end of 1999,[33] which was indeed what happened when the delay was again extended for another eighteen months, until June 30, 2001, in December 1999. In addition, Rwanda was not only facing a mathematical problem. Indeed, "Justice must not only be done, but seen to be done." The Tutsization of the judicial system (cf. supra) contributed to a perception of partiality that even the most even-handed judiciary would find difficult to beat. The feeling that Hutu suspects were prosecuted by mainly Tutsi prosecutors and judged by mainly Tutsi judges discredited the entire process and created resentment over what was seen as victors' justice, the more so since suspects of the RPA were not prosecuted (see also infra). As many Rwandans did not see justice (and the state that rendered it) as theirs, the legitimacy of the system was very limited.

Despite international condemnations and appeals for clemency, on April 24, 1998, twenty-two persons sentenced to death were publicly executed by firing squad in Kigali, Nyamata, Kibungo, Gikongoro, and Murambi. Amnesty International was "concerned that many of the defendants have been sentenced to death after an unfair trial. While the identity of all the 22 to be executed is not known, it is feared that they include individuals whose trials were grossly unfair, including some who were tried without access to a defence lawyer." More particularly with regard to the case of former prosecutor Silas Munyagishali, the

---

[30] Amnesty International, *Rwanda. Gacaca*, p. 16.

[31] United Nations, Economic and Social Council, Commission on Human Rights, *Report on the Situation*, para. 137.

[32] *Idem*, para. 140.

[33] Avocats sans frontières, *Projet "Justice pour tous au Rwanda". Rapport annuel 1997*, Brussels, 1998, p. 19.

organization noted that during his trial in Gitarama in 1997, several defence witnesses were threatened and intimidated and effectively prevented from testifying. Amnesty International was also concerned that "he may have been arrested for political reasons. In his role as assistant prosecutor, he had complained about irregularities in judicial procedures."[34] Later on, no more executions took place.

The case of Munyagishali and others drew attention to the issue of testimonies and more particularly the activities of so-called syndicates of denunciation, organized not only at the national level by associations such as Ibuka ("Remember") but also at the local level, for example, by the Association des rescapés du genocide à Butare (ARG), which threatened the good administration of justice. Money was paid for testimonies *à charge* that were often "prepared"; in a number of cases, witnesses *à décharge* turned around under threat or abstained from testifying.[35] The RPF itself participated in this denunciation drive by accusing real or perceived opponents of being *génocidaires* or of engaging in "divisionist" or "sectarian" activities (see supra). Amnesty International received numerous reports of alledgedly false genocide accusations and found that the government "frequently levied the charge of genocide in order to stifle dissent or dissatisfaction with its rule and policies."[36] Survivor organizations also attempted to derail a new attempt by the government to address the problem of the case backlog. When the cabinet decided on October 6, 1998 that prisoners without a case file or whose case file only contained data on their identity were to be released, Ibuka protested against this measure, "which consolidates the culture of impunity and aims at a general amnesty." Even the official press contested the decision: in its issue of November 15, 1998, *La Nouvelle Relève* accused the Hutu ministers to want to "arrange the question of their friends detained for genocide."

Although it became increasingly clear that the classical justice system would be unable to deal with the impasse, two contradictory evolutions

---

[34] Amnesty International, *Rwanda: 23 Public Executions Will Harm Hope of Reconciliation*, London, 22 April 1998.

[35] Liprodhor, *Procès de génocide au Rwanda. Deux ans après (déc. 96 – déc. 98)*, Kigali, 1998, pp. 20–21. In a communiqué issued by the RPF, *Ibuka* (before it was taken over by the regime, cf. supra) was accused of manipulating charges against a candidate the party proposed for the Transitional National Assembly: "The RPF asks the government to punish in an exemplary fashion whoever is found to profer false accusations" (Rwanda Patriotic Front, *Itangazo rigenewe abanyamukuru*, Kigali, 10 May 1999). After Ibuka was reined in, the regime did not utter any more complaints.

[36] Amnesty International, *Rwanda. Gacaca*, p. 6.

became visible. On one hand, there was an improvement in the quality of genocide trials. By the end of 1999, there was an increase in the number of acquittals and a decrease of death sentences and life imprisonments while more defendants were represented by counsel. On the other hand, Amnesty International remained concerned about prolonged illegal detentions, political and arbitrary arrests, torture, and killings in detention facilities (mainly in military installations, that were not accessible to outside observers), and rearrests and even the killings of persons released and members of their families.[37] In addition, the situation of released prisoners remained worrying[38], and the phenomena of denunciation and the manipulation of witnesses, both *à charge* and *à décharge*, continued. In other words, classical justice was part of the problem, not of the solution: "Rather than ending the cycles of revenge, the trials themselves were revenge."[39] As "[a]ttempts to implement an essentially unimplementable trial model in Rwanda have given rise to a gridlock,"[40] by the end of the 1990s it was clear that something else needed to be tried.

Before turning to that "something else," namely *gacaca*, a brief word must be said about the other heritage of the Rwandan justice system, namely, the crimes committed by the RPF. These were labled as crimes against humanity and war crimes by several UN reports.[41] Despite repeated pledges by the RPF that its soldiers would face justice, impunity prevailed. During the period 1994–1998, thirty-two soldiers were prosecuted, of whom fourteen were tried and convicted. Almost all were of lower ranks and received sentences not proportional to the gravity of the crime, and the crimes were called "murder," "crimes of revenge" or "human rights violations," not war crimes or crimes against humanity.[42] In addition, the regime consistently imputed RPF crimes to "rogue

---

[37] Amnesty International, *Rwanda: The Troubled Course of Justice*, London, 26 April 2000.

[38] Liprodhor, *Problématique des libérations des accusés de génocide rwandais*, Kigali, July 1999.

[39] M. Minow, *Between Vengeance and Forgiveness. Facing History after Genocide and Mass Violence*, Boston, Beacon Press, 1998, p. 124.

[40] M.A. Drumbl, "Punishment", p. 1289.

[41] For instance, United Nations, Economic and Social Council, Commission on Human Rights, *Report on the Situation of Human Rights in Rwanda submitted by Mr. René Degni-Ségui, Special Rapporteur of the Commission on Human Rights, under Paragraph 20 of Resolution S-3/1 of 25 May 1994*, E/CN.4/1995/70, 11 November 1994, para. 40; United Nations, Security Council, *Final Report of the Commission of Experts established pursuant to Security Council resolution 935 (1994)*, S/1994/1405, 9 December 1994, para.181–182.

[42] Human Rights Watch, *Law and Reality. Progress in Judicial Reform in Rwanda's Community-based Gacaca Courts*, New York, 24 July 2008, pp. 89–90 and annex 2.

elements,"although all evidence showed that massacres were widespread and systematic (see Chapter 4). Between 1998 and 2008, not a single soldier was prosecuted, and the trial that did take place in 2008 (on the murder of clerics in Gakurazo) was a blatant whitewash (see the discussion later in this chapter). The Rwandan government has consistently refused to address these crimes: "The government minimizes the nature and extent of these killings, arguing that they were isolated incidents of 'revenge killings' by a small number of rogue soldiers. The government also asserts that these rogue soldiers have been brought to justice and punished where necessary. Finally, the Rwandan government equates any demands for justice for RPF crimes with genocide denial."[43] However, despite claims to the contrary[44], this does not per se express ethnic bias. Rather the bias is political. What the RPF achieved is impunity for itself as an organization and as a "legitimate" government, not so much for an ethnic group. The proof is that RPF Hutu, as long as they were loyal to the system, enjoyed the same impunity, whereas Tutsi opponents were brutally prosecuted and persecuted.[45]

GACACA

In line with its strong belief in engineering in many fields (see Chapter 6), in 2002 Rwanda embarked on a massive experiment in transitional justice: "mass justice for mass atrocity," in Lars Waldorf's words.[46] In a move never seen elsewhere, "Rwanda decided to put most of the nation on trial."[47] Despite the initial commitment of the Rwandan government to individual and retributive criminal justice, ideas about alternative ways of dealing with an impossible situation were mooted early on. During the 1995 international conference (see supra), South African participants insisted that a truth and reconciliation commission, coupled with some form of amnesty mechanism, was an appropriate "African way" to deal

---

[43] L. Haskell, L. Waldorf, "The Impunity Gap of the International Criminal Tribunal for Rwanda: Causes and Consequences", *Hastings International and Comparative Law Review*, 34:1 (2011), p. 53.

[44] See, for example, J.N. Clark, "National Unity and Reconciliation in Rwanda: A Flawed Approach?", *Journal of Contemporary African Studies*, 28:2 (2010), p. 146.

[45] For instance, when former prime minister Pierre-Célestin Rwigema, a Hutu, returned to Rwanda in 2011 after almost a decade in exile, he was "pardoned," while during that same year, four former high-ranking Tutsi were judged in absentia and given long prison sentences (see Chapter 3).

[46] L. Waldorf, "Mass Justice".

[47] *Idem*, p. 3.

with a past of intense violence.[48] At another conference held in Kigali in August 1997, Justice Minister Nteziryayo referred again to the South African model. Acknowledging that "[i]t is hard to say what is the official view," he stated as "his own view" that "we want mechanisms over and above the institutions of justice, something which is in line with social justice," adding that a Truth and Reconciliation Commission "is necessary."[49] In early 1998, (then vice-president) Kagame said that "in the long run, this cannot go on: we will have to find other solutions, and we'll explain this to the survivors."[50] During the "Urugwiro reflection meetings" (see supra), participants agreed that, in order to break the deadlock, "it is necessary to look for and try justice which is not classical"[51]; more precisely, "Rwandans can base that new justice on the Gacaca Rwandese heritage."[52] Vandeginste noted that, after the elimination of the threat of Hutu militias in the DRC as a result of the second Rwandan invasion and the gradual neutralization of internal dissent, it was "much more 'comfortable' for the regime in power to declare that reconciliation is a policy objective."[53]

As a result of the Urugwiro discussions, a commission was tasked in November 1998 with proposing mechanisms to increase public participation in adjudicating the genocide legacy. The thirteen-member commission chaired by Justice Minister Faustin Nteziryayo (who, however, resigned during the proceedings and fled the country) produced recommendations in June 1999. It proposed to establish *gacaca* courts, a reference to a long-existing local justice mechanism. *Gacaca* refers to the grass on which these informal gatherings sat when settling disputes.[54] The report contained precise recommendations on the structure, functions, and competence of

---

[48] W.A. Schabas, "Genocide Trials", p. 884.

[49] "Comments in the Discussion of the Paper by the Minister of Justice", in Newick Park Initiative, *Le rôle de l'Eglise dans la Restauration de la Justice au Rwanda (Rapport de la Conférence tenue à Kigali du 19 au 21 août 1997)*, Cambridge, September 1997.

[50] "Les Belges sont les bienvenus au Rwanda", *Le Soir*, 20 January 1998.

[51] Republic of Rwanda, Office of the President of the Republic, *Report on the Reflection Meetings Held in the Office of the President of the Republic from May 1998 to March 1999*, Kigali, August 1999, para. 80.

[52] *Idem*, para. 81.

[53] S. Vandeginste, "Justice for Rwanda, Ten Years After: Some Lessons Learned for Transitional Justice", in F. Reyntjens, S. Marysse (Eds.), *L'Afrique des grands lacs. Annuaire 2003–2004*, Paris, L'Harmattan, 2004, p. 53.

[54] On the original *gacaca*, see F. Reyntjens, "Le *gacaca* ou la justice du gazon au Rwanda", *Politique Africaine*, No. 40, December 1990, pp. 31–41.

the new *gacaca* and on the legislative changes that were needed.[55] After national consultations, the proposal was modified several times.

The Transitional National Assembly finally adopted Organic Law No. 40/2000 of January 16, 2001, "on the establishment of 'Gacaca Jurisdictions' and the organization of prosecutions for offences constituting the crime of genocide or crimes against humanity committed between 1 October 1990 and 31 December 1994." The preamble of the law outlined five objectives: (1) establish the truth; (2) accelerate proceedings; (3) eradicate the culture of impunity; (4) punish the guilty, reconcile the Rwandans, and strengthen their unity; and (5) prove the capacity of Rwandan society to settle its own problems based on its traditions. The law thus combined the needs for justice and accountability and for truth and reconciliation. The system was very decentralized: 10,648 *gacaca* jurisdictions were created, including 8,987 at cell level, 1,531 at sector level, 154 at municipal level, and 12 at prefecture level. Justice was to be done by elected "persons of high integrity," known as *inyangamugayo* without legal training. Although the law explicitly referred to tradition, the system was not traditional – apart from its name and the fact that it was locally embedded – but in effect very much state based, as state law was to be applied and state institutions, including the prosecutors' offices, played a lead role.[56] Betts noted that the coercive, administrative, and prosecutorial functions therefore radically altered the logic of *gacaca*, molding them to facilitate the interests of the state.[57] In addition, the "new" *gacaca* was retributive or punitive, not restorative as was the old one. Government observers at *gacaca* proceedings made sure that every "actor" behaved according to the official script,[58] a behavior also induced by the presence of police and military at the trials.[59] Ordinary people realized this well, and

---

[55] A summary of the commission's proposals can be found in Republic of Rwanda, Office of the President of the Republic, *Report on the Reflection Meetings*, para. 90–99.

[56] A summary outline of why *gacaca* is only vaguely traditional can be found in F. Reyntjens, S. Vandeginste, "Rwanda: An Atypical Transition", in: E. Skaar, S. Gloppen, A. Suhrke (Eds.), *Roads to Reconciliation*, Boulder, CO, Lexington Books, 2005, pp. 118–119. The distance with "tradition" was acknowledged by Prosecutor General Gerald Gahima who referred to *gacaca* as "a concept, an inspiration we borrowed. We are not replicating *gacaca* as it has existed in the past" (interview quoted in J. Meierhenrich, *Lawfare*).

[57] A. Betts, "Should Approaches to Post-conflict Justice and Reconciliation be Determined Globally, Nationally or Locally?", *European Journal of Development Research*, 17:4 (2005), p. 743.

[58] S. Thomson, *Resisting Reconciliation: State Power and Everyday Life in Post-genocide Rwanda*, PhD thesis, Dalhousie University, 2009.

[59] Human Rights Watch, *Rwanda. Justice Compromised. The Legacy of Rwanda's Community-based Gacaca Courts*, New York, May 2011, p. 92.

they distinguished between *gacaca ya leta* (*gacaca* of the state) and *gacaca ya keera* (*gacaca* in ancient times).[60]

After the election of the judges in October 2001, a pilot phase was in place from 2002 to 2004, and the *gacaca* jurisdictions started functioning nationwide in 2005. Two types of criticism were voiced.[61] On one hand, it was clear that international norms, such as those of the International Covenant on Civil and Political Rights (to which Rwanda is a party), would not be respected, particularly in its fair-trial provisions. These concerns related to the blurred distinction between prosecuting and judging, the absence of legal assistance, the summary motivation of judgments, the risk of self-incrimination, and the vague regime of evidence and sentences. On the other hand, the social and political environment prevailing in Rwanda was seen as a threat to the proper administration of justice: freedom of expression was limited, openly challenging the regime's truth (cf. Chapter 7) was risky,[62] and local-level relations were based on fear and mistrust.[63] In addition, the government made immediately clear that the crimes committed by the RPA would not be dealt with by the *gacaca* jurisdictions. As some people raised these crimes during pilot *gacaca* proceedings, a 2004 amendment to the *gacaca* law limited their competence to the crime of genocide, thus putting the RPA at bay. This confirmed that, just as with conventional justice (and the ICTR, see the following discussion), *gacaca* was to become an instance of victor's justice.

Despite all the misgivings, there was, however, a widely shared feeling that, given the enormity of the prison problem, *gacaca* should be given a chance, and the initial assessment and outlook were rather positive.[64] The "soft consensus" among observers was summarized as follows by Peter

---

[60] S. Takeuchi, *Gacaca and DDR: The Disputable Record of State-Building in Rwanda*, JICA-RI Working Paper, No. 32, July 2011, p. 17.

[61] They are well summarized in Amnesty International, *Rwanda. Gacaca*.

[62] The law referred to the "culture of divisionism" well before the law on divisionism was promulgated.

[63] For more on these concerns, see S. Vandeginste, "Les juridictions *gacaca* et la poursuite des suspects auteurs du génocide et des crimes contre l'humanité au Rwanda", in F. Reyntjens, S. Marysse (Eds.), *L'Afrique des grands lacs. Annuaire 1999–2000*, Paris, L'Harmattan, 2000, pp. 75–93.

[64] See, for instance, T. Longman, "Justice at the Grassroots? Gacaca trials in Rwanda", in N. Roht-Arriaza, J. Mariezcurrena (Eds.), *Transitional Justice in the Twenty-first Century. Beyond Truth versus Justice*, New York, Cambridge University Press, 2006, pp. 206–228, and compare with Longman's overall negative assessment that follows.

Uvin: "The choice, then, amounts not to one between a 'clean,' satisfying, safe, or easy to achieve alternative, and a 'dirty,' risky, unsatisfying one. Rather, it is between two real-world alternatives that both violate human rights, both contain political and social risks. It is, in other words, a deeply political decision, and not a technical or legal one."[65] He added that, perhaps, "the strongest element in favour of *gacaca* is the lack of an alternative."[66] Others showed more reticence,[67] and many of the misgivings did indeed materialize, as will be seen later.

At the end of February 2011, when the *gacaca* process was nearing its end, the minister of justice announced that 1,222,093 persons had been judged, 145,255 (12 per cent) of whom were acquitted[68], a rate that is significantly lower than the 20–30 per cent range routinely mentioned. Even after the *gacaca* process was closed in June 2012, there remains uncertainty over exact figures. The final report of the National Service of the *Gacaca* Jurisdictions (SNJG) was not available at the time of writing, but a brief summary that was made public added to the confusion.[69] It mentioned that 1,958,634 cases, which translated in 1,003,227 suspects tried,[70] were conducted, fewer than the number mentioned in February 2011. No acquittal rate was given for suspects, but the overall acquittal rate for cases was said to be 14 percent. Despite the uncertainty surround-

---

[65] P. Uvin, *The Introduction of a Modernized Gacaca for Judging Suspects of Participation in the Genocide and the Massacres of 1994 in Rwanda*, A Discussion Paper prepared for the Belgian Secretary of State for Development Cooperation, s.d. (2000), p. 13.

[66] P. Uvin, C. Mironko, "Western and Local Approaches to Justice in Rwanda", *Global Governance*, 9:219 (2003), p. 227.

[67] J. Sarkin, *Using Gacaca Community Courts in Rwanda to Prosecute Genocide Suspects: Are Issues of Expediency and Efficiency More Important than Those of Due Process, Fairness and Reconciliation?*, s.d., 2001.

[68] "Les tribunaux gacaca ont acquitté près de 150.000 personnes (officiel)", Kigali, Fondation Hirondelle, 28 février 2011.

[69] Republic of Rwanda, SNJG, *Summary of the Report Presented at the Closing of Gacaca Courts Activities*, Kigali, June 2012. The confusion is further enhanced by the findings of Ingelaere, who compared the statistics of the SNJG for the sectors he observed in detail during a given period with his own figures. Those of the SNJG were a multiple of his own (B. Ingelaere, *Peasants, Power and the Past. The* Gacaca *Courts and Rwanda's Transition from Below*, PhD thesis, University of Antwerp, 2012). Whether this observation can be extrapolated for the whole of Rwanda is another question, but it suggests that the official statistics should be looked at with caution.

[70] This would mean that suspects were tried in almost two cases on average. However, a few days before the closure of *gacaca* the SNJG provided a figure of more than 1.6 million suspects convicted and 270,000 acquitted ("Gacaca: Mission Accomplished", *The New Times*, 13 June 2012).

ing the figures, it is assumed that about 1 million suspects were found guilty, which corresponded to the figure announced by the government during the last decade.[71] This tally is striking for two reasons: first, because the number of perpetrators surpasses that of the victims[72] and, second, because the number of persons condemned represents almost 70 percent of Hutu males who were adult in 1994,[73] which in effect means that the Hutu as a whole were considered guilty. It must be noted that only a minority of those convicted served prison terms. By early 2012, about 40,000 genocide convicts were in jail (out of a total prison population of 58,000). Thus, *gacaca* succeeded in its aim to reduce the problem of carceral overpopulation.

Although the *gacaca* process has been extensively and thoroughly researched, the interpretations differ. Of the scholars who have studied *gacaca* from a grassroots perspective, using similar anthropological methods, two interpretations oppose Phil Clark, on one hand, and all the other researchers, on the other. Ingelaere believes that this can be explained by the fact that Clark focuses on the design of *gacaca*, the "model," not its double, namely actual practice.[74]

Phil Clark distinguishes three types of analyses of *gacaca*: those from human rights and legal commentators, who he claims interpret *gacaca* mainly as a juridical institution; those who have conducted extensive fieldwork and criticize various aspects of its practice (this group includes the other researchers mentioned in the following discussion); and those (including some Rwandan observers) who argue that *gacaca* not only aims to punish *génocidaires* but also contributes to other post-genocide

---

[71] Despite Phil Clark's assessment that "[t]he government grossly overstates the number of suspects prosecuted by *gacaca*, citing upwards of 1 million" (P. Clark, *The Gacaca Courts, Post-genocide Justice and Reconciliation in Rwanda. Justice without Lawyers*, Cambridge, Cambridge University Press, 2010, p. 175). Straus estimated that there were around 200,000 perpetrators (S. Straus, "How Many Perpetrators Were there in the Rwandan Genocide? An Estimate", *Journal of Genocide Research*, 6:1 [2004], pp. 85–98).

[72] As the *gacaca* courts were not competent to judge other crimes, this figure is limited to the victims of the genocide against the Tutsi. They number 600,000 at the most, of course a huge figure in itself, particularly because it represents roughly three quarters of all Tutsi living in Rwanda in 1994 (see F. Reyntjens, "Estimation du nombre de personnes tuées au Rwanda en 1994", in S. Marysse, F. Reyntjens [Eds.], *L'Afrique des grands lacs. Annuaire 1996–1997*, Paris, L'Harmattan, 1997, pp. 179–186).

[73] Our calculation is summary and approximative, but the great lines are clear: Rwandan population in 1994: 7,775,000, of which 3,900,000 (50%) were males, 3,500,000 (90%) were Hutu, and 1,600,000 (45%) were adults.

[74] B. Ingelaere, "From Model to Practice. Researching and Representing Rwanda's 'Modernized' *Gacaca* Courts", *Critique of Anthropology*, 32:4 (2012), pp. 388–414.

objectives, particularly reconciliation.[75] Clark places his analysis in the third category. However, the difference between these interpretations is not as clear cut as he suggests. He does not always adequately present what he calls the "prevailing orthodoxy," which then allows him to claim that "[m]ost commentators have consequently misinterpreted the main methods and objectives of *gacaca*, leading them to criticise it for failing to achieve outcomes for which it was never intended."[76] What does distinguish Clark from other scholars is that he seems to accept at face value what his respondents tell him, without wondering whether they are not simply articulating the public transcript imposed by the regime rather than offering their own (hidden) transcript (cf. supra). Thus, for instance, he quotes an *ingando* detainee who states, "Now I know where all our problems came from – they came from the bad leaders."[77] The same respondent consulted his lesson notes to conclude that "Gacaca lets us solve our own problems. (...) Outsiders cannot help us, only ourselves." It is not surprising that Clark found that "[m]ost detainees described the *ingando* lessons as useful and believed that they would help them reintegrate more quickly and smoothly into their home communities,"[78] as he himself on several occasions writes that "[e]choing the official interpretation (...), the popular view" finds this or that.[79] Under these conditions, one must have doubts about the "widespread enthusiasm among the population for engaging in truth telling at *gacaca*."[80] One of the main weaknesses of Clark's defense of *gacaca* is that it "places much stock in the participatory 'spirit of *gacaca*' and its potential for reconciliation."[81] Thomson notes that a common thread in analyses of the whole process "is the assumption that ordinary Rwandans are willing participants."[82] In a similar vein, Rettig writes that positive assessments "are based more on the assumption that gacaca is a local, traditional, restorative judicial

---

[75] Clark lists Karekezi, Gasibirege, and Drumbl (P. Clark, *The Gacaca Courts*, p. 5). It is quite telling that there exists no Rwandan research on the actual operation of *gacaca*. Alice Karekezi and Simon Gasibirege published about *gacaca* before it started functioning, but not during or afterward. Unlike the research conducted by foreign scholars discussed below, their views are prospective and normative but not empirical.

[76] P. Clark, *The Gacaca Courts*, p. 83.

[77] *Idem*, p. 106.

[78] *Idem*, pp. 106–107.

[79] For instance, *idem*, p. 192.

[80] *Idem*, p. 195.

[81] S. Thomson, R. Nagy, "Law, Power and Justice: What Legalism Fails to Address in the Functioning of Rwanda's *Gacaca* Courts", *International Journal of Transitional Justice*, 5 (2011), p. 19.

[82] S. Thomson, *Resisting Reconciliation*, p. 238.

mechanism (...) than on the way gacaca operates or how Rwandans have received it."[83] Indeed, the first surveys that informed international support for *gacaca* were conducted during or even before the pilot phase, before most Rwandans realized what the process had in store for them.[84]

Extensive field research has since unearthed fundamental flaws in the *gacaca* process. The first is the issue of truth telling. Ingelaere arrives at findings that are diametrically opposed to those of Clark.[85] Although the "surfacing of the truth" is predominantly not considered on par with accountability or reconciliation, he argues that it is the cornerstone of the entire transitional justice framework in post-genocide Rwanda. However, the decline in mutual trust, the distorted experience of reconciliation, and the lack of active popular participation in the *gacaca* process are mainly the consequence of a problematic quest for the "truth."[86] Ingelaere observes that the search for the truth took place in a context that was doubly adverse. On one hand, Rwandans communicate strategically: what counts is not so much the "truth" in a Western sense, but rather the usefulness of what is said in an insecure and complex setting. *Ubgenge* is a virtue: it refers to "intelligence resulting in self-controlled public acts. But it also refers to elements of wisdom and trickery, caution, cleverness, prudence. It is the capacity to gain a clear understanding of situations and the capability to surround oneself with a network of profit generating social relations."[87] On the other hand, as seen earlier, the government decrees what is true. This framework is widely propagated, including in the countryside, and it "has instilled a far-reaching degree of self-censorship in the population with regard to elements not fitting in the official 'public transcript.'"[88] Thomson also observed that the *gacaca* courts served to further the state-sanctioned version of events and that the constant threat of sanction

---

[83] M. Rettig, "Gacaca: Truth, Justice, and Reconciliation in Postconflict Rwanda?", *African Studies Review*, 51:3 (2008), p. 26.

[84] For example, Université Nationale du Rwanda, Centre de Gestion des Conflits, Ministry of Justice, Johns Hopkins University Center for Communication Programs, *Perceptions about the Gacaca Law in Rwanda: Evidence from a Multi-method Study*, Kigali, April 2001. This report noted "a certain level of confidence" and an "overwhelming readiness to participate," but these did not stand the test of the actual *gacaca*.

[85] Most prominently in B. Ingelaere, "'Does the Truth Pass across Fire without Burning?' Locating the Short Circuit of Knowledge in Postgenocide Rwanda", *African Studies Review*, 53:1 (2010), pp. 41–59.

[86] *Idem*, p. 509.

[87] *Idem*, p. 520.

[88] *Idem*, p. 522. Ingelaere notes that the Kinyarwanda word *kwibwizira* entails this idea of self-censorship. It expresses the idea that people do what authorities want them to do, even without the latter asking them to do so or use coercion.

pushed people toward adopting a tactical approach, particularly as "local officials constantly remind ordinary Rwandans to 'watch themselves.'"[89] Thomson and Nagy found that truth is "largely scripted and consequently the product of roles that ordinary Rwandans perform to avoid attracting the ire of local officials."[90] Problems with truth did not just concern Hutu. Thus, "male relatives force many Tutsi survivor women to testify in ways that support interests outside those of delivering justice or promoting reconciliation."[91] Brounéus found that for Tutsi women, giving testimony involved intense psychological suffering, and that *gacaca* created a great deal of insecurity for them.[92] A case study of Sovu commune by Rettig offers a survey of all problems associated with truth in *gacaca*. People told lies or half-truths, and silences and omissions were omnipresent; *gacaca* was a forum for settling old disputes; distrust in the community was sharpened. Likewise, Burnet found that, as a result of lying and the seeking of revenge, "the legitimacy of *gacaca* has been so undermined in some communities that residents dismiss all testimony as lies or half-truths."[93]

The problem with truth telling had an understandable impact on trust. Ingelaere found that the restoration of confidence seen in previous years leveled out in 2005, when the *gacaca* tribunals started functioning nationally. He explains this based on the fact that "truth" in the popular experience, from the side of both Hutu and Tutsi, was perceived as not surfacing in the *gacaca* process.[94] In addition, noting a rise of "meta-conflicts" (conflicts about the resolution of conflict), Ingelaere found that *gacaca* activities became the most important source of conflict at the local level.[95] Like Ingelaere, Waldorf observes that "*gacaca* proceedings have caused a worsening of interethnic social relations," fearing that "the actual experience of *gacaca* has confounded hopes that it would promote reconciliation."[96] He finds that *gacaca* has been politicized and that "[t]he

---

[89] S. Thomson, "The Darker Side of Transitional Justice: The Power Dynamics behind Rwanda's *Gacaca* Courts", *Africa*, 81:3 (2011), p. 379.

[90] S. Thomson, R. Nagy, "Law, Power and Justice", p. 20.

[91] S. Thomson, "The Darker Side", p. 383.

[92] K. Brounéus, "Truth-Telling as Talking Cure? Insecurity and Retraumatization in the Rwandan Gacaca Courts", *Security Dialogue*, 39:1 (2008), pp. 55–76.

[93] J.E. Burnet, "The Injustice of Local Justice: Truth, Reconciliation, and Revenge in Rwanda", *Genocide Studies and Prevention*, 3:2 (2008), p. 183.

[94] B. Ingelaere, *Living the Transition. A Bottom-up Perspective on Rwanda's Political Transition*, IOB Discussion Paper 2007–6, Antwerp, 2007, p. 45.

[95] B. Ingelaere, "The Rise of 'Meta-conflicts' during Rwanda's Gacaca Process", in S. Marysse, F. Reyntjens, S. Vandeginste (Eds.), *L'Afrique des grands lacs. Annuaire 2010–2011*, Paris, L'Harmattan, 2011, pp. 303–318.

[96] L. Waldorf, "Mass Justice", p. 75.

gravest danger (. . .) lies in the potential imposition of collective guilt on the Hutu majority,"[97] a fear compounded by the number of those convicted mentioned earlier.

That this collectivization of guilt was not an unfortunate occurrence but an explicit intention of the regime showed in a remarkable document handed out to the inmates of Kigali prison by a religious group, Esther Vision Ministries, acting at the request and on behalf of the executive secretary of the SNJG. Two of the points made in the text are particularly revealing: "3. (. . .) the genocide is the responsibility of all Hutu, wherever they come from, whether they have killed or not. (. . .). 4. (. . .) You must accept that, as the genocide targeted all Tutsi (because the aim was to exterminate them), it also concerns all Hutu. Here is why: all Tutsi are survivors, all Hutu are *interahamwe* (. . .)."[98] Just like guilt, victimhood was collectivized. Rombouts found victim competition and eventually victim hierarchy, with unrecognized and unsupported (Hutu) victims on one side and with recognized and supported (Tutsi) victims on the other.[99] A group of Hutu women interviewed by Burnet, able to speak out after a Tutsi woman had left a focus group, told her that *gacaca* was "profoundly dividing" the population along ethnic lines.[100] Perhaps the most telling indictment was made by one of Rettig's interviewees: "Maybe there can be reconciliation when *gacaca* finishes."[101]

State control was another feature common to most analyses. Looking at the broader power dynamics behind the *gacaca* experiment, Thomson found that it is "central to a state-run legal system that produces a particular version of justice and reconciliation that reinforces the power of the post-genocide government at the expense of individual processes of reconciliation."[102] She observed that the collectivization of Hutu guilt and the politicization of Tutsi victimhood contributed to that design[103] and that

---

[97] *Idem*, p. 79.

[98] "Imiburo yagenewe abakoze ibyaha by'itsembabwoko batari babyemera ngo babyihane, banabisabire imbabazi" ("Information addressed to those who have committed the sin of genocide and who do not recognize it, so that they may repent and ask for pardon"), document distributed on October 20, 2005, in Kigali Central Prison, reproduced in G. Theunis, *Mes soixante-quinze jours de prison à Kigali*, Paris, Karthala, 2012, p. 245. The quotes used here are based on the translation in French on pages 186–187 of the book.

[99] H. Rombouts, *Victim Organisations and the Politics of Reparation: A Case Study on Rwanda*, Antwerp and Oxford, Intersentia, 2004.

[100] J.E. Burnet, "The Injustice of Local Justice", p. 186.

[101] M. Rettig, "The Sovu Trials. The Impact of Genocide Justice on One Community", in S. Straus, L. Waldorf, *Remaking Rwanda. State Building and Human Rights after Mass Violence*, Madison, The University of Wisconsin Press, 2011, p. 206.

[102] S. Thomson, "The Darker Side", pp. 373–374.

[103] *Idem*, p. 378.

"[f]or many ordinary Rwandans, the *gacaca* process represents an oppressive form of state power that forces individuals to participate in ways that are not necessarily in line with their own lived realities."[104] In other words, "local officials seek to control the *gacaca* process by forcing individuals to participate in ways that reinforce the power of the government at the expense of their own well-being."[105] For many Rwandans, "the *gacaca* courts represent a form of state control in their lives, which promotes fear and insecurity as opposed to unity or reconciliation."[106] As seen earlier, however, forced compliance with state imposed rituals does not always correspond to reality: "the *gacaca* courts are a site of everyday resistance to the policies of the RPF-led government, not one of national unity and reconciliation."[107] In other words, contrary to the official discourse, "*gacaca* courts are a contested and conflicted state space and are characterized by discord and tension between various actors."[108]

These observations were echoed by research that allowed to listen to people who were free to speak, as the respondents were interviewed in the Nakivale refugee settlement in Uganda, where most had recently fled (some for the second or third time). Interviewees described how *gacaca* developed from a community-based justice system into a mechanism for state control. In addition to observations already made elsewhere in this section (victor's justice, settling of personal differences, division and polarization of communities), interviewees talked of how they had been on local *gacaca* panels but had had to flee because they refused to wrongly convict people. One former president of a *gacaca* court said that "his verdicts that would set free (Hutu) people from prison would often be over-ridden by higher placed (Tutsi) government officials."[109] Ibuka, seen as a government-controlled mechanism aimed at keeping alive the notion of collective Hutu guilt, was feared by many: "If the *gacaca* judges don't do exactly what *Ibuka* wants, they are imprisoned because *Ibuka* is like a branch of the RPF."[110]

---

[104] *Idem*, p. 381.

[105] S. Thomson, R. Nagy, "Law, Power and Justice", p. 20.

[106] S. Thomson, "Whispering Truth to Power: The Everyday Resistance of Rwandan Peasants to Post-genocide Reconciliation", *African Affairs*, 110:440 (2011), p. 445.

[107] S. Thomson, *Resisting Reconciliation*, p. 231.

[108] *Idem*, p. 241.

[109] *A Dangerous Impasse*, p. 26.

[110] *Idem*, p. 27. In a similar vein, a *gacaca* president was given political asylum in France after she was threatened and detained because she refused to give in to orders of local officials and an army officer (Cour nationale du droit d'asile, *Contentieux des réfugiés, Jurisprudence du Conseil d'Etat et de la Cour nationale du droit d'asile*, Année 2008, pp. 27–29).

Contrary to official statements, *gacaca* was not restorative. According to Waldorf, "*gacaca* has always been an uneasy mix of restorative and retributive justice: confessions *and* accusations, plea-bargains *and* trials, forgiveness *and* punishment, community service *and* incarceration."[111] It became increasingly retributive, both in design and in practice.[112] In the communities where Burnet conducted her research, "the perception of the *Gacaca* courts is that they are entirely focused on punitive justice."[113]

Another serious obstacle related to popular participation. Attendance in this "unpopular popular justice" was poor, as *gacaca* was imposed on local communities in a top-down fashion by a highly centralized and authoritarian regime, because subsistence farmers needed to tend to their fields, whereas both Hutu and Tutsi feared the process and its potential consequences. Low participation rates led the government to use coercion, an aspect that was reinforced when the 2004 amendment to the *gacaca* law made attendance compulsory.[114]

Looking at *gacaca* from a primarily human rights angle (Clark's first category of analysts), Human Rights Watch spoke of a "mixed success," but then mainly outlined "multiple shortcomings and failures." It found that "the single most significant compromise" was "the curtailment of the fair trial rights of the accused," and dozens of cases mentioned in the report showed "how these due process shortcomings have directly contributed to flawed *gacaca* trials."[115] In an attempt to meet the end of 2007 deadline initially set for the closure of proceedings, the government pressurized *gacaca* judges into speeding up trials. As a consequence, some defendants were sentenced to life imprisonment in trials that lasted less than an hour: "the quality of decision-making was being sacrificed for the sake of speed."[116] Later on, the number of politically motivated in absentia trials increased, some aiming at securing custody over suspects living abroad,[117]

[111] L. Waldorf, "Rwanda's Failing Experiment in Restorative Justice", in D. Sullivan, L. Tifft (Eds.), *A Handbook of Restorative Justice: A Global Perspective*, Abingdon, Routledge, 2005, p. 422.

[112] L. Waldorf, "Mass Justice", p. 53.

[113] J.E. Burnet, "The Injustice of Local Justice", p. 177.

[114] L. Waldorf, "Mass Justice", pp. 64–68.

[115] Human Rights Watch, *Rwanda. Justice Compromised*, pp. 3–4. The report is based on more than 2,000 days of observing trials and conducting interviews; more than 350 *gacaca* trials were followed.

[116] *Idem*, p. 24.

[117] *Idem*, p. 56.

others at seizing their property or settling personal scores,[118] others still at silencing opponents.[119] Like others, Human Rights Watch observed problems with telling the truth, and even with speaking at all (the practice of *ceceka*, cf. supra), forced participation, intimidation of (defense) witnesses and even of judges, corruption, and external interference in trials. Again echoing a concern expressed elsewhere, the report concluded that "[o]ne of the *gacaca* laws most serious shortcomings is that it does not cover war crimes and crimes against humanity committed by the RPF."[120] Waldorf's conclusion was severe: in addition to converting local ad hoc practices into a centrally organized and ambitious undertaking, the government compounded the problem by failing to provide reparations to genocide survivors, making *gacaca* an exercise in victor's justice, restricting freedom of speech on sensitive issues, and collectivizing guilt.[121]

In a brief but excellent summary of the *gacaca* experiment, Longman argued that

far from serving to resolve conflict and promote reconciliation, as their advocates claimed, trials have allowed an authoritarian government to consolidate its power, created insecurity in the population, and heightened ethnic tensions. (…) [T]he *gacaca* process has promoted neither the restorative nor traditional judicial principles its supporters claimed. Instead, *gacaca* has been a retributive and punitive process used to promote a repressive political agenda and to settle many personal vendettas.[122]

The final verdict of Klaas de Jonge, a veteran resident observer of *gacaca*,[123] was without appeal:

the *gacaca* process has been a failure (because of) the poor quality of the justice administered; the incomplete and biased establishment of the truth; the forced participation of the population in the process; the lack of adequate reparation policy for victims; the high number of convicts in prisons and prison-like work camps; the continuing distrust between Hutu and Tutsi; and in particular, the lack of measures to ensure non-repetition.

---

[118] A *gacaca* official told Ananda Breed that "it was his belief the accused was innocent, but that he had been targeted due to his property wealth" (A. Breed, "Discordant Narratives in Rwanda's Gacaca Courts", in M. Campioni, P. Noack (Eds.), *Rwanda Fast Forward. Social, Economic, Military and Reconciliation Prospects*, Houndmills, Palgrave Macmillan, 2012, p. 40).

[119] Human Rights Watch, *Rwanda. Justice Compromised*, pp. 98–103.

[120] *Idem*, p. 119.

[121] L. Waldorf, "Mass Justice", p. 85.

[122] T. Longman, "Trying Times for Rwanda. Reevaluating *Gacaca* Courts in Post-Genocide Reconciliation", *Harvard International Review*, 32:2 (2010), p. 49.

[123] De Jonge was head of mission for Penal Reform International (PRI) in Rwanda from 1998 to 2001 and coordinator of PRI's *gacaca* research from 2001 to 2005.

According to him, all transitional justice measures but above all the political instrumentalization of the *gacaca* courts, "have been used to strengthen control over the Hutu majority." He fears that the "never openly stated objective of '*gacaca* as a tool of suppression' seems, in the short run, to have worked well," but that "in the long run it could lead to disaster."[124]

With hindsight, the caution advocated already in 1996 by the UNHCHR was prophetic. It warned that the violence experienced in 1994 "was of such a gravity that it simply cannot and should not be handled in the Gacaca" and that "[c]aution should be exercised against too much government intrusion."[125] Although it is likely that the thinking about *gacaca* started as a genuine attempt to find a solution to an impossible problem, it gradually became another tool of oppression. For instance, only after ordinary people expressed the desire for judging RPF abuse did the regime expressly adhere to the logic of victor's justice, among other ways by putting an end to the *gacaca* jurisdictions' competence for crimes against humanity. In addition, the government realized the opportunities for political control offered by procedures that were taking place at the local level, but were centrally monitored at the same time. So it is no wonder that many viewed *gacaca* as "merely another imposition of the central government on local communities and another venue in which local power conflicts can work themselves out while appearing to conform to central government policies."[126] Under the political and social circumstances prevailing in Rwanda and given the design and implementation of the *gacaca* experiment, a "shared truth" could not emerge. As seen earlier, de Lame observed a similar divergence of meaning in the genocide commemorations.[127]

---

[124] K. de Jonge, *PRI's Research on Gacaca*, Bujumbura, 1 May 2010 (mimeo). The final report of PRI was much less outspoken. It found that "the advantages of the *Gacaca* very often also revealed themselves as being its weaknesses," and it mentioned problems with "basic principles of justice" and with "the process of establishing the truth," but it avoided proposing an overall (favorable or unfavorable) verdict on the exercise (PRI, *The Contribution of the* Gacaca *Jurisdictions to Resolving Cases Arising from the Genocide. Contributions, Limitations and Expectations of the Post-*Gacaca *Phase*, London and Kigali, n.d. [2010]).

[125] United Nations, High Commissioner for Human Rights, *Gacaca: Le droit coutumier au Rwanda*, Kigali, 1996, quoted by B. Ingelaere, "The Gacaca Courts in Rwanda", in L. Huyse, M. Salter (Eds.), *Traditional Justice and Reconciliation after Violent Conflict. Learning from African Experiences*, Stockholm, International IDEA, 2008, p. 36.

[126] J.E. Burnet, "The Injustice of Local Justice", p. 188.

[127] D. de Lame, "Deuil, commémoration justice dans les contexts rwandais et belge.Otages existentiels et enjex politiques", *Poitique Africaine*, 92 (December 2003), p. 47.

Apart from Clark, who, while acknowledging that the results of the *gacaca* process have been mixed,[128] offers an assessment that is by and large supportive (albeit at times vague and confusing), all other observers, who accumulate a considerable deal of data, field experience and analysis, conclude that *gacaca* has brought neither justice, nor truth, nor reconciliation.[129] Quite the contrary, they point to the considerable risks for the future of Rwanda generated by a process that is deeply flawed and that contributes to the prevalent structural violence. For many Hutu, "the *gacaca* process is simply a means 'for this government to get rid of us. (...) It is like they are killing Hutu through excessive punishment.'"[130] The whole process therefore actually impeded the realization of the rule of law and the promotion of sustainable peace.[131] This overall failure should not come as a surprise. It was simply impossible to implement a sophisticated system of information about and control of a process that was at the same highly decentralized and strictly controlled.[132]

THE ICTR

The relations between Rwanda and the ICTR were discussed in Chapter 5. This section looks at the politics of the ICTR in which these relationships have played an obvious part. Kingsley Moghalu, a former special counsel and spokesperson of the tribunal pointed at the "dilemmas of political justice" and candidly acknowledged that "war crimes justice – and war crimes tribunals – simply cannot be understood from a strictly legal or judicial standpoint, which is divorced from an understanding

---

[128] P. Clark, "The Legacy of Rwanda's Gacaca Courts", Think Africa Press, 23 March 2012.

[129] At least in general terms. The outcome was mixed in certain locations, depending on local political and social dynamics, as shown by Ingelaere (B. Ingelaere, *Peasants, Power and the Past*).

[130] S. Thomson, R. Nagy, "Law, Power and Justice", p. 27.

[131] S. Brown, "The Rule of Law and the Hidden Politics of Transitional Justice in Rwanda", in C. Lehka Sriram, O. Martin-Ortega, J. Herman (Eds.), *Peacebuilding and Rule of Law in Africa. Just Peace?*, Abingdon, Routledge, 2011, p. 179.

[132] Peter Uvin, who initially (and cautiously) advocated *gacaca*, told me that the demands these complex systems make on international donors and on the government are too heavy: "They never work" (personal communication). The desire of the Rwandan regime to keep control is also stressed by Astrid Jamar, when she discusses the refusal to accept a donor-sponsored NGO-initiated "Gacaca Facilitation Initiative": "Rwandan authorities were less concerned about aid efficiency and coordination than about their ownership (i.e., control – FR) of the project (A. Jamar, "Deterioration of Aid Coordination in Gacaca Implementation: Dealing with the Past for a Better Future?", in M. Campioni, P. Noack (Eds.), *Rwanda Fast Forward*, p. 83).

of international relations and world politics."[133] Pierre-Richard Prosper, who was the trial lawyer prosecuting during the ICTR's first genocide trial and who once believed in "pure" justice, confirmed in a conversation with Moghalu that "war crimes justice is political."[134] As we have seen the rather cynical role he later played in the emergence of victor's justice, he was well placed to make that assessment.

Serious management problems marred the institution from the beginning. Created by UN Security Council resolution 955 on November 8, 1994, the ICTR started effectively functioning in mid-1995. Hardly a year and a half later, an internal UN inquiry conducted under the leadership of Karl Paschke in February 1997 found serious malfunctions, both at the Registry and the Office of the Prosecutor (OTP). The registrar and the deputy prosecutor were summoned to New York and asked to resign. They were replaced by Agwu Okali (Nigeria) and Bernard Muna (Cameroon), respectively.[135] In light of the continued poor performance of the tribunal, both were replaced in early 2001, Agwu Okali by Adama Dieng (Senegal) and Bernard Muna by Bongani Majola (South Africa).[136] Six years into the Tribunal's operation, the ICG's judgment was severe: it pointed at "the mediocre productivity of the judges," "incompetence in a large part" of the OTP, illegal fee splitting between lawyers and defendants, and internal power struggles.[137]

A problem from day one was the extremely slow pace of procedures. Only in 1998, three years after the ICTR started effectively functioning, were the first three judgments rendered; two of these came after a brief trial following a guilty plea. Until the start of the "Cyangugu trial" in September 2000, six of the nine judges had not sat on a substantive trial for more than a year. One of the consequences of the delays was that suspects spent time in pretrial detention for periods that would not be admissible in domestic jurisdictions or under the European Convention on Human Rights. An extreme case, between his arrest in Belgium on June 28, 1995, and the judgment in first instance on June 24, 2011, Joseph Kanyabashi spent sixteen years in prison. Although the tribunal was set

---

[133] K.C. Moghalu, *Rwanda's Genocide. The Politics of Global Justice*, New York and Houndmills, Palgrave Macmillan, 2005, p. 5.

[134] *Idem*, p. 6.

[135] "ONU-Rwanda-Tribunal: Koffi Annan convoque à New York les responsables du tribunal pour le Rwanda", New York (United Nations), AFP, 12 February 1997.

[136] Majola was appointed only in January 2003; the post was vacant for almost two years.

[137] International Crisis Group, *International Criminal Tribunal for Rwanda. Justice Delayed*, Nairobi, Arusha, and Brussels, 7 June 2001, pp. 10–13.

to close proceedings at first instance at the end of 2008, it was soon clear that this was impossible. By June 2007, ICTR president Denis Byron had to admit to the Security Council that the deadline would not be met: "[A] solution must be discussed that will allow the Tribunal or other mechanisms to proceed with such cases beyond the end of 2008."[138]

The "completion strategy" became increasingly urgent and crucial, but the transfer to domestic courts aimed at dealing with the problem ran into serious difficulties. On one hand, third countries were not eager to take on cases, and France was the only one to accept judging two indicted persons residing there.[139] On the other hand, although Rwanda was anxious to receive as many cases it could, the prosecutor initially would not require transfers because two of the conditions in Rule 11*bis* of the ICTR Rules of Procedure and Evidence, the absence of the death penalty and the guarantee of a fair trial, were not met.[140] In March 2007, Rwanda enacted legislation aimed at countering these objections: capital punishment was abolished and special provisions were made for transfer cases. Nevertheless, the trial chambers and the appeals chamber at first refused to authorize transfers on account of sentencing and fair justice concerns. Similar reasons prevented third countries from extraditing suspects to Rwanda. Not until early 2012 did transfers and extraditions take place. Léon Mugesera was extradited from Canada in January 2012, followed by Jean Uwinkindi who was transferred from the ICTR in April. Earlier, the European Court of Human Rights decided that the extradition from Sweden of a suspect would not violate the convention.[141]

Poor prosecutorial policy was another sour point. At the beginning, investigations and prosecutions lacked focus, and the OTP went for any suspect, however small, it could find. The indictment of lower-level suspects irritated Kigali, which found that "the indictments generally concern only local level officials."[142] The caseload created by the prosecution of "small fry" that would not have been tried had the OTP developed a coherent investigation and prosecution policy early on, considerably

---

[138] United Nations, Security Council, 5697th meeting, 18 June 2007, S/PV.5697, p. 8.

[139] Ephrem Nkezabera was judged in Belgium, but this was not the result of a transfer under article 11 *bis* of the Rules of Procedure, but of an agreement between the prosecutor and Belgium.

[140] W.A. Schabas, "Anti-complementarity: Referral to National Jurisdictions by the UN International Criminal Tribunal for Rwanda", *Max Planck Yearbook of United Nations Law*, 13 (2009), p. 37.

[141] Case of *Ahorugeze v. Sweden* (Application no. 37075/09), judgment of 27 October 2011.

[142] "Le Rwanda propose le transfer du TPIR à Kigali", Kigali, AFP, 20 February 1997.

delayed the tribunal's work in dealing with suspects who ranked high in the hierarchy of genocide.[143] The quality of indictments was poor, as was the way in which the OTP met its burden of proof. Judge Ostrovsky publicly complained: "I constantly have to deal with unprofessional indictments. (...) Moreover, the prosecution oftentimes does not even bother to provide evidence on a number of counts."[144]

The weakness of the OTP raised the issue of equality of arms, made very clear when in December 2000, Prosecutor Del Ponte, regretting the poor performance of some prosecuting teams, stated that "our judges are good judges, because they correct the errors of the prosecution."[145] The impression of partiality was further enhanced when, during a visit to Taba in September 2000, Registrar Agwu Okali referred to the condemnation of the former mayor of that commune, Jean-Paul Akayesu, while the judgment was not yet final. The poor functioning of the OTP again became clear in 2002, when former FAR General Léonidas Rusatira was indicted and arrested in Brussels at the request of the ICTR. Not only was he widely known to have opposed the genocide and integrated into the RPA after the war,[146] but even a cursory reading of the indictment revealed elements that were factually untrue. After some prosecution expert witnesses[147] conducted an inquiry on their own behalf, they were able (with great difficulty) to convince Prosecutor Del Ponte that she was about to commit a grave judicial error. She then asked the tribunal to authorize the withdrawal of the indictment.[148]

The quality of witness statements, crucial in these cases that were strongly based on the establishment of facts and where documentary evidence was rare, was an Achilles' heel of the ICTR, and the OTP in particular. The way in which Rwandans communicate was discussed earlier, and many witnesses lied under oath. A few examples must suffice. In

---

[143] However, from 1998 the ICTR secured an increasing number of arrests and indictments of major players, and in this field it performed better than the ICTY.

[144] "Judge Yakov Ostrovsky Criticisms of ICTR", Arusha, Internews, 13 May 2002.

[145] "Compte-rendu d'une conférence de presse tenue à Arusha le 13 décembre 2000", Arusha, Fondation Hirondelle, 13 December 2000. This led to an angry reaction by the suspects detained in Arusha. In a letter sent to the president of the ICTR on December 15, 2000, they stated that the "scandalous revelations" made by the prosecutor "have explicitly confirmed that our judges are not neutral, but that they complete the indictments and, were necessary, correct their weaknesses."

[146] As seen earlier, Rusatira went into exile in October 1995. Just as with others before and after him, it was only at that moment that Kigali launched accusations against him.

[147] Alison Des Forges, André Guichaoua, and this author.

[148] On this saga, see T. Cruvellier, *Le tribunal des vaincus. Un homme libre au Rwanda*, Paris, Calmann-Lévy, 2006, pp. 223–228; "L'erreur", *Diplomatie judiciaire*, 13 August 2002.

the "media case," the OTP wanted to submit as evidence a diary kept by the witness, supposedly in 1994. However, it was forced to withdraw it after defense lawyers pointed out that copies available to them had additional insertions made well after 1994. The witness admitted he had made later additions, and the head of the prosecution team Stephen Rapp apologized to the chamber for the handling of the diary disclosure.[149] In the same trial, prosecution witness DM stated that several other prosecution witnesses had lied: "I can assure you that one old man who came to testify here came back bragging that he had made compromising testimony against Ngeze. (...) That old man never even left his house during the genocide."[150] In the Ntakirutimana case, defense counsel argued that there was a witness syndicate aimed at falsely accusing Hutu of genocide crimes. A witness described in detail the working of a denunciation enterprise set up by Ibuka and local authorities in Kibuye.[151] The issue of false testimony became particularly clear in the case of Abdul Ruzibiza. A former lieutenant of the RPA, he fled the country in early 2001. He testified against the RPF on several occasions: in Kampala before ICTR investigators, in Paris in the Bruguière inquiry, and in Madrid before judge Andreu Merelles. He gave interviews and published memos, and even a sizable book.[152] In March 2006, he testified under oath before the ICTR in the case of Bagosora et al. All along, his statements on crimes committed by the RPF were consistent. Suddenly, in November 2008 after the arrest of Rose Kabuye (cf. supra), he claimed that he invented everything; nothing of what he had earlier stated, including under oath, was true.[153] Heard in June 2010 by French judges Trévidic and Poux, he, however, explained that his retractation "is linked to my personal security and that of other witnesses," and he confirmed his earlier damning statements about the RPF.[154] Ruzibiza died of an illness a few months later.

---

[149] "Witness Claims Nahimana's Writing Was 'Extremist'", Arusha, Hirondelle News Agency, 23 August 2001.

[150] "Prosecution Witness Says Others Before Him Have Lied", Arusha, Hirondelle News Agency, 11 September 2001.

[151] "Survivors Group Trained Genocide Witnesses, Says Defence Witness", Arusha, Hirondelle News Agency, 29 April 2002.

[152] A.J. Ruzibiza, *Rwanda. L'histoire secrète*, Paris, Editions du Panama, 2005.

[153] On this saga, see C. Vidal, "Les contradictions d'un lieutenant rwandais. Abdul Ruzibiza, témoin, acteur, faux-témoin", in S. Marysse, F. Reyntjens, S. Vandeginste (Eds.), *L'Afrique des grands lacs. Annuaire 2008–2009*, Paris, L'Harmattan, 2009, pp. 43–54.

[154] "Audition sur commission rogatoire", Oslo, 15 June 2010.

The OTP appeared more intent on securing convictions than on discovering the truth,[155] as was made clear in the sequel to the judgment of the first condemned suspect, Jean-Paul Akayezu. When an appeal against the judgment in first instance was pending, the defense filed a motion for review, based on an affidavit made on March 25, 2001, by a witness who stated in very concrete terms that a number of prosecution testimonies were made up by an organized false denunciation enterprise set up by local administrative and judicial authorities and by Ibuka.[156] Based on technical and procedural elements, the appeals chamber followed the prosecution's argument and rejected the motion in a brief judgment.[157] If it were really concerned about establishing the truth, the OTP should have worried about the possibility that several of its witnesses lied under oath in a concerted fashion. It could at least have inquired into the veracity of its witness statements, based on the defense witness's affidavit, particularly as it contained precise indications on the identity of those involved in the alleged organization of perjury and the places and dates of their meetings.[158] As far as the appeals chamber is concerned, faced with what could have been a fundamental challenge to the first judgment ever rendered by the ICTR, it could at least have proceeded to a summary verification of the allegation, rather than to declare without examination that, prima facie, the facts were not new.

---

[155] "I have received investigators of the Tribunal. (. . .) Instead of seeking the truth, they were only interested by statements charging the defendants" (Lt. Col. Augustin Cyiza in T. Cruvellier, *Le Tribunal des vaincus*, p. 209).

[156] The text of the statement of witness BBB (who was a Tutsi RPF member from Akayezu's home commune Taba) can be found in C. Onana, *Les secrets de la justice internationale. Enquêtes truquées sur le genocide rwandais*, Paris, Editions Duboiris, 2005, pp. 229–232. Onana (pp. 232–237) goes on to describe the imposition on Akayezu of a defence counsel not of his choice in a way that appears akin to blackmail, and that reminds of what happened later to Jean Kambanda (cf. the following discussion).

[157] The operative part reads as follows: "Considering that it appears *prima facie* that the plaintiff does not present new facts" (Jean-Paul Akayezu c/ Le Procureur, Arrêt [Requête aux fins de renvoi de l'affaire devant la chambre de première instance], ICTR-96-4-A, judgment of 16 May 2001). An analysis of this judgment can be found in G. Mols, "Révision et moyen de preuves supplémentaires dans la jurisprudence des tribunaux internationaux ad hoc. Une réflexion concernant l'arrêt du 16 mai 2001 dans l'affaire Jean-Paul Akayezu c/ le Procureur", in F. Reyntjens, S. Marysse (Eds.), *L'Afrique des grands lacs. Annuaire 2001–2002*, Paris, L'Harmattan, 2002, pp. 37–44.

[158] Other examples of unethical behaviour by the OTP (and by defence teams) can be found in T. Cruvellier, *Le Tribunal des vaincus*. Ethical codes in most countries would prohibit such behavior. But then, in most countries, all players (judges, OTP, registry, witnesses, journalists) do not live together in the promiscuity of the "village" that is Arusha.

Another instance of the OTP's obsession with convictions rather than with the truth occurred in the case of former prime minister Jean Kambanda. After having spent eight months in isolation in a Dodoma hotel without the assistance of a lawyer, he was brought to enter a guilty plea after being convinced by his lawyer Michael Oliver Inglis, acting in league with his personal friend and former partner in a law practice, Deputy Prosecutor Muna, that he would get away with a light sentence. The OTP added pressure by offering special protection to his family, which had been threatened.[159] Kambanda's confession was less than sincere, and in a letter of September 11, 1998, to the ICTR registrar he wrote, "I do not recognise Mr. Inglis as having been my counsel or as being one for the future. At best, he has acted at the service of the Prosecutor."[160] When he was sentenced to life in prison, he appealed and retracted his guilty plea, but the decision was confirmed.[161] Cruvellier concluded that "[b]y avoiding a trial, thanks to the agreement concluded between the defendant and the prosecutor, the Tribunal thus nourished a judicial fiction."[162] Genuine suspects were left alone by the OTP in exchange for their assistance in nailing others.[163] Some of those who refused to do so, including persons who were probably innocent, were subsequently prosecuted. It happened to General Augustin Ndindiliyimana[164] and General Gratien Kabiligi,[165] and it nearly happened to General Léonidas Rusatira (cf. supra).[166] On November 5, 2005, former minister Juvénal Uwilingiyimana wrote a letter to Prosector Jallow to complain that he was harassed by OTP staff who

---

[159] The main investigator in charge of the Kambanda file was Canadian police officer Pierre Duclos, accused in his country of perjury, tampering with evidence, and obstructing the course of justice in the famous affair of Matticks Brothers.

[160] Quoted in G. Musabyimana, *Rwanda, le triomphe de la criminalité politique*, Paris, L'Harmattan, 2008, p. 217.

[161] On the Kambanda affair, see C. Onana, *Les secrets*, pp. 238–254; J. Laughland, *A History of Political Trials. From Charles I to Saddam Hussein*, Oxford, Peter Lang, 2008, pp. 207–220 (chapter 16, "Jean Kambanda, Convicted without Trial").

[162] T. Cruvellier, *Le tribunal des vaincus*, pp. 67–82.

[163] *Idem*, pp. 83–94.

[164] On May 17, 2011, Ndindiliyimana was convicted to a prison term that coincided with the time he spent in pretrial detention. Obviously, a sentence of eleven years, three months, and seventeen days did not correspond to the gravity of the crimes he was found guilty of, but was an acquittal in disguise.

[165] Kabiligi was acquitted on December 18, 2008, after having spent more than eleven years in pretrial detention.

[166] On these cases, see T. Cruvellier, *Le tribunal des vaincus*, pp. 209–230.

threatened him with prosecution unless he testified against several defendants. He claimed he was blackmailed into providing false testimony.[167]

The lack of independence of the tribunal, and the OTP in particular, from the Rwandan government, already mentioned earlier, showed in many ways and amounted to an obstruction of justice. A few examples among many must suffice. In June 1996, a leading genocide suspect, Froduald Karamira, was deported to Rwanda from India where he lived. During a stopover in Addis Ababa he attempted to escape and was arrested by the Ethiopian authorities. The ICTR prosecutor Richard Goldstone not only wanted to indict him, but also hoped to convince Karamira, who acted on the interface between the leaders of the genocide and the killers on the streets of Kigali in 1994, to cooperate with his office. But the Rwandan government claimed custody of Karamira and started to intimidate Goldstone's staff in Kigali, whose security it said it could not guarantee if the OTP asserted its primacy in this case. Goldstone gave in, Karamira was judged in Rwanda, and he was among the twenty-two executed in April 1998.[168] By ceding to blackmail, Goldstone did two irreparable things: he gave a clear signal to Kigali that playing hardball worked, and he lost a crucial source of information that could have been of immense help in major cases, including the one against Bagosora et al. in which the prosecution failed to show conspiracy to commit genocide.[169] The stage was thus set for successful blackmail in the subsequent cases of Barayagwiza and the removal of Carla Del Ponte discussed earlier. Just like foreign diplomacies, the ICTR became a hostage of the Rwandan regime.

In a remarkable sortie, even a judge found that there was "ample evidence to show that a large number of crimes were committed by members of the RPF whose leaders today occupy key positions in the government."[170] We have seen earlier how her intention to prosecute RPF crimes was one of the reasons for the removal of Del Ponte as prosecutor, but this trend was visible from the beginning, under Richard Goldstone's tenure. In July 1996, when I asked Goldstone whether he

[167] On November 21, 2005, three days after his last meeting with OTP staff, Uwilingiyimana disappeared, and his mutilated body was found in a Brussels canal on December 17. Jallow issued an astonishing statement including that "this individual, though an indictee of the Tribunal, *voluntarily agreed* to cooperate in the search for truth and justice for the Rwanda genocide of 1994. I convey my sincere condolences to his family" (emphasis added). The assassins of Uwilingiyimana were never found.

[168] For more details on this case, see T. Cruvellier, *Le tribunal des vaincus*, pp. 25–33.

[169] *The Prosecutor v. Théoneste Bagosora, Gratien Kabiligi, Aloys Ntabakuze and Anatole Nsengiyumva*, No.ICTR-98-41-T, judgment of 18 December 2008.

[170] "Judge Yakov Ostrovsky Criticisms of ICTR", Arusha, Internews, 13 May 2002.

intended to prosecute RPF suspects, he answered with irritation that he did not see the need. After I told him that there was compelling prima facie evidence that the RPF committed crimes within the Tribunal's mandate, he replied that there was no such evidence. He continued to believe that, if elements of the RPF committed crimes, these were "revenge killings" that did not justify prosecutions.[171] In addition to uncritically accepting the RPF's line, Goldstone was also aware of the ICTR's vulnerability towards Rwanda, and he was anxious to ensure Kigali's cooperation or at least avoid its sabotage (cf. the Karamira affair).[172]

After Hassan Jallow succeeded Del Ponte as prosecutor, the ICTR decisively embarked on its road to becoming a pathetic instance of victor's justice. During the years following his appointment, Jallow bought time by systematically stating that "he was reviewing the evidence before determining whether or not he would indict elements of the RPF." With the ICTR's completion strategy in mind, I wrote a letter to Jallow in January 2005, saying that if the RPF crimes were left unprosecuted,

the ICTR will have failed to eliminate one of the root causes of genocide and other crimes –impunity. (. . .) In addition, by meting out victor's justice, the ICTR fails to meet another stated objective, namely to "contribute to the process of national reconciliation and the restoration and maintenance of peace." Under these circumstances, the ICTR risks being part of the problem rather than of the solution. While I remain committed to the cause which is at the heart of the mandate of the ICTR, on ethical grounds I cannot any longer be involved in this process. I shall, therefore, not be able to co-operate with the OTP unless and until the first RPF suspect is indicted.[173]

The publication of an article by Jallow only reinforced the apprehension that justice would not be done. From a legal point of view, he claimed an almost total discretion in prosecuting or not, and where he admitted the possibility of judicial review, the burden of proof he deducted from the existing case law was such that it would be impossible to assume for a party wishing to contest his decision not to prosecute.[174] The way in which he departed from a legal argument was revealing, as he wrote that the RPF

---

[171] V. Peskin, *International Justice in Rwanda and the Balkans. Virtual Trials and the Struggle for State Cooperation*, New York, Cambridge University Press, 2008, p. 189.

[172] V. Peskin, "Victor's Justice Revisited. Rwandan Patriotic Front Crimes and the Prosecutorial Endgame at the ICTR", in S. Straus, L. Waldorf (Eds.), *Remaking Rwanda*, p. 176.

[173] During the previous ten years, I had assisted the ICTR, and the OTP in particular, in several ways in an advisory fashion and by acting as an expert witness.

[174] H.B. Jallow, "Prosecutorial Discretion and International Criminal Justice", *Journal of International Criminal Justice*, 3:1 (2005), pp. 145–161.

"waged a war of liberation and defeated the Hutu government of the day, putting an end to genocide."[175]

The collusion between Jallow and the Rwandan government was made very clear when he transferred one case file to Rwanda. As the suspects were not indicted, Jallow did not need authorization from a trial chamber, which he would not have received, as at that very time the tribunal denied transfer requests because of fair trial concerns.[176] Faced with accusations that he refused to prosecute RPF suspects, Jallow announced in June 2008 that "[i]t has been established that on 5 June, 1994, RPF soldiers had killed 13 clergymen and two other civilians at Gitarama" and that the Rwandan prosecutor general claimed that he would shortly indict the implicated soldiers. Jallow added that his office would "monitor those proceedings."[177] Hardly two weeks after Jallow's announcement, four men were before the Kigali court martial. On October 24, a major and a general were acquitted, whereas two captains (who pleaded guilty) were sentenced to eight years in prison, a sentence that was reduced to five years on appeal. Contrary to Jallow's promise, they were tried for murder instead of war crimes.[178] Human Rights Watch wrote to Jallow that

[t]he trial proved to be a political whitewash and a miscarriage of justice, betraying the rights of victims' families to obtain justice for their loved ones. (...) Despite your commitment to the Security Council to ensure close monitoring of the trial, you sent an observer for only two preliminary detention hearings, one trial day, closing arguments, and the verdict. That cursory presence did not constitute diligent monitoring.[179]

---

[175] *Idem*, p. 156.

[176] From 2005, he did actually transfer dozens of cases, but these were related to suspects who had not been indicted nor detained, and their whereabouts were unknown. This measure was therefore symbolic more than anything else.

[177] "UN Prosecutor Finally Admits to RPF Crimes during 1994", Arusha, Hirondelle News Agency, 6 June 2008.

[178] An extensive treatment of the "Gakurazo trial" can be found in L. Haskell, L. Waldorf, "The Impunity Gap of the International Criminal Tribunal for Rwanda: Causes and Consequences", *Hastings International and Comparative Law Review*, 34:1 (2011), pp. 59–70. Unlike Jallow, many Rwandans were not fooled by this show trial. Begley's Hutu participants felt that "the government only arrested the soldiers in order to prevent the ICTR from investigating the case" (L. Begley, *"Resolved to Fight the Ideology of Genocide and All of its Manifestations": The Rwandan Patriotic Front, Violence and Ethnic Marginalisation in Post-genocide Rwanda and Eastern Congo*, DPhil thesis, University of Sussex, 2011, p. 175).

[179] K. Roth, "Letter to the Prosecutor of the International Criminal Tribunal Regarding the Prosecution of RPF Crimes", New York, Human Rights Watch, 26 May 2009.

To no avail, as the dice were cast. In June 2009, Jallow told the Security Council that "[his] office does not have an indictment that is ready in respect to [allegations against the RPF] at this particular stage,"[180] thus definitively guaranteeing impunity to the RPF. As trials are impossible if the prosecutor refuses to indict suspects, Jallow carries a major historical responsibility in this failure of international criminal justice: "He chose to acquiesce in a pretense of justice rather than recognize an absence of justice."[181] The ICTR thus stands in stark contrast to the International Criminal Tribunal for the former Yugoslavia and the Special Court for Sierre Leone, where crimes committed by all sides were prosecuted.[182]

At the end of 2011, the cost of the ICTR stood at more than US$1.6 billion. Sixty-nine persons had been judged, of whom ten were acquitted (eighteen cases were still pending in appeal). The average cost per defendant thus was more than US$23 million.

Despite its many shortcomings, the ICTR has contributed to the development of international criminal law, beyond the case of Rwanda.[183] It was the first international court that prosecuted and convicted for genocide. Thus, it "gave life to the Genocide Convention for the very first time since that treaty was adopted."[184] In doing so, it established a normative framework for judging the "crime of crimes." The ICTR also contributed to clarifying and ordering existing norms of international humanitarian law. For instance, as they share a common language and culture, Hutu and Tutsi are no ethnic groups in the strict sense of the word, a fact that could have prevented the qualification of the crimes committed as genocide. In its very first judgment, the ICTR held that

there are a number of objective indicators of the group as a group with a distinct identity. (. . .) Moreover, customary rules existed in Rwanda governing the determination of ethnic groups, which followed patrilineal lines of heredity. The identification of persons as belonging to the group of Hutu or Tutsi (or Twa) had thus

---

[180] United Nations, Security Council, 6134th meeting, 4 June 2009, S/PV.6134, p. 33.

[181] L. Haskell, L. Waldorf, "The Impunity Gap", p. 85.

[182] For more elaborate treatments of victor's justice at the ICTR, see V. Peskin, *International Justice*; L. Waldorf, "'A Mere Pretense of Justice': Complementarity, Sham Trials, and Victor's Justice at the Rwanda Tribunal", *Fordham International Law Journal*, 33:4 (2010), pp. 1221–1277.

[183] A survey of the ICTR's case law can be found in L.J. van den Herik, *The Contribution of the Rwanda Tribunal to the Development of International Law*, Leiden, Brill, 2005. Also see A. Obote-Odora, "Genocide on Trial. Normative Effects of the Rwanda Tribunal's Jurisprudence", *Development Dialogue*, March 2011, No. 55, pp. 125–151.

[184] K.C. Moghalu, *Rwanda's Genocide*, p. 202.

become embedded in Rwandan culture. (. . .) Moreover, the Tutsi were conceived of as an ethnic group by those who targeted them for killing.[185]

Likewise, the same judgment found that rape can amount to the crime of genocide:

Sexual violence was a step in the process of destruction of the Tutsi group – destruction of the spirit, of the will to live, and of life itself. (. . .) In this respect, it appears clearly to the Chamber that the acts of rape and sexual violence, as other acts of serious bodily and mental harm committed against the Tutsi, reflected the determination to make Tutsi women suffer and to mutilate them even before killing them, the intent being to destroy the Tutsi group while inflicting acute suffering on its members in the process.[186]

The ICTR also had an indirect impact on Rwandan legislation. When Kigali was seeking to obtain transfers of cases from Arusha (and extraditions from third countries), the death penalty was one of the obstacles. Although the Rwandan regime was all but abolitionist, it reacted in a pragmatic fashion. Organic Law 31/2007 of July 25, 2007, abolished capital punishment. With the same intention of securing transfers and extraditions, Organic Law 11/2007 of March 16, 2007, aimed at providing a number of guarantees in the areas of evidence, rights of the defense, witness protection, and the administration of sentences, in order to align Rwanda with international norms, including those of the ICTR. In May 2009, another organic law sought to meet concerns of the ICTR Appeals Chamber in adjudicating transfer requests, particularly by guaranteeing that a witness could not be held criminally liable for things said in the course of a trial.[187] However, Schabas's somewhat optimistic assessment of the domestic impact of the ICTR, namely that Rwanda "has made great strides in order to modernise its justice system, inspired by international standards"[188] may well be naïve: in light of the regime's practices in the area of justice, it is very likely that these "strides" were opportunistic, aimed at securing transfers, rather than inspired by a genuine intention to improve the administration of justice in an independent and impartial fashion.

[185] *The Prosecutor v. Jean-Paul Akayezu*, No.ICTR-96–4-T, judgment of 2 September 1998, § 170–171.

[186] *Idem*, § 732–733.

[187] This however still left a dangerous void, as witnesses could be prosecuted for things previously said *outside* of the courtroom. This is what the attorney of Victoire Ingabire, Peter Erlinder, was charged with (cf. supra).

[188] W.A. Schabas, "Anti-Complementarity", p. 59.

JUSTICE IN THIRD COUNTRIES

The rare cases that were treated in third countries related to three main sequels of the genocide: trials of genocide suspects in application of the principle of universal jurisdiction, demands for the extradition of genocide suspects by Rwanda, and investigations of the role played by the RPF.

Switzerland was the first country proceeding to the prosecution, judgment, and conviction of a genocide suspect. On April 30, 1999, a military court sitting in Lausanne sentenced the former mayor of Mushubati Fulgence Niyonteze to life in prison for assassination, incitement to assassinate, and war crimes. In France, a procedure was opened against Father Wenceslas Munyeshyaka in May 1999. In 2004, France was condemned for the slow progress in this case, but by the time of writing, nothing palpable had happened in this and a dozen of other investigations of suspects. A first assize court case in Belgium against Rwandan suspects took place in April and May 2001, and four defendants were sentenced to between twelve and twenty years in prison.[189] Three more assize cases, some with multiple defendants, took place later in Belgium. Other rare suspects were tried in the Netherlands, Canada, Norway, and Finland.[190]

For reasons similar to the ICTR's, courts in third countries have long refused to extradite suspects to Rwanda. This has been the case in Germany, France, the United Kingdom, Switzerland, and Sweden.[191] In countries where domestic law precluded the prosecution of suspects, the impossibility to extradite resulted in the so-called impunity gap and the violation of the Aut Dedere, Aut Judicare (extradite or judge) principle. However, the obstacles were not just legal, and one understands why so few cases have been tried based on universal jurisdiction. These procedures are costly and complicated, and overstretched prosecutors and judiciaries are not tempted by trials related to events in a faraway country.

---

[189] On this trial, see P. May, *Quatre Rwandais aux Assises Belges. La compétence universelle à l'épreuve*, Paris, L'Harmattan, 2001.

[190] The phenomenon of false testimony, noted earlier in the ICTR, also affected proceedings in third countries. For instance, a person was pressured by Ibuka to lie under oath against two of his uncles prosecuted before an assize court in Belgium. After he refused, he was arrested, but he escaped and found asylum in France (Cour nationale du droit d'asile, *Contentieux des réfugiés, Jurisprudence du Conseil d'Etat et de la Cour nationale du droit d'asile*, Année 2008, p. 29).

[191] However, Canada extradited Léon Mugesera in January 2012, and the European Court of Human Rights ruled that extraditions to Rwanda are not contrary to the Convention (Case of *Ahorugeze v. Sweden* [Application No. 37075/09], judgment of 27 October 2011).

As far as RPF crimes are concerned, the cases ongoing in France and Spain against RPF officials have been discussed briefly in Chapter 5. In Belgium, several formal complaints were lodged against Kagame, but they didn't go anywhere because of new criteria on the needs for links of victims with Belgium introduced in its universal jurisdiction law, as well as because of the immunity enjoyed by a head of state in function. Together with Spain and France, the DRC appears to have become the most likely country where RPF crimes could be judged, as the ICTR does not fulfil this part of its mandate. The International Criminal Court is competent only for crimes committed from July 1, 2002, whereas most RPF crimes took place before that date. Earlier, we have discussed the arm wrestling that accompanied the mapping report on crimes committed in the DRC between 1993 and 2003.[192] The report concluded that a number of actors, Rwanda in particular, committed war crimes and crimes against humanity, and possibly genocide (cf. supra). It suggested that a mixed judicial mechanism, made up of Congolese and international personnel, would be the most appropriate way to deal with these international crimes. Whereas Rwanda reacted in the furious way described earlier, influential quarters in the international community took the report more seriously. The *New York Times* compared the crimes committed by the RPA in the DRC to those of 1994 in Rwanda, which were covered by a conspiracy of silence.[193] An op-ed in *The Guardian* stated that "[b]y seeking to quash publication of the report, the Rwandan government is raising further questions about what it may be trying to hide. Kagame's forces played a crucial role in ending the genocide in Rwanda, but this does not absolve them of scrutiny for crimes they may have committed in the years that followed, both in Rwanda and Congo."[194]

More threateningly, one of Rwanda's most important supports came out in favor of a judicial mechanism to deal with the findings of the mapping report. Assistant Secretary Philip Crowley stated that the United States "strongly supports accountability for violations of human rights and international humanitarian law around the world, including in

---

[192] United Nations, High Commissioner for Human Rights, *Democratic Republic of the Congo, 1993–2003. Report of the Mapping Exercise Documenting the Most Serious Violations of Human Rights and International Humanitarian Law Committed within the Territory of the Democratic Republic of the Congo between March 1993 and June 2003*, Geneva, August 2010.

[193] "Dispute Over U.N. Report Evokes Rwandan Déjà Vu", *The New York Times*, 30 September 2010.

[194] "Identify the Congo Killers and Bring Them to Justice", *The Guardian*, 1 October 2010.

the DRC."[195] This position was reiterated by the U.S. ambassador-at-large for war crimes Stephen Rapp who indicated that the United States supported the idea of a mixed tribunal to judge the crimes committed in the Congo.[196] A few months later, the idea of mixed tribunals gained momentum. Although it formulated some criticisms, the reaction of the Congolese government to the mapping report was by and large positive,[197] and Congolese civil society maintained the pressure to follow up. In April 2011, the director of special procedures at the UN High Commission for Human Rights announced that the Congolese government wished to establish special chambers.[198] However, in August 2011 a bill tabled in Parliament met with resistance in the Senate, which invoked issues of sovereignty and budgetary concerns. At the time of writing, no further progress had been made.

CONCLUSION

Noting heavy international involvement in the justice process, Oomen observes that "this specific – often technocratic, decontextualized, and above all apparently apolitical – emphasis on justice might seem innocuous at first glance, but that it carries dangers with it. This becomes especially true when it takes place in an increasingly autocratic and oppressive political environment like contemporary Rwanda."[199] Indeed, as Meierhenrich argues, "[a]s in warfare, the principal function of lawfare is the defeat of the enemy, real or imagined. The aim of lawfare is the imposition of the victor's will on the enemy. (. . .) It is this critical, functional difference that distinguishes lawmaking (or the ordinary use of law) from lawfare (or the extraordinary use of law)."[200] This applies to justice, but to other uses of law as well (constitutional design,

---

[195] "UN Mapping Report on Violations of Human Rights in the Democratic Republic of the Congo", Washington, DC, October 1, 2010.

[196] "Washington soutient l'idée d'une chambre mixte pour juger les crimes de guerre et les crimes contre l'humanité", Radio Okapi, 25 October 2010.

[197] République démocratique du Congo, Ministère de la Justice et des Droits humains, *Observations du gouvernement sur le Rapport du Projet Mapping concernant les violations les plus graves des droits de l'homme et du droit international humanitaire commises entre mars 1993 et juin 2003 sur le territoire de la République démocratique du Congo*, August 2010.

[198] "Suivi du rapport Mapping de l'ONU: Bacré Ndiaye fait le point", Radio Okapi, 5 April 2011.

[199] B. Oomen, "Donor-driven Justice and its Discontents: The Case of Rwanda", *Development and Change*, 36:5 (2005), pp. 889–890.

[200] J. Meierhenrich, *Lawfare*.

legislation on divisionism and genocide ideology, land law, and other fields addressed elsewhere in this book). The technocratic approach adopted by the donor community did not allow recipient countries to see what Oomen calls "shadow book-keeping": "they comply with donor exigencies in terms of decentralization, democratization, constitution-writing, while real politics take place elsewhere and along wholly different lines."[201]

Both domestically and internationally, the RPF was remarkably successful in ensuring impunity for its crimes, and thus imposed victor's justice. As in many other areas discussed earlier in this book, it did so with the support of powerful international allies who did not heed Mamdani's ominous warning: "The price for victor's justice, in Rwanda, must be yet another round of continuing civil war."[202]

[201] B. Oomen, "Donor-driven Justice", p. 907.
[202] M. Mamdani, *When Victims Become Killers. Colonialism, Nativism, and the Genocide in Rwanda*, Princeton, NJ, Princeton University Press, 2001, p. 272.

Conclusion

This book has analyzed the successful seizure of power and the consolidation of hegemony by a group of Rwandans who came from abroad and whose social base was, and remains, very narrow. This was achieved through the elimination of counterveiling voices, both political and social, by repression, terror, and massive human rights abuse. Skillful information management and communication, as well as the imposition of a monopolistic narrative have been crucial instruments to further this project. Ambitious, radical, and rapid legal, cultural, social, and economic engineering was used to purportedly create a new Rwanda and a new Rwandan. Military might and the belief in force as a mechanism of transformation were used both domestically and in the region, thus turning a small and poor country into a powerhouse. The regime aggressively tackled the international community, helped by the genocide credit it astutely exploited and by its decent bureaucratic governance. Until recently, this allowed it to safeguard a moral high ground, to escape international condemnation and to ensure impunity.

Rwanda is not an average African dictatorship. It is a place where everything is excessive: violence during and after the genocide, human rights abuse, repression and terror, exclusion, entitlement and lack of it, resentment and rage, fast and radical engineering, good bureaucratic and flawed political governance, distance between narratives and between the spoken and the unspoken, ethnic antagonism, and so much more that may lead to a new eruption of the volcano.

The central figure in Rwanda's (and indeed the entire Great Lakes region's) destiny is Paul Kagame. He is certainly a man with vision and ambition, but at the same time he is probably the worst war criminal in office today.[1] If and when he is prosecuted (or overthrown), this will be a major embarrassment to those – in politics, academia, the press or the business community – who have given him a red-carpet treatment for so many years. It is surprising that only recently, and for one of his lesser crimes (aiding and abetting the M23 rebellion in the DRC; see supra), this support has dwindled and serious questions were asked.[2]

The RPF was extremely successful in rapidly restoring the state and imposing total control in a country that was destroyed and traumatized after the genocide. It achieved to a large extent what it set out to achieve. Regime change has heralded the emergence of a new elite at other times and in other places, but the case of Rwanda was very peculiar, as the new elite came overwhelmingly from abroad, hardly knew the country (except for idyllic projections in the Tutsi diaspora), and was seen as representing an ethnic minority by those it claimed to have "liberated." This distance was further reinforced by the way in which the regime massacred its own citizens, eliminated spaces for the articulation of dissident narratives, installed a radical dictatorship, imposed collective guilt on the majority of its population, engineered radically new social and economic relations, and again introduced a "premise of inequality."[3] It also dramatically redrew the regional geopolitical map and defined its relations with the world on its own terms.

As it came to power as a result of military victory with little external support, apart from that of Uganda, the RPF was in a position to set the terms of the post-genocide political dispensation. Despite adhering to the rhetoric of power sharing, it rapidly monopolized power and eliminated countervailing voices, but did so in an incremental way. This piecemeal approach allowed the regime to avoid condemnation by the international community, which was faced by steps considered, each on its own, to be too small to warrant a robust response.[4] The RPF explored the limits of tolerance, and it realized there were none, so it crossed one Rubicon after

---

[1] The comparison with dual-faced Janus or Dr. Jekyll and Mr. Hyde springs to mind. Until very recently, the donor community wished to privilege the Dr. Jekyll side, but the Mr. Hyde face has become increasingly visible. Dr. Jekyll is the rational man with a vision. Mr. Hyde is the ruthless killer.

[2] This episode also confirmed the implicit quid pro quo that Kagame was allowed to do what he liked inside Rwanda, provided he did not derail the Congo.

[3] J.J. Maquet, *The Premise of Inequality in Ruanda*, London, Oxford University Press, 1961, on the period before the revolution of 1959.

[4] This book has, however, shown that many of these steps were all but "small." Human rights violations in particular were massive and quite well documented at the time they were

the other. Referring to opponents, Kagame once said that a barrel can be emptied with a coffee spoon, and this holds also true for his dealing with the international community. After having eliminated individual domestic and external troublemakers one at a piece, he finished neutralizing the political opposition by 2003 and civil society by 2004. The manipulation of elections allowed to confer a layer of democratic legitimacy on what was in reality the radical closing off of political space. The introduction of legal instruments allowed to tighten the regime's grip. This piecemeal approach, coupled with the regime's moral high ground, kept the international community in a constant waiting mood. It hoped things would improve, but they kept worsening up to a point of no return, because its hesitant and confusing responses only further emboldened the RPF. This enabled the regime to pursue its own agenda, while keeping the donor community on board. Its strong stance on issues it considered crucial, coupled with divergent donor positions, gave the regime considerable room for maneuvre.[5]

The RPF's engineering project is ambitious and risky. It entails profoundly modifying not only the country's political and economic characteristics, but also its social, historical, and cultural defining traits. Particularly after 2000, it wanted to create a new Rwanda and a new Rwandan, as summarized by Straus and Waldorf: "The RPF has undertaken a series of dramatic political, economic, and social projects, including the world's boldest experiment in transitional justice, comprehensive land tenure and agricultural reform, forced villagization, a de facto ban on ethnic identity, re-education of the population, and the systematic redrawing and renaming of Rwanda's territory, among other things."[6] The regime showed a similar engineering boldness in the way it intervened in its vast but weak neighbor, the DRC, by realizing regime change there in 1996–1997 and attempting it a second time two years later, only to be stopped by regional allies intervening in support of Laurent Kabila whom Kigali had earlier made king. Despite this political and military failure, the Rwandan regime benefited economically from the control it exercised during many years over a vast territory next door. Indeed, together with

---

committed. However, for reasons explained in this book, the international community preferred to turn a blind eye after they occurred.

[5] R. Hayman, "Going in the 'Right' Direction? Promotion of Democracy in Rwanda since 1990", *Taiwan Journal of Democracy*, 5:1 (2009), p. 72.

[6] S. Straus, L. Waldorf, "Introduction. Seeing Like a Post-conflict State", in *Remaking Rwanda. State Building and Human Rights after Mass Violence*, Madison, The University of Wisconsin Press, 2011, p. 4.

the rents of international aid, this control allowed to create the basis for "developmental neo-patrimonialism."

The RPF displayed an extraordinary sense of entitlement. The combination of its having defeated the forces of genocide, its efficient and cynical exploitation of international feelings of guilt and ineptitude, and its regional military might allowed it to tackle unsympathetic voices aggressively and with arrogance. Strongly worded, indeed intimidating statements reduced to silence many of those who might otherwise have spoken out. This assertive and proactive behavior has allowed to escape judicial scrutiny both by the ICTR and the justice systems of third countries. Despite coming from a small and very poor, aid-dependent country, the regime's aggressive communication strategy has served to avoid condemnation for its human rights record, its poor democratic credentials, its dangerously flawed political governance, and its aggressive behavior in the region. The skillful use of the genocide credit even allowed the regime to present itself as the victim of genocide. As a matter of fact, the RPF did not have much of a choice, as it would simply lose power if it accepted a competitive political system, particularly as it increasingly alienated its natural base (Hutu democrats first, Tutsi survivors later, and eventually rising numbers among its own members).

Strong information management was a major weapon. The regime's performance in this field may well be traceable to the intelligence background and experience of some of the RPF's military leaders, including Kagame. Monitoring and disseminating information was part of a strategy for both external and internal consumption. Externally, the RPF successfully cordoned off the arenas of massive human rights abuse in Rwanda and the DRC and imposed a monopoly of the reading of history. In combination with the moral high ground achieved through the genocide credit, this has made the regime nearly unchallengeable for the international community. Domestically, the RPF decreed one single truth and devised instruments (legislation, intimidation, "reeducation", silencing alternative voices) to avoid it being challenged, at least publicly. By doing so, it has privileged the public transcript of the powerful, although it has, of course, not eliminated the hidden transcript of the oppressed. In all likelihood, in the privacy of their homes, in discreet conversations, and in the body language that accompanies their silence, the powerless construct their truth, which may well be more radical than the RPF believes. In Rwanda as in other places, history is a highly political stake of the present and the future rather than a way of analyzing and understanding the past.

The so-called international community bears overwhelming responsibility in allowing the RPF to successfully deploy its skills. It has been a willing hostage to Kigali's spin, as noted by Sommers: "Perhaps the most disturbing aspect of the Rwandan government's determination to deny many basic realities is that it has so many enablers."[7] This tolerance was visible from the early days after the RPF seized power. The failure to tie the pledges made at the January 1995 donors' roundtable to improvements in a rapidly deteriorating human rights situation may well have persuaded the regime that it could act without restraint and that impunity was assured. This feeling could only be reinforced when reactions were muted, to say the least, after the RPA massacred thousands of IDPs in Kibeho camp in April 1995, after the prime minister and two other ministers left the government "of national unity" in disgust in August 1995, after scores of Hutu officials were killed or went into exile throughout 1995, or after Rwanda invaded Zaire/DRC on two occasions and committed massive atrocities there. Under these circumstances, the moment soon came when dialogue was futile. Peter Uvin's judgment is severe:

In the case of post-genocide Rwanda, those who provide significant budgetary support claim to do so as part of a deliberate and respectful strategy in which both sides dialogue to produce a long-term political and economic vision for the future. (...) In practice, the Rwandan side gains greater power, partly because no one in annual monitoring exercises wants to rock the boat and undermine the nice setup.[8]

Hayman argues likewise: "The RPF continues to expand its control over political space in Rwanda, and donors have been active agents in this through their support of the regime."[9] Brown even claims, rightly in my view, that "to the extent that donors fund and legitimize the government, they can be considered in part responsible for serious problems that will probably result from the government policies that they support."[10]

As noted in a report written for AFRICOM,

[t]he government is competent and capable, and its success in maintaining stability and driving economic recovery has drawn widespread praise. A short-term visitor

---

[7] M. Sommers, *Stuck. Rwandan Youth and the Struggle for Adulthood*, Athens, GA, and London, University of Georgia Press, 2012, p. 226.

[8] P. Uvin, *Human Rights and Development*, Bloomfield CT, Kumarian Press, 2004, pp. 116–117.

[9] R. Hayman, "Going in the 'Right' Direction?", p. 75.

[10] S. Brown, "The Rule of Law and the Hidden Politics of Transitional Justice in Rwanda", in C. Lehka Sriram, O. Martin-Ortega, J. Herman (Eds.) *Peacebuilding and Rule of Law in Africa. Just Peace?*, Abingdon, Routledge, 2011, p. 191.

to the country comes away with the sense that many within its leadership ranks are genuinely committed to a vision of social transformation, a Rwandan citizenry united by economic progress and able to overcome the traumatic divisions of the past.[11]

The donor community and other external observers see decent technocratic/bureaucratic governance but ignore flawed political governance,[12] whereas the latter risks destroying the achievements of the former.[13] McDoom found that "post-conflict stability premised on economic growth and strong leadership – but without political liberalization in the longer term – may have a finite duration and a possibly dramatic ending."[14]

When they did recognize political risks, donors engaged in wishful thinking and tried to adopt "an incremental position on the matter, encouraging the GoR to take at least some steps in the right direction."[15] In its December 2003 Country Assistance Plan, DFID wrote: "We believe that the government as a whole remains committed to progressively opening up space for legitimate political debate and freedom of expression,"[16] but the opposite happened during the following years, and DFID refrained from assessing "progress." Eight years later, DFID's Operational Plan noted "constraints on rights and freedoms" and saw "mounting concern that power is too highly centralised, with unpredictable consequences for long term political stability, economic development and human rights,"[17] but kept on a waiting mood without proposing ways of dealing with these concerns.

---

[11] Center for Strategic & International Studies, *Rwanda. Assessing Risks to Stability*, Washington, DC, p. 11.

[12] This has been the attitude from early on. In early 1998, the UN coordinator in Rwanda stated that "Rwanda will not know democracy for a long time, but good governance is a more modest and realistic aim" ("'Le Rwanda n'est pas encore sorti du génocide de 1994', selon l'ONU", Kigali, AFP, 13 March 1998).

[13] This bias is by no means limited to the case of Rwanda. Hout has shown that governance-related publications from the World Bank show more frequent use of depoliticized notions (such as "management," "public sector," and "decentralization"), whereas academic publications tend to associate governance with political issues and institutions (as witnessed by notions such as "interests," "conflict," and "democracy") (W. Hout, *Governance and the Rhetoric of International Development*, Inaugural Address, ISS, Erasmus University Rotterdam, 27 May 2010).

[14] O.S. McDoom, *Rwanda's Exit Pathway from Violence: A Strategic Assessment*, World Development Report, Background Case Study, April 2011, p. 6.

[15] P. Uvin, "Difficult choices in the new Post-conflict Agenda: The International Community in Rwanda after the Genocide", *Third World Quarterly*, 22:2 (2001), p. 180.

[16] DFID, *Rwanda: Country Assistance Plan 2003–2006*, p. 12.

[17] DFID Rwanda, *Operational Plan 2011–2015*, p. 2.

International willingness to reward technocratic/bureaucratic governance was reinforced by institutional mechanisms. For instance, the Presidential Advisory Council (PAC), a group of two dozen individuals from Rwanda and several other countries (eight of whom are from the United States) "united in their commitment to love and serve the people of Rwanda," includes a number of international businesspeople who, in addition to being a strong lobbying machine, naturally adopt a managerial approach without being hindered by too much knowledge of the wider social and political environment.[18] Likewise, Tony Blair's Africa Governance Initiative (AGI) supports the Rwandan government, among others by putting young U.K. bureaucrats at its disposal in strategic spots. They have a technocratic vision and tend to "wish away" politics.[19]

There are reasons for the attitude of the international community. Like Ethiopia and Uganda, Rwanda offered the combination of a well-organized rebel movement winning a clear victory, meaning that the outcome of the war was not negotiated by outsiders, and the victorious regime embracing market economies.[20] Another reason is the way in which the donor community functions. Uvin pointed at "a lack of fine knowledge" among the donors, who largely see what they want to see, and interact with people who have a vested interest in making sure this continues.[21] Indeed donor assessments, on both facts and their interpretation, differ widely. The lack of clear evidence implies that error is not only likely, but in the case of Rwanda potentially very costly, not so much for the donors – who only risk losing money – but more so for the Rwandans, who risk losing their lives. Some main donors have invested

[18] A good example of this disconnected "business-like" assessment can be found in a piece authored by Mauro De Lorenzo for the American Enterprise Institute. After highlighting the virtues of a country among "the least corrupt, most serious, and most business-friendly environments in Africa," which "seems like a model for how Africa can go beyond aid," De Lorenzo noted – almost as an afterthought – that "the Rwandan government is *in a sense* a minority government" (emphasis added), hence the need to "achieve legitimacy by delivering results" (M. De Lorenzo, "The Rwandan Paradox. Is Rwanda a Model for an Africa beyond Aid?", American Enterprise Institute, Foreign and Defense Policy, 1st January 2008). *The Economist* was less forgiving: "Those in the West who rightly praise Mr Kagame for his achievements in development must also loudly lambast him for his loatsome and needless tendency to intolerance" ("Rwanda and Other Aid Darlings. Efficiency versus Freedom", *The Economist*, 5 August 2010).

[19] Holvoet and Rombouts point out that the denial of "politics" is one of the most serious flaws of the new aid paradigm (N. Holvoet, H. Rombouts, "The Challenge of Monitoring and Evaluation under the New Aid Modalities: Experiences from Rwanda", *Journal of Modern African Studies*, 46:4 [2008], p. 598).

[20] P. Englebert, D.M. Tull, "Postconflict Reconstruction in Africa. Flawed Ideas about Failed States", *International Security*, 32:4 (2008), p. 136.

[21] P. Uvin, "Structural Causes", p. 176.

large amounts of money and a great deal of political support in Rwanda, and they need to continue supporting the "model" to avoid its collapse and the loss of their investment.[22] So donors' and recipients' interests converge: donors need successes; recipients need aid. This comes with a price for donors, namely "a nagging fear that, in the long run, they are condoning, if not strengthening, new dynamics of social exclusion and violence."[23] Indeed, this book has on several occasions mentioned the structural violence prevailing in Rwanda and the risks of it developing into acute, physical violence, and a cross-national quantitative analysis found that Rwanda has the third-highest level of political exclusion worldwide, after Sudan and Syria, part of a configuration that carries a high statistical probability of violent conflict.[24]

It should serve as a warning that, next to many differences, there are striking continuities between the pre- and post-genocide regimes. Just like today, Habyarimana's Rwanda was seen as "a laboratory of development," and "Rwanda Vision 2020" echoes the five-year development plans in vogue under the Second Republic. Noting the existence of "lines of command branched deeply into rural life," Ingelaere reminded that "it was precisely a highly top-down, authoritarian, and non-democratic set of institutional structures and exercise of power that was of crucial importance in the administration of genocide. Such forces are still present and

---

[22] Earlier, de Torrenté observed exactly the same dynamics in Uganda, another "model" that could not be allowed to fail. He saw a "convergence of interests" and a "mutual dependence" of the NRM and donors and concluded that "the irony is that, after having invested so much in Uganda, the donors have now only feeble means left to impact on practices of which they begin to acknowledge the damaging effects on sustained stability" (N. de Torrenté, "L'Ouganda et les bailleurs de fonds. Les ambiguïtés d'une lune de miel", *Politique Africaine*, No. 75, October 1999, p. 90).

[23] P. Uvin, "Difficult Choices", p. 181. Donors may find solace in the "amplification effect" proposed by Dutta et al. They argue that aid does not have the power either to make dictatorships more democratic or to make democracies more dictatorial. Rather their findings suggest that aid may strengthen democracy in already democratic countries and dictatorship in already dictatorial regimes, and they quote Rwanda as an example of the latter, well before the RPF took over (N. Dutta, P.T. Leeson, C.R. Williamson, "The Amplification Effect: Foreign Aid's Impact on Political Institutions", *Kyklos*, 66:2 (2013), pp. 208–228).

[24] A. Wimmer, L.E. Cederman, B. Min, "Ethnic Politics and Armed Conflict: A Configurational Analysis of a New Global Data Set", *American Sociological Review*, 74:2 (2009), pp. 316–337. The data behind these findings can be accessed via Google on "Ethnic Power Relations Dataset." A caveat is in order. Like in other large-N group studies, the data are crude and unsophisticated. Thus, Wimmer et al. consider all Hutu (estimated to be 84 percent of the population) as "excluded" and all Tutsi (15 percent) as "included," a far cry from a thick description.

potentially destructive."[25] Both regimes displayed a strong belief in managing, monitoring, controlling, and mobilizing the population. However, the current regime goes much further, by radically modifying rurality and destroying peasant modes of life through agrarian and land reforms, by introducing new settlement structures, and by imposing new local political and social relations. The dislocation is such that it may prove irreversible when its perverse effects become clear.

The RPF's mode of governance is based on the short-term view of keeping power, but it may be counterproductive for that aim in the longer term, because it antagonizes ever-increasing numbers of Rwandans who see no peaceful, political ways of changing the government, thus leaving them only the option of violent means. As noted by McDoom, "continued political exclusion may force the steam of ethnic or indeed other 'grievances' to simply continue to accumulate inside the pressure cooker. This has a dangerous self-reinforcing logic: the government will feel compelled to exert even more control to counter even more pressure."[26] In addition, rather than decreasing ethnic antagonism, the regime's practice of "ethnic amnesia", coupled with violence and discrimination against Hutu, as well as the separation of "victims" and "perpetrators," has deepened the divide which however remains confined to the hidden transcript. The RPA's behavior in the DRC has even contributed to regional ethnogenesis, pitting "Bantu" against "Nilotics" or "Hamitics," thus increasing the risks faced by Tutsi across Rwanda's borders. The Burundian case, particularly under Bagaza (1976–1987) has shown that top-down prohibition of ethnic alignment does not work. Ethnic identification was forbidden there, and identity cards did not mention ethnic belonging, but during times of violent confrontation, killings followed clearly defined ethnic lines. It is no mean paradox that only after Burundi institutionalized ethnicity after 2000 it was successful in managing the divide.[27] However, the falling out of increasing numbers of Tutsi with the RPF may have a positive effect on this issue. Indeed, it shows that the regime is not that of the Tutsi, at least not all of them, a fact that may reduce the role of ethnicity and enhance that of politics.[28]

---

[25] B. Ingelaere, "Peasants, Power and Ethnicity: A Bottom-up Perspective on Rwanda's Political Transition", *African Affairs*, 109:435 (2010), p. 292.

[26] O.S. McDoom, *Rwanda's Exit Pathway*, p. 5.

[27] See F. Reyntjens, "Burundi: Institutionalising Ethnicity to Bridge the Divide", forthcoming.

[28] A similar phenomenon was seen under the Habyarimana regime and during the genocide, when Hutu were targeted by other Hutu, obviously not on account of their ethnic identity but because they were (seen as) opponents.

Mamdani's analysis of the challenges facing the Rwandan political system was ominous. When writing that "Rwanda's key dilemma is how to build a democracy that can incorporate a guilty majority alongside an aggrieved and fearful minority in a single political community,"[29] he probably inadvertently adhered to the dichotomy of guilty versus innocent, perpetrator versus victim, and Hutu versus Tutsi, exactly the bipolarization that *gacaca* and other policies later achieved. Mamdani went on pointing at the issue of "the very survival of all remaining Tutsi" and its inference, as a direct outcome of the experience of genocide, that "Tutsi Power is the minimum condition for Tutsi survival". This led him to the conviction that "the only peace possible between Hutu and Tutsi is armed peace."[30] Although this may be the situation today, it is of course an untenable position in the long term. Mamdani continued as follows:

The dilemma of postgenocide Rwanda lies in the chasm that divides Hutu as a political majority[31] from Tutsi as a political minority.[32] While the minority demands justice, the majority calls for democracy. The two demands appear as irreconcilable, for the minority sees democracy as an agenda for completing the genocide, and the majority sees justice as a self-serving mask for fortifying minority power.[33]

This dilemma would not exist in case of genuine (i.e., non-ethnic) democracy and genuine (i.e., not victor's) justice. Both aims would then be reconcilable, and this is what a responsible political leadership in Rwanda would have to strive for if the nation is to survive in the long term.

---

[29] M. Mamdani, *When Victims Become Killers. Colonialism, Nativism, and the Genocide in Rwanda*, Princeton, NJ, Princeton University Press, 2001, p. 266.

[30] *Idem*, pp. 270–271.

[31] However, rather than political, the majority is demographic.

[32] Again, the minority is demographic, not political. In addition, Mamdani suggests that the ethnic minority is in power. However, the RPF does not equal (all) Tutsi.

[33] M. Mamdani, *When Victims*, pp. 273–274.

References

C. Adamczyk, "Independent Actors or Silent Agents: Where To Go for Rwandan Civil Society?", in M. Campioni, P. Noack (Eds.), *Rwanda Fast Forward. Social, Economic, Military and Reconciliation Prospects*, Houndmills, Palgrave Macmillan, 2012, pp. 60–75.

A Dangerous Impasse: Rwandan Refugees in Uganda, Citizenship and Displacement in the Great Lakes Region, Working Paper No. 4, June 2010.

African Rights, *Rwanda. Who Is Killing; Who Is Dying; What Is to Be Done*, May 1994.

African Rights, *Rwanda. Death, Despair and Defiance*, 2nd edition, August 1995.

African Rights, *Faux pas pour le Rwanda. Remarque sur la recommandation parlementaire prônant l'interdiction de six ONG*, Kigali, 9 July 2004.

African Rights, *The Leadership of Rwandan Armed Groups Abroad with a Focus on the FDLR and RUD/Urunana*, December 2008.

Africa Watch, *Rwanda: Talking Peace and Waging War. Human Rights since the October 1990 Invasion*, New York, 27 February 1992.

Amnesty International, *Reports of Killings and Abductions by the Rwandese Patriotic Front, April–August 1994*, London, October 1994.

Amnesty International, *Rwanda: Mixed Reaction to Publication of Kibeho Killings inquiry*, London, AFR 47/11/95.

Amnesty International, *Rwanda: Sharp Increase in Killings Could Plunge Rwanda Back into a Cycle of Violence*, London, 12 August 1996.

Amnesty International, *Rwanda. Unfair Trials: Justice Denied*, London, April 1997.

Amnesty International, *Rwanda: Ending the Silence*, London, 25 September 1997.

Amnesty International, *Rwanda: Civilians Trapped in Armed Conflict. "The dead Can No Longer Be Counted"*, London, 19 December 1997.

Amnesty International, *Rwanda: "Disappearances" Reach Alarming Proportions, Say Amnesty International Delegates*, London, 12 March 1998.

Amnesty International, *Rwanda: 23 Public Executions Will Harm Hope of Reconciliation*, London, 22 April 1998.

Amnesty International, *The Troubled Course of Justice*, London, 26 April 2000.

Amnesty International, *Eastern Congo Ravaged. Killing Civilians and Silencing Protest*, New York, May 2000.

Amnesty International, *Rwanda: Number of Prisoners of Conscience on the Rise*, London, 7 June 2002.

Amnesty International, *Rwanda. Gacaca: A Question of Justice*, London, December 2002.

Amnesty International, *Rwanda: Escalating Repression against Political Opposition*, London, 22 April 2003.

Amnesty International, *Rwanda: Run-up to Presidential Elections Marred by Threats and Harassment*, London, 22 August 2003.

Amnesty International, *Rwanda: Government Slams Door on Political Life and Civil Society*, London, 9 June 2004.

Amnesty International, *Rwanda: Deeper into the Abyss – Waging War on Civil Society*, London, 5 July 2004.

Amnesty International, *Rwanda: La liberté de la presse réprimée depuis 12 ans*, London, 3 May 2006.

Amnesty International, *Rwanda: Pre-election Attacks on Politicians and Journalists Condemned*, London, 5 August 2010.

Amnesty International, *Safer to Stay Silent. The Chilling Effect of Rwanda's Laws on "Genocide Ideology" and "Sectarianism"*, London, 25 August 2010.

Amnesty International, *Rwandan Opposition Politician Jailed for Exercising Rights*, London, 14 February 2011.

Amnesty International, *Rwanda: Shrouded in Secrecy. Illegal Detention and Torture by Military Intelligence*, London, October 2012.

Amnesty International, *Rwanda: Ensure Appeal after Unfair Ingabire Trial*, London, 30 October 2012.

"Analysis: The Trial of Sendashonga's Assassins – a Trail of Missing Links", Nairobi, Internews, 18 September 2000.

A. Ansoms, "Striving for Growth, Bypassing the Poor? A Critical Review of Rwanda's Rural Sector Policies", *Journal of Modern African Studies,* 46:1 (2008), pp. 1–32.

A. Ansoms, "Re-engineering Rural Society: The Visions and Ambitions of the Rwandan Elite", *African Affairs*, 108:431 (2009), pp. 289–309.

A. Ansoms, "Rwanda's Post-genocide Economic Reconstruction. The Mismatch between Elite Ambitions and Rural Realities", in S. Straus, L. Waldorf (Eds.), *Remaking Rwanda. State Building and Human Rights after Mass Violence*, Madison, University of Wisconsin Press, 2011, pp. 240–251.

A. Ansoms, *So Where Has the Youth Gone? An Anomaly in the EICV Dataset*, unpublished note, 15 March 2012.

A. Ansoms, D. Rostagno, "Rwanda's Vision 2020 Halfway Through: What the Eye Does Not See", *Review of African Political Economy*, 39:133 (2012), pp. 427–450.

A. Ansoms, D. Rostagno, J. Van Damme, "Vision 2020 à mi-parcours: l'envers du decor", in: S. Marysse, F. Reyntjens, S. Vandeginste (Eds.), *L'Afrique des grands lacs. Annuaire 2010–2011*, Paris, L'Harmattan, 2011, pp. 261–280.

Avocats sans frontières, *Projet "Justice pour tous au Rwanda". Rapport annuel 1997*, Brussels, 1998.

Avocats sans frontières, *Recueil de jurisprudence. Contentieux du génocide et des massacres au Rwanda*, 5 vols., Brussels, 2003–2004.

J. Balzar, "Rwanda's New Leaders Accused of Harassing Refugees: Africa: Aid Official Says Actions Don't Match Words of Conciliation. New Exodus to Zaire Is Feared", *The Los Angeles Times*, 16 August 1994.

J.-F. Bayart, A. Mbembe, C. Toulabor, *La politique par le bas en Afrique noire. Contribution à une problématique de la démocratie*, Paris, Karthala, 1992.

L. Begley, "The Other Side of Fieldwork: Experiences and Challenges of Conducting Research in the Border Area of Rwanda/Eastern Congo", *Anthropology Matters*, 11:2 (2009), pp. 1–11.

L. Begley, *"Resolved to Fight the Ideology of Genocide and All of Its Manifestations": The Rwandan Patriotic Front, Violence and Ethnic Marginalisation in Post-Genocide Rwanda and Eastern Congo*, DPhil Thesis, University of Sussex, 2011.

Bertelsmann Stiftung, *BTI 2010 – Rwanda Country Report*, Gütersloh, 2009.

D. Beswick, "Aiding State Building and Sacrificing Peace Building? The Rwanda–UK Relationship 1994–2011", *Third World Quarterly*, 32:10 (2011), pp. 1911–1930.

D. Beswick, "The Role of the Military in Rwanda: Current Dynamics and Future Prospects", in M. Campioni, P. Noack (Eds.), *Rwanda Fast Forward. Social, Economic, Military and Reconciliation Prospects*, Houndmills, Palgrave Macmillan, 2012, pp. 249–264.

A. Betts, "Should Approaches to Post-Conflict Justice and Reconciliation Be Determined Globally, Nationally or Locally?", *European Journal of Development Research*, 17:4 (2005), pp. 735–752.

J. Birara, *Note sur la situation au Rwanda*, 2 January 1995.

R. Bonner, "Mass Killings by Rwandan Rebels Are Reported", *The New York Times*, 5 September 1994.

D. Booth, F. Golooba-Mutebi, *Developmental Patrimonialism? The Case of Rwanda*, APPP Working Paper No. 16, London, ODI, March 2011.

D. Booth, F. Golooba-Mutebi, "Developmental Patrimonialism? The Case of Rwanda", *African Affairs*, 111:444 (2012), pp. 379–403.

J.-H. Bradol and A. Guibert, "Le temps des assassins et l'espace humanitaire, Rwanda, Kivu, 1994–1997", *Hérodote* 86:7 (1997), pp. 116–149.

A.-M. Brandstetter, *Contested Pasts: The Politics of Remembrance in Post-genocide Rwanda*, Ortelius Lecture at the University of Antwerp, Wassenaar, NIAS, 2010.

A. Breed, "Discordant Narratives in Rwanda's Gacaca Courts", in M. Campioni, P. Noack (Eds.), *Rwanda Fast Forward. Social, Economic, Military and Reconciliation Prospects*, Houndmills, Palgrave Macmillan, 2012, pp. 29–44.

K. Brounéus, "Truth-Telling as Talking Cure? Insecurity and Retraumatization in the Rwandan Gacaca Courts", *Security Dialogue*, 39:1 (2008), pp. 55–76.

S. Brown, "The Rule of Law and the Hidden Politics of Transitional Justice in Rwanda", in C. Lehka Sriram, O. Martin-Ortega, J. Herman (Eds.), *Peacebuilding and Rule of Law in Africa. Just Peace?*, Abingdon, Routledge, 2011, pp. 179–196.

S. Buckley-Zistel, "Dividing and Uniting: The Use of Citizenship Discourses in Conflict and Reconciliation in Rwanda", *Global Society*, 20:1 (2006), pp. 101–113.

S. Buckley-Zistel, "Nation, Narration, Unification? The Politics of History Teaching after the Rwandan Genocide", *Journal of Genocide Research*, 11:1 (2009), pp. 31–53.

J.E. Burnet, "Gender Balance and the Meanings of Women in Governance in Post-genocide Rwanda", *African Affairs*, 107:428 (2008), pp. 361–386.

J.E. Burnet, "The Injustice of Local Justice: Truth, Reconciliation, and Revenge in Rwanda", *Genocide Studies and Prevention*, 3:2 (2008), pp. 173–193.

J.E. Burnet, "Whose Genocide? Whose Truth?", in A.L. Hinton, K.L. O'Neill (Eds.), *Genocide. Truth, Memory, and Representation*, Durham, NC, and London, Duke University Press, 2009, pp. 80–110.

J.E. Burnet, "Women Have Found Respect. Gender Quotas, Symbolic Representation, and Female Empowerment in Rwanda", *Politics & Gender*, 7:3 (2011), pp. 303–334.

M. Campioni, P. Noack (Eds.), *Rwanda Fast Forward. Social, Economic, Military and Reconciliation Prospects*, Houndmills, Palgrave Macmillan, 2012.

CCAC, *Rapport sur l'observation des élections communales au Rwanda*, no date.

CCOAIB, *The State of Civil Society in Rwanda in National Development. Civil Society Index Rwanda Report*, Kigali, March 2011.

Center for Strategic & International Studies, *Rwanda. Assessing Risks to Stability*, Washington D.C., June 2011.

Centre de lutte contre l'impunité et l'injustice au Rwanda, *Rwanda: Les enlèvements de civils s'intensifient à Kigali*, 19 February 1999.

Cladho, *Déclaration sur les incidents du camp des déplacés de Kibeho*, Kigali, 28 April 1995.

J.N. Clark, "National Unity and Reconciliation in Rwanda: A Flawed Approach?", *Journal of Contemporary African Studies*, 28:2 (2010), pp. 137–154.

P. Clark, Z. Kaufman (Eds.), *After Genocide. Transitional Justice, Post-conflict Reconstruction and Reconciliation in Rwanda and Beyond*, London, Hurst, 2008.

P. Clark, "The Rules (and Politics) of Engagement: The Gacaca Courts and Post-genocide Justice, Healing and Reconciliation in Rwanda", in P. Clark, Z. Kaufman (Eds.), *After Genocide. Transitional Justice, Post-conflict Reconstruction and Reconciliation in Rwanda and Beyond*, London, Hurst, 2008, pp. 297–319.

P. Clark, *The Gacaca Courts, Post-genocide Justice and Reconciliation in Rwanda. Justice without Lawyers*, Cambridge, Cambridge University Press, 2010.

P. Clark, "The Legacy of Rwanda's Gacaca Courts", Think Africa Press, 23 March 2012.

Clinton Foundation, "Former President Clinton Announces the Winners of the Third Annual Clinton Global Citizen Awards", 23 September 2009.

Coalition to Stop the Use of Child Soldiers, *The Use of Children as Soldiers in Africa*, April 1999.

H. Coffé, "Conceptions of Female Political Representation. Perspectives of Rwandan Female Representatives", *Women's Studies International Forum*, 35 (2012), pp. 286–297.

J. Cohen, *One Hundred Days of Silence. America and the Rwanda Genocide*, Lanham MD, Rowman & Littlefield Publishers, 2007

P. Collier, *Wars, Guns, and Votes. Democracy in Dangerous Places*, New York, Harper, 2009.

B.M. Collins, *The Rwandan War 1990–1994: Interrogating the Dominant Narrative*, PhD thesis, London, University of London, SOAS, 2009.

"Comments in the Discussion of the Paper by the Minister of Justice", in Newick Park Initiative, *Le rôle de l'Eglise dans la Restauration de la Justice au Rwanda (Rapport de la Conférence tenue à Kigali du 19 au 21 août 1997)*, Cambridge, September 1997.

Commonwealth Human Rights Initiative, *Rwanda's Application for Membership of the Commonwealth: Report and Recommendations of the Commonwealth Human Rights Initiative*, Delhi, August 2009.

Commonwealth Human Rights Initiative, *The CHRI Condemns Human Rights Abuses in the Run Up to Elections in Rwanda*, London, 22 July 2010.

COOPIBO, FOS, NCOS, Vredeseilanden, *Le Rwanda. Et maintenant?*, 7 November 1990.

J. Corduwener, "Wederopbouw in Rwanda, met ijzeren hand" ("Reconstruction in Rwanda, with an Iron Fist"), *NRC-Handelsblad*, 27 March 2002.

L. Côté, "Le Tribunal Pénal International pour le Rwanda: Un tribunal dans la tourmente", in F. Reyntjens, S. Marysse (Eds.), *Dix ans de transitions conflictuelles. L'Afrique des grands lacs. Annuaire 2005–2006*, Paris, L'Harmattan, 2006, pp. 415–442.

Council of the European Union, *Declaration by the Presidency on behalf of the European Union on the case of Pasteur Bizimungu*, Brussels, 9 July 2004.

T. Cruvellier, *Le Tribunal des vaincus. Un Nuremberg pour le Rwanda?*, Paris, Calmann-Lévy, 2006.

T. Cruvellier et al., *Augustin Cyiza: Un homme libre au Rwanda*, Paris, Karthala, 2004.

R. Dallaire, *Shake hands with the devil. The failure of humanity in Rwanda*, Toronto, Random House Canada, 2003.

C. Davenport, A.C. Stam, "What Really Happened in Rwanda?", Miller-McCune Research Essay, 6 October 2009.

Déclaration du conseil des ministres à l'issue de sa réunion au Village Urugwiro, le 17 septembre 2004, relative au rapport de la Chambres des Députés sur les tueries de Gikongoro et de l'idéologie génocidaire au Rwanda, Kigali, 18 September 2004.

V. DeGennaro, "Global Doc: Safe distance", *Notre Dame Magazine*, 12 December 2012.

H. Deguine, "Peut-on encore parler du Rwanda?", *Médias*, Spring 2008, No. 16, pp. 70–74.

K. de Jonge, *PRI's Research on Gacaca*, Bujumbura, 1 May 2010.

D. de Lame, "Deuil, commémoration, justice dans les contextes rwandais et belge. Otages existentiels et enjeux politiques", *Politique Africaine*, No. 92, December 2003, pp. 39–55.

M. De Lorenzo, "The Rwandan Paradox. Is Rwanda a Model for an Africa beyond Aid?", American Enterprise Institute, Foreign and Defense Policy, 1 January 2008.

C. Del Ponte, *La caccia. Io e i criminali di guerra*, Milan, Feltrinelli, 2008.

A. Des Forges, *Leave None to Tell the Story. Genocide in Rwanda*, New York and Paris, Human Rights Watch-Fédération internationale des ligues des droits de l'homme, 1999.

A. Des Forges, "Land in Rwanda: Winnowing out the Chaff", in F. Reyntjens, S. Marysse (Eds.), *L'Afrique des grands lacs. Annuaire 2005–2006*, Paris, L'Harmattan, 2006, pp. 353–371.

S. Desouter, F. Reyntjens, *Rwanda. Les violations des droits de l'homme par le FPR/APR. Plaidoyer pour une enquête approfondie*, Institute of Development Policy and Management, Working Paper, Antwerp, June 1995.

M.-E. Desrosiers, S. Thomson, "Rhetorical Legacies of Leadership: Projections of 'Benevolent Leadership' in Pre- and Post-genocide Rwanda", *Journal of Modern African Studies*, 49:3 (2011), pp. 429–453.

N. de Torrenté, "L'Ouganda et les bailleurs de fonds. Les ambiguïtés d'une lune de miel", *Politique Africaine*, No. 75, October 1999, pp. 72–90.

DFID, *Rwanda: Country Assistance Plan 2003–2006*.

DFID, Rwanda, *Operational Plan 2011–2015*.

M. d'Hertefelt, D. de Lame (Eds.), *Société, culture et histoire du Rwanda. Encyclopédie bibliographique 1863–1980/87*, Tervuren, Royal Museum for Central Africa, 1987, 2 vols.

M. Dorsey, "Violence and Power-building in Post-genocide Rwanda", in R. Doom, J. Gorus (Eds.), *Politics of Identity and Economics of Conflict in the Great Lakes Region*, Brussels, VUB Press, 2000, pp. 311–348.

M.A. Drumbl, "Punishment, Postgenocide: From Guilt to Shame to Civis in Rwanda", *New York University Law Review*, 75:5 (2000), pp. 1221–1326.

N. Dutta, P.T. Leeson, C.R. Williamson, "The Amplification Effect: Foreign Aid's Impact on Political Institutions", *Kyklos*, 66:2 (2013), pp. 208–228.

T. Eide, "Violence, Denial and Fear in Post-genocide Rwanda", in A. Suhrke, M. Berdal (Eds.), *The Peace In Between. Post-war Violence and Peacebuilding*, London, Routledge, 2012, pp. 267–286.

J. Elie, *Celui qui savait*, film, Montreal, Alter-Ciné, 2001.

N. Eltringham, *Accounting for Horror: Post-genocide Debates in Rwanda*, London, Pluto Press, 2004.

K. Emizet, "The Massacre of Refugees in Congo: A Case of UN Peacekeeping Failure and International Law", *Journal of Modern African Studies*, 38:2 (2000), pp. 163–202.

P. Englebert, D.M. Tull, "Postconflict Reconstruction in Africa. Flawed Ideas about Failed States", *International Security*, 32:4 (2008), pp. 106–139.

European Union, Election Observation Mission, Republic of Rwanda, "EU Chief Observer Refutes Allegations about Divisions in EU Election Observation Mission", Kigali, 14 September 2008.

European Union, Election Observation Mission, *Republic of Rwanda. Final Report. Legislative Elections to the Chamber of Deputies*, 15–18 September 2008, 26 January 2009.

Fédération internationale des ligues des droits de l'homme, *Rwanda. Quelle réconciliation nationale sans pluralisme démocratique?*, Paris, 4 June 2003.

Fédération Internationale des ligues des droits de l'homme, *Rwanda: La FIDH appelle à mettre un terme à l'actuelle vague de violence et demande une enquête indépendante et impartiale sur les assassinats d'opposants politiques et de journalistes*, Paris, 16 July 2010.

Fédération internationale des ligues des droits de l'homme, Africa Watch, Union interafricaine des droits de l'homme et des peuples, Centre international des droits de la personne et du développement démocratique, *Rapport de la commission internationale d'enquête sur les violations des droits de l'homme au Rwanda depuis le 1er octobre 1990*, March 1993.

B. Flyvbjerg, "Five Misunderstandings about Case-Study Research", *Qualitative Inquiry*, 12:2 (2006), pp. 219–245.

Front Line Rwanda, *Disappearances, Arrests, Threats, Intimidation of Human Rights Defenders 2001–2004*, Dublin, 2005.

Front Patriotique Rwandais, *"L'environnement actuel et à venir de l'organisation"*, n.d. (early 1994).

A. Furuma, "Open Letter to H.E. Paul Kagame, Reference: RPF/RPA Performance in the Last Ten Years", 23 January 2001.

A.E. Gakusi, F. Mouzer, "Rwanda: Contraintes structurelles et gouvernance", Paris, May 2003, mimeo.

A.E. Gakusi, F. Mouzer, *De la revolution rwandaise à la contre-révolution. Contraintes structurelles et gouvernance 1950–2003*, Paris, L'Harmattan, 2003.

R. Gersony, "Prospects for Early Repatriation of Rwandan Refugees Currently in Burundi, Tanzania and Zaire. Summary of UNHCR Presentation before Commission of Experts", Geneva, 10 October 1994.

Global IDP Project, *Ensuring Durable Solutions for Rwanda's Displaced People: A Chapter Closed Too Early*, 8 July 2005.

N. Gökgür, *Formulating a Broad-based Private Sector Development Strategy. Inception Report*, 20 June 2011.

N. Gökgür, *Rwanda's Ruling Party-owned Business Enterprises: Do They Enhance or Impede Development?*, IOB Discussion Paper 2012.03, Antwerp, 2012.

N. Gordon, "Return to Hell", *The Sunday Times* (London), 21 April 1996.

P. Gourevitch, *We Wish to Inform You that Tomorrow We Will Be Killed with our Families*, New York, Farrar, Straus and Giroux, 1998.

Government of Rwanda, "Response to the Amnesty International Report, Democratic Republic of Congo. Rwandese-controlled East: Devastating Human Toll", Kigali, n.d. (2001).

Government of Rwanda, "Response to Amnesty International's Report on Rwanda's forthcoming elections", Kigali, n.d. (2003).

Government of Rwanda, "Rwanda Response to the 2005 State Department Country Reports on Human Rights Practices, released by the Bureau of Democracy, Human Rights and Labor on March 8, 2006", s.l. (Kigali), s.d. (2006).

Government of Rwanda, "Statement by the Government of Rwanda on the report of the UN Group of Experts on the Democratic Republic of the Congo", Kigali, 15 December 2008.

Government of Rwanda, "Statement by the Government of Rwanda on Leaked Draft UN Report on DRC", Kigali, 27 August 2010.

N. Gowing, "New challenges and problems for information management in complex emergencies: ominous lessons from the Great Lakes and eastern Zaire in late 1996 and early 1997", paper presented at Dispatches from Disaster Zones conference, Oxford, 28 May 1998.

P. Gready, "'You're Either with Us or against Us': Civil Society and Policy Making in Post-genocide Rwanda", *African Affairs*, 109:437 (2010), pp. 637–657.

P. Gready, "Beyond 'You're with Us or against Us': Civil Society and Policymaking in Post-Genocide Rwanda", in S. Straus, L. Waldorf (Eds.), *Remaking Rwanda. State Building and Human Rights after Mass Violence*, Madison WI, The University of Wisconsin Press, 2011, pp. 87–100.

R.E. Gribbin, *In the Aftermath of Genocide. The U.S. Role in Rwanda*, New York, iUniverse, 2005.

A. Guichaoua (Ed.), *Les crisis politiques au Burundi et au Rwanda (1993–1994)*, Paris, Karthala, 1995, pp. 762–764.

A. Guichaoua, "Transition politique à la rwandaise: d'un totalitarisme à l'autre", *Eins-Entwicklungspolitik Nord-Süd*, 2007, No. 5.

A. Guichaoua, *Rwanda: De la guerre au génocide. Les politiques criminelles au Rwanda (1990–1994)*, Paris, La Découverte, 2010.

P. Habamenshi, *Rwanda. Where Souls Turn to Dust. My Journey from Exile to Legacy*, New York, iUniverse, 2009.

W. Harambe, *Les propriétés illégalement occupées au Rwanda: une manne pour le Front Patriotique Rwandais*, s.l., s.d. (1996).

F. Hartmann, *Paix et châtiment: Les guerres secrètes de la politique et de la justice internationales*, Paris, Flammarion, 2007.

L. Haskell, L. Waldorf, "The Impunity Gap of the International Criminal Tribunal for Rwanda: Causes and Consequences", *Hastings International and Comparative Law Review*, 34:1 (2011), pp. 49–85.

R. Hayman, "Going in the 'Right' Direction? Promotion of Democracy in Rwanda since 1990", *Taiwan Journal of Democracy*, 5:1 (2009), pp. 51–75.

R. Hayman, "Abandoned Orphan, Wayward Child: The United Kingdom and Belgium in Rwanda since 1994", *Journal of Eastern African Studies*, 4:2 (2010), pp. 341–360.

D. Hilhorst, M. van Leeuwen, "Emergency and Development: the Case of Imidugudu, Villagization in Rwanda", *Journal of Refugee Studies*, 13:3 (2000), pp. 264–280.

H. Hintjens, "Post-genocide Identity Politics in Rwanda", *Ethnicities*, 8:1 (2008), pp. 5–41.

E. Hobsbawn, T. Ranger (Eds.), *The Invention of Tradition*, Cambridge, Cambridge University Press, 1983.

N. Holvoet, H. Rombouts, *The Denial of Politics in PRSP Monitoring and Evaluation. Experiences from Rwanda*, IOB Discussion Paper 2008–2, Antwerp, 2008.

N. Holvoet, H. Rombouts, "The Challenge of Monitoring and Evaluation under the New Aid Modalities: Experiences from Rwanda", *Journal of Modern African Studies*, 46:4 (2008), pp. 577–602.

W. Hout, *Governance and the Rhetoric of International Development*, Inaugural Address, ISS, Erasmus University Rotterdam, 27 May 2010.

C. Huggins, "The Presidential Land Commission. Undermining Land Law Reform", in S. Straus and L. Waldorf (Eds), *Remaking Rwanda. State Building and Human Rights after Mass Violence*, Madison WI, The University of Wisconsin Press, 2011, pp. 252–265.

Human Rights Watch, *The Aftermath of Genocide in Rwanda*, New York, September 1994.

Human Rights Watch, *Rwanda: A New Catastrophe?*, New York, December 1994.

Human Rights Watch, *Rwanda: The Crisis Continues*, New York, April 1995.

Human Rights Watch, *Local Rwandan Leaders Assassinated*, New York, August 1995.

Human Rights Watch, *Democratic Republic of Congo: What Kabila Is Hiding. Civilian Killings and Impunity in Congo*, New York, October 1997.

Human Rights Watch, *Rwanda. The Search for Security and Human Rights Abuses*, New York, April 2000.

Human Rights Watch, *Eastern Congo Ravaged. Killing Civilians and Silencing Protest*, New York, May 2000.

Human Rights Watch, *No Contest in Rwandan Elections. Many Local Officials Run Unopposed*, New York, 9 March 2001.

Human Rights Watch, *Preparing for Elections: Tightening Control in the Name of Unity*, New York, May 2003.

Human Rights Watch, *Rwanda: Parliament Seeks to Abolish Rights Group*, New York, 2 July 2004.

Human Rights Watch, *Rwanda: Historic Ruling Expected for Former President and Seven Others*, New York, 16 January 2006.

Human Rights Watch, *Law and Reality. Progress in Judicial Reform in Rwanda*, New York, 24 July 2008.

Human Rights Watch, "Rwanda: None So Blind as Those That Will Not See", 26 November 2009.

Human Rights Watch, *Rwanda: Stop Attacks on Journalists, Opponents. Government Actions Undermine Democracy as Presidential Election Draws Near*, New York, 26 June 2010.

Human Rights Watch, *Rwanda: Silencing Dissent Ahead of Elections*, New York, 2 August 2010.

Human Rights Watch, *Rwanda. Justice Compromised. The Legacy of Rwanda's Community-Based Gacaca Courts*, New York, May 2011.

Human Rights Watch, "Human Rights Watch submission to International Development Committee (IDC)", May 2011.

Human Rights Watch, *Uganda/Rwanda: Investigate Journalist's Murder. Ugandan Government Should Ensure Safety of Rwandan Exiles*, New York, 6 December 2011.

Human Rights Watch, "Rwanda: Opposition Leader's Sentence Upheld. Bernard Ntaganda, Journalists in Prison for Expressing Critical Views", Nairobi, 27 April 2012.

Human Rights Watch, *DR Congo: Rwanda Should Stop Aiding War Crimes Suspect. Congolese Renegade General Bosco Ntaganda Receives Recruits and Weapons from Rwanda*, Goma, 4 June 2012.

Human Rights Watch, *Rwanda: Eight Year Sentence for Opposition Leader. Victoire Ingabire Found Guilty of Two Charges in Flawed Trial*, Nairobi, 30 October 2012.

Human Rights Watch, *DR Congo: M23 Rebels Committing War Crimes. Rwandan Officials Should Immediately Halt All Support or Face Sanctions*, Goma, 11 September 2012.

Human Rights Watch et al., *Rapport de la commission internationale d'enquête sur les violations des droits de l'homme au Rwanda depuis le 1ᵉʳ octobre 1990*, March 1993.

Human Rights Watch/Africa, Fédération internationale des ligues des droits de l'homme, *Communiqué*, 24 April 1995.

Human Rights Watch, Fédération internationale des ligues des droits de l'homme, *HRW and FIDH condemn new killings in Rwanda*, New York, July 1996.

B. Ingelaere, *Living the Transition. A Bottom-up Perspective on Rwanda's Political Transition*, IOB Discussion Paper 2007–6, Antwerp, 2007.

B. Ingelaere, *"Does the Truth Pass across the Fire Without Burning?". Transitional Justice and its Discontents in Rwanda's Gacaca Courts*, IOB Discussion Paper 2007–7, Antwerp, 2007.

B. Ingelaere, "The Gacaca Courts in Rwanda", in L. Huyse, M. Salter (Eds.), *Traditional Justice and Reconciliation after Violent Conflict. Learning from African Experiences*, Stockholm, International IDEA, 2008, pp. 25–59.

B. Ingelaere, "'Does the Truth Pass across the Fire Without Burning?' Locating the Short Circuit in Rwanda's Gacaca Courts", *Journal of Modern African Studies*, 47:4 (2009), pp. 507–528.

B. Ingelaere, "Living the Transition: Inside Rwanda's Conflict Cycle at the Grassroots", *Journal of Eastern African Studies*, 3:3 (2009), pp. 438–463.

B. Ingelaere, "Do We Understand Life after Genocide? Center and Periphery in the Construction of Knowledge in Postgenocide Rwanda", *African Studies Review*, 53:1 (2010), pp. 41–59.

B. Ingelaere, "Peasants, Power and Ethnicity: A Bottom-up Perspective on Rwanda's Political Transition", *African Affairs*, 109:435 (2010), pp. 273–292.

B. Ingelaere, "The Ruler's Drum and the People's Shout. Accountability and Representation on Rwanda's Hills", in S. Straus, L. Waldorf (Eds.), *Remaking Rwanda. State Building and Human Rights after Mass Violence*, Madison WI, The University of Wisconsin Press, 2011, pp. 67–78.

B. Ingelaere, "The Rise of 'Meta-conflicts' during Rwanda's Gacaca Process", in S. Marysse, F. Reyntjens, S. Vandeginste (Eds.), *L'Afrique des grands lacs. Annuaire 2010–2011*, Paris, L'Harmattan, 2011, pp. 303–318.

B. Ingelaere, *Peasants, Power and the Past. The Gacaca Courts and Rwanda's Transition from Below*, PhD thesis, University of Antwerp, 2012.

B. Ingelaere, "From Model to Practice. Researching and Representing Rwanda's 'Modernized' *Gacaca* Courts", *Critique of Anthropology*, 32:4 [2012], pp. 388–414.

International Crisis Group, International Criminal Tribunal for Rwanda. Justice Delayed, Nairobi, Arusha, and Brussels, 7 June 2001.

International Crisis Group, *"Consensual Democracy" in Post-Genocide Rwanda. Evaluating the March 2001 District Elections*, 9 October 2001.

International Crisis Group, *Rwanda at the End of the Transition: A Necessary Political Liberalisation*, Nairobi and Brussels, 13 November 2002.

International Rescue Committee, *Report on the Sustainability of the Rwandan Civil Society*, July 2007.

"Investigating Officer Calls former Rwandan Minister Assassination Political", Nairobi, Internews, 25 January 2001.

IRDP, *Reconstruire une paix durable au Rwanda: La parole au peuple*, Kigali, 2003.

IRDP, *La démocratie au Rwanda*, Kigali, n.d. (2006).

H.B. Jallow, "Prosecutorial Discretion and International Criminal Justice", *Journal of International Criminal Justice*, 3:1 (2005), pp. 145–161.

A. Jamar, "Deterioration of Aid Coordination in Gacaca Implementation: Dealing with the Past for a Better Future?", in M. Campioni, P. Noack (Eds.), *Rwanda Fast Forward. Social, Economic, Military and Reconciliation Prospects*, Houndmills, Palgrave Macmillan, 2012, pp. 76–95.

F. Janne d'Othée, "Rwanda. Elections en trompe-l'oeil", *Le Vif-L'Express* (Brussels), 12 September 2008.

N.A. Jones, *The Courts of Genocide. Politics and the Rule of Law in Rwanda and Arusha*, Abingdon, Routledge, 2010.

P. Jordan, "Witness to Genocide – A Personal Account of the 1995 Kibeho Massacre", reprint from the *Australian Army Journal* (www.anzacday.org.au/history/peacekeeping/anecdotes/kibeho.html).

P. Kagame, "Preface", in P. Clark, Z.D. Kaufman (Eds.), *After Genocide. Transitional Justice, Post-conflict Reconstruction and Reconciliation in Rwanda and Beyond*, London, Hurst, 2008, pp. xxi–xxvi.

"'Kagame Is a Killer.' Defectors Tell of Life on Run from Rwandan Assassins", *The Times* (London), 8 October 2012.

S. Kanuma, "When the Politics of Personal Destruction Get out of Hand", *Rwanda Focus*, 27 April 2012.

F. Keane, *Season of Blood: A Rwandan Journey*, Harmondsworth, Penguin Books, 1996.

S. Kinzer, *A Thousand Hills: Rwanda's Rebirth and the Man Who Dreamed it*, Hoboken, NJ, John Wiley and Sons, 2008.

S. Kinzer, "Kagame's Authoritarian Turn Risks Rwanda's Future", *The Guardian*, 27 January 2011.

D.E. Kiwuwa, "Democratization and Ethnic Politics: Rwanda's Electoral Legacy", *Ethnopolitics*, 4:4 (2005), pp. 447–464.

S.T. Kleine-Ahlbrandt, *The Protection Gap in the International Protection of Internally Displaced Persons: the Case of Rwanda*, Geneva, Graduate Institute of International Studies, 2006.

J. Kron, "For Rwandan Students, Ethnic Tensions Lurk", *The New York Times*, 16 May 2010.

A. Kuperman, "Provoking Genocide: A Revised History of the Rwandan Patriotic Front", *Journal of Genocide Research*, 6:1 (2004), pp. 61–84.

J. Laughland, *A History of Political Trials. From Charles I to Saddam Hussein*, Oxford, Peter Lang, 2008.

LDGL, *La problématique de la liberté d'expression au Rwanda*, Kigali, December 2001.

LDGL, *Dynamiques de paix et logiques de guerre. Rapport annuel sur la situation des droits de l'homme dans la région des grands lacs. Année 2002*, May 2003.

LDGL, *Deuxième rapport partiel de la LDGL sur le monitoring des élections des autorités des échelons administratifs de secteurs, districts et la ville de Kigali organisées du 20 février au 04 mars 2006*, Kigali, 15 March 2006.

LDGL, *Déclaration de la LDGL sur les élections législatives 2008 au Rwanda*, Kigali, 19 September 2008.

B. Leloup, "Les rébellions congolaises et leurs parrains dans l'ordre politique régional", in: F. Reyntjens, S. Marysse (Eds.), *L'Afrique des grands lacs. Annuaire 2001–2002*, Paris, L'Harmattan, 2002, pp. 79–114.

R. Lemarchand, "Burundi: The Politics of Ethnic Amnesia", in Helen Fein (Ed.), *Genocide Watch*, New Haven, CT, Yale University Press, 1992, pp. 70–86.

R. Lemarchand (Ed.), *Forgotten Genocides. Oblivion, Denial, and Memory*, Philadelphia, University of Pennsylvania Press, 2011.

"Le MDR face à la déception", *Le Messager-Intumwa*, 24 November 1994, pp. 7–9.

L. Lindholt, H.-O. Sano, *Rwanda 1997: An Analysis of Human Rights and Politics*, Copenhagen, The Danish Centre for Human Rights, September 1998.

Liprodhor, *Procès de génocide au Rwanda. Deux ans après (déc. 96 – déc. 98)*, Kigali, 1998.

Liprodhor, "Observations des élections locales (Région du nord-ouest du Rwanda)", Gisenyi, 4 April 1999.

Liprodhor, *Problématique des libérations des accusés de génocide rwandais*, Kigali, July 1999.

Liprodhor, "Déclaration sur les récentes arrestations", Kigali, 3 June 2002.

Liprodhor, "La Liprodhor proteste", Kigali, 16 April 2003.

Liprodhor, *Problématique des informations et témoignages devant les juridictions Gacaca*, Kigali, 2006.

T. Lizinde, *Rwanda: la tragédie*, Brussels (in fact: Kinshasa), 1 May 1996.

T. Longman, "Rwanda: Achieving Equality or Serving an Authoritarian State?", in H.C. Britton, G. Bauer (Eds.), *Women in African Parliaments*, Boulder, CO, Lynne Rienner, 2006, pp. 133–150.

T. Longman, "Justice at the Grassroots? Gacaca Trials in Rwanda", in N. Roht-Arriaza, J. Mariezcurrena (Eds.), *Transitional Justice in the Twenty-first Century. Beyond Truth versus Justice*, New York, Cambridge University Press, 2006, pp. 206–228.

T. Longman, "Trying Times for Rwanda. Reevaluating Gacaca Courts in Post-genocide Reconciliation", *Harvard International Review*, 32:2 (2010), pp. 48–52.

T. Longman, "Limitations to Political Reform. The Undemocratic Nature of Transition in Rwanda", in S. Straus, L. Waldorf (Eds.), *Remaking Rwanda. State Building and Human Rights after Mass Violence*, Madison, The University of Wisconsin Press, 2011, pp. 25–47.

D. Lorch, "Rwanda Rebels: Army of Exiles Fights for a Home", *The New York Times*, 9 June 1994.

D. Lorch, "Rwandan Rulers Warn against Violence", *The New York Times*, 2 October 1994.

M. Mamdani, *When Victims Become Killers. Colonialism, Nativism, and the Genocide in Rwanda*, Princeton, NJ, Princeton University Press, 2001.

Management Systems International, *Rwanda Conflict Vulnerability Assessment*, October 2002.

J.J. Maquet, *The Premise of Inequality in Ruanda*, London, Oxford University Press, 1961.

Z. Marriage, "Defining Morality: DFID and the Great Lakes", *Third World Quarterly*, 27:3 (2006), pp. 477–490.

I. Martin, "Hard Choices after Genocide: Human Rights and Political Failures in Rwanda", in J. Moore (Ed.), *Hard Choices: Moral Dilemmas in Humanitarian Intervention*, Lanham MD, Rowman & Littlefield, 1998, pp. 157–176.

J. Matata, "Rapport succint sur la situation des Droits de l'Homme au Rwanda", letter to Vice-President Kagame and to the chairman of the RPF, Brussels, 7 April 1995.

P. May, *Quatre Rwandais aux Assises Belges. La compétence universelle à l'épreuve*, Paris, L'Harmattan, 2001.

O.S. McDoom, *Rwanda's Exit Pathway from Violence: A Strategic Assessment*, World Development Report 2011, Background Case Study, April 2011.

C. McGreal, "Digging up Congo's Killing Fields", *Weekly Mail and Guardian*, 25 July 1997.

C. McGreal, "Genocide Tribunal Ready to Indict First Tutsis: Rwanda Is Blocking Investigations of Former Rebels Despite Pledges, Prosecutor Says", *The Guardian*, 5 April 2002.

L. McLean Hilker "Young Rwandans' Narratives of the Past (and Present)", in S. Straus, L. Waldorf (Eds.), *Remaking Rwanda. State Building and Human Rights after Mass Violence*, Madison, The University of Wisconsin Press, 2011, pp. 316–330.

M.D.R., "Position du M.D.R. sur les grands problèmes actuels du Rwanda", Kigali, 6 November 1994.

M.D.R., *Contribution du Mouvement Démocratique Républicain dans la recherche de solutions aux problèmes que rencontre le Rwanda*, 23 May 1998.

Médecins sans frontières, *Report on events in Kibeho camp, April 1995*, Kigali, 16 May 1995.

Médecins sans frontières, *Forced Flight: A Brutal Strategy of Elimination in Eastern Zaire*, 16 May 1997.

J. Meierhenrich, "Presidential and Parliamentary Elections in Rwanda, 2003", *Electoral Studies*, 25:3 (2006), pp. 627–634.

J. Meierhenrich, "Topographies of Remembering and Forgetting. The Transformation of Lieux de Mémoire in Rwanda", in S. Straus, L. Waldorf (Eds.), *Remaking Rwanda. State Building and Human Rights after Mass Violence*, Madison, The University of Wisconsin Press, 2011, pp. 283–296.

J. Meierhenrich, *Lawfare. Gacaca Jurisdictions in Rwanda*, Cambridge University Press, forthcoming.

C. Mgbako, "Ingando Solidarity Camps: Reconciliation and Political Indoctrination in Post-Genocide Rwanda", *Harvard Human Rights Journal* 18 (2005), pp. 201–224.

Z. Miller, *Constructing Sustainable Reconciliation: Land, Power and Transitional Justice in Post-Genocide Rwanda*, Cape Town, Institute for Justice and Reconciliation, 2007.

M. Milz, *The Authoritarian Face of the "Green Revolution": Rwanda Capitulates to Agribusiness*, 8 août 2011.

Ministère de la Réhabilitation et de l'Intégration sociale, *Closure of Displaced People's Camps in Gikongoro*, Kigali, 25 April 1995.

M. Minow, *Between Vengeance and Forgiveness. Facing History after Genocide and Mass Violence*, Boston, Beacon Press, 1998.

Mission d'observation électorale de l'Union Européenne, *Référendum constitutionnel, Rwanda 2003*, Kigali, n.d.

Mission d'observation électorale de l'Union Européenne, *Rwanda. Election présidentielle 25 août 2003. Elections législatives 29 et 30 septembre, 2 octobre 2003. Rapport final*, n.d.

K.C. Moghalu, *Rwanda's Genocide. The Politics of Global Justice*, New York and Houndmills, Palgrave MacMillan, 2005.

G. Mols, "Révision et moyen de preuves supplémentaires dans la jurisprudence des tribunaux internationaux ad hoc. Une réflexion concernant l'arrêt du 16 mai 2001 dans l'affaire Jean-Paul Akayezu c/ le Procureur", in F. Reyntjens, S. Marysse (Eds.), *L'Afrique des grands lacs. Annuaire 2001–2002*, Paris, L'Harmattan, 2002, pp. 37–44.

D. Moyo, *Dead Aid. Why Aid Is not Working and How there Is a Better Way for Africa*, New York, Farrar, Straus and Giroux, 2009.

J.-P. Mugabe, "Cri d'alarme au président de la République rwandaise, à tous les Rwandais tant ceux qui résident au Rwanda ou [sic] ceux qui sont à l'étranger", Press release, 19 March 1999.

J.-P. Mugabe, "Itangazo. Mbwirire Gen. Major Kagame Paul ku karubanda amarorerwa Urwanda ruzize" ("Solemn message to Major General Kagame Paul on the ills that undermine Rwanda"), May 1999.

J.-P. Mugabe, "The Killings Resume: Preparing for the Next Rwandan War", *Defense & Foreign Affairs Strategic Policy*, 1999, No. 4, pp. 4–7.

G. Musabyimana, *Rwanda, le triomphe de la criminalité politique*, Paris, L'Harmattan, 2008.

H. Musahara, C. Huggins, "Land Reform, Land Scarcity and Post Conflict Reconstruction. A Case Study of Rwanda", *Eco-Conflicts*, 3:3 (2004).

S. Musangamfura, *J'accuse le FPR de crimes de génocide des populations d'ethnie hutu, de purification ethnique et appelle à une enquête internationale urgente*, Nairobi, 8 December 1995.

P. Musoni, *Building a Democratic Culture: Rwanda's Experience and Perspectives*, Conference on "Elections and Accountability in Africa", Wilton Park, 21–25 July 2003.

National Democratic Institute, *Assessment of Rwanda's Pre-Electoral Political Environment and the Role of Political Parties, August 3–11, 2003*, n.d.

J.M.V. Ndagijimana, *Paul Kagame a sacrifié les Tutsi*, Editions La Pagaie, 2009.

A. Ndahiro, P. Rutazibwa, *Hotel Rwanda or the Tutsi genocide as seen by Hollywood*, Paris, L'Harmattan, 2008.

V. Ndikumana and J. Afrika, *Lettre ouverte au Conseil de sécurité de l'ONU sur la situation qui prévaut au Rwanda*, Nairobi, 14 November 1994.

C. Newbury, "High Modernism at the Ground Level. The Imidugudu Policy in Rwanda", in S. Straus and L. Waldorf (Eds), *Remaking Rwanda. State Building and Human Rights after Mass Violence*, Madison WI, The University of Wisconsin Press, 2011, pp. 223–239.

A. Nkubito, *Le harcèlement, les tracasseries, les menaces, bref la persécution du personnel judiciaire*, Kigali, 10 May 1996.

J.D. Ntakirutimana, Letter and memo "Le régime du FPR mène le Rwanda vers l'impasse", Nairobi, 12 June 1995.

L. Ntezimana, "De Charybde en Scylla? Point de vue d'un 'Rwandais positif' sur les événements en cours au Rwanda", Butare, 15 September 1994.

F. Nteziryayo, "Enlisement du système judiciaire et dérive des droits humains au Rwanda", *Dialogue*, 213 (November-December 1999), pp. 3–17.

A. Obote-Odora, "Genocide on Trial. Normative Effects of the Rwanda Tribunal's Jurisprudence", *Development Dialogue*, 55 (March 2011), pp. 125–151.

C. Onana, *Les secrets de la justice internationale. Enquêtes truquées sur le génocide rwandais*, Paris, Editions Duboiris, 2005.

B. Oomen, "Donor-driven Justice and its Discontents: The Case of Rwanda", *Development and Change*, 36:5 (2005), pp. 887–910.

Organisation internationale de la francophonie, *Election présidentielle du 9 août 2010 au Rwanda. Rapport d'une Mission francophone d'information et de contacts*, n.d.

Organisation of African Unity, International Panel of Eminent Personalities to Investigate the 1994 Genocide in Rwanda and the Surrounding Events, *Rwanda: The Preventable Genocide*, Addis Ababa, 7 July 2000.

P. Péan, *Noires fureurs, blancs menteurs. Rwanda 1990–1994*, Paris, Mille et une nuits, 2005.

K. Pells, "Building a Rwanda 'Fit for Children'", in S. Straus, L. Waldorf (Eds.), *Remaking Rwanda. State Building and Human Rights after Mass Violence*, Madison, The University of Wisconsin Press, 2011, pp. 79–86.

Penal Reform International, *From Camp to Hill, the Reintegration of Released Prisoners*, May 2004.

Penal Reform International, *The Contribution of the Gacaca Jurisdictions to Resolving Cases Arising from the Genocide. Contributions, Limitations and Expectations of the Post-Gacaca Phase*, London-Kigali, n.d. (2010).

A. Perry, "Q&A: Rwandan President Paul Kagame", *Time*, 14 September 2012.

V. Peskin, *International Justice in Rwanda and the Balkans. Virtual Trials and the Struggle for State Cooperation*, New York, Cambridge University Press, 2008.

V. Peskin, "Victor's Justice Revisited. Rwandan Patriotic Front Crimes and the Prosecutorial Endgame at the ICTR", in S. Straus, L. Waldorf (Eds.), *Remaking Rwanda. State Building and Human Rights after Mass Violence*, Madison, The University of Wisconsin Press, 2011, pp. 173–183.

T. Pickard, *Combat Medic. An Australian's Eyewitness Account of the Kibeho Massacre*, Wavel Heights, Big Sky Publishing, 2008.

J. Pomfret, "Massacres Became a Weapon in Congo's Civil War", *The Washington Post*, 11 June 1997.

J. Pomfret, "Congo Leader Bars Helping U.N. Probes", *The Washington Post*, 19 June 1997.

J. Pomfret, "Defence Minister Says Arms, Troops Supplied for Anti-Mobutu Drive", *The Washington Post*, 9 July 1997.

J. Pottier, *Re-imaging Rwanda. Conflict, Survival and Disinformation in the Late Twentieth Century*, Cambridge, Cambridge University Press, 2002.

J. Pottier, "Land Reform for Peace? Rwanda's 2005 Land Law in Context", *Journal of Agrarian Change*, 6:4 (2006), pp. 509–537.

G. Prunier, *The Rwanda Crisis, 1959–1994. History of a Genocide*, London, Hurst, 1995, 2nd ed. 1997.

G. Prunier, *Rwanda: The Social, Political and Economic Situation in June 1997*, Writenet (UK), July 1997.

G. Prunier, "The Rwandan Patriotic Front", in C. Clapham (Ed.), *African Guerillas*, Oxford, James Currey, 1998, pp. 119–133.

G. Prunier, *Africa's World War. Congo, the Rwandan Genocide, and the Making of a Continental Catastrophe*, Oxford, Oxford University Press, 2009.

A. Purdekova, *Repatriation and Reconciliation in Divided Societies: The Case of Rwanda's "Ingando"*, RSC Working Paper No. 43, Oxford, January 2008.

A. Purdekova, "'Even If I Am not Here, there Are so Many Eyes': Surveillance and State Reach in Rwanda", *Journal of Modern African Studies*, 49:3 (2011), pp. 475–497.

A. Purdekova, "Civic Education and Social Transformation in Post-Genocide Rwanda: Forging the Perfect Development Subjects", in M. Campioni, P. Noack (Eds.), *Rwanda Fast Forward. Social, Economic, Military and Reconciliation Prospects*, Houndmills, Palgrave Macmillan, 2012, pp. 192–209.

"Raporo ya commission yigenga ku rupfu rwa bwana Assiel Kabera", Kigali, 16 August 2000.

Rapport de la Commission parlementaire sur les problèmes du MDR, Kigali, 17 March 2003.

W.C. Reed, "Exile, Reform, and the Rise of the Rwandan Patriotic Front", *Journal of Modern African Studies*, 34:3 (1996), pp. 479–501.

Refugees International, "Rwandan Refugees in Tanzania", Sitrep #10, 17 May 1994.

T. Reid, "Killing Them Softly: Has Foreign Aid to Rwanda and Uganda Contributed to the Humanitarian Tragedy in the DRC?", *African Policy Journal*, 1 (2006), pp. 74–94.

R. Renard, N. Molenaers, *Civil Society Participation in Rwanda's Poverty Reduction Strategy*, IOB Discussion Paper 2003-5, Antwerp, 2003.

Reporters sans frontières, *Rwanda: l'impasse? La liberté de la presse après le génocide, 4 juillet 1994–28 août 1995*, n.d. (1995).

Reporters sans frontières, *Rwanda. Discreet and targeted pressure: President Kagame is a predator of press freedom*, Paris, 7 November 2001.

Reporters sans frontières, *Rwanda: un nouveau journal indépendant saisi dès son premier numéro*, 23 April 2003.

Reporters sans frontières, *Rwanda; Le chef de l'Etat inaugure une salve d'attaques verbales des autorités contre les journalistes*, 31 January 2006.

Reporters sans frontières, *RSF s'inquiète du mépris grandissant du gouvernement envers certains journalistes*, 6 May 2008.

Reporters sans frontières, "Sentiment mitigé après la réduction des peines contre deux journalistes femmes d'Umurabyo", Paris, 6 April 2012.

Reporters Without Borders, *Rwanda. The Arrest of Father Guy Theunis. An Investigation of the Charges, the Legal Action and Possible Reasons*, Paris, November 2005.

Report of the Independent International Commission of Inquiry on the Events at Kibeho, April 1995, Kigali, 18 May 1995.

Republic of Rwanda, *Etude sur les conditions de vie des déplacés vivant dans les camps du Nord-Ouest du Rwanda*, Kigali, March 1999.

Republic of Rwanda, Office of the President of the Republic, *Report of the Reflection Meetings Held in the Office of the President of the Republic from May 1998 to March 1999*, Kigali, August 1999.

Republic of Rwanda, Office of the President, *The Unity of Rwandans: Before the Colonial Period and under Colonial Rule, under the First Republic*, Kigali, August 1999.

Republic of Rwanda, Ministry of Finance and Economic Planning, *Rwanda Vision 2020*, Kigali, July 2000.

Republic of Rwanda, National Unity and Reconciliation Commission, *The Rwandan Conflict: Origin, Development, Exit Strategies*, Kigali, 2004.

Republic of Rwanda, Ministry of Foreign Affairs and Cooperation, *Rwanda Government Reaction to the Spanish Judge Indictments*, Kigali, 9 February 2008.

Republic of Rwanda, Independent Committee of Experts Charged with Investigation into the Crash on 06/04/1994 of Falcon 50 Aeroplane, registration number 9XR-NN, *Report of the Investigation into the Causes and Circumstances of and Responsibility for the Attack of 06/04/1994 against the Falcon 50 Rwandan Presidential Aeroplane, Registration number 9XR-NN*, Kigali, 20 April 2009.

Republic of Rwanda, National Unity and Reconciliation Commission, *Rwanda Reconciliation Barometer*, Kigali, October 2010.

Republic of Rwanda, National Institute of Statistics of Rwanda, *The Evolution of Poverty in Rwanda from 2000 to 2011. Results from the Household Surveys (EICV)*, Kigali, February 2012.

Republic of Rwanda, SNJG, *Summary of the Report Presented at the Closing of Gacaca Courts Activities*, Kigali, June 2012.

Republic of Rwanda, Ministry of Foreign Affairs and Cooperation, *Rwanda's Response to the Allegations Contained in the Addendum to the UN Group of Experts Interim Report*, Kigali, 27 July 2012.

République démocratique du Congo, Ministère de la Justice et des Droits humains, *Observations du gouvernement sur le Rapport du Projet Mapping concernant les violations les plus graves des droits de l'homme et du droit international humanitaire commises entre mars 1993 et juin 2003 sur le territoire de la République démocratique du Congo*, August 2010.

République du Rwanda, Chambre des députés, *Rapport de la Commission parlementaire ad hoc créée en date du 20 janvier 2004 chargée d'examiner les tueries perpétrées dans la province de Gikongoro, l'idéologie génocidaire et ceux qui la propagent partout au Rwanda*, 30 June 2004.

République du Rwanda, Sénat, *Idéologie du génocide au Rwanda et stratégies de son éradication*, Kigali, 2006.

République du Rwanda, Commission nationale pour l'unité et la réconciliation, *Manuel pour les camps de solidarité et autres formations*, Kigali, October 2006.

République du Rwanda, Commission nationale indépendante chargée de rassembler les preuves montrant l'implication de l'Etat français dans le génocide perpétré au Rwanda en 1994, *Rapport final*, Kigali, 15 November 2007.

M. Rettig, "Gacaca: Truth, Justice, and Reconciliation in Postconflict Rwanda?", *African Studies Review*, 51:3 (2008), pp. 25–50.

M. Rettig, "The Sovu Trials. The Impact of Genocide Justice on One Community", in S. Straus, L. Waldorf (Eds.), *Remaking Rwanda. State Building and Human Rights after Mass Violence*, Madison, The University of Wisconsin Press, 2011, pp. 194–209.

L. Reydams, *Let's Be Friends. The United States, Post-genocide Rwanda, and Victor's Justice in Arusha*, IOB Discussion Paper 2013.01, Antwerp, 2013.

F. Reyntjens, "Le gacaca ou la justice du gazon au Rwanda", *Politique Africaine*, 40 (December 1990), pp. 31–41.

F. Reyntjens, *L'Afrique des grands lacs en crise. Rwanda, Burundi, 1988–1994*, Paris, Karthala, 1994.

F. Reyntjens, "Sujets d'inquiétude au Rwanda, octobre 1994", *Dialogue*, 179 (November-December 1994), pp. 3–14.

F. Reyntjens, "Subjects of Concern: Rwanda, October 1994", *Issue* 23:2 (1995), pp. 39–43.

F. Reyntjens, "Un ordre constitutionnel dissimulé: la 'loi fondamentale' du 26 mai 1995", *Dialogue*, 186 (October-November 1995), pp. 13–22.

F. Reyntjens, "Constitution-making in Situations of Extreme Crisis: The Case of Rwanda and Burundi", *Journal of African Law* 40:2 (1996), pp. 234–242.

F. Reyntjens, "Estimation du nombre de personnes tuées au Rwanda en 1994", in: S. Marysse, F. Reyntjens (Eds.), *L'Afrique des grands lacs. Annuaire 1996–1997*, Paris, L'Harmattan, 1997, pp. 179–186.

F. Reyntjens, "Les nouveaux habits de l'empereur: analyse juridico-politique de la constitution rwandaise de 2003", in: S. Marysse, F. Reyntjens (Eds.), *L'Afrique des grands lacs. Annuaire 2002–2003*, Paris, L'Harmattan, 2003, pp. 71–87.

F. Reyntjens, "Rwanda, Ten Years On: From Genocide to Dictatorship", *African Affairs*, 103:2 (2004), pp. 177–210.

F. Reyntjens, *The Great African War. Congo and Regional Geopolitics, 1996–2006*, New York, Cambridge University Press, 2009.

F. Reyntjens, *Les risques du métier. Trois décennies comme 'chercheur-acteur' au Rwanda et au Burundi*, Paris, L'Harmattan, 2009.

F. Reyntjens, "Chronique politique du Rwanda, 2009–2010", in S. Marysse, F. Reyntjens, S. Vandeginste (Eds.), *L'Afrique des grands lacs. Annuaire 2009–2010*, Paris, L'Harmattan, 2010, pp. 273–298.

F. Reyntjens, *A Fake Inquiry on a Major Event. Analysis of the Mutsinzi report on the 6th April 1994 attack on the Rwandan President's aeroplane*, IOB Working Paper 2010-7, Antwerp, 2010.

F. Reyntjens, "*Burundi: Institutionalising Ethnicity to Bridge the Divide*", forthcoming.

F. Reyntjens, S. Vandeginste, "Rwanda: An Atypical Transition", in E. Skaar, S. Gloppen, A. Suhrke (Eds.), *Roads to Reconciliation*, Boulder, Lexington Books, 2005, pp. 101–127.

F. Reyntjens, R. Lemarchand, "Mass Murder in Eastern Congo, 1996–1997", in R. Lemarchand (Ed.), *Forgotten Genocides. Oblivion, Denial, and Memory*, Philadelphia, University of Pennsylvania Press, 2011, pp. 20–36.

H. Rombouts, *Victim Organisations and the Politics of Reparation: a case study on Rwanda*, Antwerp-Oxford, Intersentia, 2004.

K. Roth, "Letter to the Prosecutor of the International Criminal Tribunal Regarding the Prosecution of RPF Crimes", New York, Human Rights Watch, 26 May 2009.

E. Ruberangeyo, *Mes inquiétudes sur la gestion actuelle rwandaise des fonds publics*, Brussels, 31 May 1995.

F.K. Rusagara, *Resilience of a Nation. A History of the Military in Rwanda*, Kigali, Fountain Publishers Rwanda, 2009.

P. Rusesabagina (with T. Zoellner), *An Ordinary Man. An Autobiography*, New York, Penguin Books, 2006.

W. Rutayisire, "Gérald [sic] Prunier: A eulogy for genocide", Kigali, 24 October 1997.

W. Rutayisire, "Mugabe has stretched his opportunism too far", Kigali, n.d. (1999).

A. Ruyenzi, "J'accuse le général-major Paul Kagame d'être un criminel", Norway, 5 July 2004.

A. Ruyenzi, "Major-General Paul Kagame behind the Shooting Down of Late Habyarimana's Plane: An Eye Witness Testimony", Norway, 5 July 2004.

A.J. Ruzibiza, "Ubuhamya bwa Abdul Ruzibiza", Brennäsen (Norway), 14 March 2004.

A.J. Ruzibiza, *Rwanda. L'histoire secrète*, Paris, Editions du Panama, 2005.

P. Rutazibwa, "Cet ethnisme sans fin", *Informations Rwandaises et Internationales* 5 (November–December 1996), pp. 19–20.

P. Rutazibwa, "Crises des Grands Lacs: la solution viendra du Rwanda", Kigali, ARI/RNA, No. 104, 20–26 August 1998.

"Rwanda and Other Aid Darlings. Efficiency versus Freedom", *The Economist*, 5 August 2010.

Rwanda National Congress, *Rwanda: Pathway to Peaceful Change. Declaration of Core Values, Goals and an Agenda for a New Rwanda*, December 2010.

Rwanda Patriotic Front, *Itangazo rigenewe abanyamukuru*, Kigali, 10 May 1999.

Rwandese Patriotic Front, "Statement by the Political Bureau of the Rwandese Patriotic Front on the proposed deployment of a U.N. intervention force in Rwanda", New York, 30 April 1994.

I. Samset, O. Dalby, *Rwanda: Presidential and Parliamentary Elections 2003*, Oslo, NORDEM Report 12/2003.

E.R. Sanders, "The Hamitic Hypothesis: Its Origin and Function in Time Perspective", *Journal of African History*, 10:4 (1969), pp. 521–532.

J. Sarkin, *Using Gacaca Community Courts in Rwanda to Prosecute Genocide Suspects: Are Issues of Expediency and Efficiency More Important than those of Due Process, Fairness and Reconciliation?*, s.d. (2001).

W.A. Schabas, "Justice, Democracy, and Impunity in Post-genocide Rwanda: Searching for Solutions to Impossible Problems", *Criminal Law Forum*, 7:3 (1996), pp. 523–560.

W. Schabas, "Barayagwiza v. Prosecutor (Decision, and Decision (Prosecutor's Request for Review or Reconsideration))", *American Journal of International Law*, **94** (2000), pp. 563–571.

W.A. Schabas, "Genocide Trials and Gacaca Courts", *Journal of International Criminal Justice*, 3:4 (2005), pp. 879–895.

W.A. Schabas, "Anti-complementarity: Referral to National Jurisdictions by the UN International Criminal Tribunal for Rwanda", *Max Planck Yearbook of United Nations Law*, 13 (2009), pp. 29–60.

A. Schedler (Ed.), *Electoral Authoritarianism. The Dynamics of Unfree Competition*, Boulder, CO, Lynne Rienner, 2006.

D. Scheffer, *All the Missing Souls. A Personal History of the War Crimes Tribunals*, Princeton, NJ, and Oxford, Princeton University Press, 2012.

J.C. Scott, *Domination and the Arts of Resistance. Hidden Transcripts*, New Haven, CT, Yale University Press, 1992.

J.C. Scott, *Seeing Like a State: How Certain Schemes to Improve the Human Condition Have Failed*, New Haven, CT, Yale University Press, 1998.

J. Sebarenzi, *God Sleeps in Rwanda. A Journey of Transformation*, New York, Atria Books, 2009.

J. Sémelin, "Génocide, un discutable rapport rwandais", *Le Monde*, 18 August 2008.

A. Sibomana, *Gardons espoir pour le Rwanda. Entretiens avec Laure Guilbert et Hervé Deguine*, Paris, Desclée de Brouwer, 1997.

A. Sibomana, *Hope for Rwanda: Conversations with Laure Guibert and Hervé Deguine*, London and Sterling VA, Pluto Press, 1999.

E. Sidiropoulos, "Democratisation and Militarisation in Rwanda: Eight Years after the Genocide", *African Security Review*, 11:3 (2002), pp. 77–87.

S. Silva-Leander, "On the Danger and Necessity of Democratisation: Trade-offs between Short-term Stability and Long-term Peace in Post-genocide Rwanda", *Third World Quarterly*, 29:8 (2008), pp. 1601–1620.

S. Smith, "Rwanda: enquête sur la terreur tutsie. Plus de 100.000 Hutus auraient été tués depuis avril 1994", *Libération*, 27 February 1996.

S.W. Smith, "Rwanda in Six Scenes", *London Review of Books*, 33:6 (17 March 2011), pp. 3–8.

M. Sommers, P. Uvin, *Youth in Rwanda and Burundi. Contrasting Visions*, Special Report 293, Washington DC, United States Institute of Peace, October 2011.

M. Sommers, *Stuck. Rwandan Youth and the Struggle for Adulthood*, Athens GA, and London, University of Georgia Press, 2012.

J.K. Stearns, *Dancing in the Glory of Monsters. The Collapse of the Congo and the Great War of Africa*, New York, Public Affairs, 2011.

J.K. Stearns, F. Borello, "Bad Karma. Accountability for Rwandan Crimes in the Congo," in S. Straus, L. Waldorf (Eds.), *Remaking Rwanda. State Building and Human Rights after Mass Violence*, Madison, The University of Wisconsin Press, 2011, pp. 152–169.

S. Straus "How Many Perpetrators Were there in the Rwandan Genocide? An Estimate", Journal of Genocide Research, 6:1 (2004), pp. 85–98.

S. Straus, L. Waldorf (Eds.), *Remaking Rwanda. State Building and Human Rights after Mass Violence*, Madison, The University of Wisconsin Press, 2011.

S. Straus, L. Waldorf, "Introduction. Seeing Like a Post-Conflict State", in S. Straus, L. Waldorf (Eds.), *Remaking Rwanda. State Building and Human Rights after Mass Violence*, Madison, The University of Wisconsin Press, 2011, pp. 3–21.

A. Stroh, "Electoral Rules of the Authoritarian Game: Undemocratic Effects of Proportional Representation in Rwanda", *Journal of Eastern African Studies*, 4:1 (2010), pp. 1–19.

J. Swain, "The Riddle of the Rwandan Assassin's Trail", *The Sunday Times*, 4 April 2004.

S. Takeuchi, *Gacaca and DDR: The Disputable Record of State-Building in Rwanda*, JICA-RI Working Paper, No. 32, July 2011.

C. Tertsakian, *Le Château. The Lives of Prisoners in Rwanda*, London, Arves, 2008.

G. Theunis, *Mes soixante-quinze jours de prison à Kigali*, Paris, Karthala, 2012.

S. Thomson, *Resisting Reconciliation: State Power and Everyday Life in Post-Genocide Rwanda*, PhD thesis, Dalhousie University, 2009.

S. Thomson, "Reeducation for Reconciliation: Participant Observations on Ingando", in S. Straus, L. Waldorf (Eds.), *Remaking Rwanda. State Building and Human Rights after Mass Violence*, Madison, The University of Wisconsin Press, 2011, pp. 331–339.

S. Thomson, "The Darker Side of Transitional Justice: The Power Dynamics behind Rwanda's Gacaca Courts", *Africa*, 81:3 (2011), pp. 373–390.

S. Thomson, "Whispering Truth to Power: The Everyday Resistance of Rwandan Peasants to Post-genocide Reconciliation", *African Affairs*, 110:440 (2011), pp. 439–456.

S. Thomson, R. Nagy, "Law, Power and Justice: What Legalism Fails to Address in the Functioning of Rwanda's Gacaca Courts", *International Journal of Transitional Justice*, 5 (2011), pp. 11–30.

J.M. Tobias, K.C. Boudreaux, "Entrepreneurship and Conflict Reduction in the Post-Genocide Rwandan Coffee Industry", *Journal of Small Business and Entrepreneurship*, 24:2, pp. 217–242.

F. Twagiramungu and S. Sendashonga, *F.R.D. Plate-forme politique*, Brussels, March 1996.

UNDP, *Turning Vision 2020 into Reality. From Recovery to Sustainable Human Development*, 2007.

UNHCR, "Briefing Notes", Geneva, 12 December 1997.

UNHRFOR, *Update on the Human Rights situation during August 1996*, Kigali, n.d.

United Nations, Economic and Social Council, Commission on Human Rights, *Report on the Situation of Human Rights in Rwanda Submitted by Mr. René Degni-Ségui, Special Rapporteur of the Commission on Human Rights, under Paragraph 20 of Resolution S-3/1 of 25 May 1994*, E/CN.4/1995/70, 11 November 1994.

United Nations, Economic and Social Council, Commission on Human Rights, *Report on the Situation of Human Rights in Rwanda Submitted by Mr. René Degni-Ségui, Special Rapporteur, under Paragraph 20 of Resolution S-3/1 of 25 May 1994*, E/CN.4/1996/7, 28 June 1995.

United Nations, Economic and Social Council, Commission on Human Rights, *Report on the Situation of Human Rights in Rwanda Submitted by Mr. René Degni-Ségui, Special Rapporteur, under Paragraph 20 of Resolution S-3/1 of 25 May 1994*, E/CN.4/1996/68, 29 January 1996.

United Nations, Economic and Social Council, Commission on Human Rights, *Report of the Joint Mission Charged with Investigating Allegations of Massacres and Other Human Rights Violations Occurring in Eastern Zaire (Now*

Democratic Republic of the Congo) since September 1996, A/51/942, 2 July 1997.

United Nations, Economic and Social Council, Commission on Human Rights, *Report on the Situation of Human Rights in Rwanda Submitted by the Special Representative, Mr. Michel Moussali, Pursuant to Commission Resolution 1999/20*, E/CN.4/2000/41, 10 February 2000.

United Nations, General Assembly, *Report of the Special Representative of the Commission on Human Rights on the Situation of Human Rights in Rwanda*, A/55/269, 4 August 2000.

United Nations, General Assembly, Human Rights Council, *Report of the Independent Expert on Minority Issues, Gay McDougall*, A/HRC/19/56/Add.1, 28 November 2011.

United Nations, High Commissioner for Human Rights, *Gacaca: Le droit coutumier au Rwanda*, Kigali, 1996.

United Nations, High Commissioner for Human Rights, *Democratic Republic of the Congo, 1993–2003. Report of the Mapping Exercise Documenting the Most Serious Violations of Human Rights and International Humanitarian Law Committed within the Territory of the Democratic Republic of the Congo between March 1993 and June 2003*, Geneva, August 2010.

United Nations, Security Council, *Final Report of the Commission of Experts Established Pursuant to Security Council resolution 935 (1994)*, S/1994/1405, 9 December 1994.

United Nations, Security Council, *Report of the Secretary-General on the United Nations Assistance Mission to Rwanda*, S/1995/457, 4 June 1995.

United Nations, Security Council, *Report of the Investigative Team Charged with Investigating Serious Violations of Human Rights and International Humanitarian Law in the Democratic Republic of Congo*, S/1998/581, 29 June 1998.

United Nations, Security Council, *Report of the Panel of Experts on the Illegal Exploitation of Natural Resources and Other Forms of Wealth of the Democratic Republic of the Congo*, S/2001/357, 12 April 2001.

United Nations Security Council, *Final Report of the Panel of Experts on the Illegal Exploitation of Natural Resources and Other Forms of Wealth of the Democratic Republic of the Congo*, S/2003/1027, 23 October 2003.

United Nations, Security Council, *Report of the Group of Experts on the Democratic Republic of the Congo*, S/2005/30, 25 January 2005.

United Nations, Security Council, *Final Report of the Group of Experts on the Democratic Republic of the Congo*, S/2008/773, 12 December 2008.

United Nations, Security Council, *Final Report of the Group of Experts on the Democratic Republic of the Congo*, S/2009/603, 23 November 2009.

United Nations, Security Council, *Letter dated 26 October 2010 from the Group of Experts on the Democratic Republic of the Congo addressed to the Chair of the Security Council Committee Established Pursuant to Resolution 1533 (2004)*, S/2010/596, 29 November 2010.

United Nations, Security Council, *Addendum to the Interim Report of the Group of Experts on the Democratic Republic of the Congo (S/2012/348) concerning Violations of the Arms Embargo and Sanctions Regime by the Government of Rwanda*, S/2012/348/Add.1, 27 June 2012.

United Nations, Security Council, "Letter Dated 7 August 2012 from the Coordinator of the Group of Experts on the DRC addressed to the Acting Chair of the Committee", S/AC.43/2012/COMM.32, 8 August 2012.

United Nations, Security Council, *Letter Dated 12 October 2012 from the Group of Experts on the Democratic Republic of the Congo Addressed to the Chair of the Security Council Committee Established Pursuant to Resolution 1533 (2004) concerning the Democratic Republic of the Congo*, S/2012/843, 15 November 2012.

Université Nationale du Rwanda, Centre de Gestion des Conflits, Ministry of Justice, Johns Hopkins University Center for Communication Programs, *Perceptions about the Gacaca Law in Rwanda: Evidence from a Multi-method Study*, Kigali, April 2001.

USAID, *Rwanda Democracy and Governance Assessment*, November 2002.

U.S. Committee for Refugees, *Life after Death: Suspicion and Reintegration in Post-genocide Rwanda*, Washinton, DC, February 1998.

P. Uvin, *Aiding Violence: The Development Enterprise in Rwanda*, West Hartford, CT, Kumarian Press, 1998.

P. Uvin, *The Introduction of a Modernized Gacaca for Judging Suspects of Participation in the Genocide and the Massacres of 1994 in Rwanda, A Discussion Paper Prepared for the Belgian Secretary of State for Development Cooperation*, s.d. (2000).

P. Uvin, "Difficult Choices in the New Post-conflict Agenda: The International Community in Rwanda after the Genocide", *Third World Quarterly*, 22:2 (2001), pp. 177–189.

P. Uvin, *Human Rights and Development*, Bloomfield, CT, Kumarian Press, 2004.

P. Uvin, "Structural Causes, Development Co-operation and Conflict Prevention in Burundi and Rwanda", *Conflict, Security & Development*, 10:1 (2010), pp. 161–179.

P. Uvin, C. Mironko, "Western and Local Approaches to Justice in Rwanda", *Global Governance*, 9:219 (2003), pp. 219–231.

S. Vandeginste, "Poursuite des présumés responsables du génocide et des massacres politiques devant les juridictions rwandaises", in S. Marysse, F. Reyntjens (Eds.), *L'Afrique des grands lacs. Annuaire 1996–1997*, Paris, L'Harmattan, 1997, pp. 93–122.

S. Vandeginste, "Les juridictions gacaca et la poursuite des suspects auteurs du génocide et des crimes contre l'humanité au Rwanda", in F. Reyntjens, S. Marysse (Eds.), *L'Afrique des grands lacs. Annuaire 1999–2000*, Paris, L'Harmattan, 2000, pp. 75–93.

S. Vandeginste, "Rwanda: Dealing with Genocide and Crimes against Humanity in the Context of Armed Conflict and Failed Political Transition", in N. Biggar (Ed.), *Burying the Past. Making Peace and Doing Justice after Civil Conflict*, Washington, DC, Georgetown University Press, 2001, pp. 223–253.

S. Vandeginste, "Justice for Rwanda, Ten Years After: Some Lessons Learned for Transitional Justice", in F. Reyntjens, S. Marysse (Eds), *L'Afrique des grands lacs. Annuaire 2003–2004*, Paris, L'Harmattan, 2004, pp. 45–60.

S. Vandeginste, "Rwanda, The World Bank, PRSP and Human Rights", in S. Marysse, F. Reyntjens (Eds.), *L'Afrique des grands lacs. Annuaire 2004–2005*, Paris, L'Harmattan, 2005, pp. 119–139.

L.J. van den Herik, *The Contribution of the Rwanda Tribunal to the Development of International Law*, Leiden, Brill, 2005.

S. Van Hoyweghen, "The Urgency of Land and Agrarian Reform in Rwanda", *African Affairs*, 98:392 (1999), pp. 353–372.

M. van Leeuwen, "Rwanda's Imidugudu Programme and Earlier Experiments with Villagisation and Resettlement in East Africa", *Journal of Modern African Studies*, 39: 4 (2001), pp. 623–644.

J. Vansina, *Antecedents to Modern Rwanda. The Nyiginya Kingdom*, Madison, University of Wisconsin Press, 2004.

H. Verhoeven, "Nurturing Democracy or into the Danger Zone? The Rwandan Patriotic Front, Elite Fragmentation and Post-liberation Politics", in M. Campioni, P. Noack (Eds.), *Rwanda Fast Forward. Social, Economic, Military and Reconciliation Prospects*, Houndmills, Palgrave Macmillan, 2012, pp. 265–280.

M. Verpoorten, "Detecting Hidden Violence: The Spatial Distribution of Excess Mortality in Rwanda", *Political Geography*, 31 (2012), pp. 44–56.

P. Verwimp, "Development Ideology, the Peasantry and Genocide: Rwanda Represented in Habyarimana's Speeches", *Journal of Genocide Research*, 2:3 (2000), pp. 325–361.

C. Vidal, "Les commémorations du génocide au Rwanda", *Les Temps Modernes*, No. 613 (2001), pp. 1–46.

C. Vidal, "Rwanda. L'espoir en Trompe-l'oeil", *Le Nouvel Observateur*, 19–25 June 2003.

C. Vidal, "Des humanitaires témoins de l'histoire", *Les Temps Modernes*, No. 627 (2004), pp. 92–107.

C. Vidal, "Les contradictions d'un lieutenant rwandais. Abdul Ruzibiza, témoin, acteur, faux-témoin", in: S. Marysse, F. Reyntjens, S. Vandeginste (Eds.), *L'Afrique des grands lacs. Annuaire 2008–2009*, Paris, L'Harmattan, 2009, pp. 43–54.

C. Vidal, "Sur un emballement médiatique. L'attentat du 6 avril 1994 contre le président Habyarimana: comment la presse française a fait dire à un rapport d'expertise ce qu'il ne disait pas", in F. Reyntjens, S. Vandeginste, M. Verpoorten (Eds.), *L'Afrique des grands lacs. Annuaire 2011–2012*, Paris, L'Harmattan, 2012, pp. 337–349.

L. Waldorf, "Rwanda's Failing Experiment in Restorative Justice, in D. Sullivan, L. Tifft (Eds.), *A Handbook of Restorative Justice: A Global Perspective*, Abingdon, Routledge, 2005, pp. 422–434.

L. Waldorf, "Mass Justice for Mass Atrocity: Rethinking Local Justice as Transitional Justice", *Temple Law Review*, 79:1 (2006), pp. 1–88.

L. Waldorf, "Censorship and Propaganda in Post-Genocide Rwanda", in A. Thompson (Ed.), *The Media and the Rwanda Genocide*, London, Pluto Press, and Kampala, Fountain Publishers, 2007, pp. 404–416.

L. Waldorf, "Revisiting Hotel Rwanda: Genocide Ideology, Reconciliation, and Rescuers", *Journal of Genocide Research*, 11:1 (2009), pp. 101–125.

L. Waldorf, "'A Mere Pretense of Justice': Complementarity, Sham Trials, and Victor's Justice at the Rwanda Tribunal", *Fordham International Law Journal*, 33:4 (2010), pp. 1221–1277.

L. Waldorf, "Instrumentalizing Genocide. The RPF's Campaign against 'Genocide Ideology'", in S. Straus, L. Waldorf (Eds.), *Remaking Rwanda. State Building and Human Rights after Mass Violence*, Madison, The University of Wisconsin Press, 2011, pp. 48–66.

S. Warshauer Freedman et al., "Teaching History in Post-genocide Rwanda", in S. Straus, L. Waldorf (Eds.), *Remaking Rwanda. State Building and Human Rights after Mass Violence*, Madison, The University of Wisconsin Press, 2011, pp. 297–315.

C.M. Waugh, *Paul Kagame and Rwanda. Power, Genocide and the Rwandan Patriotic Front*, Jefferson, NC, McFarland & Company, 2004.

A. Wimmer, L.E. Cederman, B. Min, "Ethnic Politics and Armed Conflict: A Configurational Analysis of a New Global Data Set", *American Sociological Review*, 74:2 (2009), pp. 316–337.

K. Wyss, *A Thousand Hills for 9 Million People. Land Reform in Rwanda: Restoration of Feudal Order or Genuine Transformation?*, Swisspeace Working Paper 1/2006, March 2006.

E. Zorbas, "What Does Reconciliation after Genocide Mean? Public Transcripts and Hidden Transcripts in Post-genocide Rwanda", *Journal of Genocide Research*, 11:1 (2009), pp. 127–147.

E. Zorbas, "Aid Dependence and Policy Independence. Explaining the Rwandan Paradox", in S. Straus, L. Waldorf (Eds.), *Remaking Rwanda. State Building and Human Rights after Mass Violence*, Madison, The University of Wisconsin Press, 2011, pp. 103–117.

Index

Note: Page numbers with 'fn' followed by the locators refer to footnotes.

CPSIA information can be obtained at www.ICGtesting.com
Printed in the USA
LVOW06s2131251215

467875LV00010B/244/P